PENGUIN BOOKS

HUNDRED DAYS

'There is a grim fascination to the endgame, as the hopes still nursed by the Germans were finally extinguished and the Allies won a victory that seemed inevitable in retrospect' *Metro*

'Writing about the last 100 days of the war on the Western Front, Lloyd asks whether the Allies had learnt anything from the previous years of conflict and whether the Germans were really defeated in 1918' *Daily Telegraph*

'A sobering but essential read on the last days of a horrific conflict' *Washington Times*

'This is a powerful and moving book by a rising military historian. Lloyd's depiction of the great battles of July–November provides compelling evidence of the scale of the Allies' victories and the bitter reality of German defeat' Gary Sheffield, Professor of War Studies, University of Wolverhampton

'Compelling, very readable' *Books Monthly*

'Gives the reader an insight into the raw emotions of the period and lends immediacy to the more sober narrative' *Oxford Times*

'The book that the concluding campaign of World War I has been crying out for. This will become the standard work on the war's closing months in the years ahead . . . [an] excellent account of an almost forgotten episode in one of history's bloodiest wars' Military-history.us blog

'A bracing re-dramatization of the horrors that were most fresh in the minds of all concerned when those days were over' *Open Letters*

Nick Lloyd is Senior Lecturer in Defence Studies at King's College London, based at the Joint Services Command and Staff College in Shrivenham, Wiltshire. He specializes in British military and imperial history in the era of the Great War and is the author of two other books, *Loos 1915* (2006) and *The Amritsar Massacre: The Untold Story of One Fateful Day* (2011).

Hundred Days

The End of the Great War

NICK LLOYD

PENGUIN BOOKS

PENGUIN BOOKS

Published by the Penguin Group
Penguin Books Ltd, 80 Strand, London WC2R ORL, England
Penguin Group (USA) Inc., 375 Hudson Street, New York, New York 10014, USA
Penguin Group (Canada), 90 Eglinton Avenue East, Suite 700, Toronto, Ontario, Canada M4P 2Y3
(a division of Pearson Penguin Canada Inc.)
Penguin Ireland, 25 St Stephen's Green, Dublin 2, Ireland (a division of Penguin Books Ltd)
Penguin Group (Australia), 707 Collins Street, Melbourne, Victoria 3008, Australia
(a division of Pearson Australia Group Pty Ltd)
Penguin Books India Pvt Ltd, 11 Community Centre, Panchsheel Park, New Delhi – 110 017, India
Penguin Group (NZ), 67 Apollo Drive, Rosedale, Auckland 0632, New Zealand
(a division of Pearson New Zealand Ltd)
Penguin Books (South Africa) (Pty) Ltd, Block D, Rosebank Office Park,
181 Jan Smuts Avenue, Parktown North, Gauteng 2193, South Africa

Penguin Books Ltd, Registered Offices: 80 Strand, London WC2R ORL, England

www.penguin.com

First published by Viking 2013
Published in Penguin Books 2014
004

Copyright © Nick Lloyd, 2013
All rights reserved

The moral right of the author has been asserted

Typeset by Palimpsest Book Production Limited, Falkirk, Stirlingshire

Printed and bound in Great Britain by Clays Ltd, Elcograf S.p.A.

ISBN: 978-0-241-95381-5

www.greenpenguin.co.uk

Dedicated to the memory of Private G. T. Cotterill,
killed in action at Gouzeaucourt, 27 September 1918

Contents

List of Illustrations   ix

List of Maps   xi

Glossary   xxiii

Preface: Death at Gouzeaucourt   xxv

Prologue: 'Surprise was complete'   1

1. Decision on the Marne   9

2. 'Neglect nothing'   28

3. 'Death will have a rich harvest'   44

4. 'Another black day'   62

5. 'The incredible roar of massed guns'   78

6. 'The whole thing was simply magnificent'   97

7. Enter the Americans   115

8. 'A country of horror and desolation'   133

9. Return to the Wilderness   150

10. 'Just one panorama of hell'   167

11. The Tomb of the German World Empire   181

12. 'The most desperate battle of our history'   199

13. 'A last struggle of despair'   216

14. 'Cowards die many times'   234

15. Armistice at Compiègne   252

Epilogue   271

Acknowledgements   281

Select Bibliography   283

References   293

Index   331

List of Illustrations

(*NA = National Archives at College Park, MD; IWM = Imperial War Museum*)

1. Tom Cotterill, the author's great-uncle (*Author's collection*)
2. The telegram announcing Tom Cotterill's death (*Author's collection*)
3. Dead Man's Corner, Gouzeaucourt (*Author's collection*)
4. Headstone of Private Tom Cotterill (*Author's collection*)
5. The Kaiser at the Hotel Britannique, Spa, Belgium, June 1918 (*NA: Record Group 165 GB, Box 12, 12395*)
6. Hindenburg and Ludendorff in the Grand Place, Brussels (*IWM: Q240101*)
7. Captured French soldiers, Soissons, July 1918 (*NA: Record Group 165 GB, Box 12, 10218*)
8. German troops in action, 8 August 1918 (*NA: Record Group 165 GB, Box 11, 10596*)
9. Front cover of *Le Petit Journal* showing Allied commanders (*Getty Images: 144845446*)
10. Crown Prince Rupprecht (*NA: Record Group 165 GB, Box 5, 4481*)
11. Lieutenant-General Sir Arthur Currie (*IWM: CO 2120*)
12. Lieutenant-General Sir John Monash (*IWM: E(AUS) 2350*)
13. Men of Ernst Kielmayer's battery (*World War I Veterans Survey, Foreign Military, German, Kielmayer, Ernst (SC862). The US Army Military History Institute*)
14. German prisoners carrying a casualty along the Amiens–Roye road (*19930012-421, George Metcalf Archival Collection © Canadian War Museum*)
15. A German field gun in action (*NA: Record Group 165 GB, Box 13, 12899*)
16. General John J. Pershing (*NA: War and Conflict, 490*)
17. Lieutenant-Colonel R. D. Garrett at Saint-Mihiel (*NA: War and Conflict, 617*)
18. 15-inch naval gun captured by Australian troops (*IWM: Q 8289*)
19. Foch and Mangin conversing outside the French War Ministry (*NA: Record Group 111 SC, Box 213, 30035*)
20. General Georg von der Marwitz (*NA: Record Group 165 GB, Box 3, 2491*)

21. German supply column, Gouzeaucourt (*NA: Record Group 165 GB, Box 11, 11878*)

22. A selection of captured German guns captured (*NA: Record Group 111 SC, Box 214, 30083*)

23. Men of 89th US Division encamped in mud at Epionville (*NA: Record Group 111 SC, Box 187, 30014*)

24. An American tank company undergoing repairs (*NA: Record Group 111 SC, Box 213, 30012*)

25. Major Charles Whittlesey of the 'Lost Battalion' (*NA: Record Group 111 SC, Box 331, 42754*)

26. Soldiers of 116/Canadian Infantry Battalion at Canal du Nord (*IWM: CO 3289*)

27. A horse team of the Royal Artillery pulls an 18-pounder up the bank of the Canal du Nord (*Getty Images: 154419630*)

28. The Kaiser on a visit to Kiel (*NA: Record Group 165 GB, Box 12, 12608*)

29. Soldiers of 27th US Division return to Corbie (*NA: Record Group 111, Box 213, 30045*)

30. Men of the North Lancashire Regiment enter Cambrai, October 1918 (*Akg-images 105393*)

31. German infantry camping west of Le Cateau (*NA: Record Group GB, Box 12, 12249*)

32. German dismounted cavalry on the march (*NA: Record Group 165 GB, Box 12, 12395*)

33. German reserves move up to the front (*NA: Record Group 165 GB, 12797*)

34. The cathedral of St Quentin, October 1918 (*NA: War and Conflict, 699*)

35. Lens in the final days of the war (*NA: Record Group 165 GB, Box 13, 13514*)

36. Effects of shellfire on Champigneulle (*NA: Record Group 111 SC, Box 331, 42767*)

37. Second-Lieutenant Wilfred Owen (*IWM: Q101783*)

38. Second-Lieutenant James Kirk, VC (*Trustees of the Manchester Regiment and Archive: MR00712*).

39. German infantry dug in at Valenciennes, November 1918 (*NA: Record Group 165 GB, Box 13, 13325*).

40. Place de la Concorde, 9 November 1918 (*NA: Record Group 111 SC, Box 214, 30105*)

41. Allied flags on the Rue Royale, Paris, 11 November 1918 (*NA: Record Group 111 SC, Box 214, 30123*)

List of Maps

1. The Western Front, July 1918
2. Second Battle of the Marne: The Allied Counter-Attack, 18 July 1918
3. The Battles of Amiens and Montdidier, 8 August 1918
4. Saint-Mihiel Offensive, 12–16 September 1918
5. Battle of the Meuse–Argonne, 26 September 1918
6. The Allied Advance, August–November 1918
7. Operations on 27 September 1918
8. The Attack on Gouzeaucourt, 27 September 1918
9. The Assault on the Hindenburg Line, 29 September 1918

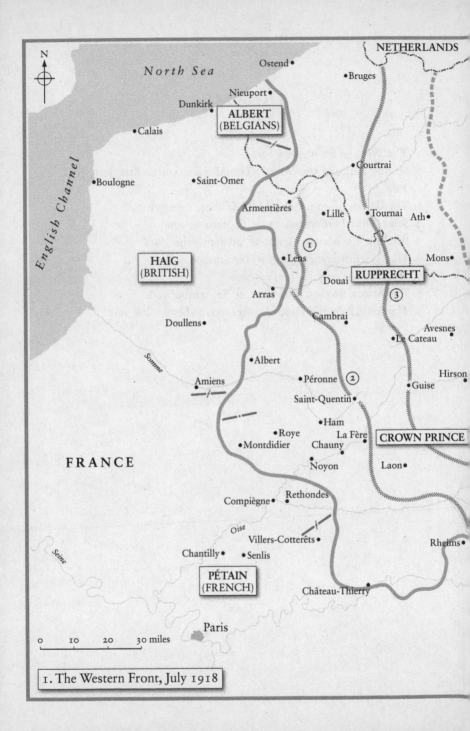

1. The Western Front, July 1918

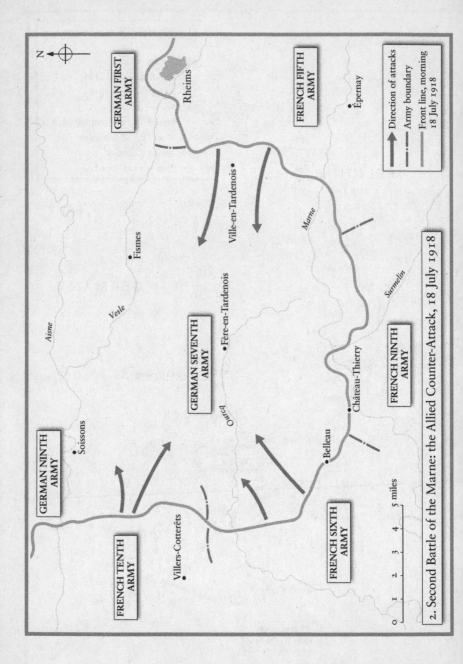

2. Second Battle of the Marne: the Allied Counter-Attack, 18 July 1918

GERMAN FIRST ARMY

Rheims

FRENCH FIFTH ARMY

Épernay

Ville-en-Tardenois

Fismes

Marne

Sarmelin

Aisne

Vesle

GERMAN SEVENTH ARMY

Fère-en-Tardenois

Ourcq

FRENCH NINTH ARMY

GERMAN NINTH ARMY

Soissons

Château-Thierry

Belleau

FRENCH SIXTH ARMY

FRENCH TENTH ARMY

Villers-Cotterêts

Direction of attacks

Army boundary

Front line, morning 18 July 1918

0 1 2 3 4 5 miles

N

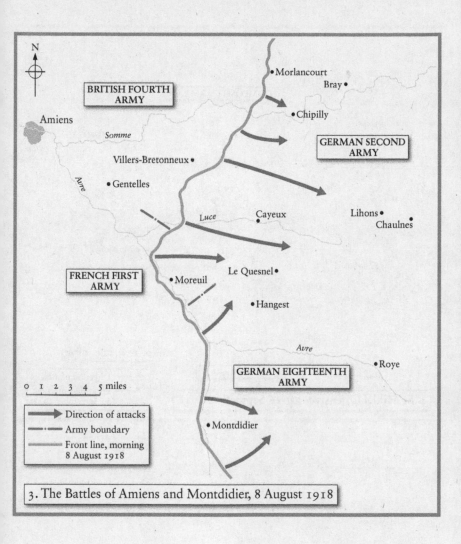

N

BRITISH FOURTH
ARMY

Amiens

Somme

● Morlancourt

Bray ●

● Chipilly

GERMAN SECOND
ARMY

Villers-Bretonneux ●

Avre

● Gentelles

Luce

Cayeux ●

Lihons ●

Chaulnes ●

FRENCH FIRST
ARMY

● Moreuil

Le Quesnel ●

● Hangest

Avre

GERMAN EIGHTEENTH
ARMY

● Roye

o   1   2   3   4   5 miles

Direction of attacks
Army boundary
Front line, morning
8 August 1918

● Montdidier

3. The Battles of Amiens and Montdidier, 8 August 1918

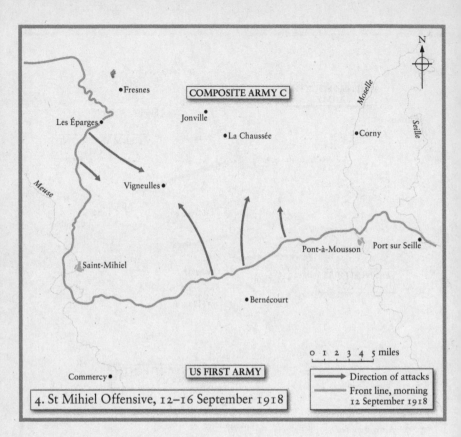

Fresnes

COMPOSITE ARMY C

Jonville

Les Éparges

La Chaussée

Corny

Moselle

Seille

Meuse

Vigneulles

Saint-Mihiel

Pont-à-Mousson

Port sur Seille

Bernécourt

0 1 2 3 4 5 miles

Commercy

US FIRST ARMY

→ Direction of attacks

— Front line, morning
12 September 1918

4. St Mihiel Offensive, 12–16 September 1918

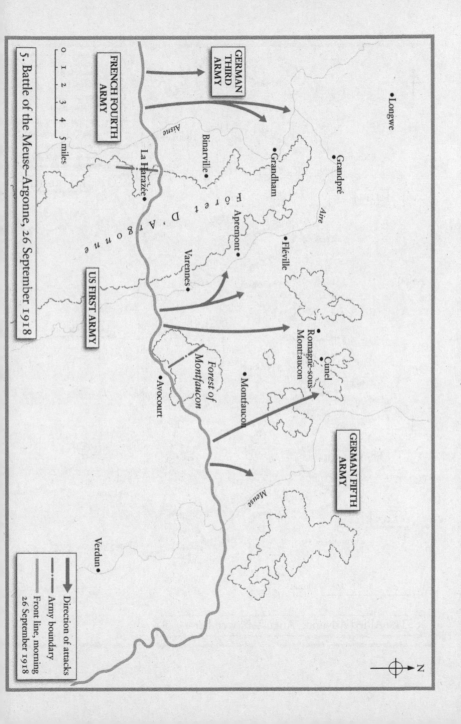

5. Battle of the Meuse–Argonne, 26 September 1918

FRENCH FOURTH ARMY

GERMAN THIRD ARMY

US FIRST ARMY

GERMAN FIFTH ARMY

0 1 2 3 4 5 miles

Longwe

Grandpré

Aire

Grandham

Binarville

Aisne

Forêt D'Argonne

Apremont

Fléville

Varennes

La Harazée

Romagne-sous-Montfaucon

Cunel

Forest of Montfaucon

Montfaucon

Avocourt

Meuse

Verdun

Direction of attacks
Army boundary
Front line, morning
26 September 1918

N

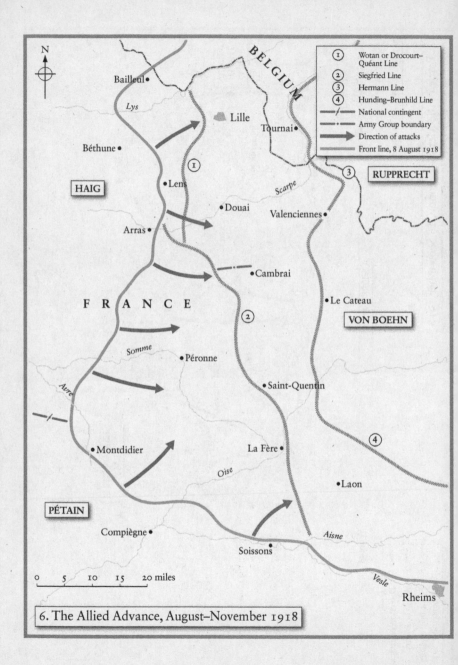

N

BELGIUM

Bailleul•

Lys

Lille

Tournai•

① Wotan or Drocourt–Quéant Line
② Siegfried Line
③ Hermann Line
④ Hunding–Brunhild Line
National contingent
Army Group boundary
Direction of attacks
Front line, 8 August 1918

③ RUPPRECHT

HAIG

Béthune•

•Lens

Scarpe

•Douai

Valenciennes•

Arras•

•Le Cateau

F R A N C E

①

②

Cambrai

VON BOEHN

Somme

•Péronne

Avre

•Saint-Quentin

④

•Montdidier

La Fère•

Oise

•Laon

PÉTAIN

Compiègne•

Aisne

Soissons•

0   5   10   15   20 miles

Vesle

Rheims

6. The Allied Advance, August–November 1918

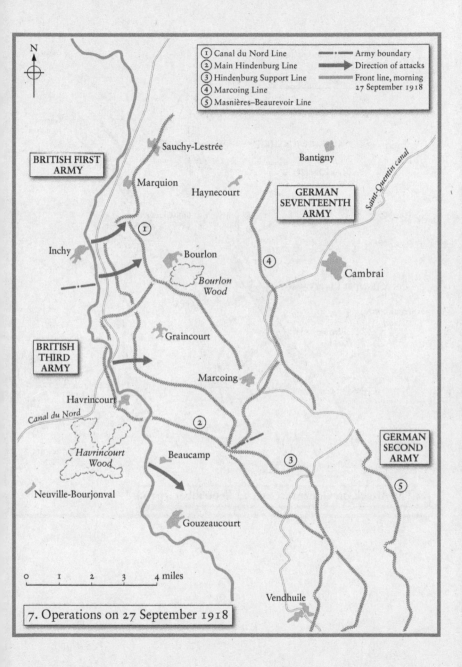

N

① Canal du Nord Line	▬ ▬ Army boundary
② Main Hindenburg Line	➤ Direction of attacks
③ Hindenburg Support Line	▬▬ Front line, morning
④ Marcoing Line	27 September 1918
⑤ Masnières–Beaurevoir Line	

Sauchy-Lestrée

Bantigny

**BRITISH FIRST
ARMY**

Marquion

Haynecourt

**GERMAN
SEVENTEENTH
ARMY**

Saint-Quentin canal

Inchy

①

Bourlon

④

Cambrai

*Bourlon
Wood*

Graincourt

**BRITISH
THIRD
ARMY**

Marcoing

Havrincourt

Canal du Nord

②

*Havrincourt
Wood*

Beaucamp

③

**GERMAN
SECOND
ARMY**

Neuville-Bourjonval

⑤

Gouzeaucourt

0   1   2   3   4 miles

Vendhuile

7. Operations on 27 September 1918

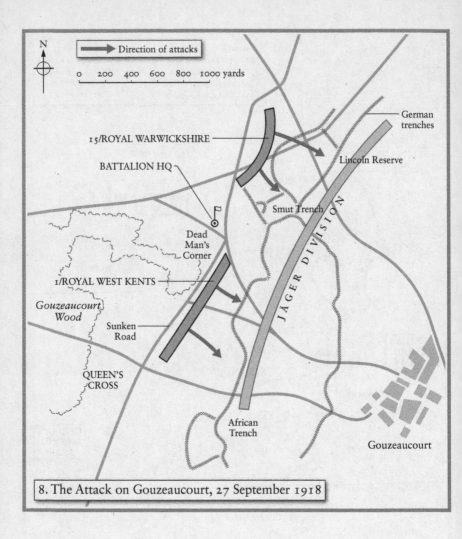

8. The Attack on Gouzeaucourt, 27 September 1918

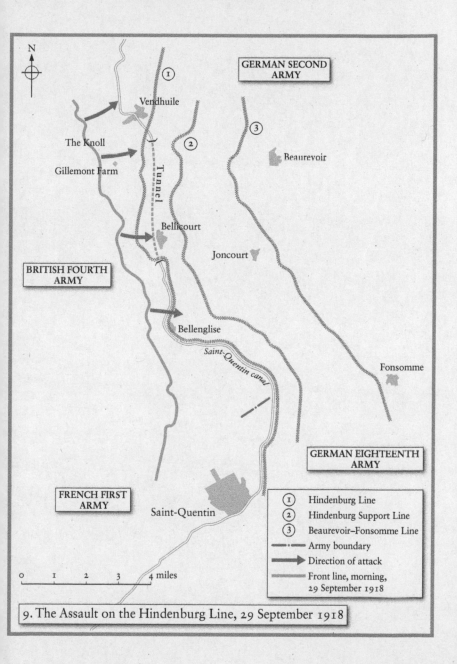

N

GERMAN SECOND ARMY

① Vendhuile

③

② Beaurevoir

The Knoll

Gillemont Farm

Tunnel

BRITISH FOURTH ARMY

Bellicourt

Joncourt

Bellenglise

Saint-Quentin canal

Fonsomme

GERMAN EIGHTEENTH ARMY

FRENCH FIRST ARMY

Saint-Quentin

①	Hindenburg Line
②	Hindenburg Support Line
③	Beaurevoir–Fonsomme Line

–·–·– Army boundary

➤ Direction of attack

Front line, morning, 29 September 1918

0   1   2   3   4 miles

9. The Assault on the Hindenburg Line, 29 September 1918

Glossary

AEF: American Expeditionary Force

Army: Collection of corps (usually between two and seven)

Army Group: Collection of armies (usually consisting of two or three)

Battalion: Unit of infantry (nominally up to 1,000 strong)

Battery: Organization of artillery pieces (usually containing between four and six guns)

BEF: British Expeditionary Force

Brigade: Major tactical formation. Three brigades made up a British division (each brigade containing three battalions). French and German brigades operated on a different system, each with two regiments

Chauchat: Unpopular French light machine-gun (extensively used by the Americans) prone to jamming in the field

Corps: A group of divisions (usually between two and five)

Creeping or rolling barrage: Moving wall of shellfire that swept across the battlefield at a predetermined pace

Division: Basic tactical unit on the battlefield employing between 15,000 and 18,000 men (although they rarely contained this number by 1918), with supporting medical, engineering and artillery arms. Owing to a lack of trained staff officers, American divisions were up to twice the size of Allied or German divisions, containing 28,000 men

Doughboy: Slang term for an American soldier

Frontschwein: Literally 'front hog'. Slang for a German soldier

GHQ: General Headquarters (British Expeditionary Force)

GOC: General Officer Commanding

GQG: *Grand Quartier Général* (French High Command)

Hindenburg Line: Major German defensive system constructed during 1916 and 1917

Jagdstaffel: German Air Force fighter squadron

Jäger: Elite German light infantry

Landwehr: German reserve units intended for garrison duties, often containing older men

Lewis gun: American-designed light machine-gun first introduced in 1915 and widely used in the BEF

Minenwerfer: German heavy trench mortar much feared by Allied soldiers

NCO: Non-Commissioned Officer

OHL: *Oberheeresleitung* (German Supreme Command)

Poilu: Literally 'hairy one'. Slang for a French soldier

RAF: Royal Air Force

Regiment: Organization of infantry battalions. French and German divisions contained four regiments (each of three battalions). The British regimental system differed from continental use and regarded the regiment as a permanent organizational unit for its battalions

Siegfried Stellung: Siegfried Line. This was the main section of the Hindenburg Line and ran from Arras to Saint-Quentin

Spartacist: Revolutionary Marxist organization founded in Germany and dedicated to ending the war

Preface:
Death at Gouzeaucourt

There war's holiday seemed, nor though at known times
Gusts of flame and jingling steel descended
On the bare tracks, would you
Picture death there.

Edmund Blunden, 'Gouzeaucourt: The Deceitful Calm'[1]

Gouzeaucourt lies nine miles southwest of the town of Cambrai. Like many villages in this part of northern France, it consists of one main street, lined by small brick buildings, and is surrounded by farmland. It sits in a flat landscape of fields, occasional copses and low slopes, which may be marked as 'ridges' on local maps, but are, in reality, barely noticeable. In the years 1914–18 this village found itself in the zone of conflict known as the Western Front; the sliver of land that was fought over repeatedly between the Allies (the French, Belgian, British and Imperial troops, and later the Americans) and the invading German forces. It had been occupied in 1914, but, given its small size, it was generally left to itself. Then, during the Battle of Cambrai in November 1917, it was fought over between British and German troops, which left it shattered, its buildings pounded into the ground and its fields pockmarked by shellfire. By the following year it was a ruin, with just clumps of shattered buildings and mounds of rubble; the home of crows and foxes, but little else.

The war poet Edmund Blunden served at Gouzeaucourt in the cold spring of 1918. 'At first the whole area was deathly still,' he wrote:

as though no war ever happened here. The civilians had not yet attempted to resume their properties and all the farms for miles were only shells of brick. It was truly a devastated area, apart from all question of the cutting down of orchards and the dynamiting of churches or cross-roads. Upon our arrival (in open trucks on a light railway) a heavy hoar-frost was loading the trees and telegraph wires and all projections and points with beards of greyish crystal – a singular sight, and the air's near whiteness thickened into the impenetrable at a few yards' distance.

No-man's-land may have been particularly wide here, with both sides remaining out of sight, but on closer inspection Blunden began to see how vicious the fighting had been. 'Strewn about this sector were relics of the Cambrai fight of the previous November,' he wrote, 'cavalry lances, guns with crumpled barrels, tanks burnt out, German machine-gun belts and carriers, and a few dead, preserved by the cold weather.'[2]

The British would return to Gouzeaucourt in the final months of 1918 as the Allied armies, now advancing on a broad front, began to approach the main German defensive position, the so-called Hindenburg Line, which lay along the Saint-Quentin canal to the east. Around this area the small villages that dotted the landscape – Villers-Plouich, Beaucamp, Trescault and Gouzeaucourt – had been turned into veritable fortresses, ringed with support trenches and dug-outs, and bristling with machine-guns. On the morning of 27 September 1918, Private George Thomas Cotterill (known as Tom) of the 15th Battalion, Royal Warwickshire Regiment, serving with 5th British Division, was killed in action here. Cotterill was, in many ways, typical of what the British Army had become after four years of war. He was just nineteen years old and had been conscripted in 1917. He arrived on the Western Front determined to do his bit in a war that had lasted longer and cost so much more than anyone had imagined. And again, like thousands of his comrades, he would never return home or live to see the Armistice six weeks later. Taken on its own Cotterill's death was hardly unique in a war that would kill over 700,000 British soldiers and take the lives of millions more, from every corner of Europe and every continent in the world. But it was unique in the grief that his death caused to the family who had lost a son and a brother. Private Cotterill was my great-uncle.

This book is, in part, inspired by Tom's story. The memory of his tragic loss, barely six weeks before the Armistice, has always haunted my family. His portrait, taken while on leave in 1918, shows an earnest young man dressed in his best suit; sitting in a chair in a photographer's studio, waiting no doubt to return to the front. As a historian, I have always been fascinated by Tom's life and death, and this book was born of a desire to learn more about how he was killed. He grew up in the village of Sealand, near Shotton, in Flintshire in northeast Wales; a thin strip of coastal land on the Dee estuary, perhaps best known as the home of John Summer's steel mill. In 1914 the steel mill at Shotton was the largest producer of galvanized steel in the country, and I imagine, like many in his family, Tom would have been destined to spend his life working there had the Great War not intervened. But in June 1914 Franz Ferdinand, the heir to the throne of the Austro-Hungarian Empire, was assassinated in Sarajevo, thus sparking off a fatal chain of events that brought Europe to war the following month. Because of his age Tom did not join the colours until late 1917, and it was only the following January that he found himself in the front line. He had been sent, not to France, but to one of the least known British deployments of the war, stiffening the Italian Army against the Austrians on the northern Italian border, where they had the novel and somewhat unique task of regularly patrolling no-man's-land in collapsible canvas boats (their front lying along the River Piave).

A letter from this period of Tom's life has survived the passage of time and offers a poignant insight into his character. It is dated 7 January 1918, and although it does not reveal his location, battalion records confirm that they were stationed in the village of Sant'Anna Morosina, northwest of Venice, over that Christmas period. The regimental history noted that 'Billets were good in barns and houses, rations were plentiful and could always be supplemented with specialities of the country, such as spaghetti and polenta.' The local 'vina rosso' was also 'very popular and cheap'.[3]

My dear Mum, Dad and all.

First a few lines in answer to your most welcome letter and parcel which I received today Monday. Hoping you are all in the best of health as I am still in the pink. Well dear Mum, I was very sorry to hear of my uncle Fred being so ill, hoping he will soon get better and also have better luck this year than last . . . I think Maud will keep on hoping for her fur till I come on leave again. We got half a quid this week, but it seems to go almost as quick as before. I think the rumour about us going away from here is cancelled at least – that is the latest – I hope it's not true, there are no signs of the boys going on leave yet . . . We have just had a little fall of snow here but it freezes as it fell [sic]. It is very cold. Hoping you are getting better weather at home . . . I am on guard tomorrow. I could do with a good pair of mittens as you can do drill better with those than with gloves and almost as warm. Hoping you are going on well with the socks. Well dear Mum, I think I have said all this time so please excuse [my] last letter, [I] will now close with fondest love to yourself, Dad and all, Bill, Maud, and all at home. Glad to hear Harry is a lot better.

From your ever loving son Tom XX

This letter, in jagged handwriting, allows us a glimpse into the thoughts and feelings of a youthful British conscript in the final year of the Great War. His thoughts, perhaps inevitably, concentrate on home: how the family are doing; his sister, Maud, and her long-desired fur coat; his Uncle Fred, who had not been well. The letter also gives us an insight into daily life in snowy Italy: the drills (which would be so much easier with mittens than gloves!); the eternal need for new socks; how his pay disappears very quickly; and the rumours of leave or where they may be sent next.

Tom's battalion, 15/Royal Warwicks, was better known as the Second Birmingham 'Pals' and had been raised in the frantic days of August and September 1914.[4] After leaving for France in November of the following year, the battalion had first seen action along the trenches of the Western Front around Arras in the cold spring of 1916. It was during this time that the battalion first experienced the realities of trench warfare: the biting cold of a winter in the open; the long marches to and from the front; the intermittent shellfire; the sight of dead French soldiers buried in the parapet; the occasional strafes from enemy aeroplanes.[5] Although it was one of the few British units to take part in the famous storming of Vimy Ridge in April 1917 (when 13 Brigade was 'lent' to 2nd Canadian Division), there was little to distinguish the second Birmingham battalion from many other British units on the Western Front. It had a sprinkling of regular officers, including the pipe-smoking Captain Charles Bill, who would write the battalion history, but the experience of soldiering would have to be learnt in the trenches for the majority of the battalion, including most of the junior officers. It was in places like the Somme and Ypres, names that have come to define the British memory of the conflict, that they would learn the meaning of war.

By the summer of 1918, after a winter on the Italian Front, the battalion was back on the Western Front, in the Forêt de Nieppe area southwest of Arras. Here it held the line, took part in the occasional trench raid, and tried to avoid the enemy snipers that were particularly pernicious on this part of the front. Its Commanding Officer was Lieutenant-Colonel G. S. Miller, a special reserve officer of the 4th Battalion, who had joined in August 1916. Some said he never wanted to command a New Army (or service) battalion – a sentiment many old regulars would have sympathized with – but, as Captain Bill later wrote, 'time brought about a change of heart. He came to appreciate that even a Service Battalion can be good, and soon developed a real pride in his command'; he was later awarded the Distinguished Service Order and bar. His Adjutant, Major George Wilmot, was a more popular man, who had, like Miller, joined the battalion in 1916, having been transferred from the Manchester Regiment. He was not only well-liked, but also terrifically brave, and was awarded the Military Cross for gallantry in January 1919.[6]

During August and September 1918, Tom's battalion was heavily employed in the final battles of the Great War. The attack in which he was killed was technically part of the Battle of the Canal du Nord, which the British official history informs me took place between 27 September and 1 October 1918. It did not involve (as far as I can find) any notable participants or any new or untried weapon; it was not interesting for any particular savagery or unique military manoeuvre. Yet from what we know, it was entirely typical of the experience of combat witnessed by the average British 'Tommy' during the last days of the First World War: battalions moving forward to flush out German positions; heavy machine-gun fire; confusion; swift enemy counter-attacks (primarily using bombs and close-quarter weapons); and then finally the German defenders vanishing like wraiths in the morning, leaving nothing but empty ration cans and piles of spent cartridges. The advance would then continue until the next defensive position was reached. As was to be expected, Tom's death caused a huge gulf in the family and a set of wounds that never healed. Family legend has it that on the morning of his death, his mother, Florence, woke up with a searing pain in her head. When she recovered, she had a dark sense of foreboding that Tom had died. And then the dreaded telegram came on 23 October – nineteen days before the Armistice – confirming that her son had been killed in action.

Tom Cotterill died taking part in one of the last great campaigns of the First World War, what has become known as the 'Hundred Days' or the 'Advance to Victory'. The term 'Hundred Days' is a British one – redolent of the last battles against Napoleon in 1815 – and refers to the period between the Battle of Amiens on 8 August and the Armistice on 11 November 1918, a total of ninety-five days. This marked the decisive moment in the course of a war that had been waged for over four years, but these battles, epic in their scale, intensity and ferocity, remain only patchily remembered.[7] While thousands of books have been written (and continue to be published) on the causes and origins of the First World War, sadly and somewhat intriguingly, the same cannot be said of how the war ended. In the opening sentence of his *To Win a War* in 1978, the British historian John Terraine complained that 'The final campaign of 1918 – the last victorious "Hundred Days" – is virtually an unknown story', and this remains the case today.[8] Private Cotterill was one of a whole generation who were wiped out in the final months of the war, but who remain lost to history.

The campaign of 1918 remains one of the most important, yet least understood, periods of the war. Writing in 2011, the historian David Stevenson claimed that 'whereas modern comprehensive investigations now exist into the outcomes of other modern conflicts, the First World War still lacks one'.[9] It had begun on 21 March, when the thunderous opening of the German Spring Offensive shattered the trench deadlock that had gripped the opposing armies for the best part of three years. Having been able to redeploy large numbers of troops to France after the collapse of Russia, Germany's leaders vowed to strike before the Allies, buttressed by powerful American support, became invincible. The aim was to conduct a massive attack in France, separate the British and French Armies, and win the war before Germany's perilous strategic situation worsened even further. But this great masterstroke failed. Although manoeuvre returned to the Western Front and the German armies advanced deep into north-ern France, the Allies evaded this knock-out blow and held on. And it was in July, when Germany's strength began to fade, that the Allies hit back, thus beginning the final campaign of the Great War: the Hundred Days.

When I began researching this period, the lack of a really satisfac-tory account of these final battles, particularly one that analysed the situation from the point of view of all the main warring sides, became immediately apparent. Although there have been many good books on 1918 – a personal favourite being Gregor Dallas's epic *1918. War and Peace* (2000) – their coverage remains patchy, selective and fre-quently drawn from a few well-worn sources. Anglophone historians have understandably focused on the battles fought by the British Expeditionary Force and have relatively little to say about the important roles played by the French or the Americans. Other writers have claimed that the war was effectively over by the summer of 1918 – meaning that the Hundred Days was not especially important – but this remains a narrow and selective approach dependent upon hind-sight. The Germans may have lost the war by July, but the Allies had certainly not won it and there was much still to do, as the staggering toll of losses reveals all too clearly. Between 18 July and 11 November the Allies sustained upwards of 700,000 casualties while the Germans lost at least another 760,000 men.[10] Indeed, casualty rates among Brit-ish units were some of the worst of the war, leading many commentators to assume that nothing had been learnt from previous offensives; that it was the same old story of fruitless slaughter and sacrifice in 1918 as it had been in earlier years. This may not have been the case, but the death toll of those final days – increased tragically by the so-called 'Spanish flu' – remains remarkable and deserves greater examination than it has hitherto received.

The reason why this last phase of the Great War has remained relatively unknown is not hard to find. For ninety years it has been overshadowed by the major trench warfare battles of the middle years of the war, those on the Somme, Ypres or Verdun in 1916 and 1917, which seem to sum up the experience and (apparent) futility of the war: the mud; the blood; the pointless slaughter. In Germany, the last battles of the war remain under-researched and little known. During the interwar period it was perhaps understandable if these battles were not greatly appreciated given the growth of a 'stab in the back' legend which claimed that the German Army had not really been beaten in 1918, but had been betrayed and sabotaged by a group of pacifists, Jews and socialists at home. The widespread belief that Germany had not really lost the war meant that the final battles were seen as being neither especially important nor as interesting as the great German offensives of the spring and summer of 1918. These operations, which restored movement to the Western Front and were notorious for the use of *Stosstruppen* (stormtroopers), have long fascinated historians and thus distorted our view of the collapse of the Army in late 1918. Therefore, for various reasons, all the combatants of the Hundred Days had their own reasons for ignoring or neglecting the last phase of the war, and this is perhaps why this period is much less well-known than others. The war had destroyed old certainties, killed millions, and this meant that the end came as a blessed relief and saw only muted celebration. It was over. That was enough.

This book tells the story of those final days, the last four months of combat on the Western Front. It begins with what would become the turning point of the war in the west, the Second Battle of the Marne in July 1918 (which preceded the Battle of Amiens), and follows the course of the fighting right up to the Armistice. It does not intend to offer a full operational history of how the war ended or the justice of the subsequent peace. David Stevenson's 2011 account, *With*

Our Backs to the Wall: Victory and Defeat in 1918, provides as comprehensive a picture as could be wished for. This book concentrates on the fighting in France and Belgium, with brief discussions of the war elsewhere, from Italy and Salonika to Palestine. It seeks to explore two main questions: firstly, to what extent had the Allies improved their so-called tactical 'learning curve' on the battlefield; and, secondly, was the German Army really defeated in 1918? It is based on the testimonies of those British, Commonwealth, French, German and American soldiers who served during those final days and left vivid, frequently haunting, recollections of what they went through. These accounts, drawn from the archives of five countries, offer a valuable and moving picture of what it was really like to experience the twilight of the Western Front: the shattering bombardments; the storm of machine-gun fire; the sight of hundreds of dead and wounded; the exhaustion of endless marches; the glow of burning French villages; the comradeship and fear. It ends with a description of perhaps the most iconic event of the twentieth century, the Armistice on 11 November 1918, when the guns fell silent.

Like millions of others, Private Cotterill did not live to see the Armistice celebrations. His war came to an end in the empty fields north of Gouzeaucourt. He was evacuated from the lines and buried in the British cemetery at Neuville-Bourjonval several miles to the rear. The cemetery is small by Great War standards and sits forlornly in the middle of a field, just a short way from the village, bordered by a low rubble wall. The British cemeteries in this part of France rarely see visitors. The main draws of the Western Front, Ypres and the Somme, attract thousands of tourists every year, but relatively few make their way to the bare ridges south of Cambrai, and those that do are often on the lonely pilgrimage to find a lost loved one. When I visited there was no one else around. It was a cold, wet day in spring, with a bitter wind blowing across the flat fields, and one could only be struck by the loneliness and sadness of the scene. Tom is buried in plot C30, alongside 200 other soldiers, most of whom were killed in the last year of the war. As I stood there I was filled with a powerful urge to write a history of those final days; to do all that I could to bring him home.

Prologue:
'Surprise was complete'

The last act of the great German tragedy of 1918 was beginning.

Jean de Pierrefeu[1]

18 July 1918

It was a wild night; wet and windy, with thunderstorms growling out over the front and sending rain lashing down into the trenches. Corporal Frank Faulkner had arrived at his sector with the men of B Company, 23rd Infantry Regiment of 2nd US Division, on the night of 17–18 July. 'I never saw so many men, guns, ambulances and various kinds of equipment,' he wrote. 'We knew that something was coming off but we did not know the importance of it till some time after. That night it rained and it was pitch dark and we hiked up to the front, the roads were congested with equipment and tanks and only a flash of lightning would show us the way.'[2] Faulkner may not have known exactly what was afoot, but he could sense the immensity of the occasion. At that moment, over 300,000 men – French, North African, American, British and Italian – were moving into their assembly positions along the front from Rheims to Soissons north of the River Marne in northeastern France. Faulkner would be present at a pivotal moment in the war on the Western Front. The Second Battle of the Marne was about to enter its most critical phase.

Two days earlier, on 15 July, the last German offensive of the Great War had broken out along a sixty-five-mile front. Three German armies had concentrated forty-two divisions and massed nearly 1,700 guns in this critical sector, aiming to capture the fortified city of Rheims.[3] But this time the Allies were waiting for them. Forewarned by accurate intelligence and well prepared by commanders who understood German offensive tactics, the Allies were confident that this time they could withstand whatever the enemy threw at them. Instead of packing their men in the front-line trenches like sardines, they moved the bulk of their forces back, intending to wait until the Germans had expended their energy before engaging them. As well as working out how to contain the enemy thrust, reserve forces specially detailed for a counter-attack were already filtering into position, hoping to strike when the Germans were at their weakest, pushing forward at the end of long supply lines, deep into the Marne pocket. Then and only then would the Allies hit back. The 'mouse trap', as it became known, had been set.

By 17 July, two days into what came to be called Operation Marneschutz-Reims, German hopes had been dashed. The long-awaited attack on 15 July went wrong from the beginning, and within two hours of going over the top the German infantry had encountered such heavy resistance that a breakthrough could not be achieved. Rheims remained in French hands and it was evident that any further advance was out of the question. And it was at this point, when the momentum of the German attack had drained away, that the Allies sprang their trap. Four large American divisions, the 1st, 2nd, 4th and 26th, were poised to strike the west face of the salient along the line Soissons to Château-Thierry on the morning of 18 July. They would be joined by fourteen French divisions, split into six corps, from their Tenth and Sixth Armies. On the opposite flank another two French corps, assisted by Italian troops that had been deployed on the Western Front, would attack the eastern face of the German lines. Their objective was the town of Fère-en-Tardenois, lying squarely in the middle of the salient. If the Allies could reach this point, German forces to the south, along the Marne, would be cut off and a major success achieved.

Getting everyone and everything into position was a monumental task. Troops, guns and supplies were brought up at night in order to prevent German observation, while aircraft buzzed overhead intercepting stray enemy planes and putting them to flight. The Allies could not know for certain whether their plans had been discovered by the enemy – the potential for word to leak out was frightening – but snippets of intelligence hinted that their plans were not suspected. The main attack was entrusted to General Charles Mangin's French Tenth Army, spearheaded by the elite XX Corps, containing 1st and 2nd US Divisions and 1st Moroccan Division; striking eastwards from the forest of Villers-Cotterêts. For the counter-attack the French had managed to mass an unprecedented amount of armour, 540 light and 240 medium tanks, the majority of which would be deployed in this sector; hidden under the trees, covered over with tarpaulin and branches.[4] In the final moments before the assault was due to go in, amid pouring rain, the crush behind the lines seemed to become desperate. A French officer, Lieutenant Charles Chenu, noted that the 'entire forest' of Villers-Cotterêts was 'on the move'. 'Troops slip ceaselessly towards the lines; artillerymen, arms bare, cut down branches, haul the guns, shift soil. As we have to be able to see, candles are lit; the forest sparkles as if enchanted, or like those towns whose twinkling lights are all that can be glimpsed at night from on board ship.'[5]

Mangin's attack would be resisted by ten German divisions, about 900 guns and 900 aircraft in total, dug in behind only weak defences.[6] Rumours and intelligence reports had been filtering in for some time of French and American troop movements, particularly on the west face of the salient around Villers-Cotterêts, but these were not taken seriously or were brushed aside.[7] Although most of the German units were well below strength and had been exhausted by constant combat, they would still be able to offer considerable resistance, hence the need for an elaborate deception plan. French commanders knew that surprise was essential. They had decided that there would be no preliminary bombardment, nothing to warn the Germans of the impending assault, only silence. At Zero Hour, a huge creeping barrage would roar into life, smoke shells would cloak the battlefield and then the tanks, followed closely by the infantry, would push on ahead. This was a novel and state-of-the-art tactic that did not go unnoticed. The number of people who had been entrusted with the plans was kept to an absolute minimum and a junior officer like Charles Chenu was not one of them. At 4.20 a.m., five minutes before Zero Hour, Chenu went and spoke to his senior officer because he was unsure what was going on.

'There's been a mistake,' he said. 'Zero Hour is in five minutes and we haven't fired a shot.'

The captain looked at Chenu wearily. 'We've changed our tactics,' he replied. 'Today, there will be no initial assault by the artillery; we take them by surprise. We will only break cover when we attack.'

Chenu was unsatisfied with this and asked his captain again, 'Isn't the artillery doing any more about it?'

'No,' he answered, 'they will cope.'

Chenu had convinced himself, whatever anyone else said, that the attack had been postponed. For years all trench attacks had only gone in after lengthy, punishing bombardments had prepared the way; smashing down defences and pulverizing the opposing forces. Understandably, anxious troops found comfort and courage in such support, but now, by 1918, things were different. Surprise – the element that seemed to have deserted the Western Front – had returned. At that moment, he heard two shots, fired calmly, lazily almost; the first rounds of the morning, echoing away on the breeze. And then, suddenly and brutally, 'the whole forest exploded with gunfire'. Chenu and his men looked at each other, stunned; mouthing swear words as they were 'surrounded by guns spitting out fire, muzzles aflame'. The barrage had begun.

'Forward, forward,' someone shouted.[8]

Elton Mackin, a Marine with 2nd US Division, recalled the moment the counter-attack began. 'One instant there was silence,' he wrote, 'then the world went mad in a smashing burst of sound.'

Men, caught off balance, were hurled to the earth, which shook against the guns. Minds, stupefied, refused all function for a moment and reeled. Everything within a hundred yards was gnawed in bitter, tearing bites at men and trees and wire. The stately forest melted beneath a raging storm of fire and steel. Heavy branches and trunks crushed the life from men who cowered among the roots for shelter. One heard a furious, awful screaming as the shell fire rolled away. Then mad waves of charging infantry came after it, mopping up.[9]

Private Ralph Williams was one of the combat engineers detailed to help the infantry get forward. 'No one could hear an order, so word was passed on from man to man, "Combat packs and follow in line!" This led to ammunition dumps where four bandoliers were given to each man plus hand grenades.' Five minutes later the leading infantry started moving out. 'The Germans were in the other half of this forest. With our rolling barrage, they either had to evacuate, or hole up. There was very little resistance the first half hour as this was a surprise attack and caught them off-guard.'[10]

Moving through the wheat, supported in places by the lumbering shapes of the tanks, the Allied infantry crept forward, rifles and grenades at the ready. The German defenders, crouching in thinly scraped trenches or sheltering in sunken lanes, were taken by surprise by the intensity of the bombardment, which made coordinating any kind of organized response almost impossible. In many cases, the only thing to do was to sit tight, check your weapons, and wait for the Allied infantry to appear – the bowed attackers that filtered towards your positions in the wake of the creeping barrage. In many sectors, machine-gunners were the backbone of the defence. The 08 German heavy machine-gun could fire up to 400 rounds per minute, meaning that unless they were taken out quickly, they could cause horrendous casualties to infantry moving in the open. When Captain Malcolm Helm, of 5th Machine Gun Battalion (2nd US Division), went forward that morning through fields 'loaded with wheat', he noticed several 'cleared out spaces' with a wrecked German machine-gun in the centre surrounded by a bunch of enemy corpses. 'Paths radiating from the centre like spokes of a wheel showed where our infantrymen had converged on the machine gun crew from every direction and had shot or bayoneted those who did not escape.'[11]

In line with the infantry were the tanks, in which so much faith had been invested. Lieutenant Chenu was the commander of a

Schneider medium tank, attached to 1st US Division. Weighing over 13 tons with a crew of six, the Schneider was cumbersome and slow, although it packed a powerful punch with a 75mm howitzer housed in its box-like chassis. Chenu's men were in the second wave and as they chugged forward, their tracks grinding along the dusty ground, they could see the black explosions of the barrage up ahead. 'The second wave of tanks has moved off. I go on foot, like all the battery commanders, to try and have an overview for as long as possible,' he wrote. 'We get closer to the Hell of a barrage. It has, fortunately, regular gaps. My battery, in twos, worm swiftly in to the left. That's done: not a single tank damaged.' Unfortunately that was where Chenu's luck ran out. As he approached another tank, a little up ahead, a shell struck it, and it exploded in a flash of yellow flame. Within seconds the driver emerged from the burning sheets of metal, terribly wounded, running to the rear, hands covering his bloody face.[12]

Chenu's battery of tanks advanced seven kilometres that day, driving through the wheat fields, supporting American infantry, firing at machine-gun nests and engaging the enemy wherever they were seen. In their sector, German soldiers gave themselves up freely. Tired and demoralized clusters of prisoners shuffled to the rear, confused at what had happened and in awe of the iron monsters that had driven over their positions. Although enemy reinforcements would eventually stem their advance, they had delivered a crushing blow to the German right flank. General Fayolle, the French Army Group commander, crowed that 'the elan of the troops was superb. Surprise was complete.' North of the Ourcq River, where Mangin's army was deployed, the Allies had gained up to ten kilometres along a twenty-five-kilometre front and taken 10,000 prisoners.[13] To the southwest, the French Sixth Army had encountered heavy resistance, but advanced between four and five kilometres and took over 1,500 prisoners and fifty guns.[14]

The Allied counter-attack stunned the German High Command. Walther Reinhardt, Chief of Staff of Seventh Army (which bore the brunt of the counter-attack), remembered how 'hell broke loose' along the front southwest of Soissons just after five o'clock that morning. What he called 'terrifying' artillery fire fell on their sector, cutting telephone wires, tearing up trenches and smashing roads and tracks leading to the front. It would be another two hours of tense waiting before they received word that a large attack had been launched with 'whole fleets of tanks' and that their front-line infantry had been overrun almost everywhere. Given the precarious situation within the salient, Reinhardt knew that it was essential to hold on for as long as possible, to redeploy their artillery and bring up ammunition, and ensure that the enemy was beaten back.[15] General Erich von Ludendorff, at the German Supreme Command, thought the same. In his memoirs he admitted that 'Our infantry had not stood firm at all points', and lamented the 'deep dents' that had been gouged out of the line.[16] He did what he could; sending volleys of telegrams to all available reserve units to march to the threatened sectors and alerting other commands that they might have to send further reinforcements in the coming days. There was nothing else he could do but wait, and hope.

The Marne fighting would place an enormous strain on the German Army. One veteran, Herbert Sulzbach, wrote in his diary on 23 July, five days after the Allied counter-attack had gone in: 'Your nerves have taken a heavy beating now, you feel physically run down, you haven't slept a second all night, you've been standing in this witches' cauldron for days . . . If someone asked me today when we had anything to eat in the last few days, I could only answer that I didn't know; because all that sort of thing just happens mechanically, and the whole of our thought and our concentration is only turned towards victory.'[17] But victory now seemed a long way off, perhaps further away than ever. The German Supreme Command knew this as well as anyone. Within days of the counter-attack they had suspended all plans for future offensives and were preparing for what the Allies would do next; waiting anxiously and hoping that they would have enough time to rest their shattered divisions and restock their depleted supplies before fighting broke out again. But there could be no denying the gravity of what had happened. It was more than just losing the Marne salient or having to break up ten divisions, it was about something much more important. *They had lost the initiative.*

1. Decision on the Marne

It remains for the living to finish the glorious work of the dead.

Georges Clemenceau[1]

18–25 July 1918

The retreat from the Marne began on 20 July. In the coming days three German armies trudged northwards in long grey columns; giving up the ground they had gained during the spring and occasionally looting French villages. One observer, Rudolf Binding, remembered being 'sick at heart' after seeing soldiers running around taking everything they could get their hands on; a dangerous illustration of the disorder and ill-discipline that was beginning to grip the German Army after four long years of war. 'In the twinkling of an eye everything was turned upside-down, as if the looters were professionals,' he wrote. 'The soldiers hacked whole beds to pieces for the sake of a length of sheeting the size of a towel and worth about one-fiftieth of their value; thousands of sheets of paper were thrown into the mud for the sake of a single picture postcard, and whole cupboards burst open for the sake of a reel of cotton.'[2] And it was not just the property of the enemy that was being grabbed; German supply trains and depots were increasingly being targeted by groups of deserters and looters desperately searching for food. 'This conduct on the part of German soldiers,' so one report read, 'constitutes a defiance of discipline, and must be repressed with the utmost vigour.'[3] Even worse, it was anything but an isolated incident and was happening right across the front. The German war effort, it seemed, was rapidly coming apart.

The morale of the Army remained steady, but it was increasingly fragile. Hope in victory was now being replaced by disillusion and weariness. Georg Bucher, a soldier who fought throughout 1918, remembered that life was viewed with 'a crazy indifference'. 'We had become hard – a frozen, inarticulate hardness which was yet an agony when, thinking ourselves unobserved, we allowed our faces to betray our thoughts.' Many had long since ceased to hate the enemy and looked upon the 'terrified agitation' of recruits – who seemed to become younger and younger with every passing week – with distrust and unease. 'We had nothing left to hope for,' he wrote, 'even our last desperate hope, the hope of victory, had deserted us.' There was nothing left to do but keep going.[4] Even the Army Group commander, Crown Prince Wilhelm, began to notice that things were not as they should have been. 'I entered every morning the office of the Army Group,' he wrote. 'I was always prepared for bad news and received it only too often. The drives to the front, which had previously been a pleasure and recreation for me, were now filled with bitterness. The staff officers' brows were furrowed with care. The troops, though still almost everywhere perfect in discipline and demeanour, willing, friendly and cheerful in their salutes, were worn to death. My heart turned within me when I beheld their hollow cheeks, their lean and weary figures, their tattered and dirty uniforms . . .'[5]

The growing problem of looting, poor discipline and desertion could be traced back, in some respects, to a simple lack of food. By 1918 the German nation and its army were starving. During the great offensives earlier in the year, in March and April, German troops had been amazed by the amount and variety of food and drink they found in British and French supply dumps; things like tinned stew and jam that had disappeared from the German diet years ago. Officers would stumble across groups of men gorging on captured rations or drunk on whisky, and unconcerned about the urgent need to press on. This lack of appropriate nutrition also meant that German soldiers were unable to resist the influenza pandemic that swept across the front during the summer. A number of divisions could only muster company strengths of around sixty men, about 30 per cent of their manpower being sick with flu, and this seems to have been entirely typical of what the German Army suffered in this period. In the Army as a whole a staggering 135,000 men were taken ill with influenza in

June; the following month another 375,000 men had to be excused duty for this reason.[6]

Given the extent of the problems facing the German Army – which had sustained nearly 800,000 casualties in the last six months – it was little wonder that a growing number of senior officers were advocating a withdrawal from exposed and over-extended lines to a shorter, more easily defensible position. Many argued that they should retreat to the *Siegfried Stellung* (or Hindenburg Line as the Allies called it), the formidable series of defences that had been prepared in 1916 as a kind of German insurance policy in the west. Here, they argued, their armies should rest and reform, and then let the Allies break themselves upon it. Major-General Friedrich Karl 'Fritz' von Lossberg, Chief of Staff at Fourth Army and one of the best defensive tacticians, admitted in the days after 18 July that the position on the Marne should be given up immediately.[7] Others advocated even more radical action. Crown Prince Wilhelm reported to OHL that the front should be immediately withdrawn to the so-called Antwerp–Meuse position, which lay far behind the Hindenburg Line. This would give their troops a breathing space, shorten the front considerably, and free precious reserves.[8] These concerns were eminently sensible and a valuable recognition of Germany's dangerously exposed position in the west, having gained large amounts of territory that was difficult to defend and strategically useless, but they would not be received well by the men who ran the German war effort: the Kaiser, Wilhelm II; the Chief of the General Staff, Paul von Hindenburg; and his right-hand man, General Erich von Ludendorff.

The Kaiser was a man who – as he would have painfully admitted – never achieved his own ambitions or truly lived up to the promise of his inheritance. He had been born in January 1859, the son of Prince Friedrich Wilhelm of Prussia and his wife, Vicky, daughter of Queen Victoria. Despite his privileged upbringing, he was always tormented by a deep-seated insecurity, particularly towards the British and his royal relatives, who were always, he would swear, scheming against him. When the war broke out, he was also increasingly sidelined by Germany's military leaders, who now held the Fatherland's destiny in their hands; something that bordered on abject humiliation and resulted in no end of frustration. He had a withered left arm, which was probably the cause of much of his insecurity, and it had become symptomatic of a man who was petty, prone to rages and hysteria, and aware that he was not what he had once seemed destined to become. His eldest son, the Crown Prince (who would command an Army Group in France), was well aware of his father's failings, even if he did his best to overlook them. The deepest characteristic of his father was, he wrote, summed up in the word *noble*.

> The Kaiser is noble in the best sense of the word; he is full of the most upright desire for goodness and piety, and the purity of his intellectual cosmos is without a blemish and without a stain. Candour that makes no reservations, that is perhaps too unbounded in its nature, ready confidence and belief in the like trustworthiness and frankness on the part of others, are the fundamental features of his character.

Yet this was not without its problems. The Crown Prince admitted that 'He has always allowed his thoughts and convictions to gush forth instantaneously and immediately without prelude and without prologue, an incautious and noble spendthrift of an ever fertile intellect which draws its sustenance from comprehensive knowledge and a fancy whose only fault is its exuberance.'[9] It was this exuberance that had tipped Germany over the edge in 1914.

Wilhelm may have nominally led Germany, but real power lay in the hands of his two military commanders: Field Marshal Paul von Hindenburg and General Erich von Ludendorff, the legendary duo who had run the war effort since the late summer of 1916. Hindenburg was the Chief of the General Staff, the pinnacle of a career that had spanned the life of the Second Reich and seen him rise to become the *ersatz* Kaiser, the most powerful man in the kingdom. His reputation as a gifted commander had been assured after his decisive victory over the Russians at Tannenberg in August 1914, when two Russian Armies had been counter-attacked in the marshes of East Prussia and been almost completely destroyed. Hindenburg's face was a mask of Prussian granite, with clipped grey hair, a hard stare and a fierce, upturned moustache; perfectly embodying the seemingly iron will of an empire and the uncompromising warrior ethos of Prussia. If anyone could do it, they would say, then surely Hindenburg could. He was known for his thoughtful composure, one German commander noting that 'If he spoke, the effect was heightened: one was then impressed not merely by the statuesqueness of his tall, broad shouldered figure, but by the depth and timbre of his voice and the easy flow of his measured, thoughtful, and deliberate speech; the conviction was confirmed that the speaker was absolute master of the situation and expressed views that could be thoroughly relied on.'[10] But there was more to him than the image of the peerless commander would suggest. By 1918 Hindenburg had lost touch with the war. His legendary calmness and composure had ossified into inaction and lack of interest. He was approaching his seventy-first birthday and spent his days either safely ensconced in the elegant surroundings of the Supreme Command at Spa in Belgium or out hunting in the forests of the east. And if Germany suffered during the war, then Hindenburg never did. Beneath his grey army tunic covered with decorations – his favourite being the Iron Cross with Golden Rays that he had received in March 1918 – was the portly gait and reddened skin of a man who enjoyed good food and helped himself to the best brandy and champagne of the pre-war years. Not that it mattered anyway, particularly when his right-hand man possessed such boundless energy and spirit.

The First Quartermaster-General was Erich von Ludendorff. He was slightly shorter than Hindenburg, with a bald head and small grey eyes, with jowls hanging over his tight collar; his mouth seemingly always turned down in a permanent scowl. He may have been Hindenburg's Chief of Staff – and at fifty-three years of age was considerably younger – but he shared his responsibility fully, and took an increasingly senior role in devising and conducting operations throughout 1918. He was a notoriously cold and serious man; even his wife, Margarethe, called him Ludendorff. Although she would claim that before the war he was often cheerful and free from anxiety – that he did not always have the expression 'of a man whose feelings had turned to ice' – by 1918 the pressure was telling. He 'never possessed any knowledge of human nature'; a serious flaw in so important a figure and which would become ever more damaging in the final months of the Great War.[11] Nevertheless, Ludendorff was a brutally effective soldier. He had begun the war as a senior staff officer who won a *Pour le Mérite* during the storming of Liège, before being transferred to the Eastern Front, where he came into contact with Hindenburg. Although the two men were great friends and formed an effective partnership ('together like one man, in the most perfect harmony'[12]), they possessed striking dissimilarities. Whereas Hindenburg was notoriously relaxed and self-possessed, Ludendorff was a fountain of energy and nervousness, a man always seemingly on the edge of a thunderous rage which scattered his attendants and required the calming influence of the Chief of the General Staff. 'Come on,' Hindenburg would say – surely and deliberately – 'I should like a word with you.'[13]

Two years had passed since Hindenburg and Ludendorff had taken command of the German war effort; now, victory, it seemed, was still as far away as ever. Her armies may have defeated Tsarist Russia, dismembered Poland, and kept the Allies at bay in the west, but Germany's strategic situation was full of danger. Bit by bit, Germany was dying; bleeding more and more every day. The great series of offensives that Ludendorff had conducted since March 1918, which had been intended as a final masterstroke to win the war in the west, had failed. The maps in the Supreme Headquarters may have shown pleasing advances into French territory and great sweeps of newly captured ground, but they could not disguise the fact that the war went on and the Allies continued to resist. Indeed, they may have been bloodied but they were unbowed, and judging from the furious pronouncements of the French President, Georges Clemenceau, were as eager for victory as ever. And they had found a powerful new ally in the United States of America, whose military power was now undeniable. Even worse, the heavy fighting had used up Germany's dwindling reserves of manpower and squandered her best troops, most of whom had been concentrated in elite storm divisions and been killed or wounded earlier in the year, at places of evil memory: trampled in the mud of the Chemin des Dames, floating in the currents of the Marne, or scattered across the fields of Flanders.

Whenever Ludendorff was handed reports from his senior officers advocating withdrawal, he would undoubtedly have given his usual scowl or snapped at his staff officers. A full-scale retreat was not possible for a number of reasons. Firstly, it would send a particularly painful signal of weakness, which might have unforeseen effects at home. It would be difficult to carry out owing to the lack of adequate (lateral) rail lines. It would mean abandoning newly won territory and great amounts of supplies. Therefore, it was unacceptable. Ludendorff's solution revealed perhaps the greatest flaw in his approach to war, his insistence that only another new offensive would do. Throughout the last days of July and the first week of August, as the Marne line was abandoned, he assiduously worked on yet another plan to shatter the British position in Flanders. Ludendorff clung to this new operation, which he called Hagen (after a character from Wagner's *Ring* cycle), like a drowning swimmer clings to a lifebuoy; fearing that if he gave it up he would cede the initiative to the Allies and never get it back. But as events moved rapidly throughout the summer, Ludendorff was forced to postpone and then cancel his cherished offensive. The unfortunate truth was that there were no military solutions to Germany's problems, only political ones. Ludendorff would come to realize this, but only when it was too late.[14]

The military situation may have been unedifying, but that was not all Hindenburg and Ludendorff had to consider. The home front, in particular, was beginning to collapse. If food could be difficult to get in Paris, with its wartime restrictions, it was much worse in Berlin. The summer of 1918 was a depressing time to be in the capital. It was always a grey, sprawling industrial city, noted for its wide streets and imposing stone buildings, but now it had a haunted, besieged feel. News of what was happening at the front was always difficult to come by so rumours and half-truths filled the vacuum. Its citizens had endured difficult periods before, the so-called 'turnip winter' of 1916–17 had been a warning that Germany could not endure for ever, but this was much worse. The Central Powers were dependent on imports of food and raw materials, supplies that had now dried up almost entirely owing to the vice-like grip of the Allied naval blockade.

It may not have been possible to see the blockade, but through the mist and the grey wastes of the North Sea its effect was certainly being felt. It had taken several years for the Royal Navy to put significant pressure on Germany and Austro-Hungary, but with the entry of the US into the war in the spring of 1917, the few remaining loopholes were swiftly closed. The noose was getting tighter.

Gradually the German people entered a dark world of *ersatz* food; substitutes that were as unappetizing as they were imaginative: coffee made from acorns; tobacco made from beech leaves; bread stuffed with sawdust; sausages made from horseflesh or rabbits. The bread ration had been reduced from seven to five and a half ounces in June and malnutrition was now becoming impossible to ignore.[15] 'You have no idea what life costs in Berlin,' moaned Leutnant Richard Schütt to his father on 12 August, echoing a common complaint. Schütt was an infantry officer based in Potsdam and was increasingly worried by how bad things were getting. In peacetime 1,000 Deutschmarks may have been a lot of money, but now in Berlin it did not go very far. 'Everything is five to ten times more expensive,' he noted. His apartment cost almost twice what it would have in 1914 and laundry was almost four times as expensive, but food remained the central problem. Before the war, he needed only fifty Deutschmarks a month to buy food – about a fifth of his salary – but now he had to pay half that amount every day. 'There are many people who have much less than me,' he wrote. 'They eat in people's kitchens, middle class kitchens or cook themselves what they can get on food stamps.' He would have liked to go to smaller, cheaper restaurants, but as an officer one had to frequent the more expensive ones ('as befitting their social standing'). He told his parents that without their weekly parcel he would have 'half starved'.[16]

For too long the German people had been fed on stories of victory, of military triumphs that surpassed Napoleon, of crushing offensives that would split the Entente. Now, as the summer of 1918 wore on – a wet, damp summer that seemed to hint at an approaching deluge – dissatisfaction with Germany's position grew. On 8 July, ten days before the Allies would counter-attack on the Marne, Richard von Kühlmann, the Foreign Secretary and man who had concluded peace with Russia at Brest-Litovsk, was forced to resign. Two weeks earlier, he had risen before a packed Reichstag and made an impassioned speech in which he had expressed doubts that victory could be achieved by arms alone. 'Without some such exchange of views, given the enormous extent of this war of coalitions and the numbers of powers involved in it,' he said, 'an absolute end is hardly to be expected from military decisions alone, without recourse to diplomatic discussions.'[17] Although von Kühlmann was right – and many in the higher echelons of Wilhelmine Germany agreed with him – the speech seemed to undermine the Supreme Command at a crucial moment, and Ludendorff panicked, shouting down a hot telephone line from Spa that the Foreign Secretary must go. The Kaiser meekly agreed, replacing von Kühlmann with Admiral Paul von Hintze, a quiet naval officer who had little of his predecessor's sense or integrity. It was a fateful decision. Germany would once more place her faith in a decision on the battlefield. Now there could be no negotiated peace, no declaration on Belgium or the League of Nations; there was only war.

The German retreat from the Marne left a nightmarish zone of devastation in its wake. Burnt-out tanks littered the countryside; trench lines lay across the landscape like huge, manmade scars; bodies lay clumped together in the wheat, which was trampled down and blown ragged by artillery fire. A French medical officer, serving with Mangin's Tenth Army, recorded the horrific sights he saw as they followed up the enemy. 'Everywhere,' he wrote, 'golden wheat and pale-gold oats hide the dead amongst the cornflowers and the poppies. We give a mental salute and pass by; inwardly very moved.' From a distance the region seemed untouched, but up close it was a different matter: 'trees broken in two, fields churned up, little dug-outs for machine-guns, abandoned munitions, dead horses, legs in the air, ridiculous and heart-breaking, with great disgusting wounds covered with enormous flies, millions of bluebottles which make a noise like an aircraft engine as they fly off.' The flies were particularly bad. 'I have never seen so many of them, you just can't imagine,' he complained. They killed hundreds with formalin poured into sweetened water, but 'just as many' were back again the next day.[18]

Casualties in the Marne sector had been enormous. The French, who had borne the brunt of Allied casualties, had lost over 2,500 officers and nearly 93,000 other ranks.[19] They had captured 25,000 German soldiers and 600 officers, and seized 3,300 machine-guns, 221 *Minenwerfer* and over 600 artillery pieces, the vast majority by Mangin's Tenth Army, but it had come at huge cost.[20] Figures for German dead, wounded and missing have never been calculated with any precision, but were, if anything, even worse. Medical reports show that the German Army suffered 165,000 casualties during the month of July, the majority of which would have been sustained in the heavy fighting on the Marne.[21] It was little wonder that many Allied soldiers would remember the battle for only one thing: the wheat fields, which were 'dotted with many rifles, the bayonets of which were stuck in the ground'. According to an American, Private Ralph Williams, who had gone over the top on 18 July, 'These were swaying in the breeze, marking spots where our fellows had fallen. It was a sickening sight. There seemed to be hundreds of them in just the small area we had covered.'[22]

As well as the thousands of broken and bloodied men that came from the front, there was a frightening surge in cases of influenza across Western Europe. This was the first wave of the great 'Spanish flu' pandemic that wreaked such havoc and caused such fear, with up to fifty million people dying worldwide before the end of 1919.[23] Influenza had always been present, but the number of admissions suddenly surged up during the last summer of the war. In the UK there had been somewhere between 2,000 and 3,000 cases each month during the spring, but over 30,000 were registered in June alone. This epidemic took the form of the so-called 'three day fever', which was extremely infectious, and, as the British Medical History noted, would strike suddenly 'so that barrack rooms which the day before had been full of bustle and life would now be converted wholesale into one great sick room'. Patients would experience a high fever, often up to 103 degrees Fahrenheit, before gradually returning to health within a short time.[24] This strain was particularly virulent in the German Army. In the two months of June and July 1918, over half a million soldiers would contract the disease, most of whom were treated in specialized 'flu infirmaries' behind the lines. The ill-ness usually began with chills and general malaise, before a fever took hold for 48–72 hours. This 'lighter' type of flu was usually not fatal – patients would generally recover within eight or ten days – and had died down by the late summer, and should not be confused with the much more lethal and dangerous strain that emerged over the winter of 1918 and into the following year.

This second strain of influenza was the killer. As the year pro-gressed, Allied and German doctors began to notice new, more terrifying symptoms in their influenza cases. They would soon become familiar with a list of complaints that included bodily weak-ness and a throbbing headache, chest pains and a hacking cough. Usually blood-stained froth would be brought up and the patient would then show the usually fatal signs of cyanosis – the blue discol-oration of the face that meant death was only hours away. 'Among the worst forms,' the German Medical History reported:

> the symptoms that dominated were not the often severe pneumonia that affected several lobes . . . but rather general infection and tox-aemia. Severe exhaustion, cyanosis, shortness of breath, slightly quickened pulse, a high, ragged fever, dizziness, and confusion were signs of these. That is why the means of circulation often failed, and pulmonary oedemas resulted in death. Bronchitis and even the melt-ing of the lung structure, both characterized by pus, were found. The spleen was enlarged. Serious relapses and mixed infections ensued.

The appearance of infected lungs was so distressing that surgeons compared them with the victims of pneumonic plague – the dreaded 'Black Death'.[25]

It was remarkable that this latest horror only produced a kind of grim resignation among the populations of Europe. For the Allies, four years of slaughter and of hopes dashed had drained their people of any optimism or *élan* they once possessed. Their armies may have marched proudly to war in 1914 confident that victory would come by Christmas, but by the summer of 1918 there were no such thoughts. The armies of the last year of the war – bar only the Americans – did not, and could not, share the illusions of their predecessors.

Eyewitness accounts from this time contain little of the enthusiasm and excitement that were shown in the frantic days of August 1914; they are, on the contrary, notable for their glassy-eyed exhaustion, cynicism and depression. To some, it seemed, the war would go on for ever; a bitter joke that was lampooned by the British humorist Bruce Bairnsfather in a cartoon featuring his favourite character, 'Old Bill'. He was still in the trenches in 1950, now with a long, white beard, noting that the 'war babies' battalion was coming out'.[26] Everyone, it seemed, was reaching the end of their limits, both physical and emotional, and if victory was to be achieved in 1918, then it would have to come quickly.

The counter-attack on the Marne may have saved Paris and snatched the initiative away from the German Army, but the war remained to be won. For the leaders of the Allied powers, the summer of 1918 was an anxious and difficult time. The French Premier, Georges Clemenceau, was, at seventy-six years old, the oldest of the major leaders of the war; a symbol of French resistance and devotion to victory that brought his homeland through the dark days of the spring.[27] His counterpart in London, David Lloyd George, was in many respects similar: outspoken, wily, untrustworthy, yet devoted to winning the war. Both men were outsiders and radicals, the kind of offbeat politicians that Western democracy often throws up in times of crisis. They had risen to power because, at times, there seemed no one else who could do the job; no one else who still had any fight left within them. For the time being they kept the flame of defiance alive, whatever the cost, hoping that Germany had overreached herself. They would put their faith – what was left of it – in four remarkable soldiers; men who now had the task of winning the war on the Western Front.

The Allied *Generalissimo* was General Ferdinand Foch. He was not at first glance a particularly impressive figure. Foch was not notably tall and had deep-set eyes, a large moustache and a high forehead. He usually wore a blue-grey French Army tunic with little adornment, and was often to be seen smoking a cigar, mainly cheap varieties. But beneath the rather unimpressive exterior was a man of quite incredible character. The words used by one biographer, 'resilient as a rubber ball', were an apt description of a man who simply would not accept defeat, no matter what.[28] Sir William Orpen, the esteemed British portrait artist, painted Foch in 1918 and in the swift, jerky movements of his brush managed to convey something of the energy and mercurial temperament of the Allied *Generalissimo*. One British officer who knew Foch described him as 'a man of relentless energy and determination. In conversation he often employed gestures to emphasize his words; two blows in the air with his fists, followed by two kicks, used to show the fate which he reserved for his enemies.'[29] He spoke in short, sharp sentences, which may have given some the impression of arrogance or impatience, but was, to those who knew him, typical of a man who was used to command and wanted things to be done quickly, without fuss. Despite his reputation as a habitual optimist, Foch knew the cost of war. In August 1914, his only son, Germain, an infantry subaltern, had been killed in action on the Meuse. After being told the news, Foch allowed himself only half an hour of sorrow, before recovering and, like a rubber ball, getting back up to fight. He straightened his uniform and emerged from his office, urging his staff, 'Now let us get on with our work.'[30]

Foch had been appointed *Generalissimo* in the dark spring of 1918 when the British and French Armies had tottered on the brink of separation, and thus defeat in detail, under the hammer blows of the great German offensive that had returned manoeuvre to the Western Front. Cooperation and coordination between the British and French had been patchy and ad-hoc since 1914, but with disagreements and defeatism now threatening to leave the Allies at the mercy of their enemies, it was essential to put in place some kind of unity of command. At a fraught meeting at Doullens Town Hall on 26 March, the British and French governments hammered out a decision that was to have immense repercussions. General Foch, the French representative on the Allied Supreme War Council, was commissioned to coordinate the actions of the Allied armies on the Western Front. He was a man renowned for his energy, decision and aggression, and had to do whatever it took to maintain contact; to make sure that the British and French commanders, Haig and Pétain, worked together in the common interest.[31]

There was never any question that Foch was the right man for the job. The only other candidate would have been the head of the French Army, General Henri Philippe Pétain, but he was not keen. In any case, there were concerns that his temperament and character were unsuited to the role because no one better epitomized French weariness than Pétain. If Foch represented the passionate Gallic spirit *par excellence*, then Pétain symbolized the earthier, resigned outlook of the French peasant. A staff officer who served at his headquarters, Jean de Pierrefeu, later remarked that 'The guiding principle of his mind, and one rarely found among soldiers, pragmatists though they be, was a sort of philosophic background, a noble fatalism.'[32] Pétain had always faced the storms of war with a calm serenity and an even temperament, unlike the more mercurial Foch. One distinguished French officer illustrated the difference between the two men by drawing a zigzag for Foch and a straight line for Pétain. While Foch went up and down, Pétain continued, serenely as ever, in a line straight as a die.[33] He had been appointed Commander-in-Chief in the bitter aftermath of the failure of the Nivelle offensive in the spring of 1917 and promised that no more large-scale attacks would come. They would wait, he said, for the tanks and for the Americans. Pétain knew that his army was a pale shadow of its former self, a gaunt and bloodied shell of an army that had fought for too long against a superior enemy. Only his dour realism could have kept it going, harbouring its strength for one final push.

Despite his impressive-sounding brief, Foch's authority was limited, and crucially he could not order anyone to do anything. The full tactical control of Allied armies was left to their national commanders, who could appeal to their governments if they felt endangered by any of his instructions. But Foch could inspire and suggest, push and prod. His position meant that he had to take a wider view of the war, above and beyond mere national contingents, and almost immediately the Allied war effort began to assume a more coordinated and focused aspect. His appointment lifted some of the crushing pressure from Haig and Pétain and meant that, at long last, Allied operations would be conceived from the brain of one man, his wishes executed by his commanders. According to Joseph Hellé, Chief of Staff to the French Tenth Army, the choice of Foch was 'singularly felicitous. Through his writings, his teachings, his expert knowledge and his optimism, Foch had made a deep impression on everyone.' He was, Hellé also admitted, 'perhaps the only French general from whom the British were willing to take orders'.[34]

The man who had been instrumental in the appointment of Foch was the British Commander-in-Chief, Field Marshal Sir Douglas Haig.[34] He had been in France since August 1914, guiding the British Expeditionary Force through its bloody rite of passage on the Somme in 1916 and throughout the heavy fighting of the following year, but was having to work increasingly hard to maintain his position against the machinations of Britain's mercurial Prime Minister, David Lloyd George. Lloyd George hated Haig. To him, Haig represented all that was reactionary and outdated about the British Army, and he would fill pages of his voluminous memoirs with vitriol about Haig and the unthinking 'military mind'.[35] In spite of the later controversies surrounding Haig's command, he looked every inch the soldier, with his stern gaze and his back ramrod straight. One of those who knew him well, his chaplain, G. S. Duncan, described his appearance as 'certainly impressive' and 'singularly handsome'. 'Preeminently he was a man of action,' Duncan wrote:

> but that broad square forehead marked him out also as the calm, concentrated and logical thinker, and the look in his eye suggested unplumbed depths of feeling and understanding. As he spoke to you, you realised instinctively that here was a man of transparent honesty, who for all his reserve had a warm heart, who in all his judgments was accustomed to look below the surface, and who brought to all his several practical tasks a strong measure of far-sightedness and idealism.[36]

Duncan knew Haig well and had served with him for many years, but others found it harder to grasp the man beneath the stiff demeanour and struggled to hold him in such warm regard. Haig was a complex man. In private he was supremely confident in his own ability, and had for many years garnered a reputation as a talented, educated soldier, but he was not a great communicator, and often struggled to get his message across. He was a curious mix of the modern and traditional: a cavalry officer who maintained the importance of the mounted arm in war, yet who had overseen the greatest expansion of artillery and firepower in the history of the British Army. A man who would later maintain that he had fought a war of attrition to wear down the might of the German Army, yet who was always drawn to the dramatic breakthrough operations that were redolent of the great Napoleonic manoeuvres he had studied as a student at Camberley. Haig embodied the contradictions, strengths and weaknesses of the British nation at war.

In June 1918 Foch's headquarters had moved to the Château de Bombon, an elegant seventeenth-century building on the outskirts of the town of Melun, twenty-five miles southeast of Paris. It had been built in the traditional French style, with elegant brickwork, a slate roof and large rectangular windows that looked out on to extensive gardens, flush with the greens of summer. Surprisingly, for such an important location, Bombon was a quiet, understated place. Foch only employed a small staff, barely a dozen officers, who were trusted to provide the general with everything he needed. Bombon was a home where Foch could think, go for walks and rides in the surrounding countryside, and direct the war that he was determined to win. On the morning of 24 July, it was the venue for an event of singular importance, a meeting of the three Allied contingent commanders: Haig; Pétain; and the American, General John Pershing. The four men had met before, but Bombon was one of the rare instances when they were all in the same room together, something that would only happen on a few brief occasions during the war. It came at a time of considerable importance.

The men arrived punctually at 10.30 a.m. and were invited in to meet Foch.[37] After the introductions, Foch instructed his Chief of Staff, Maxime Weygand, to read out a memorandum that had been prepared on the future situation in the west. It had been written by Weygand, but Foch – in his persistent wish to avoid writing things down – had agreed with every word.[38] Firstly, Weygand announced that the recent German offensive (the fifth since March) had failed.

The recent counter-attack on the Marne had turned it into a defeat, which 'must first of all be exploited thoroughly on the field of battle itself. That is why we are pursuing our attacks without pause and with all our energy.' As things now stood, the Allies had a rough equality in numbers to their enemy, but the Germans were tired and many divisions were both reduced in strength and exhausted by constant operations. Furthermore, the Allies had a great superiority in materiel, tanks and artillery. This, combined with the 250,000 US troops who were arriving in France every month, provided further proof of the changing situation. As well as the 'materiel' factor, Weygand stressed 'the moral ascendancy which had been maintained by our side from the beginning of the battle', and said that a 'turning point' had now arrived. The Allies had recovered from the enemy offensives and had rebuilt their forces. The principles of war, he said, now compelled them to seize the initiative. 'The moment has come to abandon the general defensive attitude forced upon us until now by numerical inferiority and to pass to the offensive.'

Foch had devised what he called a 'series of movements' intended to inflict a 'succession of blows' against the enemy. The main thrust of these attacks was, first of all, to clear three main railway lines that were vital to the war effort. The fighting of 1918 had brought the German Army to within striking distance of Paris and threatened a number of key logistical hubs. Railways were essential to moving troops across the Allied front, yet the Paris–Avricourt line in the Marne had been cut at Château-Thierry, the Amiens rail junction was within range of enemy guns, and German troops in Saint-Mihiel were only ten miles from the Paris–Avricourt line in the southeast. Foch was convinced that the moment to secure these positions had now arrived. He was also planning other operations to drive the enemy from the vicinity of Dunkirk and Calais in the north. Foch knew that only by coordinating the actions of the Allies as closely as possible and striking back could the German Army be kept off balance and forced to retreat.

To Foch's evident dismay, the responses of the three men were not encouraging, yet, in their own way, they summed up the positions of the three national contingents at that moment. Haig spoke first. He complained that his army had been 'entirely disorg-anized by the events of March and April' and was still 'far from being re-established'. Pétain agreed, echoing Haig's concerns and bluntly telling Foch that 'The French Army, after four years of war and the severest trials, is at present worn out, bled white, anaemic.' This was hardly encouraging, and it fell to General John J. Pershing, Commander-in-Chief of the American Expeditionary Force, to instil some optimism into the proceedings. Pershing was undoubt-edly more enthusiastic than his counterparts, speaking in a relaxed, Midwestern drawl that betrayed his origins in rural Missouri. He admitted that the Americans only wished to fight. He did, however, warn Foch that his troops were not yet ready. Although ten days ear-lier a First US Army had been created, American military power in France remained a work in progress. It may not have been battle-hardened or experienced, but it was getting there. Thousands of men were arriving at French ports every day, swarming off the jammed transport ships and slowly making their way eastwards towards the sound of the guns; the eager, young doughboys chattering nervously about what it would be like and whether the war would end before they got there. But how were these Americans to be incorporated into the war effort? The British and French commanders undoubt-edly wanted American help, but they wanted it on their own terms – in other words American units amalgamated into their own armies – and this was something that Pershing could not allow. If Americans were to fight, he continually reminded them, they would fight as a single, independent force under his command. It would be a source of constant friction.

Foch, Pétain and Haig were old acquaintances, but Pershing was, in every sense of the word, an outsider. Known as 'Black Jack' after serv-ing in an all black regiment, Pershing was, at fifty-seven years of age, slightly younger than both Haig (sixty) and Pétain (sixty-two). He had been appointed to command the American Expeditionary Force (AEF) in May 1917, the same month that Pétain had become Commander-in-Chief. At that time the AEF did not really exist; the American military was even more unprepared for war than the British had been in 1914, so it was necessary to appoint someone with administrative ability, drive and determination. Pershing had been promoted over the heads of at least five more senior officers, and understandably this aroused some jealousy. In the end he was chosen because of his recent campaign experience (in Mexico), his acknowledged promise, a strong constitution and a devoted professionalism. A senior officer of the AEF, Robert Lee Bullard, later remarked that he 'won followers and admirers, but not personal worshippers'. He was 'peculiarly impersonal, dispassionate, hard and firm . . . His manner carried to the minds of those under him the suggestion, nay, the conviction of unquestioned right to obedience.'[39] These traits were even more evident after a devastating fire had killed his wife, Frances, and three of their four children in August 1915. Pershing had always been a hard man, driven and determined to succeed, but in his youth there had been another side to his character; he was known as something of a ladies' man and was an excellent poker player. But from the moment he lost his family, there was only one side to Pershing: a cold, unyielding will. His determination would be essential to Allied victory in 1918.

At the meeting there was little sense the war would be over by Christmas. Although Haig later wrote that everyone was in 'great spirits', there remained understandable concern about what more could be achieved that year.[40] Foch took their objections calmly. He pointed out that while he agreed with their observations, he urged them to think about how a 'proper combination of our forces' could make the attacks practicable and effective. After some further discussion, no more points were raised and the commanders agreed to take Foch's note with them, discuss it with their staffs and let him know as soon as possible. With the meeting now over, the four men walked outside, into the bright sunshine, and posed for a photograph. Foch stood in the middle, a slight smirk upon his face, his hands neatly behind his back. To his right was Haig, cane in hand, and then Pétain, his dull, blue eyes staring out from beneath the peak of his *képi*, arms by his side. To Foch's left, slightly distant, was Pershing, his expression inscrutable, his eyes hidden beneath his cap.

The bulb flashed and then, shaking hands once more, the four men disappeared into the warm afternoon.

2. 'Neglect nothing'

It was therefore possible to adopt the conjurer's trick of directing the special attention of the observer to those things which do not particularly matter, in order to distract his attention from other things which really do matter very much.

Sir John Monash[1]

26 July–7 August 1918

Compared to other places in northern France – those that had been in a warzone for four years – Amiens had suffered relatively lightly. Although many of its houses had been demolished and shells had struck the cathedral, gouging out great scars in its masonry, the town had survived largely intact. Yet concern over the safety of its civilian population had forced the French Government to evacuate the town, leaving it empty and lifeless. A British officer, Charles Vince, rode through Amiens that summer. 'One went through street after forsaken street of empty, morose houses, with nothing harmed, nothing touched, no sign of destruction, except that the broken wires of the tramways trailed negligently in the streets,' he wrote. 'It was most odd and unexpected, yet they spoke more pitifully than anything else of the people who had fled and the fear that had driven them.' And while it was an odd place to visit in daylight, it was even worse at night. When darkness fell it became 'a city of the dead . . . shuttered, ghostly, and desolate, without light or sign of living except for the flash of the electric torches which the military policemen swung in their hands as they directed the dark traffic through the streets'.[2]

Amiens had been one of the main objectives of the German Spring Offensive. The capture of its railway junction would separate the Allies and allow the British to be rolled up and sent packing across the Channel, leaving the French alone to face German might.

Amiens was where the British and French Armies met and was thus the crucial link in the entire Western Front. The Germans knew that it had to be captured if the war was to be won. That summer it came under bombardment from huge railway guns that targeted the town in a vain attempt to interfere with British communications and sever its important rail links. But Amiens always remained in Allied hands. No matter how hard Ludendorff pushed, his exhausted armies could never reach it; no matter how many divisions he threw in, they always seemed to tire at the crucial moment. The town became like some floating mirage that would disappear further into the haze the nearer the Germans got to it; the perfect illustration of how limited the strategic effect of Ludendorff's offensives had really been. Amiens would also become the first great battle of the Hundred Days.

Foch's plan for a series of limited attacks had been approved by all Allied commanders the day after the meeting at Bombon. It had been agreed that the first of his 'series of movements' would take place here, in the rolling ground south of the Somme, occupied by General Sir Henry Rawlinson's Fourth British Army and General Eugène Debeney's First French Army. Foch had placed Debeney temporarily under the orders of Haig to ensure cooperation in the coming attack, but the main assault would be made by Rawlinson's troops. Plans for an attack in the Amiens sector had been maturing in Fourth Army headquarters at Flexicourt for some time. The ground was particularly favourable and intelligence reports had noted that the German troops opposite them were sheltering in light defences and suffering from poor morale. As Rawlinson's Chief of Staff, Major-General Sir Archibald Montgomery, would later write, not only were they faced with very little in the way of organized systems of defence, but also:

> the terrain was extremely favourable for an offensive with a distant objective limited only by the physical powers of endurance of horse and man. The country was open and undulating; the hard soil, with chalk very near the surface, rendered it particularly favourable for tanks and cavalry. The chances of the successful employment of these

arms were further increased by the absence of shell craters and by the dry weather of the preceding months.[3]

If the attack was to be anywhere, it would be here.

An initial outline had been sent to GHQ on 17 July and Rawlinson met with his corps commanders four days later to discuss the forthcoming operation. He was convinced that a major attack in the Amiens sector could work, and was eager to put into practice all that had been learnt over the preceding four years, including the recent fighting on the Marne. Rawlinson was particularly keen on achieving complete surprise; therefore secrecy, in his opinion, 'must be the basis on which the whole scheme is built up'. He wanted as many tanks as possible to 'save casualties to the infantry, and also, to make full use of any supply tanks that may be available, so as to reduce infantry carrying parties'. Rawlinson believed that no preliminary bombardment should take place, just a rolling barrage when the infantry and tanks got going. Reserve units would then 'leapfrog' each other on to more distant objectives.[4]

Rawlinson received confirmation from Haig on 26 July (two days after the meeting with Foch at Bombon) to go ahead with the operation, then scheduled for 10 August. Although Rawlinson initially would have preferred to attack alone without French support – fearing leaks of information – Haig impressed upon him their shortage of reserves and the need to attack in full cooperation with Britain's allies, to which Rawlinson dutifully agreed.[5] It was decided that Rawlinson's Fourth Army would push eastwards from Amiens, along the line Hangest-en-Santerre–Harbonnières–Méricourt-sur-Somme, while maintaining a strong left flank at Chipilly and on the high ground around Morlancourt.[6] The right flank would be secured by Debeney's First Army, which planned to employ three corps in the operation, beginning on the left and then gradually extending the attack to the south. The idea was for French forces to constitute what it called two 'masses of manoeuvre', one of which would outflank the town of Montdidier from the north – which was the main French objective – while the second struck from the south.[7] If this could be achieved, Amiens would be safe and out of range of enemy shelling and the important railway lines secured.

The spearhead of the attack was entrusted to two of the most powerful and experienced corps in the BEF: the Canadian and Australian Corps. Both were large, well-equipped and battle-hardened formations with a growing reputation for professionalism, ruthlessness and above all success. It had been the Canadian Corps that had taken Vimy Ridge in April 1917, successfully storming one of the most formidable positions on the Western Front in little over three hours. Although the Australians never enjoyed success on the scale of Vimy, they prided themselves on their effectiveness and aggression, specializing in large trench raids that they called – somewhat misleadingly – 'peaceful penetration'. The Australians had also recently conducted the Battle of Hamel on 4 July, a beautifully crafted combined 'all-arms' operation that took just over ninety minutes to overrun the village of Le Hamel and surrounding woodland with minimal casualties. These formations, as was rapidly becoming clear, were the 'shock armies' of the BEF. They were also semi-independent formations with powerful political support back home. Haig could not boss the Canadians or Australians around in the way that he was used to doing with British divisions.[8]

As well as containing large numbers of well-rested, highly motivated and well-equipped troops, the Dominion corps were led by two of the most promising commanders in the British Empire: Sir Arthur Currie and Sir John Monash. In many ways they were typical of their homelands, being men who could only have found success and fame in the freer air of the Dominions. There was no way Arthur Currie, a teacher and failed financier, would have risen to Lieutenant-General had he joined the regular British Army. Likewise, the Australian, Sir John Monash, came from a family of Polish Jews and he had originally been a civil engineer when he joined the North Melbourne Militia before the war. Both men possessed fierce, inquisitive minds, eagerly devouring military knowledge because they knew the lives of their men depended on it. They understood and valued firepower and logistics and also recognized the importance of patience and preparation. Currie's motto was a characteristic 'neglect nothing', while Monash described his theory of war as how 'to advance under the maximum possible protection of the maximum possible array of mechanical resources, in the form of guns, machine-guns, tanks, mortars and aeroplanes'.[9] The theory of war that emerged from the Dominion corps may not have been subtle; it may not have been as innovative as the tactical changes ushered in by the German Army, but it worked. And it worked at a tolerable cost in lives.

The attack at Amiens would be dependent on speed, surprise and the vigour with which the opening assault would be pressed. Planning went ahead in the last weeks of July and the first week of August, following well-worn routines and familiar procedures. On 31 July, Haig was driven to Fourth Army's tank grounds at Vaux-en-Amiénois, where he met Rawlinson and Hugh Elles, the commander of the Tank Corps. Haig was then shown a demonstration of the latest machines that were arriving in France and how they were used on the battlefield. Haig was impressed. 'Remarkable progress has been made since Cambrai, not only in the pattern of Tank, but also in the methods of using them,' he recalled. 'Tanks now go in first, covered by a shrapnel barrage, and break down all opposition. Enemy in strongpoints and machine gun nests are then flattened out by the Tanks. The latter then signal the infantry to "come on", and these then advance in open order and mop up the remaining defenders, and collect the prisoners.'[10] He was particularly impressed by the Mark V that was now coming into service – the culmination of British tank design in the Great War and a much-improved version of the original Mark I that had debuted on the Somme two years earlier. Like previous incarnations, the Mark V came in two types, the male and female. The male was armed with two six-pounder guns, one on each side of the vehicle, while in the female version they were replaced by six Hotchkiss machine-guns.[11] There was also the Mark V Star tank, which was six feet longer than the original Mark V and was designed as an armoured personnel carrier, with enough space inside to fit twenty men.[12]

Hopes were also high for the use of quicker, lighter vehicles, the Medium Mark A, the so-called Whippet, which would be used for exploitation with the cavalry. The Medium Mark A was very different from the rhomboid-shaped Mark Vs. It weighed only 14 tons and carried four machine-guns in a fighting turret above the chassis. Calling them 'whippets' was perhaps unfortunate. Although with a top speed of just over 8 mph they were almost twice as fast as the Mark V, they were still painfully slow and could not keep up with horses at a canter, meaning that cooperation with the cavalry would be difficult. Nevertheless, tanks would play a vital role in the assault. A total of 430 machines would start at Amiens on 8 August, the most that the British had ever employed in battle. The Tank Corps hoped that the mass use of this weapon – something it had only ever managed to do at Cambrai the previous year – would bring great success. The French, by contrast, had only two tank battalions, which were sent to Debeney two days before the attack. Most of the French tank force had been engaged on the Marne that July and had taken heavy losses, hence Debeney's insistence that without armour he would require a forty-five-minute artillery bombardment to clear the way for his troops.

As Debeney well knew, artillery had become vital to operations on the Western Front. By the Armistice the British alone had over 6,000 guns, a third of which were classified as heavy (or siege) artillery. The French had even more. They ranged from the ubiquitous British 18-pounder or French 75mm, to the heavier 8 inch, 12 inch and 15 inch howitzers that fired a bigger shell. As well as these regular types, the Western Front also saw the use of large railway-mounted naval guns that fired huge 1,500lb shells on targets up to twenty miles away.[13] Although the spirit and *élan* of attacking soldiers were still of importance – particularly when artillery or armour were not available – artillery had become the weapon that unlocked defences and allowed infantry to manoeuvre on the battlefield. Without it, they would almost always suffer crippling losses, having to advance in the face of unsuppressed enemy machine-gun and rifle fire or watch powerlessly as enemy batteries opened up on them. By 1918 the use of artillery, by all sides, was marked by a great degree of expertise, professionalism and technological prowess that allowed increasing amounts of firepower to be targeted accurately and responsively on the battlefield. In contrast to the earlier years of the war, corrections were now being made for the temperature of the air and the charge being used, the velocity and direction of the wind, the age and wear of the guns, and the type of shell and fuse. When these measurements were taken and used in conjunction with reconnaissance from the air, much greater accuracy could be achieved.

Rawlinson, for his part, could think about not opting for the kind of long, draining bombardment that had preceded the attacks of earlier years. After extensive discussion it was agreed that – as on the Marne – there would be no preliminary bombardment. The state of the enemy's defences was such that it would not be required: there were no deep dug-outs or pill-boxes and few sections of well-wired and strengthened trenches, just thin slits covered by machine-guns. At Zero Hour a creeping barrage would be fired for three minutes 200 yards ahead of the infantry, lifting up to forty times in a carefully programmed shoot that would 'cover' the infantry up to 4,500 yards into the German lines.[14] If any wire or enemy strongpoints remained then the tanks would deal with them. By keeping the guns silent until the moment of advance the precious element of surprise would be maintained and give the enemy no time to prepare for counter-battery fire. This was of crucial importance. Only by the autumn of 1917 had it become possible to fire accurately without 'registering' guns beforehand; essentially firing at specified reference points and then noting the errors in range or direction from where the shell landed. By using a complex series of mathematical equations it was possible to work out the necessary corrections for each gun to make sure they were as accurate as possible. Had Fourth Army attempted to do this before the attack, large numbers of shells would have fallen on the German positions, thus alerting the enemy to the powerful increase in artillery opposite them. By 1918, it was possible to do without this pre-registering phase of operations. Batteries would fire their guns at a special series of wired screens behind the line, from which muzzle velocity and directional errors could be identified. Armed with this information, corrections could then be made. Sir John Monash noted the 'feverish activity' at the calibration range of the Australian Corps in the early days of August. 'All day long, battery after battery of guns could be seen route-marching to the testing ground, going through the performance of firing six rounds per gun, and then route-marching back again the same night . . . So rapid was the procedure that long before he had reached his destination the Battery Commander had received the full error sheet of every one of his guns, and by means of it was enabled to go into action whenever required without any previous registration whatever.' Staff officers and other VIPs who came to see Monash were always taken to see the complex mathematical alchemy taking place in his 'calibration hut' and all left suitably impressed.[15]

A key element of the artillery preparation prior to the battle was identifying and (if possible) knocking out German batteries. Counter-battery fire, as it was called, was notoriously difficult – requiring detailed reconnaissance and pinpoint accuracy – and many Allied offensives earlier in the war had been strangled by curtains of enemy shellfire descending between the leading troops and the follow-on forces. It was estimated that the Germans had around 500 guns in the Amiens sector, far fewer than combined British and French barrels, but still enough to do considerable damage to any attack should they be left unmolested. In this important task Arthur Currie was fortunate in being able to call upon the services of one of the most outstanding soldiers of the war: his Corps Counter-Battery officer, Lieutenant-Colonel Andrew McNaughton, whose speciality, it turned out, was destroying German guns. Two thirds of the heavy guns would be devoted to taking on German batteries and making sure that they could not interfere with the infantry assault. If this could be achieved, the German defenders would be on their own.

As well as artillery and tanks, air power would play a key role in the coming battle. By the summer of 1918, after a war of technological and numerical parity, the Allies had opened up an appreciable lead over their German adversaries. Led by the French, who surpassed both Britain and the USA in aircraft production, they were able to win the battle of aerial attrition by building more aircraft and training more aircrew than their enemies. In the last year of the war, the French alone produced just under 25,000 aircraft and nearly 45,000 engines, making them the world's largest air force.[16] Although British and French aircraft may not have had the finesse or craftsmanship of the best German models, a new generation of fighters (including improved Spads, Sopwith Camels and Bristol Fighters) were very capable and were reaching deeper and deeper into enemy lines. By 7 August the Allies had attained a huge numerical advantage on this front, with 1,904 aircraft being deployed, against just over 300 German machines. Both the RAF and the French *Division Aérienne* would play a crucial role at Amiens. They were tasked with securing control of the air by bombing German aerodromes, engaging their fighters in the air, and assisting the troops in a variety of ways, ranging from ground attack and contact patrols, to spotting and even the dropping of smoke.[17]

None of these preparations would be effective, however, without the element of surprise; indeed, with the huge number of troops, tanks and guns gradually crowding into the Amiens sector, including two powerful corps packed into a front just over eight miles wide, there was a grave danger that should the Germans suspect a forthcoming attack, they could shell the approaches to the front line with predictable results – smashed artillery batteries; maddened horses; scattered battalions; and burning tanks. From the beginning of the planning process secrecy had been stressed at all levels and was the reason why a complex, ambitious and unprecedented deception programme had been undertaken. In discussions prior to the attack, both Rawlinson and Haig had been keen to achieve tactical success on the battlefield. The Canadian Corps, which Haig wanted to spearhead the attack, had been in GHQ Reserve, but if it were to enter the lines east of Amiens, alongside the Australians, then it would not take long for German High Command to realize that an offensive was imminent. The task was to get the Canadians into the line, but without anyone knowing it.

The deception plan prior to Amiens was not only imaginative and forward-thinking, it was also executed with a ruthlessness and professionalism that had never been seen before. In order to make sure the arrival of the Canadian Corps was a surprise, an elaborate series of orders were drafted that made it look like the Canadians were being deployed for an attack on the Mount Kemmel sector in Flanders to the north. Corps headquarters was packed off to the front, casualty clearing stations were set up, two Canadian battalions were detrained, and extensive wireless traffic was faked, all in order to convince the German High Command that the Canadians were there. And then, one unit at a time, the Canadian Corps began to move to its real destination. Some divisions took odd routes, initially moving north, or east, but all gradually began to track back down to the south, much to the bemusement of the officers and men, very few of whom knew the real destination. It was, as one Canadian veteran later remarked, 'a miracle of staff work'. To a casual observer, 'everything would have appeared in hopeless confusion, but such was not the case'.[18]

Secrecy was of paramount importance. Major F. J. Rice, an artillery battery commander, remembered how in the first week of August the divisional artillery staff:

> began to talk about our taking part in a 'raid'. This 'raid' became a Divisional joke during the next few days, but the secret was probably kept, I think, in spite of the conjectures as to what it all really meant. The batteries began to take up ammunition by night in positions they had selected about half a mile to a mile behind the front line. Straw was put on forward roads, ropes were wrapped around wheels, and everything possible was done to preserve secrecy.[19]

Charles Henry Savage, serving with 5th Canadian Mounted Rifles, remembered that 'It was a beautifully planned show.' A notice was posted in every man's pay book that read simply: 'KEEP YOUR MOUTH SHUT' alongside advice on how best to preserve secrecy. For example, it stated that 'If you hear anyone else talking about operations, stop him at once. The success of the operations and the lives of your comrades depend upon your SILENCE.' Indeed, such was the preoccupation with secrecy in the front lines before the attack that it often caused anger and frustration, as well as some hilarity. As battalions moved up in the dark, silently passing the guns and moving quietly along tree-lined roads, it was often difficult to work out where they were. 'To ask anyone on the road where such and such a battalion was,' Savage remembered, 'would generally bring the reply "keep your mouth shut".'[20]

The Allies had learnt about secrecy the hard way. Bitter experience had taught them the folly of attacking in full view of the enemy after long bombardments that only revealed the frontage of the coming operation. But this time, their preparation would be meticulous and imaginative. For Tank Corps HQ, the task of moving up six battalions of tanks to the front without them being noticed was of great importance. The headquarters of each unit was despatched in advance to unknown destinations and the tanks themselves were sent by rail under sealed orders. No communication was allowed between battalion headquarters and their units until they arrived at their assigned sector. Hugh Elles and his staff had also concocted a cunning series of ruses designed to throw German intelligence off their scent. Tank wireless detachments were set up in other army areas further to the north and one group of tanks were even sent to a quiet front within view of enemy observation balloons, where they then performed daily movements forward throughout the period of concentration.[21] Yet behind this ruse the main strength of the Tank Corps was on the move, concentrating near Amiens, and covered by the sound of aircraft near the front, flying back and forth every day, their engine noise drowning out the roar of the tanks. It was just like a symphony; every instrument was in its right place.[22]

German accounts of the days leading up to the opening of the offensive betray little of the frantic activity taking place on the other side of the line. The front was held by Second Army commanded by General der Kavallerie Georg von der Marwitz, a highly experienced soldier who had served on both Eastern and Western Fronts and was noticeable for his brisk white moustache. Marwitz's command held the line from Albert (opposite the British III Corps) to Hargicourt (opposite the French IX Corps), and was composed of three corps, containing fourteen divisions in all.[23] Although on paper this was an impressively strong force, Second Army was not in the best of condition. Extensive combat operations earlier in the year during the spring had drained it of manpower and dented its morale. Although it contained the extremely well-regarded 27th Württemberg Division, seven of its divisions were classified by Allied intelligence as 'third-class' that could be relied upon to hold the front but for little more. There were also worrying signs of disorder and growing discontent in some units. The Commanding Officer of 41st Division, which occupied a central position at the front, had recently noticed an increase in insubordination, with some men refusing to march to the front and officers adopting a relaxed attitude to discipline. Several men had even been shot for refusing to follow orders.[24]

Second Army did not have the luxury of sitting behind prepared positions and well-dug trench systems; the kind of defensive lines that German units had long become accustomed to holding. The ground it occupied was not particularly strong and there had not been enough time to improve it. One of the units tasked with resisting any attack was 43rd Reserve Division, which occupied the northern part of the front at Sailly-Laurette and Chipilly. One of its soldiers, Leutnant Albers, complained that his position lay 'in a very uneven zigzag line, not complete or connected but in the form of chest-high sections of trenches. There were practically no obstacles', and few construction materials available; something that was a familiar feature across the front. The positions were also dangerously isolated. It was impossible to move in daylight and the telephone lines to headquarters were continually being destroyed by shellfire. Morale was not helped by the late arrival of food, often coming in cold from field kitchens several kilometres behind the line. 'It was no wonder,' he wrote, 'that the men rapidly lost confidence.'[25]

Regular aerial reconnaissance revealed that the German defences were poor and were not being improved or maintained properly throughout July and August. Patrols undertaken by the famously alert Australians also reinforced the rapidly growing appreciation that the German defenders in this sector were soft. On the morning of 29 July, Australian units mounted a surprise raid on the German positions between Morlancourt and Sailly-Laurette, capturing 4,000 yards of front-line trench and taking over 100 prisoners. Those prisoners were 'a very poor lot of men' with low morale; their companies were very weak and they had received no drafts. One of their officers said 'that the morale of both officers and men had been very adversely affected by the success of the Allied counter-stroke on the Marne'.[26] That may have been so, but other German units were more professional and had noted signs of preparation on their sectors, sending back reports, but getting little response.

In the days before the battle, it is possible to detect the fatal signs of laziness and complacency among the German High Command. Although the few aircraft that tried to survey the Allied lines were soon brought down in flames by the powerful and ever-alert British and French air forces (that were tasked with ensuring no photographic reconnaissance could take place), suspicions gradually began to rise. Leutnant Albers remembered that they could 'clearly hear the Tommies at work; the rattling of the engines [of the tanks] was clearly audible and had already been regularly reported to those in command'. Yet little was done. Those who did report ominous preparations on the other side of the line were told to be quiet; they were merely 'phantoms of the imagination of nervousness'. For Marwitz and his staff, the idea of an Allied counter-attack was too painful to contemplate, so it was disregarded. Anyway, even if the reports were true, what could be done about it? Second Army was over-stretched, desperate for reinforcements and at the end of a long logistical tail.[27]

The Allied preparations before Amiens were a remarkable feat of care, attention to detail and sheer hard work. Statistics can provide some illustration of the scale and size of the endeavour undertaken by Rawlinson and Debeney. In Fourth Army alone, over 257,000 men and 98,000 horses had to be fed, housed and watered, while 1,242 field guns and 246 heavy guns had to be maintained and stocked with shells (600 rounds per 18-pounder and 500 rounds per 4.5 inch howitzer). This took up huge amounts of space. In the French XXXI Corps for example, nearly 8,000 tons of artillery ammunition were stacked near its batteries, enough for five days of heavy fighting.[28] As well as firepower, casualty clearing stations and field hospitals were set up, leading some worried staff officers to wonder where everything was all going to fit. Fortunately, the area behind the front line was blessed with many small copses and woods, as well as valleys and sheltered areas, where large numbers of horses, supplies, guns and trucks could move up in relative secrecy. Indeed, in the run-up to Amiens almost every area of covered ground was packed with infantry, horses and tanks. Because it was feared that German aircraft would spot any purpose-built gun emplacements, batteries were simply deployed in the open, with their ammunition stacked beside them, all netted over with camouflage or covered with cut wheat. Staff officers then buzzed between the units checking that everything was in its right place and everyone where they should be; all the time hoping to God that the Germans were not about to launch a counter-bombardment.[29] Originally scheduled for 10 August, an earlier date of attack was petitioned for by Currie and Haig agreed. By the evening of 7 August everything was in place.

In the final few hours before the attack Paul Maze, a liaison officer with Fourth Army, made his way forward. 'For a while,' he wrote:

> I stood watching the progress of the troops on the Longueau–Villers-Bretonneux road, the prolonged clatter of cavalry horses reminding me of earlier days. They were marching slowly to keep within their time. I overtook infantry and tanks moving along in weird masses in the dark, following troops all the way to the Gentelles Plateau. There the ground was taped and pegged; boards indicated the way each unit was to take as far as the approach to the line, to avoid any mix-up or delay. The whole area might have been the scene of a gymkhana. Aeroplanes were droning loudly overhead so as to drown the noise of the approaching tanks. Every object looming in the darkness hid something – the woods sheltered hundreds of silent guns awaiting their signal.

Maze tried to sleep but, like many, he could not and just lay there in his tent feeling the tension gradually increase around him like the fog that gathered in the low ground. He would doze, only to be startled awake, every now and again, by the noise of a tank engine or the scream of a lone shell. 'The atmosphere had grown hazy, the ground felt clammy. I had a hint of troops through the mist moving down the slope to their assembly position like long shadows, darker than the night. All I could see of them was their fumbling feet.'[30]

For the British, Australian, Canadian and French troops anxiously awaiting the order to go, the scene was one of great tension. A French officer, Colonel Grasset, remembered how 'with the first light of dawn a deep silence' came over the battlefield. Men had been instructed not to talk or move or leave their trenches. 'All was very calm on the surface, but feverish work in the woods, in the camou-flaged shelters, in the ruins . . .'[31] The hours and minutes before the attack were always the worst; the agonizing, ticking moments of waiting before Zero Hour when you were faced with dark thoughts of death and wounding, hoping that you and your fellows would come through alive. Some relied upon charms and amulets, bracelets and lockets of hair; others prayed to God and made vows of future service if only they would survive. One veteran of the battles of 1918, T. G. Mohan, was one of those who took solace in religion. 'Person-ally,' he would later write:

> I always believed that I should come through safely. God gave me an unmistakeable assurance that He would bring me out of the war, yet how I should get home I did not know. I never thought that I would be wounded. Yet in spite of this assurance I felt to be in England again was only a thing to be experienced in dreams – it seemed impossible ever to be a reality. To feel that I was standing on dear, solid old Eng-land – to look round and say – this is England . . . the sun shining, the neat little hedges and pretty little country cottages, all so beautifully clean and sweet . . . in the town to be able to read the good old English names, and understand what people were talking about, to feel safe again . . . it was all so impossible.[32]

Gradually time would run out. Thoughts would return to the matter in hand. Equipment would be checked once more. Final orders would be issued and the troops readied. Writing after the war, Sir John Monash would try to describe 'the stupendous import of the last ten minutes' before Amiens.

> In the black darkness, a hundred thousand infantry, deployed over twelve miles of front, are standing grimly, silently, expectantly, in readiness to advance, or are already crawling stealthily forward to get within eighty yards of the line on which the barrage will fall; all feel to make sure that their bayonets are firmly locked, or to set their steel

helmets firmly on their heads; Company and Platoon commanders, their whistles ready to hand, are nervously glancing at their luminous watches, waiting for minute after minute to go by – and giving a last look over their commands – ensuring that their runners are by their sides, their observers alert, and that the officers detailed to control direction have their compasses set and ready.[33]

The two Allied armies were like coiled springs, taut and alert; waiting to strike. The Hundred Days was about to begin.

3. 'Death will have a rich harvest'

Through the fog, I saw the outline of a tank appear . . .

Hauptmann Hatzfeld[1]

8–10 August 1918

The Battle of Amiens began at 4.20 a.m. with the roar of over 2,000 guns, which opened up a thunderous bombardment, banishing the darkness and lighting up the horizon. One witness, Private W. E. Curtis of 10th Canadian Battalion, remembered that 'you could have read a newspaper whichever way you looked' because of the light from the gunfire.[2] The bombardment would have been effective against hardened German positions, but against the sketchy and unfinished defences in Second Army's sector it was devastating. Barbed wire entanglements were torn apart; trenches were pulverized; whole companies were destroyed in a fury that came from above, shells sending great geysers of white earth up into the sky. At that moment, the leading waves of eight British, Canadian and Australian divisions were moving out of their positions and making their way towards their pre-assigned objectives, shuffling in the flickering darkness along taped lines and then shaking out into extended order as they crossed no-man's-land. To the south, another three French corps were waiting in their assault trenches, keeping their heads down as a shattering forty-five-minute bombardment pounded German positions along the River Avre.

The German defenders, many of whom were woken from an uneasy slumber by the deafening roar of the barrage, could not, at first, work out what was happening. Thick mist covered the battle-field and masked the opening movements of the attacking troops, preventing any meaningful response. In places it was also thickened by phosphorus grenades dropped from aircraft. As soon as the British barrage began, the familiar German signal flares – red and gold – fizzed up into the sky to request artillery support, but it was in vain. By the time many of the flares had been fired, Second Army's artillery batteries were already under a rain of iron, with the gun crews scattered by the violence and accuracy of the shelling and able to do nothing about it. Although there was some desultory retaliatory shelling about five minutes after Zero Hour, most of it fell on the support lines, thus missing the assaulting battalions. For the men of Second Army, 8 August was going to be a miserable day.

Despite the poor visibility, the opening assault went as well as could have been expected, the leading waves of the Canadian and Australian divisions sweeping forward behind their barrage and taking their objectives on time. German resistance differed across the front, ranging from non-existent to stubborn, but in many sectors, particularly those in the centre, the defending battalions were destroyed. Apart from some wild firing and the occasional shell, all that met the attacking troops was dazed clusters of German soldiers, their hands up, muttering, 'Kamerad'. Fourth Army's barrage was extremely heavy: a moving wall of shells, liberally sprinkled with smoke, that moved at a steady rate across the battlefield – like some kind of man-made hurricane – occasionally stopping, and then restarting exactly on time, doing everything that Rawlinson had hoped. And behind the barrage came thin lines of infantry supported by the heavy tanks, the ominous clanking and rumbling of the armoured vehicles causing many German soldiers to flee in terror. Others tried desperately to stem the attacks flooding against their positions, and Allied soldiers would sometimes glimpse their steel-helmeted foes running to and from their positions, crouching low with their Mauser rifles, their pockets stuffed full of stick grenades, desperately trying to find some cover. But before they could launch their long-cherished counter-attacks, they usually found that they were in danger of being outflanked or cut off and had to retreat.

Some German units were so badly hit by the opening salvos and the speed with which the Canadians and Australians were upon them that they had little idea what was happening. One of those who witnessed the assault was a Major Mende, commander of II Battalion of 157 Regiment (117th Division), dug in north of the Amiens–Roye road. 'As soon as the enemy artillery fire began,' he remembered, 'I rushed to the telephone to inform the regiment of the attack; but the loop was already shut down. Then I ran outside to see what was going on, but it was so foggy that I could only see two steps ahead of me. I could hear quite light infantry fire, so I assumed that the attack had been driven back or was not yet underway.' Mende could do nothing but wait for reports from his companies. He spent some time sitting nervously in his dug-out, noticing that small-arms fire had died away, but still no reports came in. He sent off despatch riders asking for news but again nothing came. An hour passed. 'Finally, Vice Sgt. Beier of 5th Company arrived with the news that the enemy was right behind him and that his company commander had apparently been killed. Hardly had he finished speaking, than the first hand grenade flew into the dug-out.' Mende was captured shortly afterwards.[3]

Others held their positions a little longer, like Leutnant Albers and his men of 43rd Reserve Division, who were captured later that morning after putting up fierce resistance against the British III Corps, which secured the left flank of the attack. At Zero Hour, they had to endure 'murderous artillery fire' from both field and heavy batteries for about fifteen minutes, during which they wrote their wills, crouched in their trenches or huddled in shell holes, hoping that they would survive. 'Nothing could be seen in the thickening fog,' he wrote. Then things began to happen. 'The artillery fire suddenly moved further back. Screams, hand grenade explosions and the eerie noise of the tank engines was audible.' As the sounds of tanks and the spatter of gunfire closed around their positions, they became aware that they had been cut off. Patrols were sent off to their right flank, but the line was broken and they were, as he put it, 'just islands in a surging sea'. The question of whether they should surrender crossed his mind, but he was unsure. 'Then we would have had to

answer to the reasons for abandoning the position before the enemy.'
Albers hoped a counter-attack would relieve them, but it never came,
only more and more British troops.

> Unfortunately our hand grenades had all been used; there was no
> longer time to operate the machine gun amid the chaos. Every man
> fired and defended himself as well as he could. But a new wave of
> English arrived in force, firing pistols and throwing hand grenades
> and killing or wounding many of my colleagues. Completely sur-
> rounded, shot at and bombed from all sides, with resistance no longer
> possible, the 20 men remaining from my company had to surrender.[4]

Albers's story was typical of the frantic action on that foggy morning
on 8 August as German units – those 'islands in a surging sea' – were
gradually swallowed up by the Allied tide.

Rawlinson's two colonial corps had conducted the main punch,
but the attack would be extended to the south by Debeney's First
French Army, which was aiming to take the town of Montdidier.
The *poilus* had moved forward at 5.05 a.m. after a forty-five-minute
'hurricane' bombardment. By the time the leading lines of XXXI
Corps had deployed, the defensive system of 14th Bavarian Division
had already been shattered by the advance of the Canadian Corps on
its right. In many cases, the incredible scenes witnessed on the Australian and Canadian sectors were repeated in the French zone. Apart
from sporadic enemy machine-gun fire, resistance melted away and
French soldiers marched across an empty battlefield, following their
creeping barrage, which stopped and restarted according to time-
table. As Colonel Grasset, historian of 42nd Division, remembered:

> When the infantry came to a halt . . . there was no further resistance
> from the enemy and we would very much have liked to push further
> forward. But the fixed barrage which was slamming into the ground
> 300 metres ahead of the front line ruled out any ill-considered initia-
> tive. Like it or not, companies split up by the march and the fighting
> had to regroup. People relaxed. The men, joyful, chatted, ate and
> smoked. The officers, gathered in friendly groups, tried to take in the
> importance of the victory.[5]

Some German units, cut off and surrounded, did what they could to impede the advance, firing all the weapons they had, but gradually, with their numbers worn down by shelling and gunfire, and often out of ammunition, they too had to surrender. One who experienced the French attack was Leutnant Stürmer. At 5.45 a.m., as 'the thundering of guns rumbled behind us like an oncoming storm', Stürmer's troops noticed shadowy blue shapes making their way across no-man's-land. Soon confused firing broke out. They retreated and tried to organize a counter-attack, but it was no good. 'The machine guns are singing, hand grenades are exploding – death will have a rich harvest . . . The right section slowly crumbled; the munitions destroyed, the trenches overrun by a superior strength,' wrote Stürmer, who was captured around midday.[6]

For those behind the front line, like Bertram Howard Cox, a former bank clerk from Winnipeg, it was an exhilarating day. He was serving with the artillery, and after three hours of constant firing from his battery he was nearly deaf. 'Within ten minutes of the start,' he wrote, 'the tanks, by the hundreds, and cavalry, by the thousands, were passing our guns. It made an awful pretty picture to see the tanks and cavalry looming up in the mist, over the crest, just about dawn. The field guns began to pass us at a gallop, too, not to mention the infantry by the hundreds of thousands.' By 5 a.m. German prisoners began to reach him; grey masses filled the road, dazed, shocked, shaking with fear. 'The thing that struck me as being most funny, was the way the prisoners would dangle right along by themselves, no escort, to the prison cage about a mile away. If there were 30 or 40 together, they would have an escort, but they mostly passed in twos or threes, all alone or four would carry one of our wounded on a stretcher. We spent a considerable part of the day checking them over; getting souvenirs and talking to those who could speak English. They nearly cleaned us out of cigarettes and emptied our water bottles.'[7]

By the time it got light and the mist had cleared – about 8 a.m. – the sight of the battlefield was suddenly revealed. One Canadian remembered how the fighting had streamed away to the east leaving it 'as peaceful as an Ontario landscape after a storm, whose bolts and flashes still play over the distant horizon'.[8] The supporting divisions, which would leapfrog the leading units, marched across the battle-field, passing the German gun line about 9 a.m.; their officers on horseback like the old days of 1914. They would come across clusters of dead Germans or straggling columns of prisoners of war, while sometimes being passed by cavalry units, their hooves clattering nois-ily over the dusty roads. Sergeant Walter Downing, a 25-year-old from Portland, Victoria, was serving with 5th Australian Division. Their progress had been 'plain sailing'. There was little enemy artil-lery or sniper fire and whenever they found themselves in trouble, 'we signalled to the tanks, and they turned towards the obstacle. Then *punk-crash, punk-crash!* As their little toy guns spoke and their little, pointed shells flew, another German post was blown to pieces.' He would always remember what he saw that day.

> For miles and miles infantry were everywhere advancing, dotted over hill and dale on either hand as far as the eye could see. Bayonets grouped and glinted in the charge as a battalion swarmed to the storming of a town miles away. Here and there thick columns of smoke and spluttering explosions told that the enemy dumps were burning. Red roofs and white walls trembled in the hot sunshine where villages drowsed beneath their lichened elms; the crops were lemon green, the pastured hillsides of a richer verdure; double rows of poplars shadowed the long straight roads.[9]

By 11 a.m. the Canadian Corps had captured its first and second objectives – four miles inside the German lines – and was waiting for 4th Division, in support, to push on to the third. Likewise, the Aus-tralians had also moved off with great speed. A wireless message received at GHQ from Monash's headquarters at 5.40 a.m. simply read 'Everything splendid'.[10] On the right, the French XXXI Corps had taken the village of Mézières at 3 p.m. – Moroccan *tirailleurs* storming forward with the cry of '*en avant*' – while to the south the two remaining corps contented themselves with maintaining heavy artillery fire on the German lines around Montdidier.[11]

For the German Army things were anything but splendid. General von der Marwitz spent 8 August at his headquarters, frantically trying to find out what was going on; he was, as he put it, 'nailed' to his telephone all day. Within hours of the opening attack, he was desperately searching for reinforcements to plug the gaps in his shattered front line. Three of his reserve divisions had already been engaged, but Marwitz immediately ordered the other three – all of which were resting north of the Somme – to march to the sound of the guns. He also spoke to General Oskar von Hutier, the commander of Eighteenth Army, on his left, and obtained permission for another division to be sent northwards as soon as possible.[12] For the Commander of Second Army – like many other senior German officers – the defeat was due to enemy tanks. He openly admitted that he had previously thought the value of armoured vehicles had been overestimated, but now there could be no denying the weapon's effectiveness. Calling it an 'evil weapon', he immediately scribbled off messages to OHL asking for motorized artillery batteries to be supplied to his men. But without these capabilities, Second Army would have to resist as well as it could. It was little wonder that he would plead in his diary, 'May God help us.'[13]

Marwitz was certainly correct to attribute much of the Allied success to the mass use of tanks. In many places they were undoubtedly effective, helping the infantry to advance, engaging German troops, crushing machine-gun nests, and crossing trenches with ease. The Tank Corps proclaimed that the 'moral effect' of the tanks emerging through the fog was 'overwhelming'. 'Many machine guns were run over and crushed, prisoners surrendered freely and on the centre and right the objectives were won with comparative ease.'[14] Infantry–tank cooperation proved a little more difficult, however, particularly during the first few hours of the assault when the vehicles had to find their own way across the darkened landscape. They maintained direction by compass bearing and were often only able to locate the enemy by the flashes of machine-gun fire.[15] When it got light cooperation improved and many tanks snaked their way across the battlefield led by section commanders who pointed out targets while infantry parties mopped them up. An incredible story of what happened when 41st Division was attacked was recorded by Hauptmann Hatzfeld of III Battalion (152 Regiment) in the German official account. After coming under fire and hearing rumours that the British were coming, Hatzfeld wanted to hold on to his command post for as long as possible – 'to give the Reserve Division time to mount a counter-attack' – but that did not happen. Instead, through the fog, he saw the awful sight of a British Mark V tank coming straight at him.

> The three machine guns immediately opened heavy fire, but failed to bring it to a halt. It drove straight over them. As Lieutenant Frantzius (Commander of 3rd Machine Gun Company) later established, a machine gun was destroyed and a number of the operating team were killed. Shortly after, the right flank and the command post came under machine gun fire from the right, whereupon the adjutant standing behind me, Reserve Lieutenant Albrecht, was shot in the face by a bullet coming from the side. At the same time, a second tank approached along the road from the front and the machine gun in front of me opened fire on it, but without success. It rolled past the command post without stopping; the machine gun team dodged to the right to get out of its way, and in doing so both gunners were killed.

By this point, Hatzfeld and his officers came under Lewis gun fire from Australian troops, but they managed to keep them at bay, until a third tank arrived. 'In the wake of this monster rolling along the road,' he remembered:

> we jumped into the tunnel entrance nearest to us and skidded quickly down the stairs, followed by hand grenades which were also already flying into both entrances. The game was up! I ordered diaries, files and cards to be destroyed. Then we waited to see what the Tommies might do next. To start with, they did nothing. It was not until around 8.00 in the morning that a man came cautiously down and called to us, then came closer upon hearing me answer and let us clamber up the steps (smashed to pieces by hand grenades) into the open air.

Hatzfeld and his men, their hands up, were taken prisoner.[16]
Hatzfeld's recollections show how irresistible the combination of

tanks and infantry was on this part of the battlefield, particularly when no anti-tank weapons were available. His men could fire their machine-guns at the Mark Vs, but the bullets would just bounce off, leaving them with the choice of continuing to fire – which some did – or getting out of the way. Even when machine-guns were loaded with special armour-piercing SmK ammunition, this did not always work. One officer of 152 Regiment (41st Division) fired 4,000 bullets at one tank, including 500 rounds of SmK ammunition, but without success.[17] It is evident that some machine-gunners continued to fire until the tanks were upon them. When Paul Maze drove up to the old front line he noticed the ghastly sight of several dead Germans who had been run over by the tanks. They were, he said, 'lying flattened out like pancakes'.[18] Nevertheless, heavy tanks, particularly the slower Mark Vs, remained extremely vulnerable on the battlefield, often when their supporting infantry had fallen away or where German batteries remained in operation. One German veteran, Leutnant Reisinger of 43rd Division, remembered seeing four tanks around Cerisy in the north. They were 'immediately dispatched by direct fire' and were, as he put it, 'burned'.[19] Indeed, even on such a success-ful day as 8 August, losses were heavy. The Mark V may have been protected by 14mm of plate armour, but it was widely noted that German artillery batteries, usually the 77mm field gun, were brutally effective against it. For example, of the thirty-four tanks that were supporting 4th Canadian Division, only six were able to reach the final objective, known as the Blue Dotted Line. 'A' Company of 1st Battalion, in particular, lost nine tanks owing to heavy anti-tank fire from Le Quesnel, and were unable to cross the open ground in front of the village without being hit. It was no surprise that after-action reports would later stress the importance of engaging field guns 'immediately they are observed, irrespective of any other targets that may present themselves', even suggesting that Whippets should be sent ahead of the heavier, slower Mark Vs 'in order to draw fire and so disclose the positions of anti-tank guns'.[20] Le Quesnel was the one objective that would remain out of Canadian hands on 8 August.

Rawlinson had placed great hopes on the use of cavalry and Whip-pet tanks to continue the advance and prevent any meaningful resistance in the rear of the German line. Although much was achieved, they did not work particularly well together. The Whippets were too slow over rough ground to keep up with horses, and the cavalry had to dismount to take on machine-guns when their armoured support was not available. Nevertheless, by late morning Fourth Army had broken into the German rear areas, overrunning a number of regimental headquarters, seizing hundreds of dazed prisoners and spreading chaos and terror. Paul Maze, who was operating with Canadian cavalry, found himself sweeping through a regimental beer garden 'with ingeniously constructed huts and tables made of branches, on which we caught a glimpse of plates with untested food still in them'; testimony to how quick and decisive the opening advance had been.[21] One soldier, Oberleutnant Schreder, Adjutant of 18 Regiment (41st Division), was at Framerville, seven miles behind the front line, where the Germans had stationed one of their infamous rail guns. Schreder had come from the front and was well aware of how devastating the attack had been. He spoke to the operator and told him to move the gun away to the east, but the man would not listen. Soon afterwards, two RAF biplanes that had been zooming low over the battlefield spotted the gun and dropped several bombs, one of which struck the ammunition wagon 'and tore the already-moving train into pieces'.

Things only got worse for Schreder and the German stragglers who were coming from the front line and heading for the rear. By this point the village of Framerville was full of soldiers, a 'rabble of people retreating further south', when 'a frantic commotion suddenly erupted'. Schreder recorded that:

> A large number of lightweight armoured cars were attacking the area from the Roman road, along with cavalry from the southwest. At the same time, 80 or 90 enemy aircraft appeared over the village at heights of no more than 100 metres, and further increased the commotion in the area with bombs and machine gun fire. No wonder then that a few officers and men with little experience of the front line joined the panicked retreat of the tradesmen companies, convoys, cars and other vehicles that were stationed in Framerville.

Schreder and his men seized a machine-gun and a few rifles and occupied the village, firing into sections of Canadian cavalry which were menacing them. Fortunately, 'as if by a miracle', they survived; 'the armoured cars also turned round and headed back towards the Roman road'.[22] Schreder's experience was typical of what happened in the German rear areas that afternoon and evening. Many other accounts speak powerfully of coming under heavy fire from aircraft flying low over the battlefield dropping bombs or firing machine-guns; of units being outflanked by squadrons of fast tanks that seemed to be everywhere, firing into them without mercy; of a situation that was as catastrophic as it was surprising. This kind of thing had never been seen in the German Army before.

8 August would be one of the most remarkable days of the war. Although the position of all units was not known, the Allied assault had driven between six and eight miles into the German lines, shattering Second Army and unhinging the flank of Eighteenth Army on its left. German casualties had been staggering. The official history estimated that they were as high as 48,000 men, including 33,000 missing or taken prisoner. Four hundred guns had been lost as well as hundreds of machine-guns and trench mortars.[23] For the battalions in the front line, often only small groups of survivors remained. 41st Division, which had faced the Australians opposite Villers-Bretonneux, was almost wiped out. It had lost all but three of its guns, and little remained of its front and supporting battalions.[24] Equally unnerving was the sight of the survivors from the opening attack. Numerous front-line battalions had been reduced to the size of companies. All that remained were clusters of shell-shocked men; their will utterly broken; their faces grimy; their eyes glassy, staring straight ahead. Their stories were always the same: horrifying accounts of iron monsters clanking out of the mist towards them; of mass infantry attacks; of being cut off and surrounded; of waiting for counter-attacks that never came. Some did not – or perhaps could not – say anything at all. Ludendorff's worst nightmare was, it seemed, coming true.

Currie's deception plan had worked perfectly. A German commander captured by 18th Canadian Battalion was horrified to find he was among Canadians. All he said to his captors was that 'we just got word that you were up in Belgium'.[25] Many others felt the same sense of disorientation and shock as more and more rumours of what had happened filtered through to the rear lines. On the outskirts of Cambrai, a pilot, Rudolf Stark, waited for what the following day would bring, watching the flashes of artillery fire on the horizon, rumbling away into the distance. At 11 p.m. his squadron was ordered to hand over every available truck to ferry reinforcements to the front. They only had four available, but they were cheerfully given. 'Well, as long as they have reserves to throw into the line, all right,' he said. Stark could not sleep that night. 'I wander along the aerodrome, sit down on the edge of a ditch and stare out into the night. The roll of the guns grows ever louder to southward. Now the rattle of wheels and the rumble of engines reach me more frequently from the road. More and more lorries, hastening southward, bringing up reserves to the threatened front. Daylight will soon be at hand; then we can fly and shall know for certain what it all means.'[26]

The Allies would continue their attack the following day, 9 August, but the speed of their advance began to slow. This was the reality of operations in the Great War, when it was difficult, if not impossible, to maintain an offensive momentum over subsequent days. But they tried their best. The liaison officer, Paul Maze, was woken at dawn by the crash of artillery fire on the village of Le Quesnel. 'There was a stir among the men,' he wrote, 'followed by the jingling of chains and the clang of stirrups as the saddles were lifted on to the horses.'[27] By the time Maze had got up, the attack had already started – the artillery that he had heard was already ten minutes late. Two battalions of 11 Canadian Brigade had made the assault, the men moving swiftly over the open ground and infiltrating into the village, covered by a barrage of machine-gun fire. Although they ran into heavy resistance, they were not stopped. Within an hour the Canadians' objective had been secured, the remaining Germans bombed out and the supporting tanks moving up through the long grass. Stage one of the attacks of the second day, it seemed, had gone to plan.

Unfortunately, the attack on Le Quesnel would prove to be the only part of the operations on the second day that went this way; 9 August was, according to the British official historian, 'a day of wasted opportunities'.[28] Given the degree of success achieved on 8 August, it was perhaps inevitable that the morning of the following day dawned with something approaching a hangover for the Allies. Getting orders out to the forward battalions and the batteries that had moved up was difficult and time-consuming because their locations were not always known and despatch riders had a habit of turning up late or not at all. Renewed attacks did not proceed at the arranged time and frequently they were either delayed or pushed forward, often going ahead without adequate flanking protection or sufficient artillery support. Because the location of units was not always known, most brigades attacked on their own in an uncoordinated fashion. It had originally been planned for 1st, 2nd and 3rd Canadian Divisions to push on to the villages of Roye and Chaulnes at 10 a.m., but it was noon before they got going. Similarly, Monash had wanted 1st Australian Division to leapfrog his 5th Division and move on towards Lihons at 11 a.m., but it was two hours later before the infantry turned up.[29]

For the tank crews, already exhausted, the morning brought new challenges. Many of them had had little sleep and much of the night had been dedicated to frantic repairs, trying to make sure the engines, the gear boxes, the steering, the machine-guns, were in working order before it got light. Even if they were fortunate most of the crews were suffering from minor ailments: cuts and grazes from bullet 'splash'; burns from the engines and exhausts; and confusion and exhaustion brought on by carbon monoxide poisoning and petrol fumes. If they were unlucky, they were likely to have sustained more serious casualties, perhaps fatalities, and already certain sections of the battlefield were littered with the ghastly remains of burnt-out tanks and incinerated crews. Moreover, because a considerable proportion of tanks had been put out of action, it was necessary to form composite battalions – often composite crews – from unfamiliar units in unfamiliar tanks. It was no wonder that the second, third and fourth days of Amiens were, in the words of Hugh Elles, 'a great test of training and the spirit of cohesion in the corps'. Considering these conditions it is incredible that the tanks continued to have success on the battlefield, yet it was becoming clear to everyone involved: tanks could only be employed in limited numbers for limited periods of time; and now the clock was definitely ticking.[30]

For the German Army, 9 August also dawned with unease and confusion. At 7 a.m. Crown Prince Rupprecht, commander of Germany's northern Army Group, was briefed on the situation. Second Army had already mounted local counter-attacks (with 79th Reserve and 221st Divisions, the former without its artillery), but the enemy was still advancing along the crucial Amiens–Roye road and General von der Marwitz's commanders were recommending an immediate retreat behind the line of the River Somme. All available reserves were being rushed to the front, but this would not be enough. After listening to his staff officers, and poring over maps of the front, Rupprecht was convinced that his Army Group would have to fall back, although he was conscious of not creating salients that would be difficult to defend. He eventually decided on a gradual withdrawal on the line Chipilly–Rosières–Roye, during which Second Army would ensure that its left would hold, so as to not uncover the right flank of Eighteenth Army. 'Yet even this is insufficient and only a temporary measure,' he opined. 'In order to preserve our strength, we must drop back further . . . and aim to link up with the Ninth Army at Carlepont. A lasting improvement in our situation can only be achieved by positioning ourselves behind the Somme and along the east bank of the Crozat canal . . .' Yet as Rupprecht knew only too well, OHL would not look kindly on this view of the situation.[31]

Scraping together reserve units was one thing, but getting them to the front, with all their equipment, and in good condition, was quite another. For the German divisions that had been rushed to the front, the situation was deeply worrying. Battalions often travelled in lorries; bumping along the narrow French roads towards the sound of the guns and the increasingly depressing prospect of getting to the front. Some were engaged by low-flying Allied biplanes and a number of columns were badly shot up. In any case, because they had been moved forward at such speed, they frequently left behind their supporting units and artillery. As soon as they reached the front, battalions were quickly formed up and marched forward, often pushed into hasty and ill-prepared counter-attacks over ground with which they were unfamiliar, and always suffering losses. When leading elements of the elite Bavarian Alpine Corps arrived at the front (to cover the junction of Second and Eighteenth Armies at Hattencourt), they found a situation of chaos and confusion. 'No one could give a clear idea of the actual position at the front; no one knew anything about troops on right and left, or above the divisions in position . . . individuals and all ranks in large parties were wandering wildly about, but soon for the most part finding their way to the rear . . . only here and there were a few isolated batteries in soldierly array, ready to support the reinforcing troops.'[32]

Given the chaos in the German rear lines, it is perhaps unsurprising that the Allies were able to make further gains. Both British and French units pushed on eastwards as best they could, mustering whatever tanks and crews were available, and capturing numerous other villages and small woods. Edward Lynch, an Australian serving with 5th Division, advanced 'across strange ground into unknown country' on the second day as they tried to keep the attack going. Every so often they would come across dazed German prisoners or clusters of dead bodies. The battlefield was, he remembered, 'littered with Fritz dead. Trees, men, war material are smashed into torn and twisted fragments. We root out forty terror-stricken wretches. They're pitiful to see. With twitching hands and bulging, blood-shot eyes, they continually fidget and flinch, unable to remain still. Fear-haunted men, they remind us of penned cattle that ever mill under the smell of blood.' After reaching their objective and digging in, they had to wait for relief. Although enemy resistance was light, soon the Germans spied their location and, with the coming of darkness, began shelling their positions with dreaded mustard gas. 'We have our gear ready to move out and are sitting around in our gas respirators, breathing through the rubber valve. Half suffocated, we sit in the darkness, our noses nearly squeezed off by the nose clips of the respirators, thinking the things we'd like to say about this gas if we only dared remove these stifling respirators.' Fortunately they were relieved that night and gratefully made their way back to the rear, stumbling along through drifting gas clouds, trying to maintain their direction through 'smoke-fogged goggles'.[33]

Moving forward in such an environment was never easy. One Canadian brigade commander, Alexander Ross, remembered that as soon as they had set off on the morning of 9 August (across 'an absolutely flat plain'), they 'ran into machine gun fire'. 'We advanced by our own firepower,' he said. 'We kept on going but the troops on the right and left had not been able to get up or advance or start on time with the result that our two attacking battalions fanned out towards the first from the flanks leaving a gap in the middle.' Although he was able to plug the gap with his reserve battalion, the lack of artillery support made him increasingly nervous about pushing on further.[34] Fourth Army gained about three miles of ground on 9 August; another two miles the following day. Debeney's forces, suffering from a similar set of problems, gained about two and a half miles, including capturing the village of Hangest, while the withdrawal of Eighteenth Army on 10 August saw them making up some progress, reaching the outskirts of Roye.[35] Yet it was evident to many of the commanders in the field that resistance was stiffening. Given the fact that almost all the heavy artillery, and many of the field guns, had not been able to get forward, artillery support was patchy. More worrying was the lack of flanking protection, which was usually a recipe for disaster in the Great War.

Gradually and inexorably the battle ground to a halt. By 10 August resistance was becoming much tougher. That day the French First Army was able to encircle Montdidier – its main objective for the battle – but recorded progressively stiffer resistance, dug-in defenders well stocked with machine-guns, and amply supported by heavy artillery.[36] The leading units were now operating far from their old front line, and although the intervening terrain was not churned into moonscape by shelling, it still took time to traverse and bring up supplies over unfamiliar ground. The Allies thus encountered an insoluble, recurring problem: how to continue an advance when everything that they needed to attack with – guns, supplies and fresh troops – took time and a great deal of effort to bring forward. Ominously, they were also now entering the old Somme battlefield

of evil memory: a tangled wasteland of shell holes and scattered
cemeteries, zigzagged by trenches and dug-outs. This was not a good
place to fight. Paul Maze remembered the increasing difficulty the
cavalry was having in advancing. 'The horses had to hop over trenches
and pick their way through belts of wire which in many places was
hidden by the long grass. Many of the horses fell into holes,' he
lamented. 'It was plain that the fighting was reverting again into
trench warfare.'[37]

German divisions were now being drawn from across the Western
Front and sent to the Amiens sector. By the third day, Seventeenth
Army had sent four divisions, Sixth Army had sent two, and
Fourth Army had handed over another five divisions. Von Hutier's
Eighteenth Army, facing the French, had also been strengthened by
three divisions.[38] These units were swiftly moving into place, filtering into the villages behind the line and setting up stronger and
thicker wire defences and digging in their machine-gun teams. On
10 August, 4th Canadian Division, supported by 32nd British Division, which had moved up to the front, continued their drive
southeast, intending to push on towards the village of Hallu. The
British and Canadians, supported by the French on their right flank,
made some progress, but enemy machine-gun fire and shelling were
becoming impossible to ignore, making any advance increasingly
costly. Forty-three tanks had been scraped together for the operation, but because of the late issue of orders, the attack went in
without the benefit of a smoke screen and in broad daylight. During
the day, over half were put out of action, mostly by German guns
firing over open sights.[39]

It was a disappointing and sobering day. 4th Canadian Division's
after-action report gloomily concluded that 'the enemy's reserves
were beginning to have their effect, and here, as on the right, the
attacking troops were confronted with the enemy's old trench system'.

Progress was naturally slow and casualties were beginning to increase.
The ground was impracticable for Cavalry and the tanks were seriously handicapped. There was an unwelcomed reversion to Trench
Warfare, and it was evident that further progress could not be made
without serious risk and unwarranted losses, unless as in a 'set-piece'

offensive, the attacking troops were to be adequately supported by
Heavy Artillery and an increased number of tanks.[40]

As might have been expected, both Currie and Monash were
becomingly increasingly unhappy about the situation on their
fronts. Almost hourly, their offensive momentum was draining
away and the Germans becoming stronger. Their men were
exhausted. They had few serviceable tanks. Most of their heavy
artillery had not moved forward. They were miles from their railheads. An unwelcome increase in enemy artillery fire had now been
noticed. Currie and Monash, committed to protecting their men
and only fighting on their own terms, were now seeing gains getting smaller and casualty lists rising; the moment – what Clausewitz
had called the 'culminating point' – had now arrived. The battle
had to be called off.

4.   'Another black day'

The ordeal of the German Army had begun.

General Georg von der Marwitz[1]

11—20 August 1918

On 7 August, as the final preparations for Amiens were being completed, Ferdinand Foch was made a Marshal of France. The great honour produced no change in the *Generalissimo*. His daily routine continued as it always had done: an early-morning Mass; lunch at noon (at which current operations were *never* mentioned); and dinner at 7 p.m., before the Marshal retired to bed.[2] One of those who observed Foch at this time was Sir William Orpen, who spent five days painting the Marshal's portrait in the long, narrow library at Bombon. They would spend ninety minutes each morning, with Orpen at his easel, while Foch sat and smoked. Foch was, at this point, trying to get used to a pipe that some of his English friends had given him, fearing that he was smoking too many cigars. But he did not take naturally to it. 'He could light it all right,' recalled Orpen, 'but after about two minutes it would begin to make strange, gurgling noises, which grew louder and louder, till it went out.' Much to Foch's delight, whenever they rested Orpen would get out some cotton wool and clean it for him.

Orpen did much more than just paint Foch. During their sessions, the painter caught a glimpse of how Foch worked and was amazed at the calmness and serenity of Bombon. Every ten minutes or so, staff officers would come and apprise him of the latest developments from the front. If there was good news he would simply mutter '*Bon!*' and nod his head; if it was bad news he would make 'a strange noise by forcing air out through his lips' and remain silent. One morning, a

French general came in (Orpen did not know who) and Foch 'very quietly, gave him times, dates, places where battles would be fought up to the end of December 1918, naming the French, British and American Divisions, and so forth, which would be used in each'. Orpen later wrote down what Foch had said and was amazed to find that 'everything went exactly as he said it would till about the middle of October, when the Boche really got on the run'. Orpen took three memories with him when he left Bombon: 'maps, calmness, and a certainty that the Allies would be victorious'.[3]

As pleased as he was by the successful initial assault at Amiens, Foch was convinced of the need to continue to push on. 'Now was the time,' he wrote in his memoirs, 'to push our advantage vigorously.' He would often tell his staff officers that they had to continue the battle; the Germans, he would swear, were just about to break. On the morning of 9 August, General Debeney received a furious order from Foch ordering him to capture the town of Roye as quickly as possible – '*move fast*, march hard, manoeuvre to the front, *reinforce firmly from the rear* with all the troops you have until the desired *result has been obtained*'.[4] Foch had never really been impressed with Debeney, who was too cautious and plodding for his taste; nevertheless the Commander of First Army was an efficient general, who would get there eventually, just perhaps not as fast as Foch would have liked. At the same time, Foch was working on plans for his Third Army to open another assault further to the south, while Mangin was also preparing to move forward on the Aisne. Foch was haunted by the retreat to the Hindenburg Line that had badly affected plans for the Nivelle offensive in the spring of 1917, and remained concerned that the German High Command would sanction a pre-emptive withdrawal and remove their armies from contact with him, shortening their line and freeing reserves. He was determined to keep on their heels.

After visiting Haig late on the evening of 11 August, Foch issued new orders to continue the push along the River Somme and the town of Bray the following morning. Writing to Haig and Pétain, he told them that 'maximum results' must be obtained from the 'deep penetration', which 'must be exploited for all its worth'. He urged that the crossings over the Somme at Ham be secured. Furthermore:

In view of the resistance offered by the enemy, there is no question of
obtaining these results by pressing uniformly all along the front; this
would only lead to being weak everywhere. On the contrary, it is a
matter of using concentrated and powerful action at the most important
points of the area, that is to say those whose possession would increase
the enemy's disorganization, in particular would disturb his communication. These operations should be rapidly and strongly mounted
by the rapid assembly and employment of the means available and
appropriate to the nature of the resistance encountered.

Foch wanted an attack to capture the road junctions near Roye, and
another to bring the main road from Amiens to Brie under artillery
fire. The flanks of the battle would be secured by further operations;
firstly by the British Third Army towards Bapaume and Péronne, and
an assault by the French Tenth Army towards Chauny. He wanted
the attacks to proceed as soon as possible. 'Since the 15th July,' he
boasted, 'the enemy has engaged 120 divisions in the battle. There is
an opportunity to-day which may not recur for a long time, and
which demands from all an effort that the expected results fully justify.'[5]

Foch may have wanted an energetic continuance of the battle, but
those commanders closer to the fighting thought otherwise. For Sir
Arthur Currie, whose corps had done so much to achieve success on
the first day, the increasing resistance at the front was troubling. One
morning, as his troops were readying themselves to push on again,
Currie met one of his brigade commanders, Brigadier-General J. A.
Clark (GOC 7 Brigade), who was at his headquarters having his hair
cut. As soon as Clark saw Currie, he got up and tried to salute, but
the corps commander told him to sit down, otherwise his hair might
get 'nicked'. 'He just stood and chatted very quietly and informally',
remembered Clark.

He chatted to me as an equal and he asked me, after he's been more or
less complimentary about the performance of the unit and the corps
in general, he said, 'Now, what's your impression of the situation
here.' Well, I said, 'I hope that you're not going to ask us to carry on

the attack in this area.' 'Why?' Well, I said, 'It's impregnable. There's nothing but wire, concrete emplacements, we are up against some-thing that we couldn't find anywhere else and we'd just be battering our heads against a brick wall if we're sent in here.'[6]

Currie thought as much. At a conference at Villers-Bretonneux on the afternoon of 11 August, chaired by General Rawlinson, he made it clear how bad the ground was. The other commanders, including Monash, all agreed with him and emphasized how much the enemy's resistance was increasing. Rawlinson was at pains to stress that there was 'no intention to try and burst through regardless of loss. Our losses up to date had been comparatively light and he did not intend to use any more men than was absolutely necessary.' Although Rawlin-son did not mind minor operations being conducted to improve the line – bearing in mind the Australians' tendency to raid – they should not involve 'useless loss'. No further attacks would be made until the bulk of Fourth Army's artillery could be brought up, perhaps some-time on 15 August. All tanks were to be immediately withdrawn and all efforts made to get as many serviceable as possible.[7]

Debeney – as cautious a commander as they came in the Great War – was also feeling increasingly queasy. While he was pleased with the capture of Montdidier, which would later become a textbook example of how to fight a positional battle, there seemed to be little chance of more far-reaching exploitation.[8] His cavalry had tried to push forward, but met 'progressively stronger resistance' and could not get very far. By the fourth day enemy resistance was stiffening, hostile shelling was much greater, and the ground was increasingly difficult to cross. On 11 August both X and XXXV Corps could only make minor progress across ground strewn with old trenches and against heavy machine-gun fire.[9] 'The combats today have shown that the Germans occupy in considerable strength the old line to the west and south-west of Roye,' Debeney wrote, 'where trenches and lines of wire are still to be found intact.' Accordingly, he had issued orders for the cancellation of his proposed operations the following day. He hoped that a postponement would allow time for his guns to cut the wire and soften up the Ger-man defences in front of him before trying again.[10]

Rawlinson relayed these concerns on to GHQ and recommended that the offensive be called off at once. On the morning of 14 August, he visited Haig and gave him a series of aerial reconnaissance photographs of the Roye–Chaulnes area that showed thick belts of barbed wire and well-dug trench systems that zigzagged across the open ground.[11] After seeing the photographs and discussing the matter with his army commander, Haig had to agree. He ordered a further postponement to the attack and wrote to Foch.

> During the past 48 hours, the enemy artillery fire on the fronts of the British Fourth and French First Army has greatly increased and it is evident that the line CHAULNES – ROYE is strongly held, while photographs show that the line is in good order and well wired. Moreover, the ground is broken and difficult for Tanks to operate. It is probable that there are at least sixteen German divisions holding the front south of the SOMME opposite the Armies under my command.

Haig informed Foch that under these circumstances he had postponed the attack until 'adequate artillery preparation' had been made.[12] He restated his position the following day. After 'careful examination' of the ground, any continuance of the attack in this sector would be 'very costly'. He had ordered his armies to continue artillery preparation (with wire-cutting and counter-battery fire) but they could only make an advance 'methodically and step by step'. Knowing that Foch would be disappointed, Haig stressed that his Third Army was soon to make its assault, and arranged to meet the *Generalissimo* at his Advanced HQ later that day.[13]

It was evident that a serious disagreement was brewing between Foch, on the one hand, who wanted the attacks to be pressed with determination, and Haig, Rawlinson and Debeney, on the other, who were all convinced of the need to desist. Foch's desire to keep going was understandable and necessary; indeed his biting, incessant aggression would be vital to the Allied war effort in 1918. Yet in this case he was wrong. Foch may have been only following conventional wisdom in demanding that the Allies concentrate their resources on key sectors of the front, but Haig was coming to a different conclusion. It seemed that he had learnt one of the most important lessons of the Western Front; that it was futile to continue to push troops against prepared positions and reinforced garrisons; much better to try and find another way round. What was needed was a series of offensives across large fronts that would stretch German reserves thinly and prevent them from concentrating their strength. Haig was convinced that if the Germans were strong in front of Amiens, well, then they would be weak elsewhere. British intelligence reports informed him that the German Seventeenth Army, south of Arras, was beginning to fall back, hence his stubborn reluctance to sanction further efforts by Fourth Army, at least for the time being.

Things came to a head on 15 August. Haig met Foch at 3 p.m. The *Generalissimo* immediately urged an attack on the Chaulnes–Roye front, but Haig refused, saying that he could only do so with heavy losses. In view of this, he had ordered Rawlinson and Debeney to postpone their attacks for the moment, while he transferred his reserves to Third Army further to the north. Foch bristled at this. With a confused look on his face, he asked Haig what orders had been issued to attack. At this point, Haig held his hands up. 'I spoke to Foch quite straightly,' he recorded in his diary, 'and let him understand that I was responsible for the handling of the British Forces.' Foch knew immediately that he had pushed Haig as far as he could. He thus backed down, smiling widely and assuring him that he only wanted information on Haig's intentions.[14] In the end Foch knew that he could not continue to nag Haig. His authority was limited and, in any case, within a matter of days new attacks would go in. So it was settled. Operations would be mounted; but they would take place elsewhere; the important thing was making sure they were properly coordinated and kept up the pressure on the German Army, which, at long last, seemed to be breaking apart.

Since the spring, the German Supreme Command had been based at Spa in Belgium, nestling in the forested, mist-mantled hills of this famous resort town. OHL was housed in (of all places) the Hôtel Britannique, one of the finest hotels in Europe. It lay along a wide, cobbled street, usually slick with the rain that frequently washed across this part of Belgium, where many staff officers were usually seen, taking the air or having a quiet smoke; trying to forget the war that went on and on. For six months it had been the nerve centre of the German war effort, humming to the sounds of clattering typewriters and the buzz of telephone calls, and busy with senior staff officers and commanders. It had always been run in an efficient and businesslike manner, but in the days after the attack at Amiens, the mood changed to one of high tension, increasing anxiety and depression. While Hindenburg was his usual stoical – almost uninterested – self, Ludendorff raged at the darkening situation, later admitting that Amiens was one of his worst experiences of the war – his 'black day of the German Army'. As soon as the news of the offensive broke, he sent a staff officer to the front to assess the condition of the divisions who had borne the brunt of the attack. What he reported hit the Quartermaster-General like a slap in the face. 'Whole bodies of our men had surrendered to single troopers, or isolated squadrons,' he raged. 'Retiring troops, meeting a fresh division going bravely into action, had shouted out things like "Blackleg," and "You're prolonging the war," expressions that were to be heard again later.' It was 8 August, Ludendorff concluded, that put the decline of their fighting power 'beyond all doubt'.[15]

Given Ludendorff's chronic anxiety and his inability to delegate responsibility, it was perhaps inevitable that in the days after the attack he regularly telephoned round senior officers and their Chiefs of Staff and told them what to do. The Army Group commander, Crown Prince Rupprecht, calmly watched events unfold from his headquarters and recorded in his diary how he 'admired the patience' of his Chief of Staff, Major-General von Kuhl, who had to deal with the constant interference from OHL.

> He remained unruffled by the continual telephone calls from Ludendorff, wanting to plan every move of the newly arrived battalions of the Alpine Corps, and just appeased Ludendorff by answering with a 'yes' or by saying to him: 'We cannot yet predict how this will turn out, everything depends on how circumstances develop,' etc. Telephone contact has so many disadvantages – there tends to be too much of it and in these direct conversations that took place between

OHL and the Chiefs of Staff of the army groups and armies, the group commanders are almost totally excluded. Just recently an army Commander-in-Chief said to me: 'I don't really know what I'm there for – everything is already decided before I am even consulted!' . . . If only Ludendorff would just telephone the Chiefs of Staff and not every individual army corps![16]

Rupprecht, always a sensible and responsible commander, had little of the manic energy and optimism of Ludendorff. He realized that the disaster on the front of Second Army was due to the exhaustion of the troops, their 'inferior organization', and the widespread despondence over the fate of the last German offensive in July. This was what he called the 'miserable fact' of what the German Army had become. Rupprecht would have liked to withdraw Second Army further back, but Ludendorff told him, in no uncertain terms, that the position must be held at all costs.

In the days after the attack at Amiens, OHL desperately tried to find out what had gone wrong. It reported on 11 August that there had been three main reasons for the 'defeat' of Second Army: 'the troops were surprised by the massed attack of the Tanks'; there were 'scarcely any positions or obstacles worth mentioning . . . to make a methodical resistance possible'; and the available artillery was 'wholly insufficient to establish fresh resistance' against an enemy that had broken through. This was all well and good, but it could not mask the serious decline in Germany's fighting power. OHL ordered more to be done to observe the enemy, expect surprise tank attacks (particularly at daybreak), and construct more trenches and anti-tank obstacles. The Supreme Command also resorted to the desperate, if understandable, exhortation that troops, 'even if they are enveloped, must, if necessary, defend their battle zone for days, to the last round and to the last man'.[17] For his part, Ludendorff preferred to assign responsibility to command failures, blaming von der Marwitz's Chief of Staff, Major-General Erich von Tschischwitz, who he believed was not up to the job. He immediately ordered the formation of a new Army Group, commanded by General Hans von Boehn (with the defensive expert, Fritz von Lossberg as his Chief of Staff), which would oversee the operations of Second, Eighteenth and Ninth Armies, and hopefully provide better coordination on that part of the front.

Despite the heavy casualties and the serious reverse in front of Amiens, Ludendorff refused to contemplate further withdrawals. At one meeting, Lossberg repeated his advice that they should occupy and extend the Hindenburg Line immediately with all available reserves instead of sending every man to the front. 'My justification for this was that the initiative for action had now without doubt been transferred to the enemy, and that this attack had hit a very sensitive spot on the German front.' But Ludendorff remained unmoved, telling him to make a reconnaissance of a new fall-back position, running from Combles to Péronne and Noyon. When Lossberg told him that it would take too long for this line to be completed, Ludendorff just ignored him. Believing that Ludendorff was now in total denial about reality, Lossberg went to see for himself. He visited the three armies and gave a detailed brief to General von Boehn at his headquarters at Le Cateau. Second Army was in a 'poor condition', and its troops had 'failed completely' on 8 and 9 August. Amiens was 'probably the greatest defeat a German Army had suffered during the war' and the Supreme Command was greatly overestimating their capacity for resistance. Although Ninth Army had not yet been engaged, the retreat of Second Army had led to the outflanking of Eighteenth Army. Casualties had also been heavy, with a number of divisions being broken up and their men sent to plug gaps in other units. It was a grave situation.[18]

On the morning of 13 August, just five days after the attack at Amiens, Hindenburg chaired a meeting at the Hôtel Britannique. The dramatic events of the past week called for a decision about what to do and the Chancellor (Count von Hertling) and the new Secretary of State (Paul von Hintze) had been invited to attend. Hindenburg would claim that he had 'no illusions about the political effects of our defeat on August 8', which revealed the weakness of the German Army on the Western Front. 'The amount of booty which our enemy could publish to the world spoke a clear language. Both the public at home and our Allies could only listen in great anxiety. All the more urgent was it that we should keep our presence of mind and face the situation without illusions, but also without exaggerated pessimism.' Although he was content that the situation had been stabilized – at least temporarily – he was only too well aware that on many sectors the defences were not up to scratch and the men were not showing the stubborn resistance of earlier years. What was worse, he lamented, the enemy had learnt much in how to attack. 'If the enemy repeated these attacks with the same fury, in view of the present constitution of our Army,' he warned, 'there was at any rate some prospect of our powers of resistance being gradually paralysed.'[19]

According to Hindenburg's memoirs, during the meeting on 13 August, he affirmed that the situation was 'certainly serious, but that it must not be forgotten that we were still standing deep in the enemy's country'. He believed that 'a successful conclusion of the war' was not impossible and 'hoped that the Army would be in a position to hold out'. 'Had not France, on whose soil the war had now been raging for four years, had to suffer and endure far more?' he asked.[20] Hindenburg may have radiated his old solidity – a rock that could never be moved – but his deputy, Erich Ludendorff, was falling apart. According to Colonel Hans von Haeften (the Supreme Command's liaison officer to the Government), when he arrived at Spa on 11 August, he found Ludendorff 'outwardly calm but very grave. It was not the loss of territory or the superiority of the tank – a weapon which we had neglected – which disturbed him; he was the man to rise to the surmounting of unexpected difficulties. What depressed the General was that he had lost confidence in the morale of his troops, the indispensable element in victory.' Ludendorff told Haeften that the men could no longer be depended on and that Germany needed peace quickly.[21] During the meeting, Ludendorff despaired of what he called Hindenburg's 'more optimistic view' of the situation.

I reviewed the military situation, the condition of the Army, the position of our Allies, and explained that it was no longer possible to force the enemy to sue for peace by an offensive . . . I sincerely hoped, however, that the Army in France would stand fast. The state of affairs on the Western Front was naturally bound to make an unfavourable impression on our Allies. In this connection, the *morale* of our Army and people became a matter of even greater importance than before.

After speaking for some time, the Secretary of State, Paul von Hintze, drew 'the logical conclusion that peace negotiations were essential and that we should have to bring ourselves to take up a very conciliatory attitude'.[22]

The Kaiser was at Spa the following day to chair a Crown Council meeting. In his presence the Quartermaster-General seemed to recover his nerve and banish the pessimism he had previously shown; a not uncommon experience for those in the presence of the Supreme War Lord. Ludendorff talked about 'moral endurance'; the need to strengthen the hopes of the Army and the people; to instil in them an unquenchable desire for victory; to do whatever it took. Von Hintze addressed the meeting with tears in his eyes and his hands shaking. He urged them to engage in diplomacy to end the war because it could not be concluded by military means; that something must be done to break the political deadlock. For his part, Hindenburg remained unimpressed, gruffly arguing that peace moves should only come when there had been some improvement in the military situation. The question was what to do about it; whether to continue to hang on at the front, hoping for an improvement in the situation, or make some kind of diplomatic move to end the war – a political manoeuvre that might result in revolution and chaos.

It would later be claimed that the Kaiser received an incorrect view of the situation on 14 August; that his generals had not presented him with all the facts, leaving him to labour on with the impression that something could be salvaged from continuing fighting. This was at least partly true, but hardly unusual; the Kaiser had been sidelined in the running of the German Empire for years. As early as November 1914, he had complained that 'The General Staff tells me nothing and never asks my advice. If people in Germany think that I am the Supreme Commander they are grossly mistaken. I drink tea, saw wood and go for walks . . .'[23] The Kaiser himself had little to say about the meetings at Spa. They were a painful reminder of his failure as Commander-in-Chief and his impotence in the face of Hindenburg and his formidable deputy. Ludendorff was certainly more optimistic than he had been the previous day (perhaps unable to bring himself to admit openly how disastrous the situation was), but Hindenburg's stand never wavered. His pride and legendary calmness prevented him from admitting what they all knew to be true: that the war had to be ended. They agreed that von Hintze should send peace feelers through the Queen of the Netherlands, but nothing else was done. The war, what was left of it, would have to go on.

It was evident in the days after Amiens that Ludendorff's nerves had suffered. From this point – mid- to late August – he seems to have become weaker. Tiredness, bordering on exhaustion, marked his features as he alternated between piteous depression and ridiculous optimism. More and more staff officers now began to notice the decline in their chief, at one point even arranging for the eminent psychiatrist and Chief Staff Physician, Dr Hochheimer, to pay a visit to Spa. When Hochheimer met Ludendorff and began to assess his condition, he found a man bordering on a nervous breakdown, who was overworked, exhausted and unable to function effectively. Rest was urgently required. Hochheimer greeted the commander 'warmly and casually' and handed him a precise daily schedule of activity that was intended to free his mind from anxiety and worry. Much to his aides' surprise, Ludendorff agreed with this diagnosis and followed his advice 'willingly and happily'. 'He accepted it,' Hochheimer noted, 'although the restriction of his long working hours, especially the night time hours, was difficult for him.' In the coming days, Hochheimer urged his patient to take pleasure in his garden, especially 'the most beautiful flowers' that were brought into his stuffy office (that Hochheimer likened to 'a dead furniture display as it does not have any pictures hanging on the wall'). While Hochheimer was certainly pleased by Ludendorff's willingness to work with him – 'the central issue is the freeing of a fossilized soul' he would write in his diary – he knew only too well that nothing short of a miraculous turn of events in the west could restore Ludendorff's nerve. As long as he stayed at his post, he would get no rest, and as the German armies crumbled, the pressure would only increase.[24]

*

The situation at the front only seemed to worsen in the weeks after the blow at Amiens. Six days after the Crown Council meeting, a new offensive opened on the Aisne, this time by Charles Mangin's Tenth Army, which blasted yet another hole in the line. The attack opened in bright sunlight at 7.10 a.m. on 20 August, General Pétain proudly reporting that 'it won the most complete success along its entire front, over-ran the whole of the centre of resistance, which for a long time the enemy had been powerfully fortifying'. Eight thousand prisoners had been taken and over 100 guns fell into French hands.[25] For the German Army, this attack would be another disaster, comparable in some respects to the defeat at Amiens. Surveying the maps at Advanced Headquarters at Avesnes, and cursing as news came in, was Ludendorff, who was stunned at the speed with which German resistance had crumbled. For him 20 August was 'another black day' with 'heavy and irreplaceable losses'. 'On August 20th a deep salient was made at Cuts,' he wrote, 'rendering the position of the troops, with the Oise in the rear, exceedingly uncomfortable. In the direction of Nouvron, also, the enemy broke into our line, but was driven back, although not completely, by counter-attacks delivered by good German Jaeger divisions.' Given the exposed position of German troops in front of the Rivers Oise and Ailette he reluctantly agreed to sanction the withdrawal of the right wing of Ninth Army behind the Oise, while moving the centre back behind the Ailette a day later. 'The battle had again taken an uncomfortable course, in spite of all our precaution,' he added, 'the nerves of the Army had suffered. In some places the men would no longer stand the tremendous artillery barrages and tank attacks which had become still more severe.'[26]

Mangin's attack was a powerful illustration of how much Allied methods of attack had improved since the grim middle years of the war. Mangin employed four corps in an aggressive thrust northeastwards towards the towns of Noyon and Chauny.[27] As on the Marne, secrecy had been stressed at all levels. Enemy aircraft were not allowed to observe French preparations, and, as was usual by now, all attacking divisions moved up to the front at night. A preliminary bombardment would take out any German batteries, blow sufficiently large holes in the barbed wire for the infantry to get through ('at least 30 to 40 metres of breach per front line company'), and destroy enemy command posts and known machine-gun nests. The French guns would also fire a powerful, but short, 'hurricane' bombardment immediately prior to the attack. As was becoming the norm by 1918, the infantry would leave behind their capes and backpacks and make sure they were as mobile as possible. Gone were the long, thick lines of infantry that had been so ineffective earlier in the war. Specially designated units were tasked with clearing up dugouts and shelters and mopping up any enemy stragglers who appeared. The advance would also be supported by tanks. Gone were the wasteful French tactics that had brought the Army to mutiny the previous year. The operation on 20 August was a sign that things had changed. This was well thought through; this was economical; this was the face of war in 1918.[28]

While the strain continued to mount for Ludendorff, the moment was particularly sweet for Charles Mangin. A square-headed man with a piercing stare, firm jaw and black moustache, he was a 52-year-old native of Moselle, whose family had fled the German Army in 1870, so it was perhaps understandable if he hated the enemy with undimmed fury. Earlier in the war, Mangin had become notorious for his apparently careless attitude towards the lives of his men; he was one of a number of generals who gained the infamous nickname of 'the butcher' and had been removed from command of Sixth Army in May 1917. Nevertheless, by the following year, Mangin's aggression, determination and vigour were once more in demand and Clemenceau had brought him back. He had masterminded the counterstroke on 18 July, outmanoeuvring his enemy, breaking the German line and imperilling their position on the Marne. But now his greatest battles were with his own army; an army whose will to fight was draining away with each passing day, and whose commander, Pétain, distrusted his aggressive, eager subordinate. On 5 August Mangin wrote in his diary:

> This army really was a bit of a deadweight to get going, not entirely believing in its success and it's the one which got things rolling because the others had even less confidence in it . . . I had to get angry

and I never do so during battle; I had to threaten, and it's the first time; had to order the Major-Generals to get on their horses with their staff and to ride at the front of the main body of the army, tearing themselves away from the disastrous headquarters where they draft the progress reports so well.

Mangin's aggression and confidence may not have been welcomed in the French Army, but he was much loved by the Americans. One captain who served at his headquarters told him that, in America, Mangin was their 'idol' and he would do well to go to the United States after the war to 'receive honours'.[29] Another observer found him to be 'quick and wiry', who constantly suggested 'an English fox terrier'. He was 'a bundle of vigour, nerve, and activity. His manner was very friendly, his words quick, brief, and incisive. He spoke with great clearness: and you knew what he had said.'[30]

Mangin was mightily pleased with Tenth Army's achievements, recording in his diary, rather immodestly, that 'my plan succeeded perfectly'. Almost smelling out German weakness, like the terrier he always reminded people of, Mangin wanted to push on. He was, however, increasingly concerned whether he would get any reserves; indeed, whether the French Army had enough left to continue the battle. He admitted on 22 August that 'it is most annoying that I did not have the necessary forces' to take advantage of the situation, and two days later at a conference with his Army Group commander, General Fayolle, he appealed for more troops to continue the attack. 'I will still be able to do something but they don't want to understand what harm is being caused by the process which consists of doling things out a bit at a time instead of putting at my disposal everything I'm asking for.' He saw Pétain on 27 August and urged him to push on, but he was increasingly aware that High Command was 'nervous' and lacked 'the steadfastness which could become necessary' in future operations. Mangin had to do his best with whatever resources Pétain gave him.[31]

For Fayolle and his chief, Pétain, there was no question of giving Mangin 'everything he asked for'. The objective was to keep the front moving and to follow the enemy, but little more. There would be no more deep penetrations into the German position, only gradual, fully supported operations that were as risk-free as possible. Let the Americans and the tanks take the strain, Pétain was fond of saying; and in August and September 1918 he was able to do this. Some of his army commanders, most notably Mangin, may have wanted to push further, deeper and more aggressively, but Pétain kept them on a tight leash. Risks could no longer be justified. On 17 August, Debeney, whose force had been gradually moving up on Rawlinson's right flank, issued orders which underlined the care with which French commanders now had to take in offensive operations.

> I stress again the importance of the artillery fire. The destruction one by one of the German batteries is a gain of absolute value. We advance as a result of superiority in fire power. Hence, the capital importance of careful regulation of the use of ammunition; we should consume only what is strictly necessary at any given moment, forbidding all useless firing. Since we have the benefit of the initiative, the artillery should carefully regulate its fire, strike hard and to the point, and expend little. We shall continue to employ the infantry in the same manner: to push into the advance what is necessary, leaving the remainder resting in the rear, but relieving the leading units before they are worn out.[32]

Foch might try and prod Pétain on every so often, urging him to grip his commanders and inject some urgency into the attack, but many of the senior command positions were held by men, like Debeney and Fayolle, who had come to prominence under Pétain and shared his caution. In the last weeks of August, French forces followed up the German retreat, and apart from minor skirmishes encountered little resistance from their rearguards. From 8 September, advance guards began to enter the German zone of fire and were thus 'obliged to become more cautious in their advance', moving forward more slowly and making sure areas were clear before pushing on.[33] It was not spectacular, but it was enough; the Allies were finally on their way.

5. 'The incredible roar of massed guns'

We're in the land of rotting men in the Year of Our Lord, 1918.

Edward Lynch[1]

21–31 August 1918

As Foch had been promised, the Allied attacks would go on. By the final weeks of August, the British and French Armies found themselves facing devastated countryside, littered with cemeteries and old dug-outs, shattered villages and splintered woods. While the British looked grimly upon the old Somme battlefield, their French allies, to the south, marched through a strip of tortured ground that had been razed by the Germans in 1917. It was a time-consuming and treacherous business. General Eugène Debeney, commanding First Army, remembered the suffering his troops endured as they moved through this awful sector. The terrain was 'full of shell holes, all the houses destroyed, ruins, nothing but ruins in the midst of which the steel skeletons of the refineries stretched their great bare arms up towards a grey sky'. They were advancing towards Saint-Quentin but the destruction they encountered was 'methodical'. Even the fruit trees, Debeney swore, had been cut down. 'For six weeks we had to fight our way forward in this dismal desert, battling at night with a veritable invasion of voles, which made sleep impossible.' His men were also 'ravaged by influenza', which, he admitted, was 'a great burden to us'. His men endured this ordeal with 'remarkable courage'.[2]

Like Pétain, Debeney was, at heart, a realist. One acquaintance described him as 'a typical-looking French officer: black hair, black moustache, military in deportment, and neat in dress; well kept, handsome, and of pleasing manners: very keen and alert and with sharp but kindly eyes'. He had apparently served so long with Pétain that he retained some of his master's 'noble fatalism'; receiving 'ill news as quietly as good . . . his judgment did not seem to be unsettled by either'.[3] Debeney was confident his troops would 'put their backs' into breaking the Hindenburg Line, which lay in front of them, but doubted whether they would be able to go much further, believing that the Germans would fall back to the Meuse, thus ensuring the war would drag on through a long winter campaign. These sober judgements stood in sharp contrast to those of Douglas Haig, whom he met regularly at this time. Despite the poor conditions and the continuing stubborn resistance from the enemy, Haig was convinced that much could be achieved before the end of the year. After Amiens, Debeney wrote, Haig 'could clearly see all the possible consequences of the victory and he immediately pursued them, in spite of all the obstacles, with conviction and a stubborn will to defeat the enemy and to finish the war before the end of the year'. By 21 August the British were ready for their renewed push.

Two days before the attack was to go in, Haig met the commander of Third Army, Sir Julian Byng, and explained his thoughts on the coming operation. Haig was upbeat and urged Byng to keep up the pressure on the German line. His objective, Haig explained, was to 'break the Enemy's front, and *gain Bapaume as soon as possible* . . . Now is the time to act with boldness, and in full confidence that, if we only hit the Enemy hard enough, and continue to press him, he will give way and acknowledge that he is beaten.'[4] For his part, Byng was a little more cautious than Haig would have liked, but prepared to do his best. Three corps would push forward between Albert and Arras against the battered Seventeenth Army commanded by General Otto von Below. Third Army had not made any alterations to its usual routine. There had been no obvious artillery preparation or extra road building, and no greater use of wireless communications. Everything was done to give the impression that it was just another day at the front. Troops were moved up at night, reinforcing artillery batteries were carefully hidden in woods and villages, while aircraft flew low over the lines drowning out the noise of approaching tanks. The 'Amiens method' was now standard operating procedure in the BEF.[5]

The attack began at dawn on 21 August, a day of mist and cool breezes across Picardy. As at Amiens, the attacking battalions were both helped and hampered by thick, grey fog that covered the battle-field like a shroud. While certainly interfering with German observation, it made it very difficult for the assaulting waves to maintain their correct direction: several tanks got lost; some groups, including two belonging to the Grenadier Guards, became hopelessly confused and were eventually found *behind* their support companies. During the day Third Army secured a number of objectives, including the villages of Courcelles and Moyenneville, and had pushed forward about three miles, but after running into heavy artillery fire, the leading units were unable to go much further. The tanks, shuffling along in support, also suffered heavy losses.[6] At first glance it might have seemed that nothing much had been achieved; after all they had not broken through like at Amiens. Gone were the mass use of tanks and the joyful sight of lines of Germans retreating over open, rolling countryside. Tanks could only be employed in small numbers, often not at all. Now the enemy could not be seen, other than the occasional glimpse of sinister grey-clad figures manning thin trenches or sunken roads, like wraiths in the distance. Nevertheless, these battles were important and effective; part of a gruelling series of engagements, messy and not always successful, that brought the Allied armies to a position where they could assault the last German defensive position in the west: the much-vaunted Hindenburg Line.

Typical of the experience of Third Army was 5th Division, which contained Tom Cotterill's battalion, the 15/Royal Warwickshire Regiment. This division was in almost constant action between 21 August and 4 September, pushing eastwards along the Bapaume Road, watching its flanks, taking prisoners, and dealing with the occasional machine-gun position. It advanced over fourteen miles, but suffered casualties of 210 officers and 4,065 men. This was, as the divisional history admitted, 'severe', but not 'out of proportion to the results gained'.[7] The division had attacked on 21 August as it pushed on towards Achiet-le-Petit and the Albert–Arras railway line that ran parallel to Third Army's front. The morning was foggy, and the division encountered the usual problem of keeping direction in the haze. Good progress was achieved, however, and the division was assisted by twelve Mark IV tanks and a creeping barrage provided by the field artillery. Two days later it was the turn of 13 Brigade, containing 15/Warwicks, to continue the advance. Its attack on 23 August was hampered by familiar problems: not enough time to reconnoitre and prepare adequately; poor ground conditions; and the need for combined arms and personal bravery. It was also conducted at night, which meant that organizing the battalions proved more difficult than usual. A brigade report concluded that:

> The artillery had been advancing during the day, and a barrage was organised. Owing to the width of the front to be attacked the barrage could only be a thin one, but what there was of it was reported after the battle to have been extremely good . . . The whole operation was rendered extremely difficult owing to the very short time available to get battalions into assembly positions, and to the fact that it was dark very early that night on account of clouds . . . [8]

On the right the attacking lines got pinned down and it was up to Lieutenant-Colonel Colt, the Commanding Officer of 12/Glosters, to act on his own initiative. He formed the men personally and led them through the village of Irles, pushing forward to the other side and gaining their objective. For 15/Warwicks, their Commanding Officer, Lieutenant-Colonel Miller, had only thirty-five minutes in which to issue his orders. He gathered his company commanders and told them that the attack would begin at 7.30 p.m. They would advance and gain the high ground commanding the village of Grévillers. Fortunately, the situation they encountered was much easier than they expected. They gained the ridge, and captured over 220 enemy prisoners and eight guns, and a large haul of machine-guns and ammunition, suffering only five casualties, all of whom were wounded.[9]

The fighting may have been less bloody than many had feared, but as Third Army continued its attacks, few units were immune from the daily toll of casualties. One British battery commander, R. C. Foot, whose guns were supporting 37th Division in its attack on

Achiet-le-Grand, remembered 23 August ('a heavy day of fighting') for two reasons: firstly that his guns were afflicted by a number of terrifying premature explosions; and, secondly, that he met the Commander-in-Chief, Sir Douglas Haig. 'Once the attack, and our barrage, started,' recalled Foot, 'we were busy at the guns, when, with a roar and a cloud of dust, the adjoining howitzer of the battery on our left blew up, one of its own shells bursting within the gun. A few minutes later the same thing happened to the adjoining howitzer of the battery on our right; in both cases, the whole gun detachment was either killed or wounded. Consequently, we all had the jitters, expecting a similar premature burst in one of our howitzers. Behind us, across the valley a line of 18-pounder batteries was firing over our heads, and, at intervals, one of their guns would have a premature shrapnel burst, peppering us with a hail of whirring bullets; and this did not add to our composure . . .'[10]

Evidently the effect of witnessing their own guns exploding had reduced some of Foot's men to a state of exhaustion and panic. As their rate of fire slackened, he withdrew three gunners from each detachment and made them shelter in shell holes to the rear, relieving the others every fifteen minutes or so. Unfortunately, after another 18-pounder had gone up in a cloud of smoke, Foot found one of his subalterns, Jack Massey-Beresford, stone dead; he had been hit by a shell case on the back of the head. Later that day, when the battery had been withdrawn and was making its way forward, Foot was called to the head of the column to find Haig by the roadside, alone except for a Sergeant of the 7/Hussars with his Union Flag lance pennon. 'He was a very taciturn man,' wrote Foot, 'but as the Battery filed by on the road and saluted him, he asked about the body on the leading gun, and I told him about Jack's death, complained, rather bitterly and brashly no doubt, about our day's troubles with faulty ammunition. After the Battery had passed, he fell in behind them on the road with me, got out a notebook and made a note of Jack's name; later I heard that he had indeed taken the trouble to write a personal note of condolence in his own hand to Jack's family . . . this did a lot to cheer us up after a horrid day.' Although you would be hard pressed to find a gunner who would swap places with the infantry, the artillery fought a war that was as demanding in its own way. While infantry battalions would be relieved from the front line at regular intervals, artillery batteries could look forward to weeks, sometimes months, of uninterrupted front-line service, often firing every day. And each day, as Foot knew only too well, could be exhausting and demoralizing in equal measure.

Despite the daily carnage, there was a growing acknowledgement that finally, after all that had passed, the British knew how to fight effectively. 'We had never previously witnessed a preparation of this magnitude; it was awesome in its enormity,' wrote Private A. J. Turner, serving with 38th (Welsh) Division, as they prepared to attack on the Somme in late August.

> On the morning of our departure significant solemnity was lent to the scene by long lines of boys kneeling in the bright sunshine whilst Padres administered absolution. When at last we moved up toward our allotted position each yard of ground was occupied by artillery of every size and shape; menacing howitzers, long-range guns with their evil snouts pointing skyward, whole families of cannon of all calibres, and the collection stretching on each side as far as the eye could see.[11]

When these batteries opened fire, the experience was both frightening and reassuring. Turner described the bombardment as one 'continuous deafening vibrating sound; a sound such as human ears could not endure, and men cowered under the pressure of it. Behind, the incredible roar of massed guns growing in intensity with each second, overhead the slithering metallic scream of passing missiles, in front an inferno of explosions, heaving earth, and pulsating vivid light.' This kind of artillery support – usually in the form of a creeping barrage – was, by 1918, a staple element of battlefield tactics. It was designed to shield the attacking infantry from enemy machinegunners and riflemen. It advanced in front of the infantry at a set pace, forcing the defenders to keep their heads down, so that the attackers would not be murdered in no-man's-land. While, with some practice, British and French troops learnt to rely heavily on their guns (to 'lean' on them), it was never a particularly comfortable experience, and there was always the fear of running into your own barrage, getting hit by stray shells, or even 'losing' the cover and being left exposed to enemy firing points.

Like Private Turner, many of those who experienced creeping barrages found it hard to adequately express the intensity of the experience. 'One writes of the thunder of the gunfire,' remembered one British officer, 'but in reality it is not like that at all. My mother once asked me what it was like, and I answered that if you stood on the platform of any railway junction as an express train roared through, and multiplied that sound by about twenty times, you would have a fairly good idea what a barrage was like.'[12] Similarly, another British veteran, T. G. Mohan, noted that 'It would be absolutely futile for me to attempt to describe the barrage. It was at once terrible and magnificent. It is impossible to convey any adequate idea of the awful and majestic hellishness of it all; only by experience can it possibly be appreciated. It was wonderful and grand from our point of view, and when we got used to it, gave us great confidence.'[13] Behind this shellfire the infantry would advance, scurrying across no-man's-land as quickly as they could. T. H. Holmes, a Private with 13/London Regiment of 56th (London) Division, remembered fighting on the Somme in this period. He got up out of his trench and gazed out into the distance: 'through the smoke, stretched vaguely a flat plain with low hills in the far distance'. He felt 'naked' – a 'long line of men, ten to twenty yards apart, extended each side of us' – but pressed on, going about the length of a football pitch before the rattle of machine-gun fire spat out at them.[14]

The British may have been fighting over familiar territory – Beaumont Hamel, La Boisselle, Thiepval – but that was where the similarity with 1916 ended. Battlefield weapons and communications systems had progressed greatly since then and allowed battalions to deal swiftly and effectively with enemy strongpoints that, two years ago, would have held them up for weeks. If tanks were available, they were ideal for this kind of work. Holmes was a battalion signaller and carried a variety of equipment with him, most importantly his lamp. After the first resistance was encountered, he dropped into a shell hole, while his officer told him to make his first signal of the day.

Opening his heavy lamp and pointing it to the rear, Holmes flashed a coded signal for 'Machine gun post active'. It was shortly answered by the reply 'aaa', which meant that the message had been received and understood. 'Soon a new sound struck our ears,' he wrote.

A deep chug-chugging. Out of the smoke giant shapes dramatically loomed up, lurching along like ungainly prehistoric monsters. They were tanks. I remember cheering, which was rather a waste of precious breath. They clattered past, and we followed a respectful distance behind them. One of them swivelled awkwardly towards where the sparks of the machine gun revealed the position of the post, and churned right over it.

Even if tanks were unavailable, by 1918 British troops carried a remarkable array of equipment to help them survive on the battlefield. Indeed, if the Western Front was anything, it was *heavy*. 'Fighting order' was 250 rounds of small-arms ammunition (for the Lee Enfield rifle), a gas mask, a water bottle, iron rations, an entrenching tool, two Mills bombs and two sandbags. Several shovels, picks, wire cutters and phosphorus grenades were also distributed among the men.[15] Although the British could never match the number of machine-guns employed by German units, they were equipped with the Lewis gun; an excellent battlefield weapon that was relatively light and portable, and provided a high rate of fire. Platoon tactics emphasized 'fire and movement', with sections conducting coordinated attacks against strongpoints, pinning them down with fire before surrounding them. Grenades and bombs were vital tools in providing infantry with the necessary firepower to do this, with the rifle grenade being particularly effective. Mills bombs would be fired from either a rod and cartridge or a special discharger fitted to the barrel. Colonel J. Durrant, a staff officer with the Australian Corps, reckoned that veteran infantry 'could hit a large shell-hole five times out of six at one hundred yards, and do very good practice at twice that distance, or even farther'.[16]

The tactical proficiency of the BEF was particularly noticeable in one of the most impressive actions of this period, the Australian Corps's capture of Mont Saint-Quentin on 31 August. After its exertions at Amiens, Monash's troops had returned to the front on 26 August and continued pushing the enemy back along the wooded valley of the River Somme. The Germans may have been in disarray, but they benefited from falling back across terrain that was an attacker's nightmare. The large town of Péronne, in particular, lay in one of the most formidable positions ever held by German troops. It was protected from the west by the river and wide stretches of marshy ground, over which General von der Marwitz had ensured that no bridges were left standing. Sergeant Walter Downing, serving with 5th Australian Division, was one of those who witnessed the attacks here. There were no tanks in support; the defences were manned by crack German units; and the terrain was open and devoid of cover. Various attempts were made to cross, but none succeeded. It was almost impossible for engineers to construct bridges across such a wide, fast-flowing river, let alone under the guns of the enemy batteries that commanded the entire area. Downing would always be haunted by the sight of Australian infantry coming under fire as they tried to cross 'a few narrow duckboard paths, twenty inches wide', which he called 'death traps'.

> Patrols, wading hither and thither on the edge of the marsh, found and followed them among the tussocks until, on turning a corner, the men found themselves in the face of enemy machine-guns, set by design to sweep the track at point-blank range. There were many gallant but futile deeds – when, attempting to push forward at any cost, or dashing into showers of bullets to the aid of comrades lying wounded and limp upon the boards with their bodies hung half in the water, our men walked one by one to death, and fell in heaps on those narrow wandering causeways, or tumbled into the marsh and sank beneath its rippling surface, as the bullets splashed in the water or struck splinters from the duckboards.[17]

Monash, the Australian Corps commander, rapidly concluded that any attack from the west, across this open ground, would be extremely costly. He therefore decided that it would have to be outflanked from the north. The only problem was that a heavily defended hill, Mont Saint-Quentin, guarded the northern approaches to the town. It was, in the words of the Australian Corps commander, 'a bastion of solid defence against any advance from the west'.[18]

The assault on Mont Saint-Quentin began at 5 a.m. on 30 August. 5 Australian Brigade was given the task of rushing forward and over-whelming the defenders on the high ground. Its objective was, according to one witness, 'just a great hill, pock-marked by shell holes and capped by stunted trees now slashed and broken'.[19] The infantry had already fought hard for two days by the time they reached their advanced trenches, all the time being under shellfire, and facing elite German troops. After swigging down their rum ration – which fortunately arrived at 3 a.m. – the tired infantry moved forward, crossing trenches, bombing dug-outs, and trying to follow their barrage as it chewed up the ground in front of them. The trenches on the Mont were held by three battalions of the Kaiser Alexander Regiment, averaging about 600 men each. They had been ordered to hold the position at all costs, but were surprised by the suddenness and ferocity of the Australian assault. 'Here there was a sharp fight with bullets and bombs: a short check; then machine gun fire from the right . . .' wrote its regimental history. One veteran remembered how 'It all happened like lightning, and before we had fired a shot we were taken unawares.' Just 550 tired Australian sol-diers had captured one of the most formidable positions on the Western Front and taken over 500 prisoners.[20] When Rawlinson's Chief of Staff, Sir Archibald Montgomery, heard the news at Fourth Army HQ, he was stunned. He would later call it 'one of the most notable examples of pluck and enterprise during the war'.[21]

Gradually, painfully but inexorably the German armies fell back through the Somme sector, leaving behind the wilderness of 1916 and the scarred hills around Péronne. For General von der Marwitz, who had hoped to make an indefinite stand here, the loss of Mont Saint-Quentin was a particularly heavy blow. On 31 August, he confided to his diary that his men had endured 'hard, very hard battles today'. They had fought off seven British divisions and managed to prevent a breakthrough, but the intensity of the fighting caused him no end of concern. 'The English are continuing the attacks with the French at so many places that you get the impression they are pushing for a decision. Facing my front today were Australians again, the same ones that came up with the tanks on 8 August . . . Stocked up with 18-year-olds through dire need, they keep on coming . . . It's a gruelling time.' He was worried about the lack of leave available to his men and dutifully told his wife, 'Don't even think of me coming home.'[22]

The Army Group commander, General Hans von Boehn, went to the front every day with his Chief of Staff, Fritz von Lossberg, to 'assess the state of battle for himself'. His main task was to assign 'the increasingly rare relief divisions to the fronts most at risk' and try to free his armies from the vice-like grip of their pursuers. Casualty rates were ominous. Lossberg noted that during these 'mighty enemy onslaughts' several German divisions had suffered so heavily that they had to be broken up. He estimated that by early September the Seventeenth, Second, Eighteenth and Ninth Armies had collectively lost more than 100,000 men.[23] Nine divisions had been in the line against Third Army's attack on 21 August, including 2nd Guard Reserve Division, which had defended Courcelles, and 4th Bavarian Division, which had fought at Achiet-le-Petit. This latter division had taken a pounding since the beginning of the offensive, suffering over 2,800 casualties, and was utterly spent. It was relieved on the night of 23 August.[24] This seems to have been entirely typical of the attrition suffered by the Germans at this time. One unit, 55 Infantry Regiment (of 13th Division) spent several days fighting at Bazentin-le-Grand on the old Somme front. According to its regimental history, by the time it was pulled out on 27 August, the strength of its three battalions had 'melted away' because of the heavy fighting, leaving the regiment 'destitute' and desperately in need of relief.[25]

German units had undoubtedly fought hard; doing enough to blunt the British attacks and then slipping away at night. Although there were still many instances of heroism and sacrifice – Marwitz decorated one junior officer who had destroyed fourteen tanks single-handedly on 24 August – the continuous attrition of the front began to take its toll.[26] Officers began to notice that the legendary cohesion and fortitude of the German Army was faltering.

They could see how nervousness and fear spread quickly through their companies, causing some soldiers to melt away in battle or run away at the first sign of enemy tanks. One German veteran remembered how the 'mere mention of a tank was sufficient to put the whole trench into a state of excitement' with men quickly tying bundles of hand grenades together in anticipation of their arrival.[27] On 27 August 2nd Guards Division complained that some infantry 'hardly made any use of their rifles', leaving the defence entirely to the machine-gunners and artillery. 'A large number of cases have also been substantiated in which companies of Infantry have passed through the artillery lines and have not observed the request of the artillery to protect them.' It urged the 'strongest measures' to be taken to ensure that such behaviour was stamped out.[28]

One morning in late August, as Third Army was inching its way towards Bapaume, the pilot Rudolf Stark emerged from the mess of *Jagdstaffel* 35, to see his fellow aviators running around the meadow 'like children'. It took him some time before he realized what they were doing. They were picking up leaflets dropped from Allied aircraft. 'It is snowing from a clear sky. Great white flakes are dancing down. The wind had carried them a long distance and sends them sailing through the air like white butterflies.' Collecting them was a profitable business. German headquarters regularly paid out money for every leaflet that was handed in. Apparently, you could earn 'quite decent sums on the large masses of them they often have to collect'. Although Stark was convinced that 'even the stupidest soldier' was not influenced by this propaganda, the fact that headquarters was prepared to pay for them told its own story. Indeed because they were valuable, they became 'a sort of paper currency, subject to the same fluctuations as real banknotes. Now they are sought for eagerly, and the result is that the information they contain always gets read.'[29]

There is no doubt that German morale – depressed by poor food and the sickness that swept through their divisions – was badly affected by Allied propaganda that was finally beginning to take effect. German trenches and rear areas would regularly be deluged with leaflets urging soldiers to give up, and telling them of the

wonderful conditions in Allied prisoner-of-war camps, of all the
food and the jolly concert performances, and how they could not
possibly win the war, particularly now that the Americans were
arriving in such strength. For Fritz von Lossberg, the German Army's
'resilience and fighting spirit were clearly on the wane'.

> The soldiers on leave who were being indoctrinated back home,
> returned to the place where their units had been. But their divisions
> had very frequently already been moved to other locations. They fol-
> lowed on but did not find them. Even the information and checkpoints
> which had been set up everywhere could not in most cases supply any
> reliable information about the whereabouts of the detachments of
> troops. The effect of propaganda leaflets which enemy pilots had
> dropped over the German front and the area behind it was very evi-
> dent. As a result a large number of shirkers emerged; their bad
> example had a negative effect on vigorous combatants. This went so
> far that enraged soldiers even shouted the derogatory word 'strike-
> breaker' at their comrades who were prepared to fight.[30]

Nervous orders, tinged with desperation, began issuing from senior
German officers at all levels from late August. Ludendorff himself
signed an order acknowledging the 'very unfavourable impression'
created by individuals who had come back to the front after home
leave and were spreading 'high treason and incitement to disobedience', threatening to deprive those found guilty of all leave.[31] Second
Army also noted the effect that rumours (spread 'by people who have
lost their nerves') were having on the men on 25 August. 'People
with anxious temperaments saw everywhere squadrons of tanks,
masses of cavalry, thick lines of infantry. It is in fact high time that
our old battle-experienced soldiers spoke seriously to these cowards
and weaklings and told them of the deeds that are done in the front
line.' This was to be read out to all units. 'Therefore, there are no
reasons for any panic.'

There were, on the contrary, plenty of reasons for panic. In Berlin,
the mood was, according to Leutnant Richard Schütt, 'quite extraor-
dinarily bad'. He wrote to his parents on 17 August and sketched out
the dismal situation Germany faced when 'the prospects of a happy

end to the war are getting worse and worse'. He urged his father to sell his war bonds as quickly as possible ('before the next subscription') because, in his view:

> the whole thing could collapse as soon as this year. Here I can see and hear more than you can, and I have also read various secret orders. The mood among the troops is quite extraordinarily bad. Many regiments that are supposed to attack are simply refusing to do so ... Troops coming back there from the field simply refuse to cooperate, and officers can barely show themselves on the streets in the evenings. In my opinion, we will have the same conditions here as in Russia within one year at most. Not one person in the officer corps believes that we will gain a victory any more, and everyone believes that there will be a collapse.

His brother, Willy, wrote to him on 24 August. 'We have had very difficult days and have to retreat further each day,' he lamented. 'On the first day of the offensive, I was almost captured. Our division has suffered a terrible number of losses from all this.'[32]

Schütt's alarming prediction, of disaster and revolution in Germany before the year was out, was remarkably prescient. Many other officers evidently shared his sense that the end was nearing. A German Army postal censor reported on 31 August that the morale of the men had 'changed drastically' from the confident tone that had been reported before the great offensives earlier in the year. 'The previous high morale and confidence of victory has given way to extremely widespread war-weariness, glumness and despondency. Such states of mind, although they are not universal, cannot be ignored.' A constant complaint was the unfair allocation of leave, with farmers being allowed to return home in the spring and summer, and the remainder being promised leave in the winter, which was almost inevitably cancelled, leaving immense resentment behind. The report concluded that:

> We are no longer dealing with the youthful soldiers of 1914. Most of the members of the army probably come from the middle and more mature years of life. These people are more serious and more sensitive! Now it is not only the events out here that have an effect on them; newspapers and letters provide them with news over some of

the situation at home, about which a cool, level-headed observer, would have to shake his head.[33]

If the strain of constant operations was bad for the Allies, it was even worse for German soldiers, who were generally poorly fed and without the combat support Allied soldiers received. They also had less time out of the line. As the fighting intensified throughout August and September, units would often find themselves 'resting' in positions much closer to the front than they would have occupied previously. This caused yet more grumbling. General Marwitz complained on 26 August that his men had endured 'unspeakably hard' conditions after being left in the front line 'for such a terribly long time' because of poor rail connections.[34]

Fever – variously called 'Flanders fever' or 'Champagne fever' – laid out increasing numbers of men. The symptoms were varied, but usually consisted of cold sweating and then a terrible, throbbing weakness. Patients would be unable to eat or drink, and would often succumb to dysenteric attacks that left them even weaker. The diarist Rudolf Binding was struck by what he called an 'extraordinary attack of fever' in August, which left him existing in 'an artificial condition of tottering weakness'. 'I'm simply collapsing,' he despaired. 'Even so, we all (officers as well as men, be it said) have to eat bread that is as damp as a bath-sponge. The cooking is done with a so-called butter which is as old and rancid as war-fever, and, to finish up with, we dig green potatoes out of the fields – not new potatoes, but green October roots. So when once you have got it this diet makes quite certain that you will not get rid of it.' The lack of proper food and drink and adequate amounts of leave had been complaints in the Kaiser's army for some time. It was, however, the increasing realization that the war could not be won that caused sagging hearts to collapse into despair and – on occasion – mutiny. Although Rudolf Binding stayed with the Army to the end, the news that his division was being sent to the Somme left him shaken and angry. 'It will be the same all over again,' he wrote, 'but without any confidence. Our troops will be thinner and worse; for days the horses have not had a grain of oats; the men are being given barley-bread which will not rise in the oven, and we have taken some knocks. Against us we shall have thousands of tanks, tens of thousands of airmen, hundreds of thousands of hearty young men, behind whom there will be an American Army which may number a million.'[35]

The constant Allied air attacks gnawed away at morale even further. German columns of infantry, marching to the front, would regularly have to scatter as British and French biplanes swooped low overhead, firing machine-guns and dropping bombs. Although the physical damage that such aircraft could do was undoubtedly limited (with only 25lb bombs), its effect on tired and nervous soldiers can well be imagined.[36] One day, when General Marwitz was being driven behind the lines, he was attacked by 'an army of fliers'. Hearing the roar of enemy aircraft overhead, Marwitz and his staff were forced to dive into the trenches and shell holes by the side of the road. While sheltering from the air attack, he found himself crouching next to one man who seemed to have lost his mind. He kept saying over and over again, 'now he has thrown his bits of chocolate and hasn't got anymore'. 'Evidently,' Marwitz remarked, 'he was a comedian.' On 24 August, Second Army counted over 120 bombs that had fallen in Cambrai during the day, and even one of the general's staff, Hauptmann von Heydebreck, was stunned to find that a 'dud' had landed in his wash cabinet next to his bedroom.[37]

By late summer the RAF was reaching further into the German rear lines, bombing railways and divisional headquarters, and – with grave implications for the German Air Force – mounting surprise raids on enemy airfields. On 17 August, 80th Wing, led by Lieutenant-Colonel Louis Strange, paid a morning visit to the German airfield at Lomme, east of Lille; the home of *Jagdstaffel* 40, commanded by Major Carl Degelow. Strange, a buccaneering spirit whose squadrons would become devastatingly effective against German airfields, led the raid in his Sopwith Camel, diving down into the attack 'with every wire screaming protest'. 'As we flattened out and streaked over those hangars,' he wrote, 'I tugged hard at the release thongs of my bomb gear, and then heard the most awful din of crashes when the whole of the Flight sent down their total of 24 twenty-pound bombs. The next good look I took at Lomme

showed me all the six hangars on one side of the aerodrome
enveloped in black smoke clouds, edged with reddish-yellow flames
that poured out of the windward side.'[38]

For those on the ground, the attack was a terrifying spectacle of
impotence and frustration. They had first been alerted to the danger
by the wailing of sirens across the airfield, but by then it was too late.
The strong westerly wind blew the formation – estimated at over
fifty aircraft – towards them with great speed. Since there was no
time to get airborne, Degelow hurriedly handed out rifles and
ordered everyone into the covered trenches alongside their hangars.

> Shortly before reaching our airfield, the lower swarm of the enemy
> squadron dived in a left turn. This was a trick, intended to devour our
> machine gun protection for, simultaneously, down out of the great
> formation of scattering single-seat units came one squadron in a dive
> on our hangars. At the same moment, the two-seat Bristol Fighters
> flying above the single-seat fighter squadron dropped their bombs in
> order to render our defences powerless, while British Sopwith single-
> seaters attacked our hangars at low altitude with concussion bombs.
> They flew the length of the sheds, which were all in a row, dropped
> their high-explosive bombs and then split up, half wheeling in a left
> turn, while the others turned right.[39]

Degelow watched as the Sopwiths flew in circles above the airfield,
firing incendiary bullets and setting two of the sheds on fire. If anyone tried to get out of the trenches, they would be spotted and
peppered with machine-gun bullets. All they could do was cower in
their covered trenches, take potshots whenever they could, and hope
that it would soon be over. The raid cost *Jasta* 40 four precious Fokker DVIIs and was another worrying indication that Germany was
losing the war in the skies.

By the end of the month, Foch, Haig and Pétain could look favourably on what had been achieved. The 'point of balance' on the
Marne had now been exploited and turned into a crushing series of
hammer blows. By 29 August French forces had driven north from
Soissons, taken the town of Noyon on the Canal du Nord, and were

closing on the line of the River Somme towards Ham. The Australians had crossed the Somme, moved into Péronne, and taken the strongly held enemy positions on Mont Saint-Quentin. British forces in the north had also made good progress towards Cambrai, although they had run up against the northernmost section of the Hindenburg Line, the Drocourt–Quéant switch – a tough series of defensive lines cloaked in barbed wire – that Haig had assigned to the Canadian Corps. Apart from small-scale counter-attacks the Germans were unable to mount any serious offensive operations at this time; they had enough on their hands trying to disengage their rapidly tiring forces from the endless Allied attacks. All they could do was throw their divisions into the furnace and hope that the Allies would tire and give in. Indeed, the cost of pushing the Germans back had not been cheap. French operations between 8 and 29 August had cost just under 100,000 casualties, including 2,390 officers killed, wounded or missing, which, to Pétain at least, justified extreme caution.[40]

Foch, having recovered his eagerness for the offensive after the disagreement with Haig after Amiens, now wanted to extend the battle line even further. In six weeks, he wrote, 'the enemy had lost all the gains he had made in the spring. He had lost heavily in men, munitions and stores. Most important of all, he had lost the initiative of operations – he had lost his moral ascendancy. Material and moral confusion must inevitably reign within his ranks.'[41] Studying the maps of the front every day at Bombon, assisted by the quiet, reassuring presence of Weygand, Foch began to think about more than just freeing railway lines from German observation. By 30 August he had drawn up an ambitious outline for future operations. The British, supported by the French on their right, would continue to attack in the direction of Cambrai and Saint-Quentin. At the same time, the main body of the French Army would push forward and move past the River Aisne. As for the Americans, they were scheduled to make an attack on Saint-Mihiel, south of Verdun, in mid-September, but would then transfer the bulk of their forces to the Meuse–Argonne for a joint Franco-American assault towards Mézières. If these could be conducted successfully, Foch was convinced that the Germans would be unable to extricate their forces and mount any kind of large-scale counter-attack. The final battle had begun.

6. 'The whole thing was simply magnificent'

Slaughter cattle for Wilhelm & Sons.

Graffiti on a German troop train (September 1918)[1]

1–11 September 1918

At midday on 2 September, OHL ordered General Otto von Below's Seventeenth Army to begin its retreat to the Hindenburg Line. It was to start that night. Other armies were ordered to do the same in the next few days; packing up their equipment, harnessing tired horses to artillery batteries; notifying infantry regiments of their routes; preparing those units which would remain in place and cover the retreat.[2] This was the ultimate result of the smashing blow the Allies had landed at the Battle of Amiens, which had unhinged the German position in France and made such a radical redeployment necessary. The one card that Ludendorff still had – *the Hindenburg Line and the prospect of holding out in the west* – had now been played. This defensive system would be manned, the armies withdrawn from the front, and the wire emplacements sealed. At best Germany could now hope that the defences were strong enough and that they would hold against the increasing Allied onslaught. If the German Army could maintain its position here, inflicting heavy casualties on their attackers and raising the prospect of yet more sapping attritional struggles, then maybe, just maybe, the Allies would tire and give in.

The news of retreat spread quickly through the German armies in the west and depressed morale yet further. 'Tonight we retreated to the Siegfried Line,' wrote Willy Schütt to his brother, Richard, on 6 September. 'Our battalion commander was severely wounded last night and his adjutant was killed. One of our drivers was also killed last night. He would have been going on leave today.'[3] Rudolf Stark, commander of *Jagdstaffel* 35, had been notified that their retreat would begin on 7 September. 'All the ground we won in the spring must be given up again,' he mused. 'Will this retirement help us like the other one did? Will the enemy launch his attack against empty air and waste months bringing up reinforcements and making preparations for a fresh offensive? Shall we be able to strengthen our front in the meanwhile?' On 10 September he heard news that Cambrai had been evacuated. Through the pouring rain and cold wind, he drove through the city and watched the long black columns of refugees squelching through the mud, making their way eastwards, drawing carts piled high with furniture. The nearer he got to the centre of town, the worse the crowds became. 'An old man pushes a crippled wife along in a hand-car. Sick people hobble on sticks along the rough cobblestones. At a crossroads a car lies in a ditch, with a broken wheel; all its contents are strewn in the mud. Two weeping women stand by it; a man stares helplessly at his household goods and then glowers at us with rage and hatred in his eyes.'

Among the crowds of refugees pulling their pathetic carts, Stark found German soldiers hurrying along, flinching as occasional shells clattered into the buildings, raising clouds of dust and sending the local pigeons flapping into the air. 'Men are carrying huge bundles of documents from the town-commander's headquarters and loading them up on to lorries. Such a mass of papers has accumulated, and now it must all be taken back somewhere.' Stark helped bring out a number of the oldest refugees in his truck, including an old lady who sat next to him in the cabin. 'She shivers as she wraps her old wool shawl about her lean body. In her hand she clutches a picture, the only thing she could rescue, the only thing that represents the sum of her many years. It is a photograph; a young man in French uniform. Underneath it a quavering cross has been drawn in ink, with a date and a single word: Verdun!' Stark shuddered: 'what misery and distress are to be seen on these roads!'[4]

The decision to withdraw to the Hindenburg Line had been taken reluctantly and in a hurry because the Allies were gaining ground quicker than expected. On 2 September, after several days of heavy and sustained combat, the British First Army, spearheaded by Sir Arthur

Currie's Canadian Corps, broke through the Drocourt–Quéant Line, thus unhinging the northern flank of the Hindenburg system and sending shockwaves through two Army Groups. Orders were issued within hours to abandon the position and man the main section of the Hindenburg Line to the east. Seventeenth Army would retreat immediately, followed by Second Army, to its left. In order to maintain conformity with these movements, OHL also reluctantly sanctioned the withdrawal of both Eighteenth and Ninth Armies further to the south. Even worse, it was agreed to give up the German gains around Lys in the north, which had been won at such cost in the spring, ordering both Fourth and Sixth Armies to fall back.[5] 'As a result of our victory yesterday, the hinge of the German system has been broken,' wrote Currie in his diary on 3 September. 'The Commander-in-Chief, the Chief of the General Staff and others called to personally express their appreciation. Today we find that the Boche is practically retiring across the Canal du Nord.'[6]

The breaking of the Drocourt–Quéant Line would be one of the finest achievements of the Canadian Corps during the war, Currie even rating it higher than the first day at Amiens. The position had been constructed at the same time as the Hindenburg Line and was built primarily to extend it northwards and shield the Douai plain from any Allied advance. It was a formidable line with hundreds of concrete dug-outs, interlinking trenches and swathes of barbed wire that was held in strength by seven German divisions, including 1st and 2nd Guard Reserve Divisions. Given the depth of the German defences and the inevitable lack of surprise, Currie decided to rely on his guns. Between 27 August and 2 September, the Canadian Corps fired over 10,000 tons of ammunition, almost twice what it had used at Amiens.[7] After several days of preliminary operations, the main assault began at 5 a.m. on 2 September, with three Canadian divisions in line, covered by 4th British Division on its northern flank. Fighting continued all day. Because only fifty-three heavy tanks were available to support the assault, much of the fighting involved platoons and companies in a traditional infantry battle.[8] Currie's troops – men from Toronto and Vancouver, Ontario and British Columbia – fought their way through this dense defensive system, using rifle and bayonet, bomb and grenade, mortar and artillery, in what was sometimes fierce hand-to-hand fighting.

In the early stages of the attack, most battalions were covered by a precisely engineered creeping barrage, that unearthly wall of shells that fell like a curtain in front of them. But at certain points they had to get forward without it, and had to rely on good leadership, smart tactics and determined courage. In this maelstrom, there were some incredible instances of valour, including the action of Corporal Walter Rayfield of 7th Battalion. He rushed 'a trench filled with the enemy, bayoneting two and taking ten prisoners. Later he located and engaged with great skill, under constant rifle fire, an enemy sniper who was causing many casualties.' Not content with his day's work, Rayfield subsequently charged a trench single-handedly and 'so demoralized the enemy by his daring and coolness that 30 surrendered to him'. He would be awarded the Victoria Cross.[9] Another remarkable tale concerned Private Arthur James Foster of 38th Battalion who would be awarded the Military Medal for his bravery that day. His men were close to their objective when they came under 'a terrible barrage of machine gun fire'. They immediately dropped to the ground and tried to get forward, but it was no use so they lay out in no-man's-land under heavy fire. Determined to do whatever he could, Foster got up and began attending to the wounded, dragging man after man across the fields through what he called 'a hail storm of bullets'. After the fighting had ended he continued carrying wounded back to the dressing station and helping those scattered over the battlefield. 'This was all done,' he remembered, 'amid considerable machine gun fire and a few heavy shells.'[10] By the evening of 2 September, through the smoke and fire, over 6,000 German prisoners had been taken as well as sixty-five guns and nearly 500 machine-guns.[11]

Despite the heavy Allied losses and the daily discomfort – the hunger and thirst, the exhaustion and danger – morale in both British and French Armies rose 'like mercury' as the advance continued.[12] They knew enough about the war to realize that something was different, that objectives that would have taken months to capture, were now falling within days, sometimes even hours. The German foe –

always so solid, determined and tough – was now cracking. Haig, for one, was delighted with how things were progressing, particularly with the achievements of the Canadians. On the evening of 2 September he rode forward and personally congratulated Major-General Archibald Macdonell, commander of 1st Canadian Division, whose troops had fought their way into the Drocourt–Quéant position. It was a rare display of emotion from the usually imperturbable Commander-in-Chief.

'Well, Macdonell, I could have long distance phoned you, but I prefer to come up and see you and shake you by the hand and personally thank your division for their magnificent work and you yourself too,' he said, visibly moved.

Macdonell thanked his commander.

'Please let your brigades know,' Haig continued, before warning Macdonell against getting killed or wounded. 'You broke the line and got through!' he exclaimed. 'The whole thing was simply magnificent and it was wonderful.'

Macdonell was deeply touched to receive such praise from his Commander-in-Chief. To him it showed the 'real' Haig – 'a kindly, loveable gentleman, first, and great commander afterwards'. 'Small wonder,' he wrote, 'that we Canadians idolized him.'[13]

Haig's relief at cracking the Drocourt–Quéant Line was plain for all to see, and was, in part, a reflection of the great pressure upon him. The previous day he had received a telegram from the Chief of the Imperial General Staff, Sir Henry Wilson, warning him of the unease in London about possible heavy casualties in future operations. 'Just a word of caution in regard to incurring heavy losses in attacks on Hindenburg Line,' wrote Wilson. The War Cabinet would 'become anxious if we received heavy punishment in attacking the Hindenburg Line WITHOUT SUCCESS'. As might have been expected, Haig was angry and disappointed at the telegram and wrote back furiously to Wilson, complaining about the 'weaklings' in the War Cabinet.[14] Although Wilson tried to mollify Haig and insist that it did not show a lack of confidence in his command and it was just a kind of friendly warning, the telegram was a niggling reminder of the concerns many in London had about Haig's command, and how much capital he had spent in earlier years with grandiose promises of breakthrough and victory. Haig had to be careful.

Following up the German armies was never easy or without cost. As well as advancing in the face of shelling, booby-traps, and machine-gun and sniper fire, the Allied armies had to operate in a terrifying and dangerous chemical environment. Although shell and machine-gun fire accounted for the majority of casualties, gas evoked a fear that was unlike any other weapon and had a significant effect on how the war was fought. It had evolved much since the first chlorine gas had been released near Ypres in 1915, maturing into a weapon that was used with a remarkable degree of ingenuity and inventiveness. By 1918 all sides had incorporated gas into their battle tactics, with both front and rear sectors regularly being deluged with gas, which poisoned the ground and caused a constant trickle of casualties. Gas shells, containing either mustard or phosgene, would often be fired alongside high explosive, in the hope that during a bombardment – with its noise and chaos – the arrival of quieter gas shells would be missed. If any soldiers survived the bombardment, then a silent, deadly killer would still await them. Gas also offered a useful and effective method of counter-battery fire. Because it was very difficult to score a direct hit on enemy gun positions, gas shells were frequently employed to force gunners to don their respirators, which often impeded their accuracy and slowed their reactions.

For the Allies, the main problem was dealing with mustard gas – 'the king of the war gases' – which was used in increasing amounts by German artillery. As the retreat gathered momentum, German gunners fired thousands of these shells at their pursuers, using it as an area denial weapon, through which the Allies could not advance, or at least not without difficulty. As the historian Tim Cook has shown, 'German gunners simply blocked out map grids and fired shells to saturate the whole sector, thereby eliminating that area from the front.'[15] Ever since its introduction in the summer of 1917, mustard gas had become notorious for its effectiveness at causing casualties because of its persistence and the lack of a foolproof countermeasure. The German chemical industry produced vast amounts of this effective and unpleasant chemical compound, while the Allies could only manufacture limited amounts by the summer of 1918. Mustard gas may not have been immediately fatal (particularly if there was only minor contact), but it caused a variety of painful wounds, including lung damage (if inhaled), blisters and burns on the skin, and conjunctivitis in the eyes. The shells would explode with a dull thud or pop, leading some inexperienced soldiers to mistake its arrival for that of a 'dud' shell. The liquid contents would then leak out, rapidly vaporize and form terrifying yellow clouds. Because it could go through wool and cotton, there was precious little protection from its symptoms, particularly if the liquid splashed you, and it lay there, settling in shell holes and trenches, often remaining active for weeks. It is little wonder that unless dealt with quickly the fear of mustard gas had a devastating effect on unit morale. All soldiers could do was put on their gas masks and try to get out of the affected area as soon as possible. Unfortunately, this was sometimes easier said than done because German gunners had an annoying habit of creeping their gas barrages forward at the same rate as a man could walk. If you were particularly unfortunate, you could be exposed for hours.

In late August, a British soldier, T. H. Holmes, was unfortunate enough to get caught in a bombardment of mustard gas. He quickly put on his small box respirator, but he disliked wearing one intensely. Holmes found any sort of activity for more than fifteen minutes to be 'irksome'. 'The goggles became clouded, and the space inside the mask, warm and wet . . . But you dare not remove them while there was gas about, and the only thing to do, apart from staying still and letting the fumes disperse, which was a long job, was to hurry through the shelling to a clear area, if you could . . .' The first response of many soldiers once they had left an infected zone was to pull their masks off at the earliest opportunity, but that could be dangerous as there was no immediate reaction to inhaling mustard gas, often only a minor tickling at the back of the throat. By the time Holmes and two companions had managed to get clear of the gas cloud, they were desperate for fresh air and pulled off their masks. Holmes had just slipped off his headstraps when a stray gas shell exploded on the edge of a nearby crater covering them in a yellow, choking cloud. Although Holmes was able to pull his mask back on again, one man could not and 'lay gasping and clutching his throat'. They managed to drag him to a Regimental Aid Post – all the time wheezing and coughing – but he died shortly afterwards. By that time, Holmes's eyes were 'completely closed up, red and swollen, and terribly painful. From my nose and mouth came a continuous stream of mucus.'[16]

The Americans – who began their own offensive in September – would also encounter the horror of mustard gas. Indeed, Pershing's forces were particularly susceptible to gas attacks as they lacked the sophisticated and well-worn anti-gas doctrine of the British and French. Whereas the Allies had been gradually improving their protective measures since 1915 (and were well aware of how deadly chemical weapons could be), there was a lack of appreciation in the US Army of how easily gas could cause casualties. Gas accounted for 27 per cent of American losses in the Great War, a frighteningly high figure that, in part, explained the speed with which large US divisions were worn out at the front.[17] One American officer, Frank Holden, a Battalion Gas Officer, experienced a gas bombardment that September. It was a terrifying few hours that revealed not only how inventive gas tactics were becoming, but also how difficult they were to combat. Holden knew that the Germans often fired tear gas (or what was known as Blue Cross gas) into areas where troops had concentrated, causing intense choking, sneezing and coughing. After Blue Cross had been deployed, German gunners would then deluge the target area with more deadly agents, many men often finding it impossible to keep their respirators on if they needed to sneeze or vomit. Holden's battalion had marched into the village of Norroy when they came under a barrage of 'sneezing gas' (most probably Blue Cross). He immediately ordered all gas masks to be worn.

> After the village was filled with this sneezing gas the shelling ceased. It was then that my Gas Sergeant and I kept busy running through Norroy, telling the men to keep on their masks; that if they did not they would be unable by inhaling the sneezing gas to keep them on in a few minutes when we would be shelled with phosgene or mustard gas.

Holden was right. Within minutes, shrapnel shells were bursting over their heads, alongside mustard gas that covered the village in poisonous clouds. Although it soon ceased, Holden kept telling his men to keep their masks on. He scrambled up a nearby hillside and saw the gas clinging 'in the valley . . . as smoke settled in lowlands on a hot summer's afternoon'. By the time he returned, the wounded were already being taken out on stretchers. One soldier caught his eye. 'He had to sit up on the stretcher. His back, chest and face were a solid, burning blister where the horrible mustard gas had spattered on him. Not only that, but the awful gas fumes had gotten into his lungs and he was breathing heavily.' It was no wonder that Holden found this soldier 'the most pitiful sight I saw in France'.[18]

It was not just the infantry that had to deal with mustard gas. Allied gunners were particularly vulnerable given the extent to which it was employed as a counter-battery weapon. One British gunner, R. C. Foot, was exposed to mustard gas on 3 September at Manancourt on the Somme. He had moved his battery into what seemed like a 'convenient hollow', close to the infantry support line, but found, to his horror, that a trap had been laid by German gunners 'seeking no doubt to deny the ground to the assembling infantry'. They 'drenched the whole battery position with mustard gas shell all night'.

> We were working, getting ammunition ready to cover next morning's attack, and inevitably nearly all of us got the mustard liquid on our clothes and hands. By the time the set piece barrage for the morning's advance was over, nearly all of us were blistered, and many had eyelids so swollen that they could not see . . . Some forty of us, myself among them, formed a 'crocodile' of walking wounded, each man with a hand on the shoulder of the man in front of him, to the nearest dressing station to get first aid treatment for our blistered skin. Many were so badly damaged that they were sent off to base hospitals.[19]

Recovery from exposure to mustard gas could take years; some victims were never really healthy again. Despite the suffering, Foot remembered that morale was good. 'The pain and irritation of these enormous blister wounds are frantic in their effect. Yet it was quite a cheerful procession: someone would make some silly joke, and a ripple of laughter, stopped often by the cracking of blistered lips, would run from front to rear as we stumbled along.' Although the German Army would increasingly experience the horror of mustard gas being fired back at them, it remained a major problem for the Allies throughout the Hundred Days as they were advancing through shelled areas. The determination, professionalism and – as Foot revealed – humour with which Allied forces kept going was remarkable.

Notwithstanding the chemical environment, to advance successfully and surely, the Allies also required immense logistical support. Indeed, as they gradually followed up the retreating German armies, they had to try and solve one of the most pernicious problems of the Great War: how to supply and reinforce an army on the move. By 1918 both the British and French were very experienced at making limited advances, often across difficult ground, but – as had been seen at Amiens – they found it much more taxing to make sustained leaps, primarily because of the seemingly insurmountable logistical problems this posed. The further troops went from their railheads – where all their supplies were deposited – the more difficult it was to keep going, usually no more than ten or twelve miles. Not only would they lack basic supplies, but they would also find that artillery support was not available. Guns, particularly the heavier varieties, took much time and effort to move, particularly across difficult ground. Their voracious appetite for ammunition presented yet more problems. It was possible to use motor vehicles to bring supplies from the railheads, but trucks had to keep to roads and bridges, and if used constantly would begin to break down. In any case, they would not get far across broken or shell-pitted ground and would have to wait until crossings – frequently demolished by the Germans – had been rebuilt, which often took several weeks.

One of those tasked with keeping the front moving was Clifford Johnston, a lorry driver with the Canadian Corps. Although Johnston was not in the front line, his occupation was just as dangerous, not to mention exhausting. A typical night shift involved joining a convoy hauling ammunition from the railheads up to the front.

Often they had to pass their own artillery batteries that were blasting away. 'The worst part of the trip though was driving over the roads full of shell holes in the black dark – and after each flash it would be darker still,' he remembered. They were forbidden from putting their headlights on lest they attract the attentions of enemy aircraft. 'Coming through Arras we couldn't see anything and ran into the side of the building once and over the pavement several times.' The following day one of his vehicles crashed and broke an axle, although he was fortunate not to join one convoy that got stuck out in the open and was shelled all day. Indeed Johnston soon acquired a reputation for luck and skill; on 5 September his lorry slipped into a shell hole and ran over a box of live hand grenades, none of which exploded.[20]

Even if trucks were available, they were not much use crossing water obstacles. The Australian Corps had great problems in getting over the Somme because all the bridges and railway sidings had been destroyed. Monash was told that the great railway bridge at Péronne could be rebuilt, but it would take two months. In the end, they managed to establish a railhead on the west bank of the Somme, and then repair all the road bridges that had been felled across the river. This entailed much traffic congestion, but after heroic amounts of hard work and spectacular improvisation, a way through was found. Monash described the 'scenes of feverish activity' around Brie, Éterpigny and Péronne in early September.

> Hundreds of tons of steel girders, of all lengths and sections, were hurried up, by special lorry service. Pile-driving gear was hastily improvised. The wreckage of the original bridges was overhauled for sound, useful timbers. The torn and twisted steelwork was dragged out of the way by horse or steam power, and tumbled in a confused mass into the river bed. Hammer, saw and axe were wielded with a zest and vigour rarely seen in peace-time construction.[21]

The efforts of the British and French engineers, who got their armies over numerous water obstacles in the last four months of the war, were essential to the Allied advance. Between August and November

1918 the Royal Engineers erected over 330 stock span or rolled steel joint bridges – approximately double the number that had been built in the preceding four years of (largely static) warfare. These heavy bridges were essential to the advance because they could take tanks, a weapon that had not even existed before the war.[22]

Almost everything was tried to help maintain the momentum of the advance. For many divisions, particularly the cavalry, finding enough water for the horses was a daunting challenge. Even in infantry divisions, the number of horses that were employed presented many difficulties, particularly when so many of the small wells in French villages had been either drunk dry or destroyed by the retreating Germans. In Major-General John Ponsonby's 5th British Division, their divisional train was able to assist by improvising water-carriers with petrol-tins and by converting several wagons to water-tanks with the use of tarpaulins. In order to supply the infantry, three gun-carrying tanks were attached to the division. They may have been slow, but they could carry forward stores behind the leading troops. Like many units in the BEF, 5th Division also benefited from the efforts of the RAF to drop boxes of ammunition by parachute on to the battlefield; indeed, in many cases, the required stores were nearly always supplied ahead of time.[23]

One of the features of the advance to the Hindenburg Line was the need for new headquarters. John Monash was reluctant to leave his luxurious château at Bertangles, but accepted it as a necessary evil. By 8 September his headquarters was situated in the devastated Somme region near Assevillers, 'where a number of tiny wooden huts served us as bedrooms by night and offices by day'. As he later wrote, 'The scale of comfort possible for all senior Commanders and Staff rapidly declined as the advance developed . . . From château to humbler dwelling house, and thence into bare wooden huts, and later still into mere holes hollowed out in the sides of quarries or railway cuttings.'[24] As the Allies had to reposition their headquarters further forward, German units found theirs being repeatedly moved back. The pilot Rudolf Stark noted that throughout August 'flights to the front became shorter and shorter'. 27 August was their last day at their old headquarters and was spent getting ready to leave.

My trunks are packed; my pictures have come down from the walls; my books have disappeared. Deprived of its cloth, the table suddenly assumes a bare, forbidding aspect. The room in which I have lived so long has become a stranger to me. The mess also looks bare. Only the scantiest necessities still remain. Pictures and lamps have been removed; the window frames stand out black in a livid light. The rooms have reverted to their former condition; they are plain, bare peasants' living quarters again.

Stark was 'loath to depart'. 'We have become gypsies,' he moaned. 'We wander from place to place and have grown used to wandering.'[25] Even senior commanders were not immune to the depressing sights of staff officers emptying their desks, packing stacks of papers and typewriters into boxes, and hitching lifts to the rear; a visual symbol of the tectonic shifts that were taking place at the front. On 6 September, Advanced OHL returned to Spa, followed by General von Boehn, who left Le Cateau and took up temporary residence at Avesnes.[26]

Logistical problems were not just confined to the British and French. Although German forces had an advantage in that they were retreating and shortening their lines of communication (which had been so stretched during the spring and summer), they suffered from an acute shortage of horses. The German officer Rudolf Binding complained that his division was 'crying out for horses' and it was the same across the Army. A veterinary inspector told him that 'The Entente has four and half million horses at the Front, while we have only one and a half.' Since June his draught horses had been fed on chopped turnip and whatever else they could graze. Fodder was in short supply, leaving them in a poor condition to pull artillery batteries.[27] Outbreaks of looting and disorder further disrupted supplies. By August the order which had been so ruthlessly enforced in the territories Germany had occupied was visibly breaking down. According to Crown Prince Wilhelm, 'In the larger camps on the lines of communication, thousands of straggling shirkers and men on leave wandered about; some of them regarded every day that they could keep away from their units as a boon from heaven; some of them were totally unable to join their regiments on account of the

overburdening of the railways.' One evening Wilhelm took a journey to the front via Hirson, a major railway junction south of the
Belgian border in Picardy.

> It was just dinner-time for men going on leave and stragglers, who
> stood about by the hundred. I mingled with the crowd and talked to
> many of the men. What I heard was saddening indeed. Most of them
> were sick and tired of the war and scarcely made an effort to hide
> their disinclination to rejoin their units. Nor were they all rascals;
> there was many a face there which showed that the nerves had given
> way, that energy was gone, that the primitive and unchecked impulse
> of self-preservation had got the mastery over all recognition of the
> necessity for holding out or resisting.[28]

The Crown Prince, shocked at how quickly the deterioration seemed
to have come, complained about the lack of 'comprehensive and
thorough measures' to restore order and determination, but it was
too late. Faith in victory – that essential component of morale – had
been shattered by the failure of Ludendorff's 'peace offensive' in
March and April. Now all that was left was either to give in, become
a prisoner or desert, or remain at your post and try to endure what
was coming.

Probably the worst thing German soldiers had to endure was the
shellfire, which scourged their lines and made the artillery bombardments of earlier years seem light in comparison. As the American
historian Scott Stephenson has written, 'To be a German defender in
the path of a major Allied attack late in the war was to experience the
horrors of Dante's *Inferno*.'[29] The firepower that the Allies were able
to bring to bear upon German positions in the last months of the war
was accurate, devastating and, at times, neverending; having a terrible effect not only on men's bodies, but also on their nerves and
emotions, leaving them shattered, quivering wrecks. Patient records
housed in Freiburg highlight the devastating psychological impact
the war was having on German troops, who were succumbing to war
neurosis and shell-shock in increasing numbers. One soldier, Guido
Hermann, began his military service in April 1918, but was evacuated
to a military hospital in late October suffering from exhaustion, heart

1. Tom Cotterill, the author's great-uncle, aged nineteen. This photograph was taken while he was on leave sometime in the summer of 1918. He came home to Sealand to see his two youngest siblings – Ben and Gladys – before returning to the Western Front in time for the Hundred Days.

2. The telegram announcing Tom Cotterill's death. Family legend has it that on the morning of the attack in which he was killed, his mother, Florence, woke up with a terrible headache. By the time the telegram arrived three weeks later, she already knew her son was dead.

3. View from the Sunken Road, Gouzeaucourt, looking north-east towards Dead Man's Corner (the clump of trees) where 15/Royal Warwickshire Regiment attacked on the morning of 27 September 1918.

4. The grave of Private Tom Cotterill, plot C30, Neuville-Bourjonval British cemetery, a few miles from where he was killed.

5. Officers of the German General Headquarters celebrating the thirtieth anniversary of the Kaiser's reign at the Hotel Britannique, Spa, Belgium, June 1918. The Kaiser stands to the left. The two figures on the right are Hindenburg (with white hair) and Crown Prince Wilhelm, the Kaiser's son.

6. Hindenburg (fourth from right) faces Ludendorff (fifth from right) in the Grand Place, Brussels, surrounded by attendants and somewhat nervous onlookers. The two men formed a quasi-military dictatorship from 1916 onwards, but were unable to save Germany from defeat.

7. Captured French soldiers march along a tree-lined road somewhere near Soissons during the Second Battle of the Marne. Although French losses were heavy, the Allied counter-attack on 18 July marked the turning point of the war on the Western Front.

8. German troops in action, 8 August 1918. This photograph is one of very few to actually show combat in the Great War. Note the size and space of no-man's-land, the smoke in the distance, and the dispersed tactical formation used to close with the enemy.

9. The front cover of *Le Petit Journal* from September 1918, showing a selection of Allied commanders: Field Marshal Sir Douglas Haig (top); General Georges Humbert, GOC French Third Army (right); General Sir Henry Rawlinson, GOC British Fourth Army (bottom); and General Eugène Debeney, GOC French First Army (left).

10. Crown Prince Rupprecht, Germany's northern Army Group Commander. In August 1918 he warned that Germany must 'make haste and approach our enemies, and especially England, with peace offers, and peace offers which both can be accepted and in view of the temper of the English people must be accepted'.

11. Sir Arthur Currie, commander of the Canadian Corps. One of the most talented soldiers produced during the war, Currie's motto of 'neglect nothing' became a hallmark of how his troops operated.

12. Sir John Monash, commander of the Australian Corps, was another astute and gifted general.

13. Men of Ernst Kielmayer's battery pose for a photograph during a brief rest period. Ernst is sitting under the barrel of a 77mm field gun. During the fighting at Cambrai in late September, three of Kielmayer's men were 'torn apart beyond recognition' by artillery fire; another was fortunately dug out alive.

14. German prisoners carrying a casualty along the Amiens–Roye road as a Mark V passes by. While tanks could be extremely effective, they remained highly vulnerable to German field guns. Of the thirty-four tanks supporting 4th Canadian Division on 8 August, only six were able to reach their final objective.

15. The sworn enemy of Allied armour: a German 77mm field gun in action. German artillery may not have been designed for taking on Allied vehicles, but its gunners proved remarkably effective at stopping the slow-moving British tanks throughout the Hundred Days.

16. General John J. Pershing, Commander-in-Chief of the American Expeditionary Force. He continually resisted Allied attempts at 'amalgamating' US troops in British and French divisions and was determined to wield American combat power into an independent, war-winning force.

17. Lieutenant-Colonel R. D. Garrett, chief signal officer of 42nd US Division, testing a telephone line left behind by the Germans in the retreat from Saint-Mihiel, 12 September 1918.

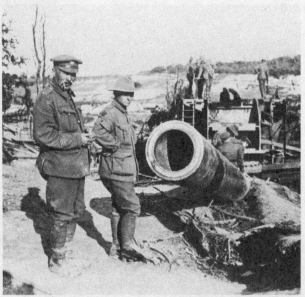

18. A 15 inch naval gun seized by 3/Australian Battalion on 23 August 1918 near Chuignolles on the Somme. This was the largest gun captured during the war and had been used for the bombardment of Amiens. Monash later presented it to the city as a gift.

19. Marshal Foch conversing with General Charles Mangin outside the War Ministry in Paris. Although Mangin had many enemies in the French Army, he proved indispensable to Foch as they endeavoured to keep French units going in the final months of the war.

20. General Georg von der Marwitz, commander of the German Second Army. Marwitz's forces were almost destroyed at Amiens in August, prompting his removal to command Fifth Army in the Argonne.

21. A German supply column in the village of Gouzeaucourt, the scene of particularly bitter fighting on 27 September 1918.

22. A selection of German guns taken by 4th US Division on 26 September 1918, the first day of the Meuse–Argonne offensive. Although this was an impressive haul, the initial stages of the offensive were characterized by frustration, delay and missed opportunities.

23. Members of 314/Field Signal Battalion (89th US Division) encamped in mud at Epionville. The exposed conditions endured by American infantry in the Meuse–Argonne were a cause of frequent complaint.

strain and what seemed like shell-shock. He lies quietly in bed, his file noted, but if a doctor approaches him 'a violent tremor begins immediately through his whole body, his teeth chatter, and he groans and writhes in the bed'. Another patient was Cyrus Karl, who broke down in the summer of 1918 after experiencing nightmares, uncontrollable body movements and an unstoppable desire to run away. The stress of the daily retreats seemed to have sparked his collapse. He became 'quite incapable of action' during this time. 'If he was alarmed, he would gather his things, and become so excited that he would start trembling, run away and wander about, completely under the influence of his compulsive movements.' He was haunted by his war service; unable to sleep, often sitting quietly; his face pale, his thoughts elsewhere.[30]

Karl was a rarity, someone who had served since the beginning of the war (he volunteered in August 1914) and only collapsed at the very end. Medical records also reveal the decreasing quality of the recruits being drafted into the German Army; those who were unfit for service and broke down much quicker than men like Karl. One of these unfortunates was Wilhelm Wilhöft, who arrived at a military hospital in Hamburg in September 1918. He suffered from fainting fits and had, since childhood, lacked control of his bladder. His doctor complained that he was a 'considerably inferior person' and 'exceptionally childish'. Although some improvement in his condition was made by treatment (with electric shock therapy), it was eventually agreed that he was unfit for future military service. Wilhöft seems to have been a regrettable case, but the authorities were understandably wary of appearing to be too lenient on those who might have been seeking a way out and there was widespread concern about the spread of malingering, which only got worse as the German Army haemorrhaged men in the summer and autumn of 1918. Electro-shock therapy was widely used in such cases. Karl Passhaus was someone who was treated in this manner. He arrived at the Department of War Neurosis in Bonn in July 1918 with 'hysterical symptoms' – a common term for shell-shock – after being evacuated from the Marne. His doctor thought he was malingering and noted that his condition disappeared after regular half-hourly sessions with the Kaufman Method, when electricity would be applied to the affected area and the patient encouraged to overcome his symptoms.[31]

The succession of hammer-blows on the Western Front did more than smash men's minds. It also forced a dramatic reappraisal of German strategy. OHL wanted new defensive areas to be set up behind the line and hosted a conference at Avesnes on 6 September to determine where they should run. The Chiefs of Staff of the three main Army Groups, including the defensive expert, Lossberg, were invited. At this meeting Ludendorff unveiled what he called the 'Hermann Line'. It would run from the North Sea along the River Escaut and the Scarpe to Tournai, through Condé, Valenciennes and Le Cateau to the west of Guise. It would then be positioned along the River Aisne north of Verdun. Another line – the Michel Line – had already been constructed between Verdun and Metz. Lossberg noted that Ludendorff 'appeared to be very nervous: in contrast to his previously assured manner'.

> He spoke very critically of the troops. He blamed them and their commanders for what had recently happened without any admission on his part that his own flawed leadership was mainly responsible for events. He announced to us that Supreme High Command had ordered the amalgamation of the third and fourth Infantry Companies because there were no further reserves of officers or men ... General Ludendorff demanded severe reprisals for shirkers.

Ludendorff then asked the opinions of those present. Lossberg spoke first. He said that General von Boehn had made daily visits to the Siegfried Line and had found it in a 'very poor state with only a few barbed wire obstacles'. Combined with the state of the troops, it was not possible to rely on this as a permanent defensive position. Work on this 'Hermann Line' had not even started yet. Lossberg recommended that as soon as the Siegfried Line was breached – he regarded this as inevitable – the German Army should be withdrawn 'at a single stroke' from the sea back to Verdun, to the shorter Antwerp–Meuse Line. Before this took place, as much equipment as possible should be withdrawn and all railways, bridges and roads should be destroyed.[32]

Lossberg's advice was sensible and realistic, but was, once again, totally unacceptable to Ludendorff, who – like Hitler a generation later – could only issue desperate exhortations to his men to hold their ground at all costs. Little was settled at Avesnes that day. There would be no radical withdrawal. Ludendorff even rejected the suggestion to comprehensively destroy all railways and bridges; perhaps a reflection of his lingering hope for future offensives. When Lossberg pointed out that only by removing the German Army from contact with the enemy could they buy enough time to regroup and consolidate their forces, Ludendorff shook his head. The Hermann Line would be constructed and that would be held even if the Siegfried position fell. The mood at OHL was now becoming progressively worse. The senior staff officers were all upset at Ludendorff's bitter words against the men and felt he was speaking out of turn and not appreciating the sacrifices being made daily at the front. Many found Ludendorff's methods intolerable and resented his constant interference, as well as his continued fantasies of new offensives that never materialized. Like Lossberg, a growing number of staff officers were recommending further withdrawals, even arguing that Germany must sue for peace.

One of Ludendorff's most trenchant critics was Lieutenant-Colonel Georg Wetzell, his Chief of Operations. By September, Wetzell had come to the conclusion that his boss was unfit for command. Several days earlier, Ludendorff had admitted withholding information from Paul von Hintze during the meetings of 13–14 August because of the bad effect it would have had on the homeland. Wetzell was horrified at this deception and urgently petitioned Hindenburg to make sure the Kaiser and the Government were fully informed of the situation. But Hindenburg remained unmoved and Wetzell's attempts came to nothing.[33] Adding to his frustration was the fact that Ludendorff was now bypassing his office and, once again, phoning the armies directly. On 9 September Crown Prince Rupprecht complained that 'The mood amongst the Chiefs of Staff had also suffered due to Ludendorff's restlessness; in the space of 3 weeks, during the Ninth Army's heavy fighting, he changed their Chief of Staff three times – to no obvious advantage. His continual interventions, coming directly to us by telephone, bypassed the Chief of Operations, and led the latter to request that he be relieved of his post.'[34] That day Wetzell's resignation was accepted and he left the Supreme Command.

By the time Wetzell had left OHL the movement of German units into the Siegfried Line had largely been completed. Although many officers had been disappointed at the state of the defences – by 1918 parts of the Hindenburg Line were in need of thorough refurbishment – units settled down in their trenches and dug-outs and awaited the oncoming storm. A curious air of anticipation settled upon the Western Front as the movement of the preceding month drew to a close. In some sectors trench warfare even restarted, as British and French battalions reoccupied old trench systems and began the nightly task of patrols and raids, sending feelers out into no-man's-land to find out where the enemy was. Some German divisions could be relieved and sent on leave, but most of the Army – or what was left of it – remained at the front and was fed a steady diet of spine-stiffening propaganda reminding the men of their duties, the importance of defending to the end, and of the horrors that would befall the Fatherland if her soldiers failed her at such a critical moment of history. Germany had played her last card. The Allies, by contrast, were only just getting started.

7. Enter the Americans

The Americans are multiplying in a way we never dreamt of.

Crown Prince Rupprecht[1]

12–16 September 1918

It was perhaps only when he reached the front, when he passed through the ruins of French villages or saw the plumes of dark smoke rising from the landscape, that the American soldier truly understood the war. The war came to him when he smelt the damp earth of the trenches, or shuddered as shells screamed down upon him, at Belleau Wood, Château-Thierry, or on some blasted hill in the Argonne. This was why, he realized, the fighting had caused so much death and misery, and gone on for so long. He felt the iron-like taste of despair and fear – so familiar to his French and British friends – when he leapt out of his trench and advanced in the open to face the rattle of Maxim machine-guns. So this was why, he would realize, so many had been unable to defeat the German Army. The essence of the war hit the American soldier in those first few frantic moments, banishing any idealism or naivety he may have had, thrusting him into a cold world of suffering, hunger and pain, revealing in all its agony, clear and bold, the greatest tragedy in European history.

For Elton Mackin, a high school graduate from Lewiston, New York, his war began at a crossroads near Marigny Château. 'Because the long-range German guns over Torcy way were spewing bits of hate in the form of high explosives, we were put into the partial shelter of the roadside hedge, allowing time to pass. The war had come down our road to meet us. We took time to study it, to note its greeting. We had an hour or more of sunny June-time afternoon through which to wait and watch and gather swift impressions.' A German battery had zeroed in on the road and the shells 'came down in perfect flights of four, always of four, and four, and four, with just enough space between blasts for the crews to serve the guns. Methodical, precise, deadly, the gunfire swept the crossing. Men and horses died. Huge old army camions and Thomas trucks crashed and smashed and burned engineers died while recklessly moving the wrecks to keep the roadway clear.' Despite the horror, despite the flaming slaughter they could see, Mackin's men were safe. 'We were enthralled', he wrote. 'We were privileged men to lie out there, short rifle range from the carnage, learning, watching how things went.' Yes, this was how, here in France, things went.[2]

American troops had seen action at a variety of locations on the Western Front since the autumn of 1917, including the famous action at Belleau Wood. Notwithstanding their important role at Second Marne, they had always fought in units no bigger than corps and as part of larger French operations. Now all that would change. The First US Army, some 500,000 men strong, would meet the war at Saint-Mihiel, a salient that jutted into French lines southeast of the fortified town of Verdun. This battle, fought between 12 and 16 September 1918, marked the baptism of fire for General Pershing's waxing force. At last they had their own battlefield; now it was time, they knew, for the doubts about Americans' capability to fight this war, to be swept away. Saint-Mihiel – a battle that remains neglected, often ignored, by French or British historians – marked a momentous occasion. The Americans were finally here; it had been seventeen months in the making.

Both British and French newspapers had fallen over themselves to welcome the US into the war in the spring of 1917 and, almost immediately, rumours of fantastic new weapons and masses of equipment began circulating, doing wonders for morale, but sadly raising expectations of the American impact to unsustainable levels. As early as May 1917, the French Prime Minister, Alexandre Ribot, cabled the US War Department, demanding the formation of a flying corps of approximately 4,500 aircraft to be sent immediately, as well as the construction of 2,000 aircraft and 4,000 engines every month.[3] Such numbers were, however, firmly in the realm of imagination; Pershing later commenting that even years later 'the primitive state' of US aviation still gave him 'a feeling of humiliation'. When he had led a punitive expedition to Mexico in 1916, he had taken 'eight of the thirteen antiquated tactical planes which constituted our all in aviation'. When they declared war on Germany, America did not have the aircraft or the facilities to support mass operations in the air. Even worse, the aircraft they did have were 'constantly in danger of going to pieces'.[4]

The depressing truth was that for all America's industrial might and technical knowhow, it did not have an army to put into the field. Although up to four million soldiers would serve between 1917 and 1920, America was woefully unready for a major continental war in May 1917, with few trained troops, small numbers of rifles and little heavy artillery. Given these limitations, it is little wonder that British and French delegations to the US were constantly talking about 'amalgamation' and always requesting the one element they required above all others: manpower. If the Americans could just send their young men to France, they explained, the Allies would see that they were trained and equipped in their armies. Soon after America declared war, the French Military Attaché even proposed to the US Government that one division and 50,000 trained railwaymen be immediately despatched to France. The British were, perhaps, a little more subtle. Major-General Tom Bridges, a member of the British Military Mission, argued forcefully that the war was at a critical stage and the only possible way for the Americans to play a major role would be to send their untrained men into British depots, where they would be drafted into Haig's armies. Anything less and the war might be over before the Americans got there.

As was perhaps to be expected, both President Woodrow Wilson and Pershing were unhappy about these proposals, Pershing later writing that 'I was decidedly against our becoming a recruiting agency for either the French or British and at that time this was the attitude of the War Department also. While fully realizing the difficulties, it was definitely understood between the Secretary of War and myself that we should proceed to organize our own units from top to bottom and build a distinctive army of our own as rapidly as possible.'[5] This was certainly a logical and reasonable political decision. It would have been very difficult, if not impossible, for Wilson to have sanctioned the overseas deployment of American troops and placed them under the command of foreign generals. It was only right that those soldiers who volunteered, or were subsequently drafted, fought under American officers under the American flag. Nevertheless, the British and French were correct in their claims that the war might be over before the United States could intervene in any strength. The problem was time, and with the menacing eruption of the German Spring Offensive in March 1918, the arguments over amalgamation suddenly became much more urgent as the Allies pleaded desperately for American support.

By the time Ludendorff launched his devastating 'peace offensive' on 21 March, only 287,000 US combat troops had arrived in France. Although much was achieved during 1917 in raising and training a huge new army, it was now openly doubted whether the British and French could hold out until the bulk of American strength was ready. American reinforcements were, therefore, of the essence. In the frantic days of March, Pershing finally gave way, agreeing that US divisions could serve under British or French command. He also agreed to an Allied suggestion that, in order to ship more men to the front, priority would be given to infantry and machine-gunners, rather than their supporting units. While this had the result of rapidly increasing the amount of US manpower in France, it meant that they were without much of their supporting infrastructure, which had a detrimental effect on their combat performance. It was a compromise, and like all compromises it satisfied no one.[6]

When the Americans finally got to France, first impressions of them were mixed. For many veterans of the Western Front, both British and French, the Americans always remained outsiders and amateurs. One British officer, Lieutenant R. G. Dixon, had first come across US soldiers in the spring of 1918 in the Ypres Salient, and was left distinctly unimpressed. One morning, a 'long column of men hove in sight', he wrote, 'infantry, all wearing very broad-brimmed hats, and marching in a very sloppy manner along the road from Poperinghe. We sat up and gawped at them. Who the hell could they be? Not Australians, not Canadians – in any case our Dominion troops would all be wearing tin hats on *that* road, and they certainly wouldn't be marching in one solid phalanx like this lot. And they would, if Dominion troops, certainly be marching better!' Presently the column of troops halted, fell out to either side of the road, and began lighting up cigarettes. Dixon approached them.

'Good morning, gentlemen,' he said.

'Say, buddy,' replied the American officer – a chunky cigar in his mouth – 'how far is it to this l'il old shootin' gallery of yours?'

Dixon did not like the man. He admitted to being 'shaken to my foundations' by the question and glared at the 'coarse-grained, insensitive lout' in front of him.

'If you mean the Ypres Salient, sir, you will be in it in about five minutes from here. And I strongly advise you to move your troops as quickly as you can, because it is now three minutes to eleven, and at eleven Jerry puts down a carefully bracketed shoot of high velocity shells upon that stretch of road you have halted upon.'

'Oh,' grinned the American, 'I guess that'll be ok.'

Within seconds the scream of German shells rent the sky and crashed down on to a nearby crossroads. The Americans scattered hastily from the road, cursing at the punctuality of the German artillery batteries and leaving Dixon with a wry smile on his face.[7]

The French perspective was, initially at least, much warmer. Aware of their weakness and of the need for American help, many French soldiers enthusiastically welcomed their new associates, and rosy memories of Lafayette and Franco-American cooperation during the War of Independence helped to smooth any teething problems. To the French tank officer Lieutenant Charles Chenu, 'we fought alongside them, admired them, loved them'.[8] Although there were concerns about American inexperience and naivety (as well as disdain about US attitudes towards black soldiers), the bravery and verve of American troops were widely admired. One French commander, General Eugène Savatier, remarked that 'their splendid courage amazed us, and we applauded their successes whole-heartedly. Our affection was not based wholly upon our admiration. We were pleased to find in them our own qualities and defects, which made our mutual liking only the more lasting.'⁹ Indeed, not all Americans were the cigar-chomping 'louts' as described by Dixon. Some, like Major Charles Whittlesey, who commanded the 'lost battalion' in the Argonne, was a deep-thinking and sensitive soldier who had been a partner in a law firm in New York when the war broke out. Another complex individual was the logger from Tennessee, Alvin York, who had originally applied to become a conscientious objector because the war was against his religious principles. Despite this, he was sent to the front and saw action in the Meuse–Argonne, and was awarded the Congressional Medal of Honor for his actions on 8 October when he led an attack and killed up to twenty-eight enemy soldiers. Others, however, perfectly epitomized the pioneering, frontier spirit of the west, and two legendary American soldiers would cut their teeth on the Western Front: George S. Patton, a fire-eating tank commander, and Douglas MacArthur, a flamboyant brigadier who struck an almost cinematic pose in France.

For their part, American reactions to Europe and the war were also ambivalent. One American officer, Captain T. F. Grady, who would go on to fight in the Meuse–Argonne, left Portland on a heavily laden troopship on 29 March and endured two weeks of hellish pitching and rolling among the heavy seas of the Atlantic. 'Waves just like mountains,' he wrote on 8 April. 'Quite a few sick. All drills called off. Plenty of vacant seats at mess.' By the following day, only a few of his men were down for breakfast. Most were sick and drill was cancelled yet again. As if the seasickness was not bad enough, because of the danger of U-boats they had to sleep in their clothes with their life belts on. Eventually they reached Liverpool and sheepishly went up on deck for their first view of England. 'Fine view of the city and the docks were very neat,' he wrote. 'The ferry boats are very different from ours . . . the trains were funny little box cars with six compartments each . . . fine farming country and the towns were very odd – but very neat. Young girls and women do most of the work and they waved to us as we rolled by. We were welcomed all along the line.'¹⁰

American soldiers were known as 'doughboys', a term, so they

said, originating from the Mexican–American War of 1846–8, when
US troops got so caked in dust that it looked like they had been
covered in unbaked dough.[11] The doughboys may have been welcomed in England, but they could clearly see how much it was
suffering from the war. One officer, Lieutenant William Carpenter,
arrived at Winchester station one evening to see a hospital train draw
up on the other side of the platform. 'There were boys with their
heads tied up, boys that were blind, those with legs and arms off,' he
remembered. 'Those able to sit up shouted greetings to us: "Hi there
Yank. Hi sir, are you going to France? Well give 'em 'ELL!" Up to
this time the boys had been skylarking on every possible occasion,
but this touch of the real thing put a damper on the nonsense, and it
was a very thoughtful bunch of young soldiers that followed me up
the High Street of Winchester.'[12] Indeed, for many Americans the
novelty of being in a foreign country quickly wore off. Doughboys
often found themselves cold and hungry in England: bored with regular muddy hikes; annoyed that they could not buy bread because of
the rationing restrictions; and sick of the taste of coffee made from
chlorinated water – making them long for home.

For those who went straight to the Continent, things were little
better. Most of the Americans expected France, particularly Paris,
to be something straight out of the much-thumbed pages of *Vie
Parisienne*: a mysterious land of culture and fun, with well-dressed,
dark-eyed beauties on every street corner. One soldier, Herbert
McHenry, had often dreamed about meeting 'handsome, willowy,
French girls', but recorded his disappointment that the only French
women he saw 'were haggard and emaciated from hardships'.[13] They
found France to be an exhausted country, drab and grey, where
women dressed in black and there were few young men to be seen.
When Frank Holden landed at Le Havre in May 1918 the first thing
he saw was a hospital train full of wounded soldiers; a bitter reminder
of the daily cost of the war and a sober illustration of what the
Americans were about to enter.[14] Within days of their arrival many
American units had been assigned to British or French training
camps, where they were supposed to be introduced to the ways of
their allies and hone their fighting skills. Lieutenant-Colonel Ashby

Williams, who would command 1st Battalion, 320th Infantry, in France, remembered being sent to a gigantic 'rest' camp outside Calais. It consisted of 'row upon row of conical army tents so constructed that the floor of the tent was about twelve inches below the surface of the ground to protect the occupant against the lateral burst of aerial bombs'.[15]

For Ashby Williams, like many other Americans, it was at these rest camps that they first came into contact with British drill sergeants and officers who were tasked with ensuring they had the skills to survive on the Western Front. For many, the shock of this period – days of repetitive bayonet drill, exhausting gas training and exposure to bawling, sometimes brutal NCOs – left bad memories that never went away. For Ashby Williams:

> It was at Calais that we first came in touch with the British army. Our men seemed to take at once a violent dislike for everything that was British. It is difficult to analyse the reasons for this first impression. It was doubtless due in large part to the fact that the British Tommy had been at the game a long time and he assumed a cocksure attitude toward everything that came his way; perhaps to the fact that most of the Britishers with whom the men came in contact were old soldiers who had seen service and had been wounded in the fighting line and sent back to work in and about the camp, and they looked with some contempt on these striplings who had come in to win the war. Perhaps it was due to the fact that on the surface the average Britisher is not after all a very lovable person, especially on first acquaintance. At any rate our men did not like the British.[16]

It was perhaps little wonder that so many Americans hated British training camps. Indeed, many 'Tommies' would have agreed with them. The gigantic base at Étaples was notoriously tough and had seen a mutiny in September 1917 when tensions between new recruits and military police had spilled over into violence. Gradually, however, initial disgust gave way to respect. For Ashby Williams, cultural differences were to blame.

> Most of the Americans had been imbued with the idea that we must rush into the war and whip the Germans and have the thing over

with, and they could not understand what they thought were the slow, methodical and business-like methods of the British. Many of our officers were particularly struck with the fact that here under the very guns of the enemy, the British officers had a commodious club and music and all that sort of thing, and the best of wines and whiskies, and they went in and about as calmly and serenely as if they were in London or in Kalamazoo. Later on we had occasion to be convinced that the Britisher knew how to make a business of war and that he was an expert in running that business.

Whatever the Americans thought about the British or the French, they soon acquired a healthy respect for the Germans: for their ability as soldiers; for their ruthlessness; for their professionalism wherever they fought. Within days of reaching the front with his division, Captain Grady saw a German plane fly low over the lines and drop a note addressed to their Commanding Officer. 'Goodbye 42nd Division,' it read, 'hello 77th'. 'Jerry sure is there with the humour,' wrote Grady. For Frank Holden, his respect and admiration for the German soldier was summed up in his experience at Boucanville with 82nd Division. It was commonly said that the location of their battalion headquarters was well-known to the Germans, and that they could probably shell it any time they wanted. The divisional staff would joke about the time when three large shells – huge 210mm rounds – landed in a direct line near to the battalion headquarters; two shells behind, one in front. But no matter what the Germans did, they never moved their headquarters, simply because 'we thought if we did then the Germans would drop a 210 on us just to show us that they knew that we had moved'.[17]

At first glance the doughboys looked little different from their British and French associates. They wore a version of the British tin helmet and used the small pattern box respirator. They ate bully beef. They fired French or British weapons, often Lee Enfields, Lewis guns or Chauchats, and threw Mills bombs. They went into action alongside French tanks – Renaults or Schneiders – flew French or British aircraft – Spads or Sopwith Camels – and grew to love the French 75mm field gun, the legendary *soixante-quinze*. But in other respects the Americans were remarkably different. While both British and French Armies recruited mainly from remarkably cohesive home societies (excepting, of course, their colonial contingents), Pershing's men were drawn from the full spectrum of US society, and included many recent immigrants from Europe, Russia and Latin America, as well as Native Americans. A considerable number of black Americans also went to France, and although they were not permitted to serve alongside white soldiers and continued to suffer horrific racial prejudice, they did yeoman service on the lines of transport in France, helping to unload equipment and supplies, and doing the menial jobs without which Pershing's army could not have survived.

The Americans were different in other ways too. They were much richer than their cousins in other armies. They could draw $30 a month, about ten times the pay of a French private, thus gaining the eternal jealousy of the *poilus*, who looked upon the arrival of the Americans with concern and insecurity.[18] And in another odd, but still tangible way, the Americans differed from their British and French counterparts. They were big; *physically big*. Numerous commentators at the time noticed the physical presence of the first US soldiers, tall, well-built troops with high morale and an instinctive, almost cocky pride; the kind of soldiers that had not been seen on the Western Front since 1916, when Britain's New Armies had entered the fray. For their commander, this was the key point. Pershing was confident that American valour – her aggressive frontier spirit – would be the answer to the stalemate in the west. When he had first travelled to France and met British and French commanders, Pershing had quickly come to the conclusion that their methods would never win the war. They were stuck in their ways, he would tell his subordinates, and obsessed with limited, artillery-heavy trench attacks. He wanted his troops to be trained, first and foremost, as individual soldiers and riflemen, able to think for themselves on the battlefield and engage the enemy on their own terms. 'If the French doctrine had prevailed our instruction would have been limited to a brief period of training for trench fighting,' Pershing wrote, dismissively, in his memoirs.

It would probably have lacked the aggressiveness to break through the enemy's lines and the knowledge of how to carry on thereafter. It

was my opinion that the victory could not be won by the costly process of attrition, but it must be won by driving the enemy out into the
open and engaging him in a war of movement. Instruction in this
kind of warfare was based upon individual and group initiative,
resourcefulness and tactical judgment, which were also of great
advantage in trench warfare. Therefore, we took decided issue with
the Allies and, without neglecting thorough preparation for trench
fighting, undertook to train mainly for open combat, with the object
from the start of vigorously forcing the offensive.[19]

Had Pétain been privy to Pershing's thoughts, he would probably have
sighed deeply and shaken his head. The French Army had trusted in the
offensive earlier in the war, but all it had brought were long casualty
lists and a handful of square miles of shell-smashed countryside. What
was required, Pétain would claim, were limited advances, exhaustive
preparation and the employment of a great deal of heavy artillery.

In truth, the training of American units did not always proceed
on the strict lines Pershing had laid down. Once soldiers got to
France, the emphasis on the rifle and the bayonet, as he had wanted,
tended to give way to the realities of modern combat, with French
and British trainers rapidly acquainting their American students
with trench mortars, machine-guns, grenades and everything else
the Allies were using. The experience of combat also tended to
shake off any pre-war naivety and reinforce the necessity for traditional trench warfare methods. Relatively quickly, a number of
American commanders began to adopt British and French tactics in
their attacks, making strictly limited 'set-piece' advances based on
extensive preparation and overwhelming firepower, and quietly
discarding the traditional emphasis on the 'offensive spirit' and the
bayonet. Two of the most operationally successful US formations,
1st and 2nd Divisions, were fortunate in having intelligent commanders who recognized the limitations of Pershing's approved
combat doctrine and evolved their own methods, showing an
impressive ability to learn. Major-General Charles Summerall,
commander of 1st Division, became well-known for his reliance
upon comprehensive fire-plans in his attacks, even attracting criticism from GHQ for this. Similarly, the senior Marine Corps officer

in the AEF, Major-General John A. Lejeune, had been a brigade commander at Belleau Wood in June, and saw for himself how the lack of artillery support had proved fatal to numerous attacks, leaving American officers and men at the mercy of entrenched German machine-gunners and riflemen. Lejeune took over command of 2nd Division in late July and transformed the way it fought, only mounting attacks with as much firepower as possible and giving the infantry limited objectives. 2nd Division's capture of the formidable Blanc Mont ridge on 3 October was emphatic proof of the success of his methods, and was regarded by many, including Pétain, as one of the finest actions of the war.[20]

The effort to raise what would become the US First Army was an epic story of hard work, improvisation, courage and determination. Like the British before them, the Americans had begun the war with a small, professional army more used to hunting insurgents and rebels than waging major combat operations. Like the British too, they had to go through a long and sometimes painful journey of growth and development to bring their forces up to the standards of the Western Front, where any mistake – any weakness – would be ruthlessly punished. Indeed, when the Americans entered the war, few believed it could be done, or even if such efforts could be made, they would take so long as to be irrelevant. Yet within eighteen months of the US declaration of war, American forces had begun to turn the tide on the Western Front, providing vital reinforcements, not just of men and materiel (including powerful naval strength), but of morale. For every month that Ludendorff's offensives were held off, for every month that the German stormtroopers were beaten back, another nail was hammered into Germany's coffin. It may have seemed like a close-run thing in March and April 1918, but the war had been decided a year earlier. The American declaration of war on Germany in April 1917 had settled it. Kaiser Wilhelm had lost; the only question was when it would happen and in what way.

Ever since the US had been in the war, Pershing had wanted an American sector of the Western Front where his army could fight.

The German Spring Offensive had delayed this for some time, but by the late summer of 1918 his patience was running out. On 10 July, Pershing met Foch and told him that with the various US divisions scattered across the front, 'we were postponing the day when the American Army would be able to render its greatest help to the Allied cause'. The time had come, he believed, for a definite American sector, served by its own lines of communication. Looking at the front, the British were 'compelled to remain in the north' and the French would undoubtedly stay in the centre to cover Paris and Verdun. It seemed logical, therefore, to put the Americans into the south and east, around the salient of Saint-Mihiel that jutted into French lines southeast of Verdun, across the plain of the Woevre.[21] Pershing was confident that once American troops were concentrated in their own army under their own commanders, decisive results could be achieved; this was what he had spent months working towards.

Both Britain and France officially supported Pershing's aspirations, but, unofficially, hoped to put them off for as long as possible. They were loath to give up the services of American divisions that had proved so useful during the heavy fighting of the summer. Foch would often try to mollify Pershing by shaking his hand and nodding vigorously.

'Yes of course,' he would say, 'America must have her place in the war.'

The only problem was that it was difficult to justify the withdrawal of US troops from key sectors (where they had been relatively effective) at a crucial time, and concentrate them into what was regarded as a relatively insignificant corner of the Western Front. After the Battle of Amiens, Pershing had requested the withdrawal of five US divisions then serving with the BEF. An agreement was eventually hammered out to send three, but Haig was not pleased, writing to Pershing on 27 August:

> As regards the movement of your divisions from the British area, I was glad to be able to meet your wishes at once, and I trust that events may justify your decision to withdraw the American troops from the British battle front at the present moment, for I make no doubt but

that the arrival in this battle of a few strong and vigorous American Divisions, when the enemy's units are thoroughly worn out, would lead to the most decisive results.[22]

Haig, for his part, regarded the concentration on Saint-Mihiel as 'eccentric' and unnecessary and, like Foch, would have preferred to see US forces put under French command east of Rheims for a push into the Argonne. Tension was never far beneath the surface of their relationship.

For much of the war, the salient at Saint-Mihiel had been regarded as a nasty thorn in the side of the French sector of the Western Front, a seemingly impregnable position that flanked the town of Verdun and interfered with France's lateral communications. Much blood had been spent in this area in earlier years, but this time it would be different. Pershing was determined that this battle would be a clear-cut success, an undeniable expression of American military might that would justify the decision to form an independent army and send a clear message to the world that now they were serious. Pershing concentrated his most experienced units against the salient, and Pétain provided him with 3,000 guns, 150 tanks and over 1,400 aircraft to ensure success. On the southern face of the salient, US I and IV Corps would drive north towards Thiaucourt, while V Corps would move in from the west towards Vigneulles, thus pinching out the German defences and, theoretically, trapping any enemy survivors within it. The attack would go in on the morning of 12 September.[23]

The salient was held by General-Leutnant Georg Fuchs's Composite Army C. This was under the authority of General der Artillerie Max von Gallwitz, whose Army Group held the front between Apremon and Metz, and included Third and Fifth Armies. As the American presence opposite Saint-Mihiel became more noticeable throughout August and the first weeks of September, Gallwitz's concerns grew. By 9 September, intelligence reports concluded that 'it can be assumed with certainty that the Americans are accumulating ammunition and material, perhaps also heavy guns, on the south front of Composite Army C for an attack to be launched there at a not too-distant time'.[24] Although Gallwitz wanted to conduct a lightning spoiling attack to dislocate the American plans, as each day passed it became clear that his men would not be ready, and in any case the forces against them were looking increasingly ominous. The Germans in the salient – possibly around 50,000 men – were greatly outnumbered. The front trenches were held by seven under-strength divisions, with four more in reserve, and had, as with much of the German Army, been suffering from poor morale and disciplinary problems.[25] Of these divisions, four were noted as 'fourth-class' by Allied intelligence, with the majority gaining 'third-class' status, with often mediocre morale. Only 10th Division was regarded as being of 'first-class' merit, but intelligence also revealed that it had been virtually destroyed on the Marne during the summer and had been filled with inferior drafts, considerably affecting its quality.[26] On 10 September, Ludendorff agreed that at the moment no counter-attack would go in and told Gallwitz to begin to abandon the salient, moving back to a series of prepared lines to the north (known as the Michel position). He was, however, ordered to postpone the withdrawal for as long as possible.[27]

Pershing watched the battle with a small collection of staff officers at Fort Gironville, a commanding height overlooking the southern sector of the battlefield. It was an awful night, with sheets of rain coming down, and a chill wind that hinted at the onset of autumn. Not much could be seen through the mist, but they could all hear the sound of artillery fire, booming and crashing out over the salient. And then, at 5 a.m., the attack began. Pershing wrote:

> The sky over the battlefield, both before and after dawn, aflame with exploding shells, star signals, burning supply dumps and villages, presented a scene at once picturesque and terrible. The exultation in our minds that here, at last, after seventeen months of effort, an American army was fighting under its own flag was tempered by the realization of the sacrifice of life on both sides, and yet fate had willed it thus and we must carry through. Confidence in our troops dispelled every doubt of ultimate victory.[28]

Of the American soldiers in their forming-up trenches, almost all were soaked to the skin, tired from their approach marches, and cursing the orders against smoking or talking. It had been an ugly night, but the bombardment did much to raise spirits. One witness, Corporal Earl Searcy of 78th Division, remembered the horizon 'leaping forward in a mad blaze of jumping flashes', leaving everyone stunned and silent, all watching the incredible spectacle, and inviting the inevitable references to the Fourth of July.[29] After a few hours, Pershing returned to his headquarters, watching as columns of dazed German prisoners were marched to stockades in the rear. Reports filtered in from the front divisions: ground had been gained; losses had been light.

In the end the Battle of Saint-Mihiel was something of an anti-climax. Some called it a 'picnic'; others even doubted whether there had been a battle there at all. By the afternoon of 13 September, all of Pershing's objectives had been secured. Sixteen thousand prisoners and 443 guns had been taken.[30] The main attack was on the southern face of the salient and here enemy resistance was weak. The toughest thing – at least initially – was getting through the tangles of barbed wire that ringed the German defences, some of which had been in place since 1915. One member of 2nd US Division remembered seeing up to a third of his men without trousers, because they had all been torn away.[31] Most of the defending divisions were practically destroyed, and many American soldiers helped themselves to scores of battlefield souvenirs to proudly show off to their friends: Lugers, helmets, and bits and pieces of German uniforms. Douglas MacArthur, commander of 84 Brigade, recalled that in the village of Essay he saw 'a sight I shall never quite forget':

> Our advance had been so rapid the Germans had evacuated in a panic. There was a German officer's horse saddled and equipped standing in a barn, a battery of guns complete in every detail, and the entire instrumentation and music of a regimental band.[32]

In truth, almost everything that could have gone wrong did so for the German Army that day. The Americans struck at the exact moment when two divisions were withdrawing to their reserve lines, catching them in the open and causing heavy casualties. The poor weather interfered with aerial reconnaissance and meant that commanders in the rear had little idea what was going on and no clue as to the seriousness of the situation. Even more unfortunately, American shells destroyed the entire telephone network in the salient, meaning units had to rely on Morse lamps and runners all day.[33] The attack on the western face was led by V Corps, with two divisions, including the French 15th Colonial Division, attempting to sever the neck of the bulge. Here resistance was tougher as German units fought hard to keep the salient open, at least until the bulk of their forces could get away. Nevertheless, the overwhelming advantages possessed by the Americans meant that they were able to secure their objectives on time, pinching out the Saint-Mihiel salient with fewer than 7,000 casualties. Newton Baker, the bespectacled Secretary of State who had been staying at Pershing's headquarters, was delighted. This was the great battle they had promised; the battle had actually gone to plan; they had achieved victory.

For Pershing, Saint-Mihiel was nothing less than a triumph. 'An American Army was an accomplished fact,' he enthused, 'and the enemy had felt its power. No form of propaganda could overcome the depressing effect on the morale of the enemy of this demonstration of our ability to organize a large American force and drive it successfully through his defences.'[34] Whatever criticisms Haig or Foch had made about Pershing and his determination to form an independent American army, there was no doubt that at Saint-Mihiel he was proved right because the mood at German Supreme Headquarters slumped again as news of the battle came in. Losing such ground to the Americans was nothing less than a humiliation and a disaster. On 17 September, Hindenburg, now seemingly roused from his usual lack of interest, sent a furious telegram to Gallwitz complaining about his 'faulty leadership' and reminding him that he would bear full responsibility for holding his present position. 'I am not willing to admit that one American division is worth two German,' he wrote, angrily. 'Wherever commanders and troops have been determined to hold their position and the artillery has been well organized, even weak German divisions have repulsed the mass attacks of American divisions and inflicted especially heavy losses on the enemy.'[35]

For Gallwitz, the truth of the matter was more complex. Although defending the salient from a converging attack was not easy, he felt that tactically the Germans had been outfought. German armies had long relied upon a system of defence in depth, with the forward zone being held with relatively few troops, with progressively greater resistance being offered deeper into their lines. This had been very effective at saving their men from heavy artillery bombardments and leaving them to counter-attack when the enemy were at their weakest. But it was different now. The problem at Saint-Mihiel was that 'the main line of resistance was too thinly occupied'. When troops were unsteady or lacked sufficient manpower, spreading them out only resulted in disintegration. 'The method of attack often used by the enemy nowadays, that is, a brief artillery preparation and a surprise attack with masses of troops, allows, in fact demands, a stronger occupation of the main line of resistance contrary to former procedure.'[36] Gallwitz would later write in his memoirs that he had 'experienced a good many things in the five years of war'. Yet Saint-Mihiel stood out. 'I must count 12 September among my few black days,' he admitted.[37] Black days, it seemed, were becoming almost daily occurrences for the Kaiser's army.

8. 'A country of horror and desolation'

Halted against the shade of a last hill
They fed, and eased of pack-loads, were at ease;
And leaning on the nearest chest or knees
Carelessly slept.
But many there stood still
To face the stark blank sky beyond the ridge,
Knowing their feet had come to the end of the world.

Wilfred Owen, 'Spring Offensive'[1]

17–25 September 1918

The Western Front may have been entering its final stages, but it still exerted a powerful emotional and psychological pull on all those who served in it. Major H. J. C. Marshall of 46th (North Midland) Division, the unit that would break the Hindenburg Line, returned to France that autumn, cramped in a slow train that rolled past Amiens up the line to Villers-Bretonneux. 'We passed through Amiens in the moonlight,' he wrote. 'The buildings showed marks of bombardment, and the Station, usually so thronged and active, seemed quite deserted, the platforms glittering in the moonlight from broken glass from the skylights overhead. Onwards the troop train crawled, into a country of horror and desolation.' Perhaps the first thing you noticed as you got nearer the front was the smell.

Every now and then a strong gust of mustard gas would blow into the windowless carriages, accompanied by that extraordinary odour, reminiscent of burnt wool, which seems to pervade a battlefield. The whole gave the impression of a nightmare – the few trees left being mere stumps, slashed with white scars from the shells and the entire landscape a mere distortion. This went on from weary mile to wearier mile, the dawn breaking while we passed through Rosiers and Puseaux, at the reckless speed of a mile an hour.[2]

Despite the desolation, despite the smell, despite the fear that would gradually increase the nearer you got to the line, some could find a kind of beauty in the Western Front. T. H. Holmes recorded in his memoirs the experience of night marches up to the trenches.

> On some of those night marches when the moon was up, the land-scape took on an eerie sort of beauty. The poor stumps of trees, and the fingers of ruined buildings, would stand up sharp against the sky, and the muck and muddle of no-man's-land would be hidden in the darkness, and you fell to wondering whether it was ever going to end, and whether you'd come through it, and what you'd give to be able to walk along upright, and whether the man outlined in front of you was thinking the same thing. And you'd plod on, silent, except for the clump clump of your heavy boots.[3]

The poet Wilfred Owen had rejoined his battalion on 15 September at the town of Corbie on the Somme, with its grand seventh-century abbey that looked out on to miles of open ground that had recently seen much fighting. Owen had been here before. In the spring of 1917 he had visited it and 'listened under the nave . . . for the voice of the middle age'.[4] This was typical, romantic Owen; the kind of man who stuffed a copy of Keats's poems in his tunic and saw beauty in every-thing around him. But there was little beauty behind the lines. The tide of war had washed out and left scattered debris everywhere, with burnt-out tanks lying like milestones marking the advance. One observer remarked that 'The whole country is littered with rub-bish or as we call it salvage – guns and ammunition, trench mortars, equipment and so on – all the litter of war: tanks derelict and deso-late by the roadside, and lorries upside down.'[5]

That September the rear lines of the Allied armies teemed with activity and the mundane business of supplying the front with every-thing it needed: troops, ammunition, food, water and a thousand other things. Paul Maze remembered how 'Train-loads of ammunition came up every day; they had to be unloaded and every shell reloaded on to lorries which in long columns made their way through the inevitable congestion of moving troops and transports, the forerunners of an attack.'[6] The weather was wet and there was a growing chill in the air. On 22 September, Owen wrote to his friend and fellow war-poet, Siegfried Sassoon. 'You said it would be a good thing for my poetry if I went back', he joked. 'That is my consolation for feeling a fool. This is what shells scream at me every time: Haven't you got the wits to keep out of this?' He gave Sassoon his mother's address in Shrewsbury and told him, somewhat ominously, 'I know you would try to see her, if I failed to see her again.'[7] Enclosed with the letter was the poem 'Spring Offensive'; one of Owen's most haunting last works, contrasting the coming of spring and the renewal of life with the slaughter on the battlefield. Although it had originally been written about the Arras offensive of the previous year – when Owen had been concussed from shellfire – it could have equally applied to the situation that faced the British and French forces in late September 1918 with its ominous references to a 'stark blank sky beyond the ridge' and the 'end of the world' – metaphors perhaps for the Hindenburg Line.

The nearer the Allies got to the enemy's main defensive system, the slower their advance became. 5th Division, like most of the British Third Army, saw Cambrai as its great objective; indeed on some days, through the smoke and mist and cloud, the tower of its baroque cathedral could be seen on the horizon like some kind of beacon. By 18 September Third Army was closing in on the city, but progress had been slow for the past ten days. It had got within four miles of the Saint-Quentin canal, where the Hindenburg Line lay, but needed to secure a number of villages on the high ground to the west of it before any assault could be made. For the past week the weather had been poor, which hampered ground and air observation and turned the roads, which had been dry and dusty in August, into muddy bogs, which did little to help the harassed logistical services bring up supplies to the front. German artillery had also become more active, particularly mustard gas shells that settled in the hollows and proved both annoying and deadly.[8]

The men of 15/Royal Warwicks had been in reserve for most of the month, spending their time resting, cleaning their kit, having lectures, and every so often being inspected by their officers. The battalion practised making platoon attacks on strongpoints; engaging enemy positions with fire, while flanking units were despatched to get around and force them to surrender. Their time out of the line was coming to an end, however. On 12 September the brigade received orders to be prepared to move off and the following day it marched to the small village of Ytres to relieve part of the New Zealand Division, which had been at the front. On 14 September 15/Royal Warwicks relieved the Wellington Battalion, spending the next few days in the front lines opposite a German position known as Smut Trench. Patrols were frequently sent out to ascertain what resistance lay in front of them. At 4.20 a.m. on 16 September a four-man patrol crawled out into no-man's-land and made their way to the enemy front line. They realized very quickly that the trenches were manned and held strongly. That afternoon another small patrol was sent out in daylight, and once again found out that enemy units were holding the line. In this sector at least, it looked like the advance had come to a halt.[9]

On 16 September General Pershing closed down the Saint-Mihiel operation and began moving his divisions to the Meuse–Argonne, northwest of Verdun, a distance of about sixty miles. It was a decision that still rankled with many American soldiers, who were incensed at having to redeploy after waiting so long to concentrate their forces.[10] Pershing had originally envisaged continuing Saint-Mihiel far after the reduction of the salient, with American divisions driving north to secure the city of Metz, severing German lateral rail communications, and then occupying crucial iron- and coal-producing areas. However, after a series of tense meetings with Foch on 30 August and 2 September, it was agreed to limit the Saint-Mihiel operation to just the reduction of the salient and then switch the bulk of US strength to the Meuse–Argonne for a joint attack towards Mézières. At the time Pershing had not been happy, complaining bitterly to Foch that 'on the very day that you turn over a sector to the American Army, and almost on the eve of an offensive, you ask me to reduce the operation so that you can take away several of my divisions . . . leaving me with little to do except hold what will become a quiet sector after the Saint-Mihiel offensive. This virtually destroys the American army that we have been trying so long to form.'[11]

Pershing's frustration was understandable. He had spent months working for a unified American Army with its own sector, and was anxious to get going, envisaging Saint-Mihiel to be the start of a grand, war-winning offensive. Although he recognized that there were important objectives north of the Argonne, including the Mézières–Sedan–Metz railway and the Briey iron basin, he could perhaps be forgiven for thinking that this was just the latest Allied attempt to limit his independence; just another French push for amalgamation. It was finally settled at Bombon on 2 September that Pershing's First Army would mount an attack west of the Meuse, with the French Fourth Army covering its left flank, sometime between 20 and 25 September. Foch had initially suggested that the French would lead the attack and be reinforced by American divisions, but Pershing made it quite clear that he could 'no longer agree to any plan which involves a dispersion of our units' and said that if the Americans were to be involved, then they would do so as a whole army, even if they were dependent on French guns, aircraft and tanks. The decision, however, left the Americans praying for a logistical miracle to move their men and supplies from Saint-Mihiel to the Argonne within a matter of days before launching another large offensive.[12]

What was Foch thinking of? His decision to limit the Saint-Mihiel operation and mount a new Franco-American attack in the Argonne was puzzling. It jeopardized American plans and gave too little time for them to redeploy further north. Yet Foch felt it was the right thing to do. After being impressed by the success of Allied operations at Amiens, the *Generalissimo* was coming to the conclusion that perhaps more could be achieved from the remainder of 1918 than he had previously anticipated. He was also concerned that should the Saint-Mihiel operation prove successful, the American Army would 'get carried too far in an offensive of its own', and head in, what he believed, was the wrong direction.[13] He knew that the focus of operations remained on the Franco-British front, but wanted to find some way of bringing the Americans into a converging attack from the south, pushing through the Argonne in a gigantic pincer movement across France, cutting deeply into the German rear lines and destabilizing their entire front. It was certainly ambitious, but could it be done? Although Pershing remained deeply concerned about moving the bulk of his First Army from Saint-Mihiel to the Argonne in little over a week, he was confident that only his troops – with their inherent aggression and initiative – could advance across the difficult ground west of the Meuse and through the German defences.

With American operations now settled, Foch could determine how the other forces would operate. With help from the staff at Haig's headquarters, a four-stage concentric offensive was planned to take place in the last days of September, with the hardest task – that of breaching the Hindenburg Line at its most critical sector – falling to Haig's armies. Because of logistical constraints it was not possible to launch all of Foch's offensives on the same day, which were, in any case, designed to draw off enemy reserves so that significant gains could be made at the most important points. Foch initially hoped to begin the attacks with the Franco-American offensive west of the Meuse on 20 September, but that proved to be over-optimistic and it was eventually settled for 26 September. The following day the First and Third British Armies would attack in the direction of Douai and Cambrai. A northern offensive, with British, French and Belgian troops, would begin on 28 September, before the final push opened a day later. This was be undertaken by Rawlinson and Debeney's armies against the Saint-Quentin canal, possibly the most difficult sector of the front.

There was a sense that the war was approaching its climax. The question of whether the Allies would be able to get through the Hindenburg Line was frequently asked. If the Western Front had been a series of hard lessons for the British and French, then breaking the final German defensive position would be the ultimate goal. On 21 September Haig had lunch with Alfred Milner, the Secretary of State for War. Milner was in a depressed mood, telling Haig that recruitment was drying up at home and, if the British Army was used up, 'there will not be one for next year'. Haig tried to dispel his gloom. 'I pointed out the situation was most satisfactory and that *every available man should be put into the battle at once*,' he told Milner. 'In my opinion it is possible to get a decision *this* year: but if we do not, every blow that we deliver now will make the task next year much easier.'[14] Haig's belief that a decision could be made before the end of the year was, at this time, almost unique among his senior colleagues. By late September, with the Allies still to cross the foreboding Hindenburg Line, many observers were sceptical of the war ending any time soon. Most felt that 1919 or even 1920 would see the end of the war, only after the bulk of American military strength had been deployed. Commanders speculated that the German Army would retreat as far as the Rhine, and there, with its lines of communication secure and its front shortened considerably, would be almost impossible to dislodge. Stalemate seemed the only likely outcome.

The day after Foch's meeting with the three Allied commanders at Bombon the British Government had circulated a memorandum, 'British Military Policy, 1918–1919', which stated that the war would probably continue until the following summer. It estimated that by 1 July 1919 the Allies would have a superiority on the Western Front of approximately 400,000 men, meaning that the 'supreme military effort' should be made no later than this date.[15] Haig's French counterpart, Philippe Pétain, took a similar view. He remained deeply concerned about the state of the French Army and knew that it needed careful shepherding in its operations, making limited advances and trusting in the power of its heavy artillery. In a letter dated 8 September, Pétain stressed that the war would probably continue into the following year. By using the winter as an opportunity to withdraw its front line and re-form its shattered divisions, Pétain stressed that the German Army could still offer continued resistance well into 1919. He believed that the Allies would need to mount a series of preliminary operations designed to fix the enemy's reserves, before a decisive battle took place sometime in the summer.[16] For his part, Haig was unimpressed with such dire predictions (scribbling on his copy of the memorandum, 'Words, words, words!') and he remained bullishly confident that, this time, the Germans really were breaking. The only problem Haig had was convincing the British Government. He had been telling them consistently for almost two years that the Kaiser's empire was about to crumble and that the German Army was running out of men. Over-optimism and confidence, bordering on arrogance, had been Haig's chief character flaw in earlier years. He had been wrong before, and during 1917 it had nearly cost him his job. But this time there was a difference: he was right.

The day that Haig lunched with Milner, Foch was out looking over the old American sector with Weygand and Pershing. They drove out to the town of Saint-Mihiel and were pleasantly surprised to see that it had not suffered as much damage as they had feared. As he always tended to do, Foch – a devout Catholic – visited the cathedral. 'When we entered,' remembered Pershing, 'he reverently knelt, and following his example all of us did likewise, remaining some minutes at our devotions.' For Foch, there was no doubt that they would be victorious. His faith gave him a certainty and a calmness that amazed those who came into contact with him and who knew of the great responsibility on his shoulders. After a few moments deep in prayer, Foch got up, crossed himself, and then returned to his car, confident that all was well again.[17] His directive had been issued; the plans had been made. The Allies would mount a series of massive attacks beginning on 26 September that would usher in the final crisis of the war. 'Tout le monde à la bataille!' as Foch was fond of saying – everyone to the battle. Now the time had come.

By mid-September Dr Hochheimer seemed to have worked a minor miracle at Spa. Hindenburg personally thanked him for the 'transformation' in Ludendorff's demeanour, which had been improved by less work in the afternoon and more sleep, which the doctor carefully observed. 'My patient is doing better each day; today, breathing deeply, he literally fell asleep under my hands,' Hochheimer wrote on 11 September. 'The calming effect of my work and my words has made me quite happy. I am opening the door for him to worlds he has never seen before.' Ludendorff read a short chapter from *Rhapsodies of Joy* by Paul Steinmüller, but found it 'hard to understand' and 'incomprehensible'. Nevertheless, Hochheimer concentrated on Ludendorff the '*human being*'; trying to move him out of his habitual moods and temper his cold ferocity. 'The man really has become a quite different, fresher, freer and happier person,' he wrote. 'His stiffness is softening, he became relaxed and personal, asking me about my background and my family ... When I tell him about our children, he stares at me like a child being told about India – I steer clear of anything official or military.'[18]

Hochheimer may have been able to lighten Ludendorff's mood, but old habits died hard. In sharp contrast to the serenity and calmness of Bombon, OHL was a hive of activity. 'I hear from other people how he is working and giving orders again,' Hochheimer admitted. The Quartermaster-General usually worked late into the night, discussing military matters with his staff officers, often bent double over maps of the front for hours at a time. 'His sleep at night is geared to events at the front, to which he is always listening with half an ear; he sleeps from 12 midnight to 5 a.m., sometimes even less! Then the thoughts – strategic, tactical, political, economic – start to order themselves again ... The man is completely alone, he is married to his work.' When day broke he was up to his usual tricks, telephoning his commanders and inquiring what units were available and what orders they had been given. Ludendorff's impatience and inability to delegate responsibility were to blame, and it irritated many commanders across the front, but, as Crown Prince Rupprecht admitted, it was 'understandable given the present situation' and did at least give the impression that the military situation was being tackled energetically.[19] His staff were less keen. On 15 September, when Ludendorff was away, Colonel Heye, Chief of Operations at OHL, spoke to Hochheimer about this constant 'pent-up energy'. Although he was glad about Ludendorff's improvement, he asked the doctor, if possible, 'to keep detaching him from the telephone and let him work even less in the afternoons'. Hochheimer agreed to do what he could, but the situation at the front was darkening with each passing day, which put yet more pressure on the embattled Quartermaster-General and strained his already tired nerves to breaking point.

Despite the loss of Saint-Mihiel, which had been written off as a freakish accident, the Western Front seemed to be holding. News from other parts of the Central Powers was deeply worrying, however. On 15 September, a major Entente offensive began at Salonika, on the front against Bulgaria. This front had been opened in 1915, when the British and French, allied with the Greeks, had landed on the northern coast of Greece and tried to push through to Serbia. It had been a campaign composed in optimism and naivety; instead of finding the 'soft underbelly' of the Central Powers, the British and French ran into tough resistance in awful, broken country, full of hills, defiles and mountains. The ground was perfect for defence and gaining offensive momentum there was almost impossible. The war at Salonika had been deadlocked ever since, but with the weakening of the Austro-Hungarians and Ottoman Turks, combined with mutiny at home, the Bulgarian war effort began to break apart. Although the news from Bulgaria had been of concern for some time – there had been strikes, food shortages and political unrest – it was felt that the Bulgarian Army would be able to hold firm. Yet the cancer of disobedience had spread throughout its ranks with devastating effect, and in the face of a renewed Allied offensive troops began slipping away.

The news of the collapse of two Bulgarian divisions hit both Hindenburg and Ludendorff hard. Local German reserves were immediately despatched to the front, but they could do little. The Bulgarian Army simply went home. Hindenburg lamented that 'a great gap was torn in our common front', while the Quartermaster-General collapsed into hysterical wails of betrayal and surrender. 'The Bulgarian Government did nothing whatever to keep up the *morale* of the troops and the population or to maintain discipline,' complained Ludendorff. 'They gave free rein to enemy influences, and took no steps against any of the anti-German agitations.'[20] Even worse, the situation in the Middle East was now becoming desperate. Since 1914 the Ottoman Empire had been Germany's staunch and dependable ally in the region, but it had been tottering for some time. In December 1917 the British had captured Jerusalem – what Lloyd George called 'a Christmas present for the empire' – and then moved north, chasing the retreating Turkish forces out of Palestine and Mesopotamia. By the last months of 1918, they were closing in on Damascus, and ripping up what was left of the Ottoman Empire.

In the light of these sudden developments, Ludendorff had come to the conclusion that he must act. On 26 September – the day that a massive Franco-American offensive opened in the Argonne – he sent a telegram to the Secretary of State, Paul von Hintze, urging him to come to Spa immediately.[21]

Much now depended on whether the German front in the west would hold; whether the Hindenburg Line would stem the Allied attacks and restore confidence to the Army. German newspapers proudly proclaimed the impregnability of the position. The *Frankfurter Zeitung* reported in late September that 'The excellent line of the SIEGFRIED position will afford first-rate support for our Armies; by their aid our troops will be able to defend all the assaults of the enemy, and will force them to recognize in the inexhaustible fighting power of the Germans the same limits to success which we encountered during the great German campaign in the west.'[22] These defences, which now seemed Germany's only hope of holding on in France, were not, in truth, a line at all, but a series of four main defensive positions that ran across the Western Front from Armentières in Flanders down to Pont-à-Mousson on the Moselle. In the late summer of 1916 – as the German Army was being pounded at the Battle of the Somme – Hindenburg and Ludendorff began to plan the construction of a new series of defences behind the line, specially built to be difficult to shell and to allow the German Army to conserve its manpower. During the last months of 1916 and the spring of the following year, a vast system was built. The first, the Wotan Line (which included the Drocourt–Quéant switch), ran from Armentières southwards to Arras, where the main Siegfried Line was to be constructed. This went from Arras, in front of Saint-Quentin, and along the Aisne River. A third line, Hunding, ran from the Dutch border to a section of the front northeast of Verdun, where it linked up with the Michel Line, which had been constructed along the northern side of the Saint-Mihiel salient and then further on to the south. In order to avoid, as far as possible, enemy artillery fire – which was becoming increasingly difficult to combat – the defences were built on the reverse slope of hills; in other words, out of sight of the Allies. Two main trench systems would be dug with the bulk of the defending forces holding the second position and protected by acres of barbed wire, dug-outs, and pill-boxes wherever possible.[23]

There were flaws in its design, however. The necessity for siting trenches on the reverse slope to escape artillery fire could not be followed in all sectors. Along the British front, it had been decided to take advantage of a number of canals that lay parallel to the British line by incorporating them into the defensive belt, most notably the Saint-Quentin canal and the Canal du Nord. As well as being an obvious point of resistance, the canals provided a partial solution to the increasing menace of tanks, which were threatening to make Germany's barbed wire defences useless. Tanks may have been able to go over shelled ground and crush wire, but they could not cross canals. The only problem was that in many areas canals were not sited on the reverse slopes; they were, on the contrary, excavated in low-lying ground, meaning that the German line would be overlooked on both banks – ideal for artillery observation. Therefore, German commanders had often been forced to build a whole new line to the west of any canal, thus shielding this main line of resistance from observation.

One of the toughest sectors ran from Saint-Quentin northwards to Cambrai – the area that Rawlinson and Debeney would strike. Here the Saint-Quentin canal was deep, somewhere between fifty and sixty feet, and ringed with support trenches and barbed wire. It passed through a series of tunnels, most notably at Bellicourt, where a 6,000-yard tunnel had been converted by the Germans into an invulnerable, if somewhat gloomy, place to store equipment and house troops. Because the tunnel would be the obvious, and perhaps easiest, way of crossing the canal, the Germans had built extra defences to protect it, meaning that here the Hindenburg system was about *five miles* in depth. It was no wonder that Sir John Monash described it as 'an excellent military obstacle'. Furthermore:

> Deep communication trenches led back to the canal banks, in the sides of which tier upon tier of comfortable living quarters for the troops had been tunnelled out. Here support and reserve troops could live in safety and defy our heaviest bombardments. They could be secretly hurried to the front trenches whenever danger threatened.

There was, indeed, a perfect tangle of underground shelters and passages. Roomy dug-outs were provided with tunnelled ways which led to cunningly hidden machine-gun posts, and the best of care was taken to provide numerous exits, so that our occupants should not be imprisoned by the blocking of one or other of them by our bombardment. But it was the barbed wire which formed the groundwork of the defence. It was everywhere, and ran in all directions, cleverly disposed so as to herd the attackers into the very jaws of the machine-guns.[24]

Some German commanders would later claim that the defensive prowess of the Hindenburg Line had been overestimated, while whining about the need for a full refurbishment. Although in certain sectors this may have been true, the Hindenburg Line was still a formidable series of prepared positions that presented any attacker, however strong, with an enormous array of challenges. Five miles of labyrinthine dugouts, underground shelters and trenches, with fields full of rusty barbed wire; five miles of concrete machine-gun and mortar emplacements; five miles of murderous defensive fire that would make even the staunchest commander blanch; five miles of the most formidable defensive position in the history of warfare. The problem was not that the Hindenburg Line was not strong enough; the problem was that the Army that would garrison it was a shadow of its former self.

The German Army in the west was divided into five Army Groups that ran from the North Sea to the Swiss border.[25] Split between them was a total of 197 divisions, although many were considerably under-strength and urgently required rest and reinforcement. By late September the bulk of German strength lay in the north, in the critical sector between the sea and the Oise River. The Army Groups of Crown Prince Rupprecht and General von Boehn commanded approximately ninety-five divisions, including forty-three in reserve. The largest Army Group belonged to Crown Prince Wilhelm in the centre of the front against the French Tenth and Fifth Armies. As had been the case since early on in the war, the further south and eastwards you went the fewer units were in the line and the poorer their quality. The Army Groups of Max von Gallwitz and Duke Albrecht could muster only forty-two divisions, again many of them being of poor quality.[26] By this point German divisions were much weaker in manpower than their Allied counterparts (particularly the Americans who stuffed their divisions with 28,000 men, the equivalent of a British or French corps). Officially each battalion had a strength of 880 men, giving each division approximately 8,000 infantrymen, but this was rarely seen in the final months of the war, and by the end of September the average field strength of a German battalion barely reached 600 men (and this had only been achieved by dismantling fifteen divisions).[27]

To a certain extent the German Army was able to compensate for its manpower shortages with the lavish issuing of machine-guns and the new machine-pistols, the highly effective MP18, which had originally been designed for the stormtroopers. This meant that even though German divisions contained far fewer men than their enemies, they could still bring an impressive amount of firepower to bear on the battlefield, something that all too many Allied soldiers would have testified to. Nevertheless, heavy casualties throughout the spring and summer, combined with disease, a lack of food and desertion, meant that many units were wasting away at an impressive rate. The German official history bemoaned the 'extraordinary' losses throughout August and September that amounted to 230,000 men.[28] Those that went into the line were frequently exhausted because of insufficient rest, which did little for their morale or fighting spirit. Indeed, so bad were the problems over manpower that even first-class assault divisions could be reduced to near-mutiny after being almost constantly engaged at the front. By the end of September, the men of 2nd Guard Division – one of the best in the entire army – was described as being 'very dispirited' after returning to line without time to recover. In another case, one battalion of 153 Regiment (belonging to the excellent 8th Division) even refused to mount a counter-attack, the men complaining that they had suffered heavy losses without reinforcement. These were far from isolated incidents.[29]

Desperate attempts were made to shore up the men's morale. Soldiers would regularly be reminded of what would happen to them if they were taken prisoner. To give themselves up was 'a dishonourable act equivalent to treachery'. Pamphlets issued by OHL warned soldiers that if they were captured by 'our inhuman foe', they would be 'slowly tortured to death'. Should they be questioned about military subjects, they were to parry them with stock responses such as 'I'm just back from leave', 'I only joined the unit a few days ago', or 'I've been sick in quarters' and so on.[30] On 6 September, General-Leutnant Curt von Morgen, commander of XIV Reserve Corps at Bapaume, issued a proclamation to his men, urging them to realize the importance of the moment and the need to fight harder in the coming days.

> Up till now, owing to military reasons, we have allowed the British to occupy a devastated enemy country. In rearguard battles we have inflicted heavy losses on him. Now, however, you have taken up a strong defensive position and not one foot of ground is to be given up. The British are seeking a decision here, and the XIV Reserve Corps holds a most important part of the line. Remember, then, that you are defending your own homes, your own families, and your own beloved Fatherland, and think, too, what it would be like if the war, and with it the hordes of the enemy, entered our dear Home-land. If you stand fast, the victory, as before, will be ours. You are more than a match for the enemy, who only attacks with dash when accompanied by Tanks, and these we will destroy. Therefore, use your rifles coolly, and, with the blood of battle in your veins, use cold steel – the bayonet.

On 16 September, the officers and NCOs of 119th Division, holding the front at Pontruet, northwest of Saint-Quentin, listened to a lecture on the importance of holding their ground and how:

> there can be no question of going back a single step further. We want to show the British, the French and the Americans that any further attacks of theirs on the SIEGFRIED Line will be completely broken, and that this Line is an impregnable rampart; with the result that the Entente Powers will condescend to consider the peace terms which are absolutely necessary to us before we can end this war. In other words, each step backward now means a lengthening of the war.[31]

Nothing is known of how the officers and NCOs took the lecture, but it was unlikely to have restored morale significantly. Feelings in the division were already poor. Like many units in Second Army, it had been almost continually engaged since the summer and had suffered heavy losses.

No matter how much faith they had in the Supreme Command, the unceasing fighting wore men down. Crown Prince Rupprecht went on leave in late August having been advised by his doctor that he needed six weeks' rest to cure his insomnia. Owing to the continuous Allied pressure he had to cut short his leave and return.[32] For General von der Marwitz, he could only wonder at the stupidity of Europe. 'France is becoming an American colony,' he opined. 'England is handing over her mastery of the world to them and to Japan. If the Monroe doctrine: "Europe for the Europeans" counted, our old part of the earth would be a better place, but we are not capable of this.'[33] Others wrote similarly vain expressions of disgust and fear at the state that Germany – and the world in general – had been reduced to. Rudolf Binding, an officer who was terribly weak from fever, had a dream that the Kaiser, 'bareheaded and on foot', came into their camp 'to give himself up to their mercy'. He could see and feel, he wrote, 'mysterious powers rising out of the deep'. Since the counter-attack on the Marne, he had always known Germany was finished. 'How are we to recover ourselves?' he would ask, but there was never an answer.[34]

As was perhaps to be expected, both Hindenburg and Ludendorff had no time for such musings, and they became increasingly frustrated by what they saw as the indecision and incompetence around them. General-Leutnant Fuchs, the commander of Composite Army C, which had been defeated at Saint-Mihiel, was sacked soon after the battle, and on 22 September Marwitz was removed from command of Second Army, apparently because of his failure at Amiens. Although he was awarded the Order of the Red Eagle with Oak Leaves and Swords – one of the highest Prussian decorations – he was depressed at the news. 'Physically I am fresher than ever,' he wrote, 'but if one is not satisfied with my leadership, I would gladly let a better leader take my place and hope that he will achieve victories

with the Second Army.'³⁵ He was informed by the Kaiser that he
would take command of Fifth Army, under the Army Group of Max
von Gallwitz, in the Argonne. Only the most ruthless commanders
could survive on the most important fronts and Marwitz would have
to prove himself again on what had long been seen as a quieter area.
But, in a wicked twist of fate, by the evening of 25 September fifteen
large US divisions and seven French corps were moving into place in
this sector, supported by over 2,700 guns and scores of aircraft. At
that moment the US First and French Fourth Armies were ready to
go, two daggers poised to plunge deep into the German flank. Far
from coming to a quiet front to see out the war, Marwitz was headed
straight for the biggest battle in American history.

9.   Return to the Wilderness

*It was a battle pursued more by ear and sense of touch than with the eye. Troops
moved by dead reckoning of pocket compasses, as ships in fog.*

Major-General Hunter Liggett[1]

26–30 September 1918

The window panes were shaking in General Max von Gallwitz's headquarters at the medieval village of Montmédy on the Franco-Belgian
border. It was nearing midnight on 25 September and the artillery
barrage that would precede the Franco-American attack was in full
swing, rumbling away across the forested hills on the front of Third
and Fifth Armies, and making everybody anxious. For days intelligence officers had been reporting extensive movement at the front,
with large fleets of trucks and lorries bringing in men and supplies,
while they had counted no fewer than 380 aircraft at enemy airfields.
A number of American prisoners had also fallen into German hands,
revealing that French troops had been relieved from their usual positions, and that Americans were now in this sector in strength. In the
last few days Gallwitz had issued final deployment orders for his
reserves – and there were not many of them – and awaited developments with calmness and surety. Yes, it was true that the artillery fire
might signal the beginning of a major attack northwards, but perhaps
it was just a ruse, a diversion, before the Americans struck at Metz or
into Lorraine, as his spies were informing him. In truth he just did not
know. The Americans, it seemed, were an unknown quantity.[2]

Like many Prussian officers, Gallwitz had initially been sceptical
that much could be expected from the United States. The American
soldier, it was confidently explained, was cowardly and weak; constantly in thrall to finance and business interests; lacking the enduring

Kultur of Germany. It is true that some observers shivered in apprehension of the great, latent power of the Americans – their industrial
strength, their financial power, their vast population – but these were
the exceptions. Regarding the Americans, a kind of fatal amnesia
ruled German hearts. Any worries were soothed with the thought
that America would not be able to fight; that her large German com-
munities would hinder the war effort; that it would take years for
them to marshal their strength. In short, it was not Germany's fault
and it would probably not matter. The key thing was to win the war
in the meantime. Yet, over the course of 1918, Gallwitz was forced to
reconsider his earlier dismissal of American capability. Saint-Mihiel
had been a warning. Now, on the Meuse–Argonne front, it looked
like something much bigger was taking place.

Gallwitz was one of the most well-respected and experienced
commanders in the German Army. He had first seen action in 1870,
commanding an artillery battery during the Franco-Prussian War,
and had served almost everywhere since: Belgium, Galicia, Serbia,
the Somme. He knew as well as anyone what his troops were up
against and what would happen should the Allies attack. It would be
like the Somme again: the endless, ravaging bombardments; the thin
lines of infantry moving forward, fear masking their faces; the
shocked German defenders doing whatever they could to hold their
lines against the seemingly unstoppable forces ranged against them.
His Army Group could muster little more than 190,000 men, strung
out along a vast front with too few reserves immediately available.
Fifth Army in particular was weak. It was situated north of Verdun,
had lost heavily in the summer, and had much of its infantry and
artillery stripped from it at Saint-Mihiel. It consisted of just seven
divisions, many of which had only nine battalions. The ground and
defences in their sector may have been strong, and would certainly
present any attacker with major obstacles, but given enough time and
willpower, not to mention the growing firepower the Americans
could muster, they would get through. The important thing was to
hold on for as long as possible.[3]

In the days after Saint-Mihiel, the US First Army began to concentrate northwest of Verdun, relieving the French Second Army along

a section of the line between the Meuse and the Aisne rivers. They moved into difficult terrain. On their left lay the Argonne forest, a nightmare of thick woodland, hidden defiles and thin, winding tracks. In the centre the country was more open, with scattered woods and hills, but it was dominated by the forbidding rise of Montfaucon, bristling with defences and an ideal observation point from which to spy on any attacker. On the right, the dominating heights on the far bank of the Meuse also allowed oblique fire to be directed on any Allied advance. No one liked the ground, particularly in the Argonne, but it was in a position of great strategic significance ('second to none on the Western Front', Pershing had said), guarding the southern flank of the great German bulge into northern France. All supplies for the German armies ran through two rail systems, one in the north at Liège and the other in the south from Carignan to Mézières. This latter section was critical to German survival. The newly appointed commander of Fifth Army, General von der Marwitz, described it as their 'most vital artery' on the Western Front, and if this could be severed, the war would be over.[4]

For those American soldiers who knew their history, the one battlefield that the Meuse–Argonne was reminiscent of was the Wilderness of 1864. During this battle – one of the worst of the Civil War – General Robert E. Lee's outnumbered Confederate forces had engaged Ulysses S. Grant's Union Army in the tangled undergrowth of the Wilderness, Virginia, using the terrain to mask their inferiority in men and artillery. Because the ground was so poor, commanders found it difficult to coordinate their units effectively, meaning that combat often degenerated into scattered groups of men becoming lost in the trees, struggling to catch sight of a hidden enemy that was seemingly everywhere. It would be even worse in 1918 as the attackers attempted to cross ground that had been held by the German Army for four years. Since then they had constructed an elaborate series of defences with scores of dug-outs, blockhouses, connecting trenches and switch lines, all covered by thickets of rusting wire. One doughboy remembered seeing 'acres of barbed wire' and crossing ground that had been so torn up by shellfire that it 'resembled the turbulent waves of a stormy ocean'.[5] From no-man's-land to the German rear line, there were four main fortified systems within just eleven miles, meaning that nowhere on the Western Front was there as dense a defensive system as here. Perhaps inevitably, this sector had been quiet for some time, with many French commanders regarding military operations here as nothing short of suicidal. For Pershing, although he was still upset at abandoning Saint-Mihiel, he recognized that if his troops could punch through the German line and drive north, a great victory would be gained and the war would surely be over; the final and irrevocable proof of the superiority of American aggression and the wisdom of an independent army.

Pershing's plan was simple. After an intensive, but brief, artillery bombardment, three American corps – perhaps as many as 375,000 men – would drive north towards Mézières, aiming for a complete break in the enemy line in the centre at Montfaucon. They would be assisted by the French Fourth Army, which would jump off on the left of the Argonne forest, and by their swift advance compel its evacuation, hopefully without getting bogged down in it. First Army orders stated that the line Stenay–Le Chesne–Attigny–Rethel would be the main objective for the day, thus clearing the thick belt of enemy defences and turning the River Aisne.[6] Unfortunately, many of Pershing's most experienced divisions had been employed at Saint-Mihiel, meaning that they would be unavailable for the start of the battle. Instead, the main assault would be entrusted to Major-General George Cameron's V Corps, comprising 79th, 37th and 91st Divisions, none of which had much battlefield experience. Yet these troops, men from Maryland and Pennsylvania, all the way to Ohio and the Pacific Coast, would have to storm some of the toughest positions in France, maintain their cohesion, and – above all – keep going. As Pershing knew only too well, any delay could be fatal.

Good logistics and smooth planning were central to Pershing's plan. The task facing First Army's planners was not only unprecedented, but was also taxing in the extreme: how to move a vast army in secret from one part of the front to another and keep the men supplied, equipped and ready to launch a subsequent offensive. The man behind the plan was George Marshall, assistant to Pershing's Chief of

Staff, Hugh Drum. Marshall was a supremely gifted staff officer with a ruthlessly logical and balanced mind, although he did admit that the news of the shift to the Meuse–Argonne 'disturbed my equilibrium' as he racked his brains trying to think how it could be done.[7] Transport was the major problem. There were only three routes between Saint-Mihiel and the Argonne, one of which was in German hands. All movement had to be made at night – not an easy task given the primitive state of the roads in this part of France. Many of the horses attached to artillery batteries were already exhausted, which played havoc with their movement schedules. Troops had to march across the rear zone of those units involved at Saint-Mihiel while that battle was still going on and, at the same time, large numbers of French units also had to shift eastwards to join Fourth Army, which would cover Pershing's left flank. It was like learning to swim after being thrown in the ocean.

Given the lack of experienced staff officers within First Army it was something of a minor miracle that the move was accomplished at all. In just two weeks, 500,000 men, 2,000 guns, 90,000 horses and up to a million tons of supplies were moved from Saint-Mihiel to the Argonne, a distance of over sixty miles.[8] American troops were marched and bussed to the front and then filtered quietly and secretly into the lines. Officers and scouts borrowed French greatcoats and helmets (to maintain the ruse that the French were still in the line) and peered into no-man's-land, urgently trying to familiarize themselves with their new sectors before the attack went in. One scouting party from 77th Division was led by Major Charles Whittlesey, accompanied by his three lieutenants. Their French guides could not stop laughing when Whittlesey tried to squeeze into his borrowed overcoat, which had obviously been taken from a small man. Whittlesey was over six feet tall.[9] Undeterred they crept out of their trenches, down a valley and through a village that had been demolished by shellfire. Once through this area they would pass on into the Argonne forest itself; its black pines and thin tracks looking almost medieval, haunted even. Somewhere out there was the enemy.

Covering the Americans' left flank was the French Fourth Army, commanded by Henri Gouraud, a battle-hardened, if somewhat eccentric, soldier who had lost his right arm at Gallipoli. Fourth Army was impressively big, consisting of seven corps and, as usual, a mass of artillery, tanks and aircraft. It met the Americans just west of La Harazée and was tasked with attacking the enemy from the left bank of the Aisne to the River Suippe. It was to push north towards Grandpré thus outflanking the Argonne forest, before linking up with the Americans again and heading off, on the final march, up to Mézières and Sedan.[10] Although the ground was not as forbidding as the hills and woods faced by the Americans, the French sector was far from ideal. The German front-line position was protected by extensive belts of barbed wire and reinforced with concrete shelters. Behind that was the second position, lying on the reverse slope of a large, forbidding rise known as Blanc Mont, and covered with the usual network of deep trenches and dug-outs, all swathed in barbed wire. Nevertheless, their Commander-in-Chief, Philippe Pétain, was confident that together their attacks would present great problems for the enemy. One morning he visited Major-General Hunter Liggett, commander of US I Corps, and together they studied the map. Quietly and calmly, as was Pétain's way, he put his finger on the town of Étain, behind the German lines just north of Saint-Mihiel. 'That is where the enemy is holding his heaviest reserves. That is where he expects us to attack him. Instead we shall attack almost everywhere but there.'[11]

The three-hour bombardment that Pershing had planned reached crushing intensity just before Zero Hour: 5.30 a.m. on 26 September. For those American and French troops sheltering in their forward positions, the hours before they went over the top were nerve-wracking and intensely stressful. Everyone dealt with the uncertainty in his own way. It was true that for many soldiers a resigned fatalism was accepted, but others found it a maddening experience; trying to get the body and mind ready for the experience of combat, for the possibility, even probability, of being killed or wounded. According to an American battalion commander, Lieutenant-Colonel Ashby Williams, 'No men who have not passed through the experience can realize how it feels to wait for the beginning of an attack. There is excitement, of course, but it is suppressed, and there are anxious moments of speculation and anticipation as to what the attack will bring forth.'[12] Even for commanders – those maligned 'château generals' – the stress was not easy to deal with. Hunter Liggett was at his headquarters waiting for the first reports to come in. 'The nervous strain is difficult,' he admitted. 'I have learned to have two packs of cards by me and to lay them out in double solitaire position when an attack has started. That is as good an anodyne as I know. It saves you from nail biting and pacing the floor until your nerves are shot.'[13]

At the appointed time, whistles blew across the line and thousands of tired, damp and cold men got up out of their trenches and marched off, in artillery formation, into the early-morning fog, nervously scanning the ground in front of them for signs of the enemy. Despite the high hopes in Allied headquarters, it was to be a day of disappointment. On the left, Gouraud's Fourth Army proceeded slowly and surely, as was the French method by 1918. That day the French advanced four kilometres and captured 7,000 prisoners. This may have sounded impressive, but much more had been expected of the operation than this, which was supposed to sever Germany's main rail arteries into northern France. Foch was appalled. This was not how his grand offensive was supposed to look; at this rate it would be years before the Germans gave in.[14] On the American sector, initially at least, things seemed to promise more. Within five hours of pushing off, Liggett's I Corps had secured its objectives, about four miles into the German position, while III Corps also reached its designated line. In the centre, however, the heights of Montfaucon – which the Germans called 'Little Gibraltar' – held out and slowed everything else down, with hidden defenders cutting the attackers to pieces with heavy machine-gun and artillery fire. This delay would have serious implications for Pershing's goal of breaking through the German line.

First-Lieutenant Clair Groover was one of those who witnessed the attack on Montfaucon. Originally hailing from Lewisburg, Pennsylvania, Groover belonged to 313th Infantry Regiment of 79th Division. His men went forward that morning behind the bombardment and covered by smoke shells. The shelling was 'like a succession of express trains passing overhead'. Although they made progress, by the time the sun had risen and the smoke had dissipated, their advance had 'slowed down to nearly a snail's pace' across 'the roughest ground that troops ever had to fight over'. Not only was the terrain broken by shell holes and barbed wire, but they were also up against heavily entrenched defenders who were committed to holding on. Groover was amazed to stumble across a map of the defences they faced, which showed 113 machine-guns in fixed positions, many of them in concrete pill-boxes, supported by at least half as many moveable weapons. Whatever training Groover and his men had received had not prepared them for fighting of this intensity and, perhaps inevitably, their unit rapidly splintered apart. As Groover later admitted, 'In the confusion of the attack, barbed wire across no-man's-land, continuous shell holes, forests, machine gun fire; companies had been broken up into little groups; men were separate from their unit[s]. Officers assembled stragglers, and kept advancing.' By 4 p.m. they reached the southern slopes of Montfaucon, but had been badly hit. That day Groover's regiment lost three majors, two captains and six junior officers, and during the next two days suffered over 1,200 men killed, wounded or missing.[15]

Others reported similar scenes of chaos and confusion. Sergeant James Meehan (also of 313th Infantry Regiment), remembered no-man's-land being 'full of men pushing ahead through barbed wire, jumping trenches and across shell holes'. They had barely gone one hundred yards when they suffered their first casualty, one of their gunners hit in the leg. When they finally reached the slopes of Montfaucon and moved over the brow of the hill, they were met by what seemed like 'a hundred machine guns', which rapidly stopped their advance. The rest of the day was spent trying to work around the position, flanking enemy machine-guns, and avoiding the persistent shellfire, both German and American.[16] The problem was that having been slowed up by the difficult ground and the unexpectedly heavy resistance, American units lost the protection of their creeping barrage, which bounded away to the north. Lacking the training and experience that had long been drilled into their British and French counterparts, American units found it very difficult to move forward on their own, resulting in heavy casualties, confusion and attacks that rapidly came to a juddering halt. Soon the fields and woods of the

Meuse–Argonne, crisscrossed with barbed wire entanglements, would also be strewn with American bodies and bleeding wounded.

Over the next month, the Argonne would come to symbolize Pershing's lost hopes for the offensive. The experience of combat here was exhausting and draining. US soldiers would frequently have to advance uphill through a hellish landscape of shattered trees and shell holes, dragging their tired limbs and heavy equipment through barbed wire entanglements and past thinly dug trenches, while frequently coming under fire from German snipers and machine-gunners, their bullets clipping violently through the trees. At night, they would often have to get down where they could, scraping thin holes in the ground or occupying old bunkers, and drift into an uneasy sleep that was all too often broken by gas alerts or odd shrapnel shells. After three days of unceasing combat, one American officer, Captain T. F. Grady (305th Machine Gun Battalion, 77th Division), was exhausted and angry. On 28 September he recorded in his diary that he was 'very cold and couldn't get to sleep at all ... Up another heartbreaking hill so steep we had to help each other up.' After a night of rain, he woke up the following morning 'chilled to the marrow and soaked to the skin ... Everybody sore and growling.' Their rations were almost running out.

> Dad told me once that I would see the day when I would be glad to get a crust of bread – and this was the day. These damned woods are full of hills and ravines and I guess the French knew it too. Cleaned up a couple of nests and had some trouble with snipers. Bullets were whistling over our heads and we had to take cover from shrapnel. We got ahead of our objective for the day and ran into our own artillery fire and had to fall back.

By 30 September, Grady's men were becoming increasingly tired and fractious. They marched down another ridge only to get caught in an American artillery bombardment, which 'shot away' half the face of an officer and severed the legs of another 'poor fellow'. They sent up rockets to signal to their guns to stop firing, but German observers spotted them and fired a bombardment of high explosive on their positions. Grady's men dug in and took what cover they could. 'Very cold and I would give a month's pay for a cup of coffee,' he wrote in his diary. 'No tobacco and a bum outlook.'[17]

As with everything else in First Army, its medical staff worked wonders of improvisation to cope with the unprecedented demands of the front. One of those who witnessed this was Miss C. W. Clarke, a nurse with the US Evacuation Hospital at Toul. It received 200 men on the opening day of the offensive, but gradually more and more wounded arrived, particularly on 30 September, when it was 'simply deluged' with patients.

> For four weeks from 1,000 to 1,500 passed through our hospital each day. The Red Cross trains came in two or three times a day, each one taking away 500 wounded . . . In the operating room, twelve tables were in constant use day and night. There was a complete staff of doctors and nurses for day work and another for night . . . For four weeks an unbroken line of ambulances rolled up our main street, emptied its human load onto our receiving ward and rolled back to the lines to get another. We never refused to take a patient . . . The beds would all be full. We put stretchers on the floor. Sometimes the floors and corridors were so full it was hard to get around. Then a train would come. It would be loaded quickly. There would be a little respite. We would start to make up the empty beds but before we got far new patients would come and the beds would be full again and the floor and the corridors.

Upon arrival, the wounded were given anti-tetanus injections to prevent lockjaw and crosses were marked on their foreheads with iodine. They were then put into the receiving ward, where their injuries were assessed (A to D in decreasing order of severity). If they could be saved, they were cut out of their uniforms, bathed and given Red Cross pyjamas, before being sent to the X-ray section or operating theatre as required. Although Miss Clarke did not serve at the front, soon she knew everything about the battle because patients swapped stories every day. 'They, the boys, would talk about "the woods",' she remembered.

> One day the Germans didn't budge, the next day they'd be retreating, the next 'the woods' were ours. We who cared for the boys lived

through each battle as it was retold for us, either by a conscious patient right from the scene or by one under ether, whose descriptions were often more vivid. We lived through the war from Château-Thierry to the Argonne only a few hours behind the actual events, only a few miles behind the lines and we learned the spirit of our American men, kind, home-loving and unconquerable.[18]

One of those wounded in the Argonne was Colonel George S. Patton, the 32-year-old commander of 1 Provisional Tank Brigade. On the morning of 26 September, before they had reached the village of Cheppy, Patton and his men came under heavy fire from entrenched German machine-guns dug in on nearby high ground. Working with a small number of tanks – small, light Renaults – Patton tried to take his men with him and rush the crest of the hill, but was shot in the leg before he could make it, with most of his men being killed or wounded around him. He limped on for about forty feet, all the time under intense fire, before collapsing into a shell hole. For Patton, the Argonne was the proving ground for armoured warfare and for the American Tank Corps. From his wheelchair, he wrote to his wife two weeks later. 'I had seven captains, two majors and myself in the fight. Of these all are hit but one captain and two majors . . . Two lieutenants were killed and 15 wounded. But the Tank Corps established its reputation for not giving ground. They only went forward. And they are the only troops in the attack of whom that can be said.'[19]

Patton's feelings of pride in the accomplishments of his men contrasted sharply with his belief that other units had not shown the same determination. Pershing agreed. The failure to secure a clean breakthrough on the first day was highly disconcerting. It brought up all the old arguments again about the wisdom of an independent American army, as well as providing seeming proof that many of his divisions had received training that was too focused on limited advances and the old habits of trench warfare. Pershing dealt with the crisis in the only way he knew: by pushing, cajoling and threatening. On the morning of 27 September, the four corps of the US First Army received an urgent telegram from his Chief of Staff, Hugh Drum, ordering divisional and brigade commanders to 'place themselves as far up toward the front of the advance . . . as may be necessary to direct their movements with energy and rapidity in the attack'. The enemy was in retreat and there should be no hesitation or delay. 'All officers will push their units forward with all possible energy. Corps and division commanders will not hesitate to relieve on the spot any officer of whatever rank who fails to show in this emergency those qualities of leadership required to accomplish the task that confronts us.'[20] It did not take long for Pershing to deliver on this threat. The first commander, Brigadier-General Evan Johnson, was relieved on the morning of the second day. Sadly, he would not be the only officer whose reputation would be ruined in the hills west of the Meuse.[21]

American commanders may have felt uncomfortable under Pershing's cold, unyielding gaze, but the pressure on their German counterparts, at all levels, was even more intense. The first day of the assault had been one of great difficulty. Facing nearly fifty battalions of US soldiers were just eighteen German battalions. Heavy artillery fire on the roads behind the lines interfered with communications and the movement of reserves. As was the usual German practice, Gallwitz ordered a number of counter-attacks to go in, to regain ground and unsettle the attackers, but they never went ahead as planned. He had originally wanted 5th Bavarian Reserve Division to push forward, but it was 'terribly handicapped by the barrage fire of the enemy', which delayed its arrival on the field. 37th Division was also unable to counter-attack at Varennes. Only one of their regiments made it to the front, the other two being unable to get forward because of extensive traffic delays behind the lines.[22] Nevertheless, by the end of the day the German position along this sector had held, giving Gallwitz precious time to concentrate his forces and urge his men to dig in.

The experience of defending from the seemingly endless Franco-American attacks was a nightmare of heavy bombardments and strong infantry assaults, forcing German *Soldaten* to rely heavily upon the traditional weapons of defence, machine-guns, stick grenades and rifles, as well as their deepest reserves of courage and determination. One soldier who fought here was Paul Ludwig of 2nd Landwehr

Division. His unit may have been only rated 'fourth-class' by American intelligence, but it fought hard. On 13 October, Ludwig wrote to his father:

> Since the 26th we have been in close contact with the Americans, with increasing success and in conditions that require the last bit of resistance and toughness from our men. My boys are doing amazing things – I'm grateful for the stability and lack of weariness of my unit. Our situation, however, by now has a somewhat desperate air – we have honourably fought our way out of the stranglehold of a brave enemy. Since our retreat behind the Aire the regiment has again won some elbow room. We've had a bit of a breather in terms of action, but the quietness is misleading. Our losses, especially the absence of the sick, are especially grave for military reserve formations. Many a good friend of mine has bled. Good fortune has so far prevailed over myself and my company. May it remain that way. The leader of the 3rd Machine Gun Company fell beside me (Second-Lieutenant Fulda), the leader of the 1st was heavily injured. Developments on the inside are promising – however, we get too little information on this. I do not want to comment on the possibilities, especially of a military nature that the next few weeks will bring. We are ready for everything and know that they are prepared to make use of the formations down to the last man. If only the end leads to our salvation.[23]

Ludwig's regiment retreated behind the Aire River on 9 October before finally being relieved eight days later. They entered the battle with twenty-two officers and over 720 NCOs and men, but by the time they were relieved the regiment contained only ten officers and 175 men, a casualty rate of over 70 per cent.

German commanders were particularly concerned about their men's morale, and as the battle wore on there were increasing fears that something was going to give. Between 21 and 30 September, Fifth Army suffered losses of 264 officers and 8,043 other ranks; not as bad as had been feared, but worrying none the less.[24] The commander of 3rd Guard Division, his men fighting desperately at Blanc Mont, complained that 'The heavy losses, the superhuman demands placed on the physical capacities of the men during the past few days, have reduced the combat value of the division, not entirely satisfactory even before employment in lines, to a most dangerous degree. Physically and morally, the troops have now arrived at the extreme limit of their endurance.' The division now had a trench strength of barely 350 men, holding a front of two kilometres.[25] On 28 September, Gallwitz's fellow Army Group commander, Crown Prince Wilhelm, visited his younger brother, Fritz, who was serving with 1st Guards Division:

> I know my brother to be a very brave, intrepid and cool-headed man, and one whose care for his troops was exemplary. He was accustomed to affliction and distress; the First Guards had all the time been posted where things had been about as hot as they could be, at Ypres, in Champagne, at the Somme, the Chemin des Dames, Gorlice, the Argonne. This time I found him changed; he was filled with unutterable bitterness; he saw the end approaching, and, together with his men, fought with the courage of despair.

Fritz's division consisted of only 500 rifles. So bad was the situation that staff officers and their despatch carriers were fighting in the front line with their men. The artillery was worn out, their gunners exhausted, and no reinforcements were likely. The Crown Prince was dismissive of US military abilities ('they showed ignorance of warfare'), but recognized the Americans' great superiority in guns and tanks. Indeed, he even believed that the bombardments which shook the forests of the Argonne 'greatly exceeded in intensity and heaviness anything we had known at Verdun or on the Somme'.[26]

On 29 September, the Commander of Fifth Army, General von der Marwitz, drove to the front to meet some of his divisions. On the way back to his headquarters he took a wounded NCO with him. The man had been shot by the machine-gun of a tank, probably one of the Renaults the Americans were using. Marwitz recalled in his diary:

> The men supposedly retreated in part once the tank appeared (stupid, because that's when they'll really get hit), so he stayed alone and while

'catching up' he was hit by the bullet. Of course he also ran away, perhaps a bit later than the others. 'So, were there any big losses in the company?' 'No, not at all, I was the first one wounded', so it's just the fear of those things and not their actual effect. Time and again you have to tell the men that, and where they are defending themselves it's possible. The American infantry that followed came to a halt (or retreated) immediately in the face of the machine-gun fire. That's what our people and officers now always say, but still the enemy comes slowly creeping closer. I would prefer it if they overestimated the enemy and then beat him anyway. Well, the main thing is that it held.[27]

Marwitz's concern that his men were running away from the enemy tanks may not have always been true – something Colonel Patton would have testified to – but it revealed the fears that haunted senior German officers as the Franco-American attack continued to drive north. As Crown Prince Wilhelm was heard to remark upon visiting the Argonne front, 'How long yet?'

After three days of fighting, the Americans had pushed forward in places up to seven miles, but found themselves in contact with more German forces than they had envisaged; up to six extra divisions were thrown into the line by 28 September.[28] Clair Groover's battalion was still trying to advance northwards and, although Montfaucon had fallen, it encountered familiar problems. The troops 'moved down into the valley and started up the hill on the north side' before being held up 'by a withering fire from machine guns and German artillery'.

Aided by French Whippet Tanks, and a few large tanks, the regiment advanced up the hill toward Montillois. There were direct hits on several of the tanks and put them out of action. On Saturday afternoon I met Captain Edward Howard, Commander of Headquarters Company, on the battlefield. The Germans laid down a barrage with artillery. We took refuge [at the] back of a large tank. There were several direct hits. Captain Howard said, 'Clair isn't this a hell of a place for the father of two boys, to be.' My reply was: 'Right now it is a pretty good place.' We stayed there until the shelling ended. The 313th had advanced to about one mile and a half north of Montfaucon.[29]

Groover's men – 'exhausted from continuous fighting, lack of food and shortage of water' – were finally relieved on the night of 30 September. This was how it went, on and on, back and forth, through shattered woods and pock-marked slopes across the southern edge of the Western Front. Official communiqués to Washington claimed that everything had gone well, and all objectives had been secured, but they could not mask the disappointment that washed over AEF headquarters. Far from resulting in Pershing's beloved 'open warfare', the Battle of Meuse–Argonne was reproducing some of the ghastliest episodes from earlier battles: the Somme, Verdun and Passchendaele. Whether he liked it or not, Pershing was now involved in a brutal attritional slog.

American casualties mounted rapidly. By 30 September, after only four days of combat, US First Army had sustained over 45,000 casualties, seriously imperilling Pershing's grand ambitions for the offensive.[30] The logistical situation, which had been precarious at the beginning of operations, now began to break down; Hunter Liggett gloomily recording that the 'miserable roads began to have their effect on the second day'.[31] The urgent need to relieve the front-line divisions, evacuate the scores of wounded, and restock ammunition and equipment for a renewed push strained First Army almost to breaking point. The few roads in the area and the huge number of troops jammed into the American sector meant much disorganization and chaos occurred – something that George Marshall had foreseen all too clearly. One soldier, Sergeant Hakon Anderson of 107th Ammunition Train, remembered the long days and nights trying to keep the front-line troops supplied, driving up to the front, 'in pouring rain and pitch darkness':

> In the dark we tried to find roads that were no longer there, over grades, around shell holes and booby traps. Never knowing when an enemy shell would make a direct hit, and when it sometimes did it was goodbye for everyone. Ours was the heavy ammunition, 155s. 6 inch, weighing 80 lbs each. You can imagine what an explosion a

truck load would make when hit. Once one of the drivers in my convoy got off to take a short walk to answer the call of nature, and his
truck was hit in his absence.[32]

On the fourth day of the offensive the French Premier, Clemenceau,
had, rather unwisely, decided to take a look for himself and ordered
his chauffeur to drive up to Montfaucon. Needless to say, he did not
reach his destination, but got stuck in massive logjams on the muddy
roads leading up to it. Clemenceau was horrified at the scenes he had
witnessed, complaining bitterly to Foch and muttering darkly about
petitioning the President to replace Pershing.

On 29 September – the day the British would cross the Saint-
Quentin canal – Pershing was forced to suspend active operations in
the Meuse–Argonne. It was a bitter humiliation for a man who had
long been convinced that only his army could unlock the stalemate
on the Western Front. Indeed, it was rapidly becoming clear that a
new approach, new tactics and new objectives would be needed if
Pershing was to prevent his army from getting sucked into the kind
of inconclusive and agonizing attritional struggle that he had long
feared. A report by the Inspector-General of First Army revealed
numerous problems, including a communication breakdown between
units, and a shortage of rifles, gas masks and helmets. A lack of tank
support compounded matters. The offensive had only been allocated
189 light French tanks; within ten days only eighteen were still func-
tioning.[33] Lacking the amount of firepower that the Allies were able
to throw at enemy defences, and the sophisticated logistical system
that supported it, the Americans were forced to rely on their manpower. Yet, as had been proved time and again, throwing men at
barbed wire under fire would not do. This was tough; it made the
Wilderness look like a walk in the park.

10.   'Just one panorama of hell'

It seemed impossible that anyone could come alive through that cyclone of destruction.

Guardsman Frederick Noakes[1]

27–29 September 1918

The battle in the west increased in intensity in the last days of September. It was, in the words of Crown Prince Wilhelm, 'like a vast conflagration that had long smouldered in secret, and that, suddenly getting air, now burst into flame in innumerable places'.[2] The unending rumble of artillery fire could be heard across the front from Flanders to the Meuse. The Allied armies were now face to face with the main German defensive line in the west and on 27 September the second of Foch's sequence of offensives began: a crunching series of attacks that punched towards the key German logistical centre of Cambrai. This would be followed up on 28 September with an attack from Ypres – a place of bitter memory – before Foch's fourth blow landed on the Saint-Quentin canal. If all went well the Germans' hopes of making an indefinite stand on the Western Front would be ended. Their main defensive position would be smashed, their armies in retreat. Finally the road would be open all the way to Berlin.

Sir Arthur Currie, the portly commander of the Canadian Corps, was not, as yet, thinking of Berlin. He was more concerned with how his men were faring, having been placed in one of the most difficult parts of the front, astride the Canal du Nord west of Cambrai, in low-lying, partly flooded ground that was dominated by Bourlon Wood and the German trenches east of the canal (known as the Marquion Line). He knew that if any advance on Cambrai was to be successful this high ground would have to be secured. A day after the Drocourt–Quéant Line was breached, Currie began looking at future operations, rapidly concluding that a frontal attack on the German defences in this sector would be unwise. The canal itself was a serious obstacle. The marshy ground would make progress slow; his men would have to get through defences littered with machine-guns; and they would have to do so while under heavy enfilade fire.³ Eventually Currie came up with a plan, but it would be something of a gamble. Although he had acquired a deserved reputation for thoughtfulness and the care with which his operations were prepared – his policy of 'neglect nothing' – the difficulties he faced in late September forced a less cautious approach.

Currie knew that large sections of the Canal du Nord were filled with water and could not be crossed, but there was a part – about 2,600 yards wide – that was dry because it had not been finished. He ordered two divisions to cross here, and then as soon as they were over this obstacle to fan out north and east and push on through the German defences. The Canadian Corps would usually take up a front-line position of approximately 30,000 yards in width; therefore, what Currie was proposing was remarkable. Half his corps would advance on a fraction of this front across the dry canal, before two more divisions leapfrogged them further into the German defences. The audacity of Currie's plan raised some eyebrows at GHQ. Haig even asked Sir Julian Byng, Third Army commander and someone who knew Currie well, to have a quiet word with the Canadian.

'Do you realise that you are attempting one of the most difficult operations of the war?' asked Byng, when he visited Currie three days before the attack.

Currie looked at him sullenly.

'If anybody can do it, the Canadians can do it, but if you fail,' Byng warned, 'it means home for you.'⁴

Currie understood. He knew the odds and the risks. Because the attacking brigades would be squeezed into a tiny area before Zero Hour, the danger, as always, was that the Germans would somehow find out and shell the assembly positions with high explosive and gas, playing havoc with the men about to go over the top. Nevertheless, Currie's staff were happy with the plan. Everything that could be done was being done. Andrew McNaughton, Currie's counter-battery expert, was authorized to unleash his guns if the Germans shelled his men. Currie was confident that with his battle-hardened and experienced troops, thoroughly acquainted with what they were doing, supported by crack engineering and bridging units, and sheltered by a formidable barrage, all would be well. The attack went in at 5.20 a.m. on a misty, cloudy morning; the horizon lit up with the flashes of British artillery blasting away with crushing intensity. One witness said it was like 'All hell let loose. Heavy guns, smoke screen shells, flaming oil shells and tanks as far as the eye could see were all moving along ahead of us. Just one panorama of hell!'[5] Private Guy Mills would always remember the intensity of the bombardment that morning. 'It was just like a furnace door opening,' he remembered. 'There was nothing but guns, you couldn't hear anything else but guns. You couldn't hear yourself shout.'[6]

Into the smoke and fire the leading waves moved out, in long lines of heavily laden soldiers, bowed down with their equipment, including rifle, ammunition, gas mask, shovel and pick. Lieutenant-Colonel J. W. H. Joliffe, of 4th Canadian Battalion, remembered how 'the Canal du Nord, on the map, looked like a very formidable barrier and we had been provided with, in addition to entrenching tools, shovels and picks and so on . . . in each company, with a number of ladders which were carried forward during the attack and which were supposed to be lowered and raised on either side of the canal after we had crossed it'. The men could not run – the amount of equipment they were carrying precluded anything but the most urgent manoeuvre – but they pressed on as quickly as they could, each following the man in front of him as they closed with the canal – those carrying their ungainly scaling ladders looking like something out of a previous war, perhaps from the great age of sieges in this part of Europe. 'We moved from our jumping-off trenches under a very heavy barrage which certainly kept the Germans under cover,' wrote Joliffe, 'and it was only after we had crossed the Canal du Nord that we encountered any real resistance, mainly machine gun fire which caused a great many casualties but the battalion moved forward on schedule and I believe that we obtained our objective within a few minutes of the time set for us in the attack.'[7]

Joliffe was right; Currie's plan succeeded brilliantly. It was, in many respects, his masterpiece; a triumph of expert preparation, imagination and hard work; of knowing what to do and doing it. The German defenders could do little against such intensive artillery fire, with large shells tearing up their barbed wire entanglements, smashing in dug-outs and bursting over their lines in black explosions. Leutnant Hans Krieghoff of 188 Regiment, occupying the high ground at Bourlon Wood, recalled that 'Each connection with the companies is immediately severed, our runners don't return. Due to the powder fumes and smoke, visibility is zero . . . the enemy artillery fire blocks our rear and the British release their armoured vehicles and tanks upon us, their victims. Infantry columns staggered in-depth followed.'[8] In places the canal walls had been broken down and shattered by the pounding shellfire, so the attackers were able to cross without difficulty, but in other sectors they had to secure bridges where progress was less assured. Nevertheless, Currie's men plunged on into the battle, his divisions fanning out as planned, and pushing their way through the dense network of German trenches and tunnels to the east. Within twelve hours, First Army's line had advanced nearly five miles on a front of nine miles. Four thousand prisoners had been taken and over a hundred guns fell into British and Canadian hands.[9] It was another stunning blow; yet another chunk had been bitten out of the Western Front.

To the south lay Julian Byng's Third Army, which was to extend the attack and continue the push through the Hindenburg Line to the southwest of Cambrai. Apart from on the northern sector, the Canal du Nord would not be a problem – it ran away to the southwest behind Byng's lines – but the British were up against the tough defences of the Hindenburg Line and strongly dug-in German divisions that had been ordered to stay put. There were few tanks available (at least one division had only four machines allotted to it), so Byng relied on his guns to blast his infantry on to their objectives.[10] Although Third Army did not achieve a breakthrough, it gained ground and chewed up more German divisions, as had been Haig's plan. But it was not easy. 27 September 1918 would be one of the toughest days in the history of the Western Front. Haig's armies won seven Victoria Crosses that day – a fitting tribute to the tenacity of German resistance and the need for courage and determination of the highest order. Two of the most extraordinary acts of valour were undertaken by Captain Cyril Frisby and Lance Corporal Thomas Jackson of 1/Coldstream Guards for their actions on the Canal du Nord. Frisby, who commanded No. 2 Company, was detailed to take the canal crossing on the Demicourt–Graincourt road. The attack went in, only to founder in the face of what his citation called 'annihilating machine-gun fire' from a strongpoint known as Mouse Post. Realizing that unless it was captured, the attack would fail, Frisby gathered three volunteers, including Jackson, and climbed down the canal. Here the bank was dry so they were able to cross, but they had to do so under intense enemy fire. Frisby and Jackson stormed the machine-gun position, killed its occupants and secured the position. Sadly Jackson was killed later that day: typically while leading an attack into an enemy trench. Both men would be awarded the Victoria Cross.[11]

Heavy resistance was to be found not only at Graincourt. To the south, the area around Gouzeaucourt and Beaucamp – which lay in front of the Hindenburg Support Line – was quickly gaining an infamous reputation. The trenches in this sector were close together, interlocking in certain places with the German line lying along a series of ridges. They were held by the *Jäger* Division, which had occupied Gouzeaucourt on 12 September, and was one of the best German units in the field.[12] The attack had been entrusted to Major-General John Ponsonby's 5th Division, which was to take a number of enemy trenches before pushing off towards the village of Beaucamp. This would secure the high ground, break the back of any German resistance, and allow Third Army to close with Cambrai. The attack went in behind the standard creeping barrage, but German defensive fire proved too great. Few accounts have survived from those who took part in the attack, but the horror of what happened can be imagined. According to the divisional report, 'owing to the intensity of enemy machine-gun fire from AFRICAN TRENCH and SMUT TRENCH, which the enemy were holding very strongly, the 1/Royal West Kents were only able to get forward a short distance'. Corporal Piggott distinguished himself by rallying his men, and, although wounded, led them to within twenty yards of the German line. But this was as far as they got, and they were hounded out of their gains by showers of stick grenades as the Germans counter-attacked. All company officers of the attacking battalions became casualties. The tanks could offer little support. The four machines supporting the brigade appeared to start well, but soon attracted the attention of German machine-guns and artillery batteries. Very quickly all were put out of action: one fell into a trap and caught fire; another ditched in the sunken road; one was hit by an anti-tank gun; and another had engine trouble and had to return to the rear.[13]

For my great-uncle Tom Cotterill's battalion, 15/Royal Warwick-shire Regiment, it was an equally bleak story. Ever since the British guns had opened up, intermittent enemy shellfire had been falling on their trenches, unsettling the troops waiting to attack, showering them with dirt and sometimes causing casualties. It soon became evident that, in this sector at least, the defenders were alert, aware and very much determined to stay put. As soon as the Warwicks went over the top, they were immediately held up by heavy fire and made little progress, machine-gun and rifle fire scything through the attacking lines with deadly effect. One company managed to enter the German trenches but, as had occurred elsewhere, they could not hold on to their gains for long. In what was called 'a noteworthy act of courage', Sergeant T. J. Jones led a bombing party in repeated attempts to get forward, managing to cause 'heavy casualties' to the enemy.

> All the men of Sergeant Jones' party were wounded, but this NCO continued to bomb the enemy alone until his supply of bombs was exhausted. He then came back and organised a second party and placing himself as first bayonet man of the party, succeeded in penetrating the enemy's position and scattering an enemy bombing party which he forced to withdraw.[14]

Jones was subsequently awarded the Military Medal. Further to the north, 14/Royal Warwicks managed to capture some ground, but were, similarly, bombed out of their position. 15 Brigade experienced better luck, however, by securing Beaucamp village and holding it against repeated counter-attacks.

As dawn broke over the Western Front – a miserable, grey, chilly day – it was apparent that progress had been achieved, but at a cost. Third Army secured most of its objectives, but remained short of its final line, having to advance over difficult ground against some of the best units in the German Army.[15] By 4 p.m. precise information on the location of Major-General Ponsonby's brigades was unavailable, but he knew 13 Brigade had encountered heavy resistance and suffered many casualties. Despite the considerable losses, Ponsonby wanted to press the attack. He instructed his reserve unit, 95 Brigade, to push on through to the main German line (known as African Trench) as soon as possible. Orders were issued, but because not all the battalions received them, the night witnessed disjointed and unsuccessful attacks, and much heavy fighting, with the gas shelling of Gouzeaucourt Wood and the approaches to the front line doing much to disorganize the reliefs of units from the front.[16] Fighting continued throughout the night and it was only by noon on 28 September that all the objectives of the previous day were in British hands, the remnants of the *Jäger* Division having withdrawn in the darkness. 15/Royal Warwickshire Regiment reported Smut Trench clear and patrols pushed forward into African Trench, finding groups of German wounded, some British prisoners, ten machine-guns, and many boxes of ammunition.[17]

Despite the fall of African Trench and Gouzeaucourt, it had been a sobering day for 5th Division. It was not until the evening that a battery officer, Arthur Impey, found out how the attack had progressed. A runner told him that the 'Huns' had broken through and 'our fellows' were running. Although this information was incorrect – the runner had a 'bad wind up' – he later received confirmation that the 'Huns had got back in African Trench', a position to which, as Impey conceded, 'they seem to attach an extraordinary importance'.[18] In 15/Royal Warwickshire, three officers had been killed, one was lying mortally wounded, and five others had been hit. Thirty-six other ranks were dead, ninety were wounded and twenty-nine others missing.[19] By the afternoon, the brigade's front was a mess with the wounded from the Regimental Aid Post 'coming in quicker than they could be dealt with and evacuated'. Much good work was done by the men of the field ambulance who 'arranged for the carrying of stretcher cases over 1½ miles of broken and hilly ground which owing to the wet had become very slippery, and at the same time under heavy shell fire organized a squad from parties of German prisoners to help in evacuating the wounded'. In terms of senior officers, 27 September was one of the worst days in the battalion's history: Major P. C. Edwards, the second-in-command, was killed and Captain E. F. Ball, the Padre, was wounded. Edwards died after coming under heavy shelling at the battalion headquarters, which was situated at the aptly named 'Dead Man's Corner', a clump of trees lying along a sunken road on the Beaucamp Ridge.[20]

It may have been scant consolation for the battered ranks of 15/Warwicks, but the enemy had it no easier. For the German armies in the west, 27 September was another harrowing day of seemingly endless Allied attacks, always preceded by those crushing bombardments that tore up the ground and made it seem like a sinister, flickering thunder was playing across the landscape. To stand firm against such a metal onslaught took incredible amounts of courage and resilience. Ernst Kielmayer, a German gunner with 26th Reserve Division at Cambrai, recorded in his diary the experience of coming under sustained British bombardment, including a direct hit. Three men were 'torn apart beyond recognition' and another was buried by earth, but fortunately dug out alive. 'O Lord, what a Monday morning!' he wrote.

> I am firing on gun no. 4 all day long. In between we picked up the pieces of bone and flesh, and put them in a box. I marked them with a red pencil, my companion at all times . . . so the cemetery official will know . . ., as their metal plates with names and rank could not be found. Try to pick up three heads, six arms, and feet and whatever else there is left from your friends.

Kielmayer was understandably traumatized by his experiences. 'If that is how three of us die,' he wrote, 'I hope their families will never find out.' The following day his battery was back in action. They fired 200 shells ('the barrel gets red hot') but ran out of ammunition, and had to defend their position with rifles and pistols. Fortunately, they were able to withdraw after reinforcements moved up.[21]

The situation facing German commanders was extremely difficult. General von Boehn, whose Army Group faced the bulk of British strength, could do little. Aerial reconnaissance of the enemy lines was impossible owing to the limitations of the German Air Force, while his defence was 'very much impaired' by the weak and exhausted state of his divisions. In Second Army, he reckoned that there were only three divisions completely fit for action. In Eighteenth Army there was only one.[22] His subordinates tried to be optimistic. General von Carlowitz (Marwitz's replacement at Second Army) reported to the Supreme Command his pride in the tenacity of his divisions. 'Today the army has held all its positions against heavy enemy attacks,' he wrote. 'It is evacuating Gouzeaucourt, which it has bravely defended, only by order. I desire to express my deep appreciation to the brave defenders, particularly to the German Jaeger Division and the 84th Infantry of the 54th Infantry Division, whose superb achievements I have reported to the Supreme Headquarters by name.'[23] Indeed, the defence of Gouzeaucourt had been exceptional; another example, if any was needed, of the tenacity that some German units still possessed.

The British may not have made rapid advances – certainly when compared with the rush at Amiens – but the struggle in front of Cambrai was an indication of how important this sector was and how hard the Germans were fighting for it. Third Army faced thirteen enemy divisions, including some excellent units such as the *Jäger*, 6th Cavalry and 3rd (Naval) Divisions, all of which had reputations for tenacity and determination, and had been specially moved in to head off the British attacks in this sector. The only problem was that the German Army had a limited (and rapidly dwindling) number of such units that could be sent to the threatened fronts, and in order to hold the crucial Cambrai–Saint-Quentin line Ludendorff had been forced to thin out other parts of the front. To the north lay Flanders and the plain of Belgium and it was here that German reserves were at their thinnest, having been sent south in the preceding weeks. For the exhausted survivors of the attacks on 27 September, the results of their efforts may have seemed meagre, but the Western Front was crumbling. Ludendorff might be able to hold the centre, but he could not hold the flanks. On the following morning, 28 September, the Allies attacked at Ypres, and finally, this time, they broke through.

The front in Flanders was held by the German Fourth Army and although heavily outnumbered by the combined Belgian, British and French forces — about six divisions to ten — it occupied what high ground there was, and lay behind a wilderness of shell holes and waterlogged fields that had been fought over so intensely the previous year.[24] Like most of the German Army, Fourth Army was now manned by a motley collection of teenagers and older veterans who all hoped that the battle, raging to the south, would pass them by. But it was not to be. At 2.30 a.m., in the blackness of a wet night, German sentries, peering out from beneath their heavy steel helmets across the wasteland in front of them, were rocked by a thunderous bombardment that suddenly burst upon them, lighting up the darkness as if the sky had been ripped apart. What they were witnessing were the opening salvos of a three-hour preliminary bombardment that signalled the beginning of the Fourth Battle of Ypres, when Allied forces, spearheaded by General Sir Herbert Plumer's Second British Army, broke out of the salient where so much blood had been spilled since 1914.

The day that followed saw some of the most dramatic gains of the war. Plumer's forces — split into four corps from Armentières to Ypres — with Belgian divisions on their left, pushed forward behind their creeping barrage and gained much ground. Despite the difficult conditions, and tough resistance in places (particularly in Houthulst forest, which was simply a 'nest of cannons, machine guns and devices of every kind'), the German position in Flanders crumbled with alarming speed, and within hours 6,000 prisoners were being shepherded to the rear.[25] Major Carl Degelow, commander of *Jagdstaffel* 40 at Lille, was woken by the sound of artillery fire that morning, and soon became aware that something very bad had happened.

> Drowsily I rub my eyes, searching my thoughts just to catch the military bearing of the still tired body that is enjoying a state of equilibrium in which reality is surrounded by a dream-like presence.

The barrage increases in intensity, the windows clatter and the wooden barracks that serve as our shelter vibrate to the tune of this hellish music hitting us from the front. That which apparently registers as cold on the senses in this twilight condition is no figment of the imagination, no illusion.

The drumfire continued throughout the day ('muzzle flashes of the heavy artillery blaze across the front like bolts of lightning') as the rain, a fine grey drizzle, came down incessantly. In such poor weather, it was impossible to fly so Degelow and his men haunted the mess, dressed in their flying suits, drinking endless cups of tea. For his compatriots in their trenches, there would be little support from the air that day.[26]

Ludendorff spent 28 September at Spa following his usual routine: poring over maps of the front, ringing around his commanders, asking them what units they had available and telling them where they should be deployed. One of those who saw him at this time described him as like 'a cat on hot bricks'.[27] But no matter how much energy he commanded with, no matter how many telephone calls he made, or how many telegrams he dashed off, the front seemed to be on the verge of collapse. The heavy British attacks around Cambrai and the crossing of the Canal du Nord were bad enough, but now his northern flank had been broken and there seemed little in the way to prevent the Allies from liberating all of Belgium. It was at this point that something in him snapped. The previously manic commander, who had planned and conducted Germany's military operations since 1916 with an iron determination and unquenchable thirst for victory, just seemed to give up. At 6 p.m. that day, as news came in of the collapse in Flanders, he shuffled in to see Hindenburg and told him that an armistice offer must now be made. Hindenburg, getting up from his desk to greet his colleague, recorded years later that 'I could see in his face what had brought him to me.'[28] Reluctantly, he agreed with Ludendorff's appreciation of the situation. Even if the Western Front could be held, the disasters elsewhere meant that Germany's position would only deteriorate. Her allies were falling away. The situation in the homeland teetered on the brink of revolution. Yet there was still time to get something out of negotiations. 'Our one task now,'

Ludendorff said, banging the table with his fist, 'was to act definitely and firmly, without delay.'

Ludendorff's *volte face* was a dramatic moment – one of the most dramatic of the war. He would later claim that he came to this conclusion 'bit by bit', 'from the beginning of August onwards and through many hard inward struggles', but there were rumours that he had collapsed in his office, suffering some kind of nervous breakdown, clawing at this throat and foaming at the mouth.[29] His psychiatrist, Dr Hochheimer, who had been pleased at the apparent improvement in Ludendorff's condition during September, wrote cryptically to his wife on 28 September that 'It storms at Ludendorff from all sides.' Hochheimer always denied that his patient had suffered some kind of collapse, but it remains difficult to be certain of anything at this time, particularly given his fragile mental and emotional condition. When he saw Ludendorff a week later he noted that 'although the world is collapsing in ruins all around him', he was 'relaxed, released, redeemed and is breathing and sleeping again'. On 5 October, he saw Ludendorff for the last time. Sitting on his bed, the general 'spoke to him about the most darkly concealed part of his soul, his dismal loneliness'. Hochheimer found him 'secretive and mistrustful, full of bad experiences with people, yet physically, he is once again fresher and healthier and likely to live longer than anyone'.[30]

The breakthrough in Flanders seems to have been the point at which Ludendorff's will broke. Whether he had collapsed is impossible to say, but his inability to remedy Germany's dire situation – one that he was, in part, responsible for – produced some kind of nervous breakdown. Mendaciously as ever, he lambasted the failure of Germany's diplomats to make any progress in bringing the war to an end after the council meetings of 13–14 August – despite concealing the truth as best he could. Therefore, he reasoned, it was up to him to take the necessary measures. He wanted to make some kind of approach, directly, to President Wilson. The American may have been derided, but he was likely to favour what some called a 'peace of justice'; in other words allowing Germany to keep some of her territorial gains in the east. Pride and vanity prevented the Quartermaster-General from contacting Marshal Foch directly – he hated the little Frenchman with a passion – so it was obvious that their hopes lay with Wilson. There may have also been a belief that by contacting the President, fissures between the Allies could be opened, thus allowing Germany more room to manoeuvre. Wilson was someone they had long scoffed at and ridiculed but who now held the fate of Germany in his hands.

For Hindenburg, there was no dissent. He did not quarrel with Ludendorff or tell him to pull himself together; he simply accepted that if his friend and colleague believed an appeal must be made, then there was little use in prolonging the inevitable. It was a moment that the 'wooden titan' had long dreaded, but he recognized that anything was preferable to the complete destruction of the Army, which was now looking increasingly possible. Like Ludendorff, he hoped for armistice conditions that would allow them to evacuate occupied territory quickly and then, if peace terms were harsh, resume hostilities on the German border. There was something touchingly sentimental – romantic even – about their faith in an Allied response that would be a kind of grand sporting gesture, allowing them to break off contact in the west and then resume fighting when it suited them. These two hard, stony-faced Prussians, men who had subjugated Eastern Europe and western Russia and bled Belgium and eastern France dry, now expected mercy and understanding from their enemy. 'The Field Marshal and I parted with a firm handshake,' wrote Ludendorff, 'like men who have buried their dearest hopes, and who are resolved to hold together in the hardest hours of human life as they had held together in success.'[31]

Paul von Hintze, the Secretary of State, whom Ludendorff had called to Spa several days earlier, held a conference at ten o'clock the following morning, 29 September. Hintze made it clear that any appeal to Wilson would have to be followed by immediate political reform – a kind of 'revolution from above' as he called it – something that Ludendorff was naturally horrified by, but which Hintze stressed was absolutely essential. 'Revolution was standing at our door,' he argued 'and we had the choice of meeting it with a dictatorship or concessions.'[32] Hintze had a much clearer appreciation of the political situation back home, something that Hindenburg and

Ludendorff had long ignored, so it was essential that certain steps be taken by forming a new parliamentary government, bringing in the Socialist and Independent parties, and by appointing a new chancellor. When the Kaiser was told he said nothing, receiving the news with the 'utmost calm'. He issued instructions that peace should be sued for without delay and that preparations must be made for the evacuation of the Belgian coast. Then everyone went to the Kaiser's villa (the Château de la Fraineuse, a short walk from the Hôtel Britannique) for lunch; 'everyone tried to be nonchalant', one witness recorded. 'They did not succeed.'[33]

Despite the lack of a breakthrough in the Argonne, Foch's plan was succeeding perfectly; indeed it was surpassing even his expectations. There was only one question left: could the Allies cross the Saint-Quentin canal and get through the Hindenburg Line?

11. The Tomb of the German World Empire

In five weeks you'll have peace, though you swine don't deserve it!

Note dropped over German lines by a British pilot, 30 September 1918[1]

29 September–5 October 1918

Like a boxer who seeks to land the knockout punch, the Allied armies continued jabbing away at the German line, keeping the enemy under remorseless pressure. On the day that von Hintze arrived in Spa, the fourth part of Foch's sequence of offensives began – the assault on the main Hindenburg system along the Saint-Quentin canal. The preliminary bombardment had opened on 26 September and over the next three days a carefully planned shoot with every available gun fired over 750,000 shells into the German lines. It was a devastating illustration of the firepower now available to Haig's armies. Barbed wire entanglements were targeted by thousands of shells – including many armed with the new 106-type fuse that allowed for instantaneous detonation – while heavy guns methodically and mercilessly searched out enemy gun positions, the roads and tracks leading to the front, and other areas of concentration. Thousands of newly arrived gas shells were also thrown into the mix, deluging dug-outs and bunkers with 30,000 rounds of mustard gas and making the lives of the German defenders utterly miserable. Indeed, those who had hoped the Hindenburg Line, with its miles of bunkers and acres of concrete, would be a place of safety and refuge were to be disappointed. Far from being an unbreakable bastion, this last line of defence was fast becoming an anvil upon which the remaining German armies would be broken.

Unbeknown to the Supreme Command, Fourth Army staff had got their hands on a complete plan of the German defences. The documents had originally been stored at a corps headquarters at

Framerville on the Amiens battlefield and had been captured by an enterprising member of the Royal Tank Corps, Lieutenant Ernest Rollings, on 8 August.[2] Quickly realizing the importance of the files, they were sent to Fourth Army HQ and pored over by Rawlinson's staff, who were amazed at the completeness of the find. Now they knew where every trench and barbed wire entanglement was; the position of every artillery and infantry headquarters; the location of every battery (including its calibre and observation post); map references of divisional sectors and supply dumps, billets and camps; accommodation for men and horses; and communication and electric power installations.[3] With this information Fourth Army fine-tuned its bombardment to make sure it hit every key point again and again, destroying, neutralizing, and rendering useless the elaborate defences in front of it. For the German defenders, supplies had only arrived intermittently, if at all, since the bombardment had begun. I Bavarian Corps, holding the front southeast of Bellicourt, reported that 'heavy harassing fire of all calibres is continuously falling on the north half of the corps sector, particularly on rear areas, rear villages, canal crossings, and approaches'.[4] In the garrison, morale was poor, the food was terrible, and there was little hope of either reinforcement or relief. For those battalions sheltering in the dank Bellicourt tunnel, the booming of the shelling shook the nerves and tried the patience. The weather was poor, with rain, low cloud and mist, which obscured the skies and prevented aircraft from operating, leaving the defenders in a kind of isolated Hell, anxiously awaiting the inevitable end, which would come at dawn on 29 September.

The night before the attack was predictably tense. On the other side of the line not much could be seen through the thick, grey fog, but the occasional shell could be heard. British artillery had spent the night simulating 'normal activity' so as not to arouse any special concerns, every so often shelling well-known concentration areas. The German artillery responded fitfully, giving what one observer called 'a hush of expectancy' over the battlefield, and leaving those men who would be going over the top at Zero Hour a little time with their own thoughts. Some tried to sleep, but most could not. Officers studied their trench maps, NCOs repeated warnings to their men not to bunch up in no-man's-land, and soldiers cleaned their weapons. Whatever they were doing, all shivered in their muddy forming-up trenches and wondered what the day would bring. For one witness, 'We had to lay there all night and worry . . . it is impossible to describe the feeling a man has with that in front of him. I always said I knew how a man felt that was condemned to die, for we all thought that was our last night. We thought of our families and the ones we loved.'[5] And then at 4.50 a.m., in a dim, misty dawn, the bombardment began, the flashes of hundreds of guns lighting up the sky as a torrent of shells flew towards the German lines. Perhaps with a sense of relief, now that the waiting was finally over, the assaulting formations exited their trenches and stalked out into the darkness, following the creeping barrage that would escort them through the German positions, the dull roar of shells exploding in front of them like the distant crash of surf.

It would be a day of hard fighting, with German units trying desperately to maintain their hold on the canal and equally intensive efforts to push them off. Attached to Fourth Army was Herbert Read's II US Corps, which had been brought in to spearhead the attack. Unfortunately, the men got bogged down in the high ground around Gillemont Farm, which overlooked the canal, and ran into fierce resistance, heavy shelling and regular counter-attacks.[6] One of the combat engineers detailed to help the tanks get through in this sector was Walter J. Strauss (attached to 27th US Division), whose squad was to hunt for anti-tank mines. 'They were round,' he remembered, 'about 10" with a short fuse sticking to one side, the top of which was even with the ground level so that when the tank rolled over it, the fuse would ignite the mine.' Here the Hindenburg position was protected by 'an extraordinary mass of wire' and the trenches west of the canal had been 'perfected with dugouts, concrete machine-gun and mortar emplacements and underground shelters. They were protected by belt after belt of barbed wire entanglements, in a fashion which no-one understood better or achieved more thoroughly than the Germans.' Strauss was fortunate to survive his perilous work, which consisted of sticking his bayonet into the ground and rummaging around until he found something. At one point a sudden rain of shells forced him to dive into a shell hole. As Strauss jumped in, he felt 'a thud in my side'. He found, to his amazement, that a machine-gun bullet had pierced his backpack and lodged into his copy of the New Testament. 'A quarter of an inch to the right would have punctured my lung and I would have died quickly,' he later admitted.[7]

As the battle wore on, the lack of a breakthrough became increasingly worrying. Monash, who had a reputation as a calm and methodical commander, even lost his temper with his aides, frustrated at the slow progress of the attacking divisions. During the morning, the liaison officer, Paul Maze, entered an American dugout to find out what was going on.

> The muggy atmosphere outside made the deep dug-out absolutely stifling. At a table sat a Colonel and two staff officers, in stiff jackets with high collars facing a map at which the Colonel kept glancing through tortoise-shell glasses attached to a silk cord, which he kept putting on and taking off his big nose. They had no news of their attacking regiments. 'Waal,' he drawled adjusting his glasses, 'I have no news yet of how the boys have gotton [sic] on, but they went over at scheduled time, and I am confident that they have done their dooty [sic].'

Maze was unimpressed, knowing from experience that no news often meant bad news. He expressed his surprise to the colonel and suggested that he should go and try to find out what was happening. When Maze left the dug-out, he saw groups of soldiers returning from the front. He got on his motorbike and drove over to them, finding stragglers coming back without any officers, most of whom, they said, had been killed. Barking orders, Maze got them to stay where they were and place their machine-guns to face the enemy, while ordering the rest to rejoin the battle, which they did. Pleased with his work, Maze returned to the dug-out shortly afterwards, only to find that it had been heavily shelled in his absence, 'shattered as if by an earthquake'. Three corpses – a sentry and two officers – were lying together covered by a sack. Maze stepped into what remained of the dug-out and found the colonel, sitting alone, mopping his brow. The man looked up at him and said, with a sigh, 'Say, Captain, this certainly is war.'[8]

Had the difficulties encountered by the Americans been replicated across the front then Fourth Army's attack would have been deemed an expensive failure and, more likely than not, cost Rawlinson his job. It would be redeemed, however, only in the south, where Lieutenant-General Sir Walter Braithwaite's IX Corps faced the canal at the village of Bellenglise. And it was here, of all the sectors of the front, where the Hindenburg Line would be breached. Braithwaite had assigned his main attack to 46th (North Midland) Division, but few of its officers thought it would be possible. Major H. J. C. Marshall, who served with the North Midlanders, had returned from leave only a few days previously and found his divisional headquarters a gloomy place. Although morale was generally high, there was no doubt in the minds of the divisional staff that the main attack was to be delivered on their left by the Americans and Australians. That meant that their task would be what he called a 'sacrificial stunt'. 'At the best we might get a foothold on the further bank of the canal, but at a cost which would leave us no longer a fighting force. The division was indeed well used to these affairs, having in past years been given attacks to carry out across belts of uncut wire, in which it had suffered severely.' The divisional headquarters busied itself with getting everything ready for the attack, including making sure bridging supplies were available to cross the canal. If that failed, it was suggested that the infantry would just have to swim, so a lorry-load of life belts was taken from the cross-Channel ferries at Boulogne. Nobody wanted to do it, but it just had to be done.[9]

Undeterred, the division attacked an hour later than the Americans, pushing forward quickly behind the barrage, desperately hoping to be upon the enemy before they knew what hit them. Marshall was in the first wave. Under cover of 'a cyclone of shells' his company dashed to the nearest enemy trench only to find a hundred dead bodies 'mostly from the fire of the 800 machine-guns, which had been arranged to rake these trenches immediately the attack commenced'. As at Amiens, the darkness and mist of the first few hours masked much of what went on, making it difficult to maintain direction, yet also blinding German observers. Indeed, the fog was so thick that one of Marshall's friends, Captain Percy Teeton, 'was much disgusted to find that he had swum across the canal, in ice-cold water, while a tiny footbridge existed within ten yards of him which had been invisible owing to the mist'.[10] In this sector it was essential not just to cross the canal, but also to secure the road bridge at Riqueval that supplied German positions on the western bank. This task had been assigned to a party of nine men under the command of Captain A. H. Charlton of 1/6th North Staffordshire Regiment. According to Private George Waters (who was in Charlton's company):

> The bombardment was terrific as we went forward at 5.50 a.m. in a mist that started coming down. The companies had been told to move forward quickly. Captain Charlton [of] 'B' Company had to use his compass to get to the bridge. The men were on top of the Germans before they knew what was happening. A corporal, Crutchley, suddenly came to a German machine gun post protecting the bridge and he shot the German crew down before they could get their guns into action.[11]

The defenders had placed explosive charges on the bridge and were preparing for demolition when Charlton's men turned up. Waters remembered that 'The Germans at the other side of the bridge apparently heard the firing and two or three of them came forward to fire the charge to the mine which had been fixed on the bridge. Before they could get to it they were all shot down by Corporal Crutchley.' With their bayonets fixed, B Company stormed across the bridge and started cutting all the charges they could find; doing everything they could to make sure that the bridge was not destroyed. Elsewhere the attack was also succeeding and men in life jackets were splashing their way across the canal, all the while under shells and machine-gun fire, and no doubt cursing the Kaiser all the way to the far bank. Within three hours the first and second objectives had been secured and over 5,000 prisoners were making their way to the rear. It had been a brilliant success. Rawlinson and Monash, anxiously awaiting news in their headquarters, were thrilled.[12]

By 6 p.m. it was growing dark. Fighting continued on most sectors, but in other areas relieved and exhausted British, Australian and American soldiers could remove their helmets, wipe their brows, and survey the scene. The detritus of war lay everywhere. Dead German and Allied soldiers lay in clumps across the front, *feldgrau* and khaki-clad bodies lying together on the shell-smashed ground that was littered with lost equipment, body parts, fragments of shell and spent cartridges. In the canal sector, corpses bobbed in the murky waters. For the scattered German units along the front – belonging to 51 Army Corps and IV Reserve Corps of Second Army – it had been a day of confused, somewhat inconclusive, fighting. The thick fog had masked much of the attackers' preparations and meant that the infantry's warning flares were not seen by their supporting batteries, leaving them to face the attack alone. Nevertheless, there was no dramatic collapse of German resistance on 29 September. Second Army may have been pushed off the canal, but its units fought with remarkable determination. Numerous tanks were taken out by concealed anti-tank guns and elite machine-gun teams had caused scores of British, American and Australian casualties as they crouched in their rifle pits and shell holes and tore into the advancing lines.[13] Indeed, when 46th Division counted up the spoils of war after the battle, it collected over 1,000 German machine-guns, with as many as six in each shell hole. In this chaotic battle, with such an intensity of rifle, machine-gun and shellfire tearing the air apart, it is little wonder that casualties on both sides were heavy. At that time it did not feel much like a victory and several more days would elapse before this sector was, in military parlance, 'mopped up'. Nevertheless, as the Allied soldiers tried to find some rest or shelter from the persistent shellfire, some would have noted with a smile when enemy artillery began pounding their long-evacuated forming-up trenches. The Germans, it seemed, had no idea Fourth Army had established itself on the canal.[14]

Several weeks later, His Majesty King George V would visit the tunnels at Bellenglise and pay tribute to the Midlanders who had stormed this great rampart of the German defences. It was somewhat fitting, poetic perhaps, that it should fall to 46th Division to cross the Saint-Quentin canal and break the Hindenburg Line. Its officers had thought their mission was a 'sacrificial stunt', but pressed on regardless with professionalism and good humour. It was not an elite unit; it was not a member of the powerful Canadian or Australian Corps; it was not even a fashionable British division. It was, on the contrary, a provincial Territorial division from the shires of England that had been present at some of the worst disasters of British arms on the Western Front.[15] That the division managed to rebuild and become a competent fighting unit was testament to the abilities and hard work of its men and officers. Major Marshall never went back into the tunnel; he had seen too much death and horror in that gloomy, dark place to ever want to venture there again.

> Streamers of the dry-rot fungus, descended from roof to floor, in six foot pendants. The timber supports appeared to be in imminent danger of collapse, and the weird aspect of the caverns, viewed by a flickering candle, made me chary of venturing very far into their dismal recesses. The very airs which came from them, dank and tainted by the fungus breath, seemed fitting to this tomb in which were interred the hope of the German World Empire.[16]

Here, in a dank tunnel north of Saint-Quentin, the dream of German victory ended. If the Great War was anything, it was a war of surprises.

The Hindenburg Line may have been pierced, but it took British and French forces several days of hard fighting to clear the deep belt of German defences that lay in front of them. By 1 October the furious attacks launched by Haig's troops were slowing down. The usual factors were to blame: growing disorganization and lack of planning; stubborn enemy resistance; and logistical delays, which meant there would have to be a pause before pushing forward again. Casualties were not as heavy as had been feared, but units were worn down quickly in such intensive combat. After four days of brutal fighting, having outrun its supplies and beaten off innumerable counterattacks, the Canadian Corps was exhausted. Sir Arthur Currie reflected in his diary: 'Today we met nine German Divisions and must have inflicted very heavy casualties on the Boche. The Artillery never fired as much ammunition as today and many of the targets were fired on over open sights . . . The Germans have fought us here very, very hard, and when it is considered that this is one of their most important strategic flanks the reason for the violence of their counter-attacks can be appreciated.' Currie estimated that since 8 August his corps had engaged forty-seven German divisions and captured 450 guns. It was little wonder its men thought of themselves as elite troops.[17]

On 1 October, after a risky and somewhat perilous approach march over pontoon bridges that had been hastily erected across the Saint-Quentin canal, Wilfred Owen's battalion, 2/Manchesters, went into action. Its mission was to break through what was known as the Beaurevoir–Fonsomme Line – essentially the Hindenburg reserve line – a position that the battered German defenders had been told to hold at all costs. The ground in this area was open and broken with trenches and rifle pits, with scattered wire lying about. They had to move south of the village of Joncourt and take the German lines that lay along the ridge to the east. The battalion went over the top at 4 p.m. and, covered by the usual creeping barrage, managed to achieve its objectives and get astride the ridge. Nevertheless, resistance had been fierce and a further attack on the next village, Ramicourt, by 16/Lancashire Fusiliers, was unsuccessful and with that the attack bogged down. The few tanks that had been in support had been stopped – suffering the usual fate of being knocked out by German guns – and the tired, wet soldiers had to hold on, retrieving their gas masks as the inevitable retaliation of mustard gas shelling began.[18]

For Owen the experience was what he called 'sheer', and he would write to both his mother and Siegfried Sassoon of his endeavours, for which he would be awarded the Military Cross. During the day his company commander had been wounded and Owen had taken charge, successfully beating off several ferocious counter-attacks and capturing a machine-gun position, where he shot an enemy soldier with his revolver. 'It passed the limits of my Abhorrence,' he boasted to his mother. 'I lost all my earthly faculties, and fought like an angel.' More details were provided in a letter of 8 October.

All one day (after the battle) we could not move from a small trench, though hour by hour the wounded were groaning just outside. Three stretcher-bearers who got up were hit, one after one. I had to order no one to show himself after that, but remembering my own duty, and remembering also my forefathers the agile Welshmen of the Mountains I scrambled out myself and felt an exhilaration in baffling the Machine Guns by quick bounds from cover to cover. After the shells we had been through, and the gas, bullets were like the gentle rain from heaven.[19]

Owen may have been pleased at his performance, and aware of how useful his MC would be after the war, but he was left shattered by the loss of his servant, Jones, who was shot in the head while crouching next to him, and whose blood soaked Owen's uniform.

That day news arrived that 15/Royal Warwickshire Regiment, the battalion that had suffered so heavily in the attack at Gouzeau-court three days earlier, was to be disbanded. On 28 September the battalion – or what was left of it – had marched back to the village of Ytres, where it entered divisional reserve. Unfortunately, as it was leaving the trenches it got caught in a vicious mustard gas bombardment that caused heavy casualties, including the CO, Lieutenant-Colonel Miller, and his Adjutant, Major Wilmot. The Medical Officer and his staff were also incapacitated. Rumours about the possible reorganization of the division had been circulating for some time, and now, with manpower at a premium, there was a growing recognition that it would make sense to ditch some battalions and use the men to bolster the remaining units. Major Wilmot had initially been told by his brigadier that 'One battalion has to go, but I promise you it won't be yours.' Perhaps in response to the loss of almost the entire battalion headquarters staff, it was decided that, contrary to what Wilmot had been told, the battalion should go. When Wilmot was in hospital, he was visited by a staff officer from brigade, who told him that after a final inspection on 4 October the men of the battalion would be transferred to 14 and 16/Royal Warwickshire battalions.[20]

15/Royal Warwickshire was not the only battalion to be disbanded in the first days of October. Manpower was now stretched so thinly throughout the BEF that a number of battalions were being wound up and the men sent to reinforce other units. It was an unsatisfactory and unsettling thing to happen to soldiers who had grown to love their battalion, to feel at home with its ranks, and who felt they had done their time. To be suddenly moved into another unit, to be thrust into a new battalion with strange officers and unfamiliar routines, was a difficult and sometimes frustrating experience. Henry Wilson's warnings to Haig about sustaining heavy losses at the Hindenburg Line may have annoyed the Commander-in-Chief, but they were a sensible and realistic appreciation of how exhausted the British were becoming. If the war continued at this intensity for much longer, Haig would be forced to disband more than single battalions – entire divisions would have to go. It was no wonder that many in the War Cabinet in London, including the Minister of Munitions, Winston Churchill, were planning for 1919 on the assumption that hundreds, if not thousands, of tanks and aeroplanes, and the mass employment of poison gas, would be required to offset the shortages of men that would increasingly afflict the British and French Armies.

Foch visited Haig's headquarters the day after Fourth Army had crossed the Saint-Quentin canal. Haig was keen to keep pushing, but knew how tired his divisions were becoming. Debeney's First Army had not attacked on 29 September, only supporting Rawlinson's attack with artillery fire and the long-range shelling of German positions, leading to some unkind mutterings that the French were 'hanging back' when they should be attacking vigorously. Foch agreed and ordered Debeney to capture Saint-Quentin immediately. Although French patrols occupied its streets on 1 October, they went little further, with strong resistance from German rearguards on the canal slowing their advance.[21] Other French forces were on the move to the southeast, but, as in the previous month, they were generally confined to following up retreating enemy forces and conducting small-scale operations. Mangin's warnings about the fighting power of the French Army were now obvious to all. Foch, desperately trying to urge Pétain on, sent him a brusque message on 4 October, complaining about the lack of progress from Gouraud's Fourth Army in the Argonne. 'Yesterday, 3 October . . . we witnessed a battle that was not commanded, a battle that was not pushed, a battle that was not brought together . . . and in consequence a battle in which there was no exploitation of the results obtained.'[22] It was absolutely essential that the enemy was continuously engaged.

For German soldiers, there was nothing but chaos, disorganization, shellfire and endless fighting at the grey, smoke-filled, shell-torn front. 'We are in a daily battle with fate, with death, and it is a hard struggle, hopeless and sad,' wrote one German soldier, Alfred, on 29 September. He had heard news that his brother, Richard, had been severely wounded and lost a leg in the recent fighting. 'It is too miserable to imagine . . . that Richard must now return as a cripple from the heroic battle that we are fighting for our survival. We can only be consoled by the fact that it could have turned out even worse.' He himself had only escaped 'by a hair's breadth in a gigantic artillery battle' at the front. 'When I was leaving the completely churned-up, smoky trenches, a small splinter injured me (though not seriously) in the knee.' Alfred had been taken out of the line for a few days to recover, but knew that, soon, he would return to the battlefield. 'War is everywhere, and there is no end in sight for this horrific struggle,' he lamented. 'No victory can be achieved by either side.'[23]

On the Hindenburg Line, divisions – now frequently no larger than regiments – were rushed forward, often given little direction other than to mount counter-attacks or to dig in. In one German unit, 34th Division, which defended the area southwest of Saint-Quentin, the average strength of its companies was now down to twelve men and those who had survived were completely exhausted. Reports described captured prisoners from 21st, 119th and 121st Divisions as being 'quite ignorant' and 'hopelessly confused', being hurriedly thrown into the line with no orders other than to hold on.[24] A German officer from 13/Hussar Regiment, part of what had once been the elite 6th Cavalry Division, complained that his men were in a 'dreadful state', some of them having no rifles and others no packs. 'We received seven machine-guns. Our regiment is an extraordinary sight as owing to the casualties, the strength of our transport was greater than the actual fighting strength of the regiment.' It had received drafts from Potsdam, but half of these disappeared and the remainder called the infantry 'war prolongers' because of their loyalty to the High Command.[25]

On the evening of 30 September, Crown Prince Rupprecht gathered his officers together and tried to make sense of the situation. 'The fighting in and around Cambrai was very heavy,' he recorded in his diary.

> The enemy managed briefly to advance through Cambrai northwards and penetrate into Ramillies but was then pushed back after Tillon. On the Second Army's front, the enemy broke through southwards into the Siegfried 1 position. The breach points were blocked at the sides and we are putting up resistance in the less extensive Siegfried 2 position.[26]

Given the paucity of reserves and the grim international situation, there was little OHL could do other than shuffle tired and exhausted divisions from army to army. Hindenburg bluntly informed his commanders that 'No further reserves can be counted upon' and that an enemy breakthrough 'must be prevented at all costs . . . In this connection it is of paramount importance to gain time, to inflict heavy losses upon the enemy, to constitute reserves, to transport our equipment to the rear, and to destroy thoroughly the railroad and telephone installations.'[27] This was all well and good, but by 2 October Eighteenth Army reported that of its fifteen divisions, six were 'completely exhausted'. 'If battle is to be accepted in such a position,' it warned, 'then the army must be assigned to its 5 divisions equal in value to those still usable at the present moment . . . If that is not done, then the condition of the army, which recently has already given up 4 of its best divisions, will deteriorate to such a degree on moving into the HERMANN Position, that no responsibility can be assumed for even temporarily holding the position.'[28]

Work only started on the Hermann Line on 30 September, but Second Army assured General von Boehn that within eight days artillery positions could be posted, sites selected for anti-tank guns, and dug-outs and machine-gun nests built.[29] The only question was: would there be enough time to get it ready before the Allies were upon them? Fortunately, by 3 October the situation at the front seemed to be stabilizing. Cambrai remained in German hands and Crown Prince Rupprecht was pleased to discover that 'there were only local attacks in the direction of Roselaere' that morning. 'On the Sixth Army's front, all is peaceful; the enemy is edging forward only tentatively; on the Seventeenth Army's front all is also quiet, the enemy having no further fresh reserves there. The English have massed the majority of the reserves at their disposal against the Second Army.' Yet this was only a temporary pause in what was a merciless, irrevocable decline. When Rupprecht heard that the Chancellor was going to be replaced and that a new man ('who had no links with the past') would be put in charge, he was unimpressed. 'It would have been better if this had happened in the spring when we were not yet defeated – indeed, our military position at that time was more favourable than that of our enemies.'[30]

Such ceaseless combat was having a dire effect on the Army and even the morale of previously excellent divisions began to crumble under the strain. The gunner Ernst Kielmayer recorded the first appearance of mutineers among the ranks on 1 October. A group of drivers refused to ride up to the front to recover their gun. 'Can you blame them?' he asked. 'The fire from Tommy is murder. He must have gotten a big new supply of guns and ammunition.' The men from Kielmayer's battery eventually volunteered to pick it up and were all recommended for decorations, but the spectre of mutiny had been a sober reminder that the end was drawing near. 'Our losses are great. We blame only their overwhelming majority which we have noticed lately. It is only because Americans take over some of their places and have enough men and material to squeeze together the lines against the few Germans who were faithful, standing and defending their positions against overwhelming odds. That can only be because of the immense manpower coming in from over the big sea. So with an English, American, and French combination it should not take long anymore to kill off the few Germans still remaining.'[31]

Amid the intensity of battle, news was fragmentary and unclear, with rumours and gossip filling in for the lack of detail. On 5 October, Leutnant Karl Uhrmacher, serving in Flanders with 208th

Artillery Regiment, finally got his hands on a newspaper, although, as he told his father, 'There was not much good news in it.' The collapse of Bulgaria was what concerned him. Its loss boded ill for the Central Powers, which now seemed to be surrounded, more than ever, by hostile foes. He was convinced that Bulgaria was exhausted, but wondered whether their experiment with what he called 'Parliamentarization' would work.

> There is a lot of hustle and bustle here. Every man and his dog is on the run; everything is being evacuated. Thousands of men are standing around on the streets. Their mood is of course not bright and the situation for us with so few soldiers on the ground does not really inspire confidence. This is how I imagined it the evening before a revolution . . . Obviously, we do not hear much from the outside.[32]

Another German soldier, Herbert Sulzbach, who was one of the fortunate few to be granted leave, was in Frankfurt when the Hindenburg Line was breached and noted the 'dreadful, highly alarming reports' in the newspapers, from Bulgaria, from France, from everywhere, it seemed. He had a disturbing experience one morning when he passed a soldier in the street, who did not salute him; a worrying indication of how far the Army had fallen in German society. Sulzbach lost his temper. 'If these stupid youths back at home make a show of letting discipline go to pieces, you have to do something about it!'[33]

The Secretary of State, Paul von Hintze, for one, was determined to do something about it. If his 'revolution from above' was to work, then there needed to be a new government and a new Imperial Chancellor. It was obvious that the current incumbent, the ageing Count von Hertling (who was now seventy-five years old), would have to go. He was too close to the old regime, and too associated with the past, to be able to continue in this new age of parliamentary government. On 30 September he was invited to lunch with the Kaiser, awarded the Order of the Black Eagle, and then unceremoniously told that his resignation had been accepted.[34] His replacement was the 51-year-old Prince Max, heir to the Grand Duchy of Baden. Max had spent most of the war concerned with the welfare of prisoners and was well thought of. He was a liberal yet a monarchist, a modernizer but not a radical, and it was hoped that he could hold the country together through this transitional phase. He found out about the offer of an armistice shortly after 4 p.m. on 1 October. He was ushered in to see the military liaison officer, Colonel Hans von Haeften, who told him that the situation on the Western Front had worsened and that the Supreme Command wanted to appeal to President Wilson to begin negotiations for an armistice. Max was stunned. He may have been known as a moderate, but he was not prepared for such a shocking admission. He gaped at Haeften in silence for some time before asking, urgently and angrily, whether they could not wait until the following month before making the offer. Surely this was not to be done immediately? Haeften shook his head. 'It was absolutely necessary to give the tired army a rest,' he replied, repeating the Supreme Command's words and assuring Max that he was confident Wilson would see that negotiations would proceed swiftly. Max was initially of the opinion that he must decline the offer of the Chancellorship. He had no idea the situation was so poor and, in any case, their entire policy was based upon holding out, at least through the winter.[35]

After two further days of tense deliberation, Prince Max eventually accepted the Chancellorship, but not without severe misgivings. His father had warned him that their family could become tainted with the stain of surrender, but the Prince felt that he could not ignore an appeal from the Fatherland and he was, in any case, hopeful of manoeuvring events in his favour. He repeatedly argued his case before the military officers in Berlin and in telegrams to the Supreme Command that they must wait before making such an offer. Max was of the opinion that not only did their situation not justify such a suicidal act, but it would also worsen if any concessions were made. In any case, there were better ways of going about it. As he recorded, bitterly, in his memoirs years later – perhaps remembering the fate of Richard von Kühlmann – 'every official peace feeler up to now had horrified the Supreme Command' because it weakened German morale and strengthened the enemy. Yet now, the generals were all for throwing down their arms while 'the enemy pack dashed triumphantly in to the kill'. Pacing up and down in his office like a caged tiger, Max spent hours deliberating on the question, pondering why Ludendorff had made such an odd decision, reading report after report on the war and convincing himself that the Quartermaster-General had overreacted, panicked, lost his grip.[36]

Ludendorff was, however, not to be moved. Haeften spent over ninety minutes talking with him in the early hours of 2 October, explaining Prince Max's concerns and appealing to him for a delay, at least until the new Government was formed. But Ludendorff remained defiant. 'I want to save my army,' he constantly repeated, thinking only of his worn-out troops and remaining convinced that only if an armistice was granted would he be able to restore his army's morale and ready them for another battle. That afternoon, the Kaiser – newly arrived in Berlin with Hindenburg by his side – chaired a Crown Council meeting. When Prince Max tried to win over the Emperor and implore him not to make a peace offer, to persuade him that more time was needed to prepare the public before any negotiations should begin, the Kaiser rebuked him. 'The Supreme Command considers it necessary; and you have not been brought here to make difficulties for the Supreme Command.'[37] There would be no discussion; the decision had been made. As such, Max was isolated and there was little he could do. The other officers present, bowed and submissive before the Kaiser and the Field Marshal – the latter as calm and as unperturbed as ever – said little; the spell of Spa remained unbroken.

Despite this show of strength and authority from the Kaiser, Ludendorff's demand for an armistice and the beginning of negotiations with the Allies in early October was a crushing personal blow for him. By this point his health had suffered noticeably and he was often seen out walking with difficulty with a stick, complaining about his arthritis, his rheumy eyes staring into space, pondering on what had been lost. One of those who saw him often in this period was Georg von Müller, the Chief of the Naval Cabinet. On 1 October he was ordered to lunch at the Kaiser's villa in Spa, with royal aides perhaps hoping that the guests would cheer him up. 'His Majesty is in a very depressed state of mind,' Müller recorded. 'At lunch he kept clutching at straw[s] – the flu in France of which the

Chancellor has given him some details.' Four days later the Kaiser
was confined to his bed with arthritis and rheumatism. He stayed
there for three days, leaving the Imperial Court in a state of tense
anxiety, nervously awaiting news and worried about His Majesty's
health, with aides having whispered conversations in the corridors at
which the unmentionable subject of abdication was increasingly
raised.[38]

Frantic discussions continued over the following days over the
wording of the note to Wilson and the formation of a new government at home. Prince Max was so distressed at being forced into
making a peace offer that he wrote to Hindenburg demanding a
statement from the Supreme Command that the military situation
no longer admitted of any postponement to the beginning of negotiations. The Field Marshal gruffly obliged, confirming 'that a peace
offer to our enemies [must] be issued at once . . . The German army
still stands firm and successfully wards off all attacks. But the situation becomes daily more critical and may force the Supreme
Command to take momentous decisions . . . Every day wasted costs
thousands of brave soldiers their lives.'[39] On the evening of 3 October, the new Chancellor sent the 'First German Note' to Wilson,
requesting him 'to take steps for the restoration of peace, to notify all
belligerents of this request, and to invite them to delegate pleni-
potentiaries for the purpose of taking up negotiations'. The German
Government accepted Wilson's Fourteen Points 'as a basis for the
peace negotiations', and in order to avoid further bloodshed requested
measures for the 'immediate conclusion' of an armistice.[40] Thus
began the complex, delicate process of negotiating an end to the
worst war in world history.

12. 'The most desperate battle of our history'

Dante's description of Hell was too mild for this agony.

Second-Lieutenant Harold Woehl[1]

4–15 October 1918

On 4 July 1918, the US President, Woodrow Wilson, had given a speech at the tomb of George Washington in Virginia. Wilson, with his sharp, bird-like manners and thin, clear voice, a pince-nez clipped to his nose, elaborated on the reasons why America was fighting in France and confirmed the idealistic underpinning of US involvement. He reiterated his desire for the 'destruction of every arbitrary power anywhere that can separately, secretly and of its single choice disturb the peace of the world'. He wanted 'the settlement of every question, whether of territory or sovereignty, of economic arrangement or of political relationship, upon the basis of the free acceptance of that settlement by the people immediately concerned'. Thirdly, he outlined his wish for the 'establishment of an organization of peace' – what would become the League of Nations in 1920 – that would uphold justice in the world and provide international security. 'These great objects can be put into a single sentence – What we seek is the reign of law based upon the consent of the governed and sustained by the organized opinion of mankind . . . And I stand here to speak – speak proudly and with confident hope of the spread of this revolt, this liberation, to the great stage of the world itself.'[2]

Wilson had talked of his ideas about a kind of new world order before. On 8 January he had outlined to Congress his so-called Fourteen Points, when he claimed that America had entered the war because 'violations of right had occurred which touched us to the quick and made the life of our own people impossible unless they were corrected and the world secure once and for all against their recurrence'. He demanded a 'programme of the world's peace', based upon partnership, justice and fair dealing against 'force and selfish aggression'. This would be based upon freedom of the seas, equality of trade, and a general association of nations that would investigate disputes and make impartial judgements upon them.[3] Wilson may have been an idealist, but his view of human nature was shaped by growing up in a South that had been devastated by the Civil War and by the fierce, uncompromising Protestant ethos of his father, Joseph. Wilson believed that his ideas would reshape the world; a wind of change from the west that would revitalize and renew the promise of Europe, and spread freedom and liberation across the globe. The only problem was persuading his allies.

Whenever Wilson talked of his beloved Fourteen Points, the British and French Premiers, David Lloyd George and Georges Clemenceau, would undoubtedly have rolled their eyes or shrugged their shoulders. They had seen too much death and slaughter to be impressed by Wilson's rhetoric and too much of the reality of Great Power politics to believe that it could be wished away. In any case, they did not agree with many of his ideas, seeing them as impractical and unrealistic, even dangerous. For the British, they had certainly not fought the war for 'absolute freedom of navigation on the seas', nor for the 'adjustment' of their colonial empire on the lines of self-determination. Neither had the French. Clemenceau – old warrior that he was – did not think much of the idea of 'open covenants of peace'; his idea of open diplomacy was whatever resulted in a weakened Germany that would never be able to threaten France again. Yet for all the simmering tension between the Allies, and even if America remained only an 'associate power', they shared a common goal of breaking the German Army and ensuring that, in the west at least, she would lose the war. Now all their hard work seemed to be getting somewhere.

Prince Max's telegram arrived at the White House through a communiqué from the Swiss Government on 6 October. After two days of frantic discussion, during which Wilson was persuaded to issue a stronger note than he had originally intended – requesting guarantees that certain conditions would be fulfilled[4] – the President's response reached Berlin on the evening of 9 October. Wilson was understandably wary of saying too much and requested further clarification on the 'exact meaning' of the note from the Imperial Chancellor. In particular, he was concerned whether the German Government accepted his Fourteen Points fully and whether any discussions over them would only be about 'the practical details of their application'. He also asked whether Prince Max was 'speaking merely for the constituted authorities of the Empire who have so far conducted the war'; an understandable question reflecting his distrust of the men who had held power in Germany for so long.[5]

In Berlin the response to Wilson's note had been better than expected and was one of cautious optimism, Prince Max noting that it 'spoke in a different tone from the howl of rage to which the yellow press of the Allies had given vent'. He met Ludendorff on 9 October in what was a difficult and tense meeting. Neither was impressed with the other, the Quartermaster-General noting that 'We had not much in common', while Prince Max acidly reminded Ludendorff where the armistice demand had originated from. Despite the frostiness between them, they discussed the options available to Germany: to agree to both an evacuation of occupied territory and to accept the Fourteen Points unconditionally; or to consent to one of these but not the other. It would have been too difficult to repudiate all the Fourteen Points at this stage, so Ludendorff was asked about the military situation and whether it was possible to begin an evacuation of the Western Front. To Prince Max's frustration, Ludendorff – who 'did not give the impression of being shaken in health' – admitted that the Army was holding on. The situation was certainly better than it had been at the beginning of the month, but his men desperately needed a breathing space. He was convinced that if they could retreat in good order, he would be able to hold a line along the German frontier.[6]

The second German note was eventually despatched three days later:

The German Government has accepted the terms laid down by President Wilson in his Address of the 8th January and in his subsequent

addresses as the foundation of a permanent peace of justice. It declares
itself absolutely ready to comply with the parts of the President's
note regarding evacuation. The German Government suggests that
the President call a meeting of a mixed commission for making the
necessary arrangements concerning evacuation.[7]

Prince Max knew that Germany had to agree to an evacuation *in
principle* – to prevent Wilson from breaking off negotiations – but
there needed to be some guarantee that the Allies would also keep
to the Fourteen Points. When Germany's reply was being drafted,
the Supreme Command pressed for an addition that presumed the
Allied governments were also bound by these terms, something
that they believed would help in Germany's search for 'justice'.[8]
During the drafting of the second note Prince Max was also keen to
assuage Wilson's concerns about whether he could trust those in
charge. 'The present German Government which has taken this
step towards peace, has been formed by a large majority in the
Reichstag,' it noted. Furthermore, 'The Chancellor is supported by
the will of this majority, and speaks in the name of the German
Government and of the German people.' But whether this would
be enough remained an open question for several days as Prince
Max waited for Wilson's response, a period of 'suspense and apprehension' that one cabinet member described as 'the worst I have
ever lived through'.[9]

The weather worsened in the first week of October. The days
were now damp and chilly, with frequent squalls of rain that depressed
the morale of the thousands of troops squelching up to the front in
their sodden, woollen uniforms. On the day that Prince Max's first
note arrived in Washington, an American officer, Second-Lieutenant
Frank Holden, marched to the front with his regiment, 328th Infantry (82nd Division). They made progress, but in the village of
Varennes (in the Argonne), they met columns of mud-splattered
troops coming back from the line, which slowed them down. Every
few minutes motorcycles would rumble by, followed by trucks of all
descriptions, all to the sounds of MPs trying to maintain some kind
of order. Everything was in total darkness and the doughboys had

been given strict instructions against the lighting of matches or cigarettes in case the road was shelled. 'Broadway and Fifth Avenue were
never more crowded,' Holden wrote. 'The confusion, congestion,
jam and push cannot be fully described. The skill with which truck,
motorcycle, and ambulance drivers made their way through the
darkness over the front line roads was remarkable.' When they got to
their assembly position, they saw their first Germans – 'war-weary
and war-sick' prisoners – and noticed the occasional corpse or dead
horse, victims of the endemic shelling.[10]

For those in the front lines, the problems with supplies meant they
often went hungry and thirsty. Indeed, for Pershing's men, just keeping warm and dry, and perhaps finding something to eat, was always
the foremost thing on their minds. Elton Mackin, a veteran of the
Marne, recalled a damp, cold October morning in the trenches near
Blanc Mont 'that chilled our bones'. 'Hunger pangs of more than
forty active hours dulled our resistance. Men lay about in huddled
groups in mounds of dew-wet blankets, keeping warm. We had not
thought to sleep at all, but animal heat, soaked in from blanket mates,
and weariness put most of us to dozing.' They were shouted awake
by a senior officer calling for runners, followed soon after by the
opening pounding of a preliminary bombardment. 'What do men
think about at such a time?' Mackin pondered. 'Food. How good
those blankets were. And casually, sometimes, is my number up
today? Is this the place I've waited for?'[11]

If the Meuse–Argonne was what the Americans had waited for,
then perhaps it was all a waste of time. By the first week of October
the American offensive was going nowhere. No matter how many
times Pershing shouted at his subordinates to push on regardless of
loss, and no matter how many senior officers he removed, the front
lines of the US First Army stubbornly refused to move in the way he
wanted. For the past few days the American situation seemed to be
epitomized by the plight of what became known as the 'lost battalion', a group of 679 men from 308th Infantry Regiment, belonging
to 77th 'Liberty' Division, under the command of Major Charles
Whittlesey, the tall New York lawyer who had caused much hilarity
when trying on a French greatcoat in the days before the offensive.

On 2 October, his men had been cut off on wooded slopes north of the village of Binarville and, having been ordered to stay put, held their positions against increasingly ferocious attempts to wipe them out. The 'lost battalion' would become an American legend of the war as exhausted and parched doughboys fought desperately against veteran German soldiers in the scarred woodland of the Argonne.[12]

After the cessation of what became known as First Meuse–Argonne on 29 September, the Americans reinforced their lines, improved their logistics, and restocked their depleted ammunition supplies. Now more than ever, Pershing had to achieve success – to push on through the wooded, hilly country to his north and deliver a crushing blow to the enemy. At this point First Army had driven roughly eight miles into the German line, but still faced formidable obstacles. It had not been able to clear the Argonne forest – where Whittlesey's men remained – and, in the centre, its divisions were facing the ominous Romagne Heights, where the enemy's third main line of defence was situated. As Pershing would later write:

> In the entire area on our front, as well as on the dominating heights mentioned, the large groups of woods were staggered in such a way that local flanking manoeuvres caused excessive losses. Concealed in each group of woods were machine guns without number, covering the flanks and front of adjacent woods, and the timber lessened the effectiveness of our artillery fire.[13]

Even worse, they were still under flanking fire from German batteries on the east bank of the Meuse, watching every move Pershing made, shelling his men mercilessly.

Despite their success in maintaining their position, the German situation in this sector remained precarious. On 3 October, General von der Marwitz drove out to an observation post belonging to one of his divisions and spent several hours looking over the ground. In stark contrast to the US First Army, which had spent most of its existence fighting uphill, the Germans occupied the critical high ground.

> You need to climb perhaps an hour from the foot of the hill to the steep heights, but then you get a great view. The hills rise steeply out

of the plains, scattered with villages and crossed with streets. Each of the hilltops looks different from every side, so that you often get lost if you've driven on for a bit. Scattered all over the far-reaching hill-sides are built-in machine guns, individual guns, mortars, surveillance posts and so on. There is only one connected trench at the actual line of defence, but it isn't valued as much as the scattered machine gun clusters. How tactics have changed, a complete turnaround![14]

Marwitz's men were holding on, but the rumours of peace began to sap morale and make soldiers question whether they should continue to fight. Fifth Army's censor reported that morale was 'relatively bad'. 'War weariness and despondency have the upper hand as before. Numerous statements on this matter often take on forms that make the censor question whether he should let such highly demoralizing information pass into the home country.' There were increasing indications that Austro-Hungary would soon offer peace – it would send its first note to President Wilson through the Legation of Sweden on 7 October[15] – but this was 'received with mistrust and criticized disparagingly by the troops right from the start. Although in some letters, renewed hopes of a speedy peace are kindled, others are so bluntly resigned to their fate that they do not even mention the offer.'[16]

Pershing's renewed assault began at 5.30 a.m. on 4 October, the massed fire of his French 75mm artillery batteries dropping a rolling barrage about 600 yards in front of the waiting infantry. It was one of those black, dark mornings with the fields thick with dank fog – a perfect day for murder. Five divisions went forward and gained some ground, but progress was slower than expected against murderous fire and the usual obstacles. Army Group Gallwitz crowed that the attacks collapsed 'under the brave and obstinate resistance of our infantry and the performance of our artillery'.[17] The Americans were now paying the price for trying to do too much, too soon. As Second-Lieutenant Harold Woehl of 136th Infantry Regiment (32nd Division), who went over the top on 5 October, later explained, 'Everyone was exhausted and sick, and muddy, and hungry . . . There was no information about our objective; there was no artillery support; there was no liaison with the regiment on our right.'[18]

Whittlesey's 'lost battalion' was finally relieved on 7 October – although only 194 shattered survivors made it out alive from 679 officers and men – but that was a lone speck of good news in what was rapidly turning into an unrelieved nightmare. Over the coming days, fighting would spread to the east bank of the Meuse, where Major-General Henri Claudel's XVII French Corps, bolstered by two US divisions, went into action, aiming to clear the high ground of German batteries and outflank the remaining defenders west of the river. Despite determined attacks, the offensive met with the same fate as the others had. An American officer, Second-Lieutenant Joseph Lawrence of 113th Infantry Regiment (29th Division), witnessed the chaos and confusion on this sector, having to endure an exhausting approach march through mud and rain, constant shellfire and a chaotic rush through woods where he was nearly killed. At one point, during a fierce exchange of fire between his men and the enemy about twenty yards away, Lawrence noticed what he called 'a few interesting and amusing sidelights'.

A man named Gilbert, a few yards from me, had a rifle grenade that he was clumsily trying to fire . . . Finally he got it into the cup on the muzzle of his rifle and, to my horror and before I could stop him, fired it straight up. I draw up in a knot waiting for it to fall on us. It fell a few yards behind us with a loud crash, but fortunately without doing any damage. I noticed that the man next to me was cocking his rifle and pulling the trigger vigorously but the rifle was not firing. It was not loaded. I stretched my leg around and gave him a kick. That seemed to bring him to his senses. I noticed the two Heiser brothers, not over eighteen and twenty years old, operating a Chauchat automatic rifle vigorously and apparently with deadly effect. One fired the gun while the other fed the ammunition. It did not take them long to exhaust their ammunition at the rate they were firing. When the last round was fired they tossed their gun aside, jerked out their 'forty-five' automatic pistols, and carried on with them. On the end of the line to the left of me I observed a big Company K sergeant . . . moving back and forth on his hands and knees keeping order on that end of the line and generally stimulating the men.[19]

24. An American tank company undergoing repairs in the Bois de Hesse, north of Récicourt on the Meuse, 12 October 1918. Although the US First Army began operations in the Meuse–Argonne with 189 Renault tanks, within ten days only eighteen were still in action.

25. Major Charles Whittlesey (left), commander of the 'lost battalion', with Major Kenny of 3/Battalion, 307th Infantry Regiment, whose unit was the first to relieve Whittlesey's men on 7 October, near Apremont in the Argonne.

26. Men of 116/Canadian Infantry Battalion (3rd Division) move up to the front during the Battle of the Canal du Nord, 27 September 1918. According to a veteran, Private Guy Mills, 'It was just like a furnace door opening. There was nothing but guns, you couldn't hear anything else but guns.'

27. A horse team of the Royal Artillery pulls an 18-pounder field gun up a slope through the bank of the Canal du Nord near Moeuvres. Making sure the artillery kept up with the advance was absolutely vital. One gunner remembered being 'on the go for days and days and nights and nights, pulling our guns out, pulling them into some new position three or four hours later.'

28. The Kaiser standing on the bridge of the submarine tender *Meteor* on a visit to Kiel, 2 October 1918. The strain on his face is clearly visible. Four days earlier Ludendorff had told Hindenburg that the war must be ended as soon as possible.

29. Soldiers from 106th Infantry Regiment (27th US Division) return to the village of Corbie on the Somme, 25 October 1918. Some are carrying souvenirs taken from German prisoners captured on the Hindenburg Line.

30. Men of the North Lancashire Regiment make their way through the burning streets of Cambrai, 9 October 1918. One witness wrote: 'The dastardly Hun is burning what he cannot plunder or carry off. It just makes my blood boil to contemplate his villainy. I am reminded by the sight of Cambrai ablaze of the burning of Moscow.'

31. German infantry camping in Caudry, west of Le Cateau, while a French girl looks on, 15 October 1918. By mid-October large parts of the German Army were in full retreat. The pilot Rudolf Stark remembered seeing marching columns and long trains of wagons moving eastwards day and night.

32. German dismounted cavalry on the march, 9 October 1918. This mixture of aged veterans and youthful recruits was typical of what the German Army had become by 1918.

33. German reserves being brought up to the front for a counter-attack, 28 October 1918. As the front crumbled throughout October, German reserve units increasingly found themselves being pushed forward with no orders, little intelligence, and often under air attack.

34. The heavily damaged cathedral of Saint-Quentin, October 1918. The French commander, Charles Mangin, complained that 'the Boche is leaving Saint-Quentin in flames. Only the threat of reprisals will be able to prevent it from being ransacked before they leave.'

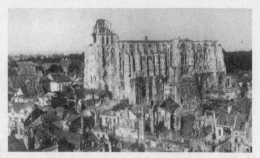

35. The town of Lens in the final days of the war. A householder watches from a balcony as streams of refugees pour through the streets.

36. 'The horrors of Dante's *Inferno*': the shattering effect of heavy shelling on the village of Champigneulle, north of Saint-Juvin, in the Ardennes.

37. Second-Lieutenant Wilfred Owen, the war poet, was killed in action on 4 November 1918 on the Sambre–Oise canal. Several days earlier he had written to his mother, 'I hope you are as warm as I am; as serene in your room as I am here . . . you could not be visited by a band of friends half so fine as surround me here.'

38. Second-Lieutenant James Kirk, aged twenty-one, served in Owen's battalion (2/Manchesters) and was awarded a posthumous Victoria Cross for his actions on 4 November. His citation commended his 'supreme contempt for danger and magnificent self-sacrifice'.

39. German infantry dug in along the canal at Valenciennes, November 1918. According to one regimental history, the positions 'consisted of rifle-pits connected up irregularly. There were no dug outs. There was no field of view owing to hedges, houses, walls and gardens. The battle headquarters were in small cellars, hardly splinter proof.'

40. The Place de la Concorde, Paris, 9 November 1918, showing some of the captured German guns on display. One witness remembered seeing 'mountains of Kraut helmets' on Armistice Day.

41. French girls decorate every possible corner of their windows with Allied flags, Rue Royale, Paris, 11 November 1918. According to Elise Bidet, who was in Paris that day, 'All the windows are decked out with flags. I have never seen so many flags and they are all in the colours of the Allies, the view is magnificent.'

Lawrence would earn a citation for his bravery on 10 October during heavy fighting around Molleville Farm. Although his men were trying their best, they could make little progress in such difficult circumstances. Pershing later called this phase 'the most desperate battle of our history' and it was easy to understand why, as his men, shelled, gassed and shot at from three sides, gradually clawed their way through some of the worst ground on the Western Front and inched ever closer to their objectives, Sedan and the railway that fed the German Army in the west.[20]

In contrast to Pershing's stalled offensive, further to the north British, French and Belgian forces continued harrying the retreating German armies as energetically as they could. 'Weeks went by,' wrote one British officer. 'The pattern was predictable. For a number of days we would make attacks, some easy, some not so, followed by a few days rest, then back again. The elusive enemy fought a skilful rearguard action with all the advantages. The only glimpses we had of them were of figures skulking behind distant hedges or on a far-off road. Noisy, but ineffectual rifle and Lewis Gun fire would hasten them on their way.'[21] By 4 October, Armentières had fallen and the British were through the dense belt of defences that had once been the Hindenburg Line. Two days later, Haig visited Foch and found him upbeat. As he entered the Marshal's study, with its maps pinned to the walls, he saw Foch reading from a newspaper spread out on his desk. It had printed the note from the Central Powers asking for an armistice.

'Here,' said Foch triumphantly to Haig, stabbing the paper with his finger, 'here is the immediate result of the British piercing of the Hindenburg Line. The enemy has asked for an armistice.'[22]

In 2/Manchester Regiment, Wilfred Owen now led D Company with four junior officers under his command. He led his men out of the front line on 3 October ('by the stars, through an air mysterious with faint gas') and back to the rear, where the usual grumbles resumed: leave, food and the war. Rumours were a feature of trench life – indeed they could spread with remarkable speed – but now, more than ever, the troops were feverish with news of the peace offers. Fourth Army had insisted that peace talk 'in any form' was to cease immediately, but inevitably the men talked. For his part, Owen felt shattered by his experiences on the Beaurevoir Line and every day looked in vain for parcels from home; anything to improve his mood. While censoring letters, he was buoyed by the positive comments about him by some of his men. They were 'more pleasing than any military medals with many bars', he told his mother. 'No change of situation,' he wrote a few days later, 'except that I now live in a tent, and a change of weather has made the place more miserable. On the night when the news was officially sent us of the German "Acceptance" we spent a merry enough night; I even discovered I could sing. We still hope something may be concluded by the Mixed Commission before we go into the line again.'[23]

The great prize that the British First and Third Armies had been fighting for since August – the city of Cambrai – finally fell to troops of 3rd Canadian Division on the morning of 9 October. This was 'a fitting climax to all the hard fighting of the Corps in this section that to us has fallen the honour of being the first troops to enter and pass through the city', wrote Sir Arthur Currie, proudly, in his diary that evening.[24] The capture of Cambrai was a remarkable feat for Haig's armies. Celebrations were only muted because of the large number of fires that had been started and which lit up the sky for miles around. A Canadian, Albert West, saw the city in flames. It was, he wrote, 'one big fire'.

> The dastardly Hun is burning what he cannot plunder or carry off. I could see four or five villages also burning. It is possible he will lay waste with fire all the country before us. Surely not! It just makes my blood boil to contemplate his villainy. I am reminded by the sight of Cambrai ablaze of the burning of Moscow. I watched it till I shivered with cold.[25]

French officers and men were understandably appalled at the scale of the damage that was being inflicted on their towns and villages during the German retreat. General Mangin, commander of Tenth Army, had visited Saint-Quentin soon after its liberation and 'shook with anger' at what he found. 'The Boche is leaving Saint-Quentin in flames,' he wrote. 'Only the threat of reprisals will be able to prevent it from being ransacked before they leave.' He wanted the Government to make an official announcement that German prisoners of war would only be returned once they had rebuilt French villages, but this was unlikely. Those he captured were immediately put to use clearing roads, repairing houses and erecting headquarters. Although Mangin was pleased to see some local farmers returning to their land, he was distressed because 'The Boche systematically removed all the furniture, except in some houses that were inhabited by officers . . . No house was left intact by the bombardment. The town is absolutely uninhabited.'[26]

British and French troops were now becoming used to liberating towns and villages as they pressed on eastwards. For some, it was one of the most abiding memories of the war: marching through the shattered ruins of homes and streets to be greeted by destitute, half-starved civilians who had suffered four years of occupation. This is what they had come to France to do; this was a visible sign that their fortunes were changing and that peace might be possible. On 10 October, a British battery commander, Major F. J. Rice, passed through the villages of Bertry and Troisvilles, just outside Le Cateau. 'The men lifted their caps to us as they had been made to do to the Boche,' he remembered. 'There were one or two of our cavalrymen lying dead in the streets, and we also passed a number of them and their horses before reaching Bertry. All the civilians waved or cheered or cried, and lots of houses had a French flag flying . . .' Unfortunately for Rice, what had been a memorable occasion at Troisvilles was soured when 'a Boche shell crashed through the wall of a house just in front of us, and as we passed an old man came out, wringing his hands which were covered in blood'. Shortly afterwards two soldiers carried out a girl who had been badly wounded. 'It was a terribly sad sight on the day of the liberation of these people.'[27]

As if the danger of German shelling was not bad enough, Allied soldiers soon became aware that the enemy may have retreated, but they had often left nasty surprises behind. As the pace of the retreat quickened, German units had to find some way of delaying the enemy as much as possible; anything to keep them from being able to launch major set-piece operations against unprepared groups of their men that might have resulted in total collapse across the front. There were scores of different booby-traps planted by the Kaiser's forces during the Hundred Days, and they all displayed the hallmarks of imagination, ingenuity and ruthlessness that the German Army had become notorious for. Random items would often be left in vacated buildings, inviting the unwary Allied soldier to pick them up or touch them, usually with fatal results. Books rigged with grenades would lie on window ledges; poisoned food and drink would be laid out ready to be eaten; even pianos would be left intact, waiting to be played, but with keys linked to explosives. It was little wonder that veteran NCOs made it their business to repeatedly tell their men not to touch anything in French villages until it had been checked by the engineers.

Charles Henry Savage, of 5th Canadian Mounted Rifles, remembered that houses were ideal places for booby-traps. 'Nearly all of us had seen the unpleasant results of setting off one of these traps and we had the greatest respect for them,' he wrote. 'Therefore visiting and inspecting houses for the first time was not the casual affair one might think.' According to Savage, the simplest type of trap was to be found on staircases. A step would be loosened so that when weight was placed on it, it dropped about an inch or so and detonated a bomb. Although it was possible to spot these traps from inside the cellar, often the only way of getting into the cellar was via the staircase. 'We were dependent on flashlights or candles for our light, and looking at a set of steps from above and by such light it was practically impossible to see anything suspicious,' he remembered. 'First we would both look each step over as carefully as we could, then one of us would feel gently on the first step to see if it seemed loose, then a little weight on the step, then the full weight. If nothing happened, the procedure would be repeated with the next step.'[28]

The crossing of the Hindenburg Line may have marked the climax of Foch's sequence of offensives, but fighting continued relentlessly throughout October as the German armies fell back. Debeney's First Army had been criticized in the ranks of Rawlinson's Fourth Army for 'hanging back' – or what they jokingly called 'debbing along' – but it fought a tough series of battles throughout the month, pushing northeastwards from Saint-Quentin as it kept on the heels of von Hutier's Eighteenth Army. They were up against the same obstacles the British were encountering – machine-guns, delayed-action mines, shell-pitted roads, poisoned wells – and progress was anything but easy, particularly when the weather began to worsen. On 11 October the war diary recorded that the advance had been 'very hampered by the resistance of the enemy'. The defenders were 'very vigilant' and the numerous machine-guns across the front slowed their progress. Five days later they had taken a bridgehead over the Oise River, but ran into fierce German counter-attacks. During October, First Army suffered nearly 15,000 casualties (about three times more than they had sustained in the previous month), but took over 10,000 German prisoners, 1,500 machine-guns and over 100 artillery pieces.[29]

French soldiers may have been physically exhausted and tired of life at the front, but they would see it through. Many were undoubtedly sustained by a desire for retribution, which became more marked as they saw the pitiless destruction meted out to their homes and businesses by the Germans. In one of his army orders, Debeney praised his men for fighting through a devastated region and having to see 'our poor villages in ruins, our mutilated arbres, our houses mined and ransacked', the sight of which he believed had increased their strength tenfold. An anonymous *poilu*'s letter, picked up by the postal censor of Fifth Army, spoke for many when he claimed that:

There is not one single ordinary French soldier who does not have a relative or friend to avenge, not counting those who have had neither house nor family for the last four years ... We want to avenge the crimes, the assassinations, the fires, the thefts committed by these modern-day Huns. The sight of villages systematically destroyed, fruit trees stupidly cut down, churches blown up with dynamite or turned into stables, inflames our anger and gives rise in our souls to violent desire for vengeance.

Others were more philosophical. A survey of French Army opinion in mid-October recorded that although an 'important mass' of soldiers advocated continuing the war until Germany was completely crushed, the majority supported armistice discussions until they had received sufficient guarantees. Given what France had suffered, and their distrust of the enemy, it was probably unsurprising that only a small number of correspondents wanted an immediate peace, regardless of conditions.[30]

The advance may have been tough for Allied soldiers, but the German experience of retreat was little easier. 'Thank you very much for the parcel you sent with the plum cake — it was nice. I got it on the day of the retreat,' wrote one German soldier, Josef, from Flanders on 9 October. 'We are now at Thielt and our division has suffered heavy losses again, but most of them were captured . . . There was a terrific air battle today and a large English fighter plane was shot down in flames close to us. The three occupants jumped out of the burning aeroplane, one after the other. You can imagine how they fell from about a thousand metres up. Then the aeroplane burnt right down the middle and fell down in two parts. Apart from that, there's no news . . .'[31] The pilot Rudolf Stark had been billeted in Maubeuge and 'day and night' he watched 'the tramp of marching columns, they are all going back. With them are long trains of wagons and crowds of refugees who have been evacuated from the front and are drifting eastwards.' He was so weak with cold that he could hardly move. His temperature was soaring and it gave him terrifying visions of being left alone and captured by the enemy. Fortunately, he was being looked after by a French family who nursed him with wine, fruit juice and books. Every day he would chat about the war with the father of the house, who brought him a map of France and Belgium. Each morning the old man would come into his room and trace the position of the front line. 'He draws thick lines in ink — always more and more lines to eastward, and each of them is marked with a date.' Stark was disappointed when the old man drew a ring around Cambrai and told him that it had fallen. 'His lines are always correct,' he grumbled. 'They leer at me from the wall, writhing their way into my brain like black serpents.'[32]

For officers and men the retreat soon became part of their daily routine. The infantry would march or be bussed to their new sectors, while gunners hauled their guns out, limbered them up and went off to find suitable ground to pitch them. As soon as they arrived, men began the seemingly endless task of preparing their new positions, digging trenches, building shelters, rolling out coils of barbed wire and hooking up telephone lines with their headquarters. For the gunners, camouflage was particularly vital at this time. Ernst Kielmayer, whose battery had taken a pounding at Cambrai, remembered pulling large sheets of wire over their guns, which would then be covered daily with fresh grass, making them 'observation proof' against their worst enemies: aircraft and reconnaissance balloons. 'We cut down small trees, if there are any left,' he wrote, 'and make garden posts out of them. We drive them into the ground around our guns and then put chicken wire over them covered with twigs and grass.' Attention to detail was vital. Kielmayer knew that their survival depended on remaining unspotted for as long as possible and their precautions included laying the wire over the battery at a precise angle not to throw a shadow, as well as ensuring that their tracks were covered up so as not to give them away.[33] It was hard work, but it was important. Sweat would save blood.

Even if appropriate measures were taken, the sheer scale and ferocity of the Allied bombardments inevitably took a daily physical, as well as psychological, toll on the German Army. On the night of 13 October, an NCO, the 29-year-old Adolf Hitler, was caught in a British mustard gas bombardment at Comines on the Franco-Belgian border. Hitler was serving as a runner with 16 Reserve Infantry Regiment (6th Bavarian Reserve Division), whose troops were already 'more like ghosts than men', encrusted with mud, their ranks thinned by the ceaseless attrition of the front. Hitler endured several hours of drumfire 'with gas shells which continued all night more or less violently', bursting on to dug-outs, splintering into roads and covering whole sections in sickly clouds of yellow gas. 'As early as midnight, a number of us passed out, a few of our comrades forever,' he recalled. By morning, he was feeling the effects of mustard gas exposure, the dreaded symptoms so familiar to Allied soldiers: a violent, hacking cough; the eruption of painful blisters all over the body; loss of sight and an intense pain in the eyes. Hitler was fortunate to have only received relatively minor exposure. His eyes, which had been temporarily blinded, burnt 'like glowing coals', but he received no long-term damage and his symptoms seem to have been worsened by his intense psychological reaction to news of the Armistice.[34]

Despite the professionalism that many units showed at this time, demoralization and indiscipline were bubbling to the surface and becoming impossible to ignore. The Crown Prince complained that individual divisions now began to fail him more often, partly from exhaustion, but more seriously from what he called 'contamination by international and pacifist ideas'. This led to them putting up disappointing resistance and having their flanks turned repeatedly. His commanders then had to sanction the premature deployment of over-fatigued but reliable troops who would plug these gaps. And it was these units – the ones who had proven their worth repeatedly – that were now distrusted by the rank and file and known as 'war prolongers'.[35] Even worse, it was evident that German loyalty, so strong throughout most of the war, was now beginning to fracture along state lines. As Cambrai was being evacuated – its shops looted and its buildings pillaged and burnt – fighting broke out between groups of soldiers eager to pocket their gains. In one bloody incident Bavarians and Prussians clashed in the streets, leaving fifteen soldiers dead, including an officer who was thrown from a third-floor window and broke his neck.[36]

By the second week of October, with the front narrowing by the day, German corps and divisions were moving back on to their last defensive positions, doing everything they could to impede their pursuers. Now that the main section of the Hindenburg Line had been crossed, the Army Groups of Rupprecht, von Boehn and the Crown Prince had no option other than to pull back their forces, occupy the Hermann Line (running north–south along the front behind the River Scheldt) and the Hunding–Brunhild position (from La Fère down to Verdun), and hope for the best. None of these positions were really worthy of the name; they had been marked out on maps, but nowhere had there been the time to construct the concrete dug-outs and pill-boxes and string out the acres of barbed wire that might have held the Allies up for any extended period. Because of this, much emphasis had been placed on siting the line behind 'natural obstacles', particularly watercourses (improved by damming), which it was hoped would economize on troops and prevent any large-scale breakthroughs.[37] Nevertheless, the shortening length of front meant the German Army was more concentrated now than it had been for months, years even, and when combined with the exhaustion of their pursuers, this meant the front gradually began to stabilize, to recover its equilibrium, which had been disturbed by the great attacks of July, August and September.

Apart from local, small-scale counter-attacks, the Germans could not muster enough forces to conduct anything larger. On 13 October, Crown Prince Wilhelm wrote to the commander of Eighteenth Army, General Oskar von Hutier, and confirmed his belief that an aggressive defensive should be conducted. But this was impossible because his Army Group only had 'extremely few reserves' at its disposal. 'These are just barely sufficient to fill up the existing gaps even if they are alerted and conducted with the utmost dispatch to the desired point.' Three divisions were available for immediate deployment, but if they were used the Army would have to 'abandon any idea of relieving front line divisions'.[38] This was the great dilemma that now wracked German commanders. Should they use their reserves strategically, to conduct counter-attacks and spoiling raids – something that their training and doctrine pushed them towards – or should they use what few men they had available to relieve those units at the front? In truth, it was an impossible question, the only logical answer being an end to the war; something that many officers could barely contemplate, but which the German Government was now trying to broker. But, as they would find out in the coming days, peace would come at a price.

13. 'A last struggle of despair'

There can be no conclusion to this war until Germany is brought to her knees.

General John J. Pershing[1]

16–25 October 1918

President Wilson's second note arrived in Berlin at 5.20 a.m. on 16 October, a crisp, autumnal morning in the capital. Any lingering hope that Germany could win some kind of diplomatic coup by negotiation was extinguished by Wilson's reply, in which he made it clear just what Germany would have to do if she wanted an armistice. Whatever Wilson's indecision in the first note, his reply was the death-blow to the Kaiser's Germany; a stunning diplomatic punch which dispelled any illusion that Germany could gain her 'peace of justice'. For President Wilson's closest adviser, Colonel House, 14 October – when Wilson finalized the words of his second note – was 'one of the [most] stirring days of my life'. He met the President shortly after breakfast and 'never saw him more disturbed'. It reminded him of a maze. 'He said he did not know where to make the entrance in order to reach the heart of the thing . . . If one went in at the right entrance, he reached the centre, but if one took the wrong turning, it was necessary to got [sic] out again and do it over.'[2]

Whatever the President's unease about how to respond, he knew that clear conditions would have to be set down and enforced by the Allies. On 5 October a conference had been held in Paris between Lloyd George, Clemenceau and the Italian Prime Minister, Orlando. They agreed that an armistice could only be concluded with Germany if eight points were fulfilled, including the total evacuation of Belgium, France and Alsace-Lorraine, the retreat of the German Armies behind the Rhine and the cessation of submarine warfare.[3]

When they heard of the German communiqué to Wilson, all their old fears and suspicions returned. Having not yet been consulted, the Allies, particularly the French, dreaded the Americans dictating a peace without taking sufficient account of their sacrifices and wishes. After all it had been the French who had endured so much since 1914, having to bear the cost of resisting the German Army, which had occupied some of her most valuable industrial areas. Likewise the British may not have suffered as many losses as the French, but they had taken on the burden of the naval war, loaned enormous sums to their Allies, and now looked upon the growing might of their former colony with envy and fear.

For the moment at least, the Allies need not have worried. While serious disagreements over the fate to be meted out to Germany would emerge later on, Wilson saw through Germany's obvious deception – that he would be flattered into concluding a favourable peace behind the backs of the British and French – and thwarted it. Having gone to war to defeat German militarism, Wilson could not be seen to countenance anything less, and his response would be heartily approved of in the Allied capitals. In his note Wilson made it clear that no arrangements would be entered into unless they could guarantee the 'present military supremacy' of the Allied armies in the field. Neither the United States nor the Allies would consider an armistice 'as long as the armed forces of Germany continue the illegal and inhumane processes which they still persist in'. Furthermore:

> At the very time that the German Government approaches the Government of the United States with proposals of peace, its submarines are engaged in sinking passenger ships at sea . . . and in their present enforced withdrawal from Flanders and France, the German armies are pursuing a course of wanton destruction which has always been regarded as being in direct violation of the rules and practices of civilised warfare.

Wilson reminded Berlin that fighting would not cease until these actions were stopped.[4]

Prince Max read what he called the 'terrible document' alone in his apartment on the Wilhelmstrasse. He was furious, accusing Wilson of bowing to the Allied commanders, of abusing the German Army and Navy, and of appealing for an uprising from the German people. Max feared that the fragile 'internal peace' would now be broken, as he put it, 'like the bursting of a dam'.[5] His response, angry and bitter, was typical of how Germany's leaders, both civilian and military, would react to what one cabinet member called the 'bombshell'.[6] Loudly professing their shock and disgust at Wilson's note, they raged against this betrayal: that he had dared to demand guarantees from them; that the submarine war should be a subject for discussion; that he had irresponsibly libelled the honour of the Army. The Crown Prince called Wilson's demands 'implacable and arrogant' and accused him of interfering in Germany's internal affairs and of being pressured into them by Foch.[7] But such special pleading was only testament to how out of touch Germany's leaders were, of how utterly devoid of imagination they were in failing to see how necessary these conditions were to Allied security. Germany's ruthless bid for European domination and her puritanical search for total victory had only succeeding in uniting her foes against her. It was too late to beg for a compromise peace now.

Ludendorff arrived for a Council of War the following day. Prince Max told him that a response could only be sent after a full appreciation of what was going on at the front had been made. Therefore a series of questions had been prepared for him to answer on this matter. This was something that Ludendorff typically found distasteful, and he immediately launched into a patronizing defence of his position (that he had borne for 'four long hard years') and of the impossibility of predicting what would ultimately happen. This was not particularly helpful, and did nothing to salvage Ludendorff's declining reputation in Berlin. Various ideas were aired about transporting German divisions currently stationed in the east to the Western Front. There were twenty-four divisions in total, including five in the Ukraine and another twelve in Romania, but these were regarded as being so physically and morally weak (being men between thirty-five and forty-five years of age and not possessing sufficient offensive spirit) that the idea did not get very far. Perhaps twelve divisions could be moved, but this would take up to three months and there was a danger that leaving the east without sufficient troops would interfere with German economic exploitation and lead to a resurgence of Bolshevik activity.[8]

Turning to the Western Front, Ludendorff stressed that he felt a breakthrough was possible, but not probable, and that more men were required. The Prussian War Minister, Heinrich von Schëuch, said that he might be able to provide a single, strong reinforcement to the Army of about 600,000 men, mainly by combing out more men from industry and by calling up the remaining members of the 1900 class. Ludendorff jumped at the idea and claimed, somewhat ridiculously, that had these men been available then 'we should have had no crisis'. The situation at the front took up the rest of the meeting, with Ludendorff answering questions about how long the line could be held, whether the Allies would continue with their offensives, how the Americans should be countered, what the morale of the men was like, and so on. Ludendorff shrugged and grimaced his way through it, admitting that he did not know how things would turn out, only that more must be done to provide reinforcements and shore up the men's morale. Although some of those present came away from the meeting optimistic at the news that the military situation was better than they had expected, or at least not as bad as had been feared at the beginning of the month, it was still a grim story. No matter how many times they asked the same question – could the Army hold out? – the Chancellor and his ministers, Ludendorff and his generals, all came to the same conclusion. The situation at the front may not have been as critical as it was on 28 or 29 September, when Foch's sequenced offensives had reached their climax, but, as Prince Max realized, it was only going to get worse. They might be able to hold the front for some time yet, they could hope for outbreaks of war-weariness or disease in the Entente, but it was clear that Germany's powers of resistance were crumbling. Therefore, there was only one thing to do: to continue with the negotiations, to do what Wilson wanted, and if that did not secure a 'peace of justice' then let it be so. Prince Max was confident that if it came to the worst, the people could be called upon to make what he called 'a last stand . . . a last struggle of despair'.

The news from the front was almost uniformly bad. Lille and Douai were abandoned on 17 October, and within two days the Allies had liberated large swathes of western Belgium, from Bruges and Thielt to Courtrai. Morale remained poor across the Army as news of the peace offers gnawed further into men's depleted reserves of courage. 'The yearning for peace is very strong and no one knows when the hour of the armistice will finally arrive,' wrote a German soldier, Alfred, on 20 October.[9] This seems to have been a fair reflection of opinion at the front. On the day that Lille fell an army censor confirmed that 'As late as the spring of this year it was possible to say of the majority of letter writers that they would not support peace at any price. Now they vehemently demand peace at any price. "We can't go on, we don't want to go on, we want to go home." The number of people who are writing home: "I won't stick my neck out any more, I'm not going to be so stupid to put my life at risk for nothing" is alarmingly big.' Although some officers and men 'continued to support the cause without fail . . . these voices cannot deceive us of the true feelings of the majority. Despondency, war weariness and strong yearning for peace still have the upper hand.'[10]

Day after day the retreat went on. 'Tired, worn-out horses trot along in front of the wagons and stagger when they come to a halt,' wrote Rudolf Stark as he arrived at his new air base at Gosselies, a suburb of Charleroi in Belgium. 'More columns loom up in the mist and roll by us, away into uncertain distances.' By now it was difficult to find suitable aerodromes to operate from, given that they were moving through dense urban areas, very different from the wide open spaces of northern France. The thick mist and deep mud, which swallowed all sound, gave the place a haunted, unearthly feel and Stark described the columns that passed them as being like 'an army of ghosts'. They tried their best to support the ground troops, but they had no precise details on their location, which changed every day. There was little for them to do: no artillery support or reconnaissance missions; very few escort duties to take care of. His men, he recalled, felt 'lonely' and 'superfluous'. 'When we take off in the morning and fly over the ground where the front lines ought to be, according to our map, we see English troops below us and know that

our men have been forced to give up yet another piece of ground . . .
We feel that the end is near, but we dare not speak of it.'[11]

For many soldiers, news of the darkening scene was hard to bear.
Within days of the bombardment at Comines, Adolf Hitler was on
his way to a hospital in Pomerania, and in his blind and distressed
state he raged against what was happening to Germany. When he
arrived, he was relieved to discover that he would probably regain his
sight quite soon, but found the news from the front almost intolerable. For some time, he wrote, there had been 'something indefinite
but repulsive in the air'. There were rumours that some kind of strike
would happen in the next few days, as well as dark mutterings that all
was not well with the Navy, but Hitler refused to believe them.
Unable to read the newspapers, he tried to bolster the morale of his
fellow patients, telling them not to listen to the rumours of such
treason and continue to believe in the war, and in victory, which
must surely come.[12] Another soldier, Leutnant Karl Urmacher, felt
the same sense of frustration and despair. 'We do not hear much from
outside,' he wrote to his father on 17 October. 'Often, when I consider the facts and their consequences, my heart tightens. How much
trust did we place in the God of Peace and in Wilson's common
sense?' His heart revolted at the great injustice that was taking place.

> Are we really the criminals, as we have been labelled, do the German
> people who suffered and bled for their existence, unlike any people
> before, really deserve this? . . . I have faith in our new men, but I am
> also concerned about their future. Perhaps it will be possible to
> achieve peace, but under what conditions? . . . We have lost the pos-
> ition of power, but let both the Army and those at home remember
> that we have not yet lost our honour. A defeat does not require dis-
> honour, but they can become this way through the way in which they
> are created and fostered. Now, we need to grit our teeth and every
> person must perform their duty to their utmost while our ability runs
> its course. May our destiny be not so hard, it is only unbearable when
> it is self-inflicted. In order for us all to give our grandchildren a clear
> conscience? Hopefully the events of the past few weeks have made
> everyone aware of their duty and responsibility.[13]

Bit by bit the German Army began to falter. The debilitating effect of the influenza pandemic, which had devoured huge numbers of men in the summer, began to grow again in the autumn. One officer, Leutnant Hans Mahler, recorded that each company in his battalion had about twenty men sick with flu during October. By the end of the month between ten and twelve people were dying each day.[14]

The Crown Prince would later claim that the intensity of the fighting meant that the German Army underwent a kind of 'self-purification' at this time, with the weaker falling away or surrendering, leaving only those of true heart and courage at the front. This was almost comforting: the feeling that through the furnace of war a hardier German race would emerge which could face the coming storms with impunity.[15] But it was just wishful thinking. The Western Front was a lottery of life and death, with shellfire and bullets, gas and grenades, taking life every day. Skill and judgement, experience and wisdom, could help in evading death in the trenches, but most killing was random with no way of predicting when it could come: the fall of a shell that would slice a man in two or leave him horribly wounded in no-man's-land; the thud of a sniper's bullet that killed one man but not another. There was no logic to it, no obvious rule of survival, and this is what caused men to break down. Ernst Kielmayer witnessed the randomness of death on 18 October when his battery suffered a premature explosion that killed one and wounded four of his friends. They had fired 200 Blue Cross gas shells ('which kept Tommy pretty quiet for awhile') when No. 2 gun blew up. 'A shell of ours exploded right after leaving the barrel and hit a leveller, Sergeant Elser, fatally.' He was dead within thirty minutes. Kielmayer was understandably distressed by what had happened. 'We see the power of our shells. It certainly is terrible. We blame our factories at home for faulty ammunition and sloppy workmanship. We get enough grief from Tommy without getting some from our own gun.'[16]

After extensive and agonized discussions, the cabinet finally issued a reply to Wilson on 21 October, agreeing to the evacuation of occupied territory and ordering the cessation of U-boat attacks on passenger steamers. While the note denied that German troops had conducted a scorched-earth policy on the Western Front ('Some destruction will always be necessary to cover a retreat') and contested any suggestion that the Navy had destroyed lifeboats on sinking ships, it was now clear that Germany must do whatever it took to secure an armistice.[17] That day the Kaiser was in Berlin meeting the new cabinet, trying no doubt to put the best possible gloss on a rapidly deteriorating situation. Philip Scheidemann, Minister Without Portfolio, was in the drawing room of the Bellevue Palace when the Emperor came in. 'He took his stand a few paces from us, supporting his withered left arm, under which he held his helmet on the hilt of his sword, then bowed and said: "Gentlemen, I have just put a few lines on paper."' The Kaiser then read out a speech, welcoming the new cabinet, and talking about the constitutional rights that would be given to the German people, which he was sure would 'consolidate the structure of the Empire at home on new and broader foundations'. He told them that the citizens of the Fatherland would now be called upon to cooperate in working these new structures and in maintaining unity through the challenges that lay ahead. Afterwards Prince Max introduced him to the cabinet, including Scheidemann, a Social Democrat, who had long been unimpressed with Prussian royalty. 'I was almost prostrate with remorse,' he later admitted. 'The Kaiser seemed quite unconcerned. His placid face was perhaps only the result of admirable training. But what effect was such a free and easy manner, such a happy-go-lucky expression to have on us? Did he imagine he could pose before us as a hero, imperturbable in his confidence of success?' Scheidemann thought not. 'His chattering jarred upon me.'[18]

Within days, the Kaiser's quiet, placid confidence that the constitutional changes he had outlined would ensure the survival of his dynasty had been shattered. The US Government responded swiftly to the German note of 21 October. Three days later Robert Lansing, the Secretary of State, replied, and although the letter took up barely a page of text, it was another devastating blow to German hopes of their 'peace of justice'. Lansing made it clear that after the German acceptance of the Fourteen Points and their solemn promise to respect 'the humane rule of civilized warfare', an armistice would now be considered by the United States and her associate powers.

Nevertheless, he warned Germany that any terms would give them the 'unrestricted power to safeguard and enforce the details of the peace to which the German Government has agreed'. However, because it was feared that the principles of responsible government had yet to be finalized in Germany, there were understandable concerns that 'the German people have no means of commanding the acquiescence of the military authorities of the Empire in the popular will' and that the power of the 'King of Prussia' to control such a policy was unimpaired. As such, the US Government could not deal with any representatives of the German people unless they were the 'real' rulers of Germany. If it had to deal with the 'military masters and the monarchical autocrats', then America would demand not peace negotiations but surrender.[19]

Lansing's note raised the stakes yet again. Although not specifically requesting the abdication of the Kaiser, the ominous references to 'military masters' and 'monarchical autocrats' was clear enough for Prince Max and most of the cabinet to understand. It was evident that the power of the Kaiser and the generals at OHL would have to be toppled before peace with the Allies could be made. For Scheidemann, all doubts were now dispelled; as he put it, 'Wilhelm II's days as Emperor were numbered.'[20] Ludendorff's position was little better. Most of the cabinet, including Prince Max, had now lost any confidence in the judgement or ability of the Quartermaster-General, and blamed him for panicking and landing them in this mess. More worrying, Ludendorff was now slipping back into his earlier rage and confusion, refusing to accept the situation at the front and indulging in ridiculous optimism. On 22 October, he telephoned Crown Prince Rupprecht's Chief of Staff, Major-General von Kuhl, and told him that the retreat from the Hermann Position to the Antwerp–Meuse Line was going to happen 'slowly', presumably as part of some kind of managed and organized pull-back. When von Kuhl told Rupprecht, the latter was predictably dismayed, believing that only a swift redeployment to the rear could help them.

> I am convinced that this would be the wrong thing to do, we should not allow the enemy any opportunity for easy victories but withdraw our troops as quickly as possible to get them out of enemy reach and

re-group them while at the same time detaching reserves in the
shorter Antwerp–Maas position. General Ludendorff is now talking
as if we can keep this war going for a long time and, if this proves
impossible, and we lose the war, it would be the fault of the Reich's
leaders. If we do not have a ceasefire soon, we must withdraw behind
the Maas and thus shorten the front considerably. Ludendorff will
not hear of this but Colonel Heye feels, quite rightly in my opinion,
that this would be absolutely the right thing to do. My group would
then be removed from the northern front and employed in Lorraine.
I don't think that it will come to that, though.[21]

By now Ludendorff had stopped listening – the news from the front
was so bad, and the fears that the Allies would not be satisfied with a
compromise peace weighed him down and darkened his mood. On
the evening of 24 October, as the third American note arrived in Berlin, Hindenburg and Ludendorff left the capital and headed back to
OHL in Spa, a bitter snub to the frantic efforts of the new German
Government to secure peace.

For the ill-fated duo, Wilson's third note was hard to accept. At
ten o'clock a proclamation was issued to the Army that made it clear
what the Supreme Command thought of the President's offer. It bore
Hindenburg's signature, but it was probably Ludendorff's doing. It
was a wild, angry document that denounced Wilson's latest response
and his threat of unconditional surrender, which was 'unacceptable
to us soldiers', and claimed that the Allies had no interest in securing
a 'peace of justice', only complete victory. 'Wilson's answer can thus
be nothing for us soldiers but a challenge to continue our resistance
with all our strength.'[22] Ludendorff tried to claim that the note was
perfectly consistent with cabinet policy and assumed that any question of the Kaiser's position would immediately result in a suspension
of negotiations, but he knew what he was doing. With this document, the Supreme Command single-handedly undercut the
authority of the Chancellor and the civilian government and brought
to a head the crisis that had been brewing for over a month.[23] For
Prince Max the tipping point had now been reached. He was furious
at what one cabinet member called Ludendorff's 'political stunt', seeing it as yet another example of an over-mighty military command

interfering in the running of the country. In a tense meeting with the Kaiser he put it simply: either Ludendorff went or he did.[24]

For so long the various theatres of war in Europe, Italy and the Middle East had seemed frozen and immobile; stalemated and deadlocked. And then in late autumn, with surprising suddenness, the thaw finally set in. By 30 September, Bulgaria had signed an armistice, which opened up the southern flank of the Central Powers. Austro-Hungary was already on the verge of capitulation, and it took only a limited offensive by the Italian Army in the final week of October – the Battle of Vittorio Veneto – to push it over the edge. In the Middle East, the Ottoman Empire was now entering its final death throes. What remained of the Turkish Army in Palestine had been routed at the Battle of Megiddo in late September, and over the following month General Sir Edmund Allenby's troops pushed north, mercilessly harassing the retreating Turkish columns. Aleppo fell on 26 October and within days an armistice was signed on the island of Mudros – thus bringing the war in the Middle East to a victorious conclusion.

Back on the Western Front, things remained promising, but difficult to foresee. As David Lloyd George wrote, 'It was clear that the end was now in sight. It was no less clear that we must move with the utmost care at this critical juncture, making sure of our footing at every stride, lest by a false step we should imperil the full harvest of our long effort.'[25] The day after Ludendorff had issued his proclamation urging a continuation of the struggle, a meeting of the Allied Commanders-in-Chief was held at Foch's headquarters, which had now moved from Bombon to the town of Senlis, thirty miles north of Paris. Foch had been asked by Clemenceau to prepare a report on the military terms of a possible armistice, so the *Generalissimo* had sent for Haig, Pétain and Pershing. It would be the first time they had been in the same room together since 24 July and it allowed them an opportunity to digest the great changes that had occurred on the Western Front since those frantic days of July when the Allies had begun their grand counter-attack. Although the situation was deeply promising, both Haig and Pétain harboured doubts about how hard they could continue to push, as well as understandable pessimism about how long the Germans would resist. Haig was concerned that although 'a very great part of the German forces had been beaten', they were still capable of effective resistance, particularly if they were able to cross the Meuse and destroy the railways during their withdrawal. He was also worried about the exhausted state of the British and French Armies. In such circumstances, Haig feared that Germany would not accept an armistice. He believed that they should make relatively minor demands, such as the evacuation of occupied territory (including Alsace-Lorraine) and the repatriation of their inhabitants, which would leave them on the German frontier in case hostilities broke out again.[26]

Foch, ever the fighter, was somewhat perturbed by Haig's pessimistic series of points, arguing that 'we are dealing with an army that has been beaten every day for three months' and an army that had lost over 250,000 prisoners and 4,000 guns since mid-July. 'When one hunts a wild beast and finally comes upon him at bay,' he added, 'he then comes in the face of greater danger, but it is not the time to stop, it is the time to redouble his blows without paying any attention to the ones he himself receives.' At that point, Pétain got up and spread out a map of the Western Front on one of the tables, showing the current Allied positions and the projected stages of a German retreat to the Rhine. If the Germans could be forced to withdraw to his schedule, quickly, then it would be impossible for them to move out all their heavy guns and ammunition, which would give the Allies a great advantage in any future campaign. Pershing spoke next. Reflecting his position as the only commander of an army that was getting stronger by the day, the American commander was bullish and talked about the guarantees they needed and the possibility of resuming fighting under the most favourable conditions. He advocated occupying bridgeheads over the Rhine, the restitution of all rolling stock that had been seized in France and Belgium (estimated at over 126,000 railway cars and 2,500 locomotives), as well as the unrestricted transportation of the US Army across the Atlantic, the immediate repatriation of foreign nationals, and the surrender of all U-boats.[27]

Foch did not expressly give his opinion at the meeting, but delivered his report to Clemenceau and the French Prime Minister, Raymond Poincaré, in person the following day. It repeated, in large part, the suggestions that Haig, Pétain and Pershing had made, and stated that seven conditions would have to be fulfilled before an armistice could be concluded. When Poincaré remarked that these conditions might be unacceptable to the Germans, Foch shrugged: 'Then we will continue the War; for at the point the Allied Armies have now reached, their victorious march must not be halted until they have rendered all German resistance impossible and seized guarantees fully ensuring peace – a peace we will have obtained at the price of inestimable sacrifices!'

Foch was not, however, keen to continue fighting for the sake of it. When Colonel House – who had just landed in France – asked the *Generalissimo* several days later whether he thought it was preferable to continue the war or conclude an armistice with Germany, Foch was appalled. 'I am not waging war for the sake of waging war,' he snapped. 'If I obtain through the Armistice the conditions that we wish to impose upon Germany, I am satisfied. Once this object is attained, nobody has the right to shed one more drop of blood.'[28]

This sentiment would have been shared by the thousands of Allied troops at the front. They were just trying to survive each day and adjust to a war of movement, which was a novel experience for men long used to static trench warfare. Between 17 and 24 October the British Third and Fourth Armies, assisted by Debeney's First French Army, mounted a series of major operations to cross the River Selle. In the teeth of bitter resistance and the usual obstacles – wire, fortified villages and heavy shelling – the Allies pressed forward; brutally smashing up any counter-attacks that came their way. It was war of manoeuvre now, requiring skill, judgement and endurance in equal measure. Lieutenant R. G. Dixon, an officer with the Royal Artillery, remembered being 'on the go for days and days and nights and nights, pulling our guns out, pulling them into some new position three or four hours later, laying out new lines of fire at first light – for we often moved in at night, and often enough to some farmyard or other that gave some cover to our gunners'.[29] Guns were moved, often by sheer brute force, under the direction of NCOs, while officers studied new maps and tried to find landmarks from which lines of fire could be drawn up. As the pursuit continued, the habits of previous years had to be broken because there was not the time or the opportunity to prepare the elaborate set-piece barrages that had accompanied earlier attacks. Now field artillery batteries were attached to battalions and provided close support whenever it was needed, doing just enough to frighten the German rearguards and send them on their way.

For the infantry, the challenges were more familiar: how to cope with the long marches to the front, the lowering temperatures and the worsening weather that sapped their strength. An officer with 154th French Division – advancing with Fourth Army towards the Aisne River – recorded in late October that they had been on the march for twenty-five nights with little rest. The cold weather made it almost impossible to sleep. 'We have only our canvas: having dozed off for one hour or two, they realize that they are covered with hoarfrost. Finally twenty days when they have not had hot food, neither washed, nor shaved, nor had clean linen. If this goes on we are going to be devoured by the vermin,' he complained. Understandably, his men were awaiting their relief with impatience.[30] The American forces, advancing on their right, were approaching a similar level of exhaustion. The men of Second-Lieutenant Harold Woehl's regiment were relieved on 20 October after nineteen days of 'continuous fighting, and digging, and starving, in the shell torn Argonne forest'. His company, now numbering fewer than sixty men, stumbled their way to the rear, exhausted beyond measure. 'Every man was covered with mud and soaked to the skin and [their] teeth were chattering in the freezing weather,' he recalled. Two days later the regiment received 600 replacements, mostly from the Southern states, but they had little military training. 'Drilling in our hellish area was impossible. So we hurriedly gave the new men personalized training in adjustment of gas masks, instructions in throwing grenades, and firing practice on improvised rifle ranges.'[31]

Despite the hardships of the advance, there were occasional moments of joy and excitement. On 20 October, Sir Arthur Currie drove up to the front to the headquarters of 1st Canadian Division at

Lewarde; proud to have liberated over 40,000 French citizens in the last few weeks. 'All the houses are decorated with French flags and the people seem overjoyed to greet the British soldiers,' he wrote. 'In many cases last night they dug up wine they had buried for years to share it with the troops. Many of the men had a bed to sleep on again but whether alone or not I cannot say.' One story doing the rounds was of a Colonel Peck who was apparently the first British soldier to arrive in the village of Hornaing. He was 'set upon' by the inhabitants, 'who hung garlands about him and pinned flowers on almost every part of his coat'. It was even said that every woman in the town had kissed him.[32] Currie remained concerned at the pace of the retreat and at not really being able to get to grips with the enemy, but he was pleased at the large numbers of prisoners now coming into their hands. By mid-October the Allies had taken over 250,000 prisoners since the summer. This marked a huge shift in the dynamics of war, proof of the collapse of German morale and a sure sign that the balance had now tipped in their favour. Long columns of German soldiers shuffled their way to the rear, where they were then given food, water and cigarettes. Lieutenant Dixon remembered seeing some on the Arras–Cambrai road and being shocked at their appearance. Did these pathetic specimens, he wondered, belong to the much-vaunted German Army? 'Lots of them were mere boys,' he wrote, 'whose immature faces peered at us from under steel helmets that seemed too large for them, frightened young faces; mingled with them were much older men, whose proper place was with their wives and children.'[33]

But not all Germans were like this. Indeed, as every soldier knew, for every group of cowed, shivering soldiers, there were others in the German Army who would not give in; those who were disputing their progress every day, inch by inch: the spine of the German defence, her machine-gunners. These men were both feared and respected. 'The gunners were brave men,' wrote T. H. Holmes, a Private with 56th (London) Division, 'because firing the gun meant revealing the position of it, and up would come a tank and invariably shoot the post to pieces, and then trample it flat. I saw a ghastly mass of crushed heads and limbs tangled up with twisted iron. They said some of these machine-gunners were chained to their weapons.'[34] Another British soldier, a member of the Machine-Gun Corps, recorded in his memoirs how these men repeatedly occupied the best positions with the most deadly fields of fire, and consequently always proved extremely dangerous. Like many soldiers, he soon became used to the sight of machine-gunners crushed beneath tanks.[35] Although it was not true that these men were chained to their weapons – the strap that the gunners wore was often mistaken for some kind of restraint – their courage was legendary. On one occasion, a Canadian, R. H. Camp, came across a gunner who had fired off all his ammunition. There was nothing particularly unusual about this, but Camp was amazed by what happened next. 'He stood up in his hole and started taking his gun to pieces and he was throwing the pieces at us, anything he could get a hold of. We knew then of course that he was out of ammunition and we up and rushed him.' Just as the Canadians were about to get to grips with him, their officer ran up shouting. 'Don't stick him boys! Don't stick him.' He got out a piece of paper, scribbled something on it, and then put it in the German's pocket. 'Don't touch this man, he's brave.' He then told the German to make his way back to the rear. The note was a signed declaration of the machine-gunner's courage and a guarantee that he would not be harmed.[36]

What to do with these hardcore elements was a source of constant discussion. Frederick Noakes, a Guardsman who had seen Captain Frisby win his Victoria Cross on the Canal du Nord, remembered an argument the men of his platoon had one evening as they were marching back up to the front. The question was whether the German rearguards who stayed behind and resisted without hope of survival or relief should be allowed to surrender or whether they should be killed. 'One or two men said they ought to be wiped out, even if they put up their hands; they had killed many of our men to no purpose, and should pay the price, the dirty bastards! But the great majority disagreed. They were brave men, they asserted, who had sacrificed themselves so that their comrades might get away.'[37] It is difficult to say whether Noakes's belief that there was little hatred

towards these Germans was widely shared. Keith MacGowan, serving with 47th Canadian Battalion, thought not. Showing remarkable
candour, he admitted to his mother that 'Every Hun who fights is
killed by my boys, but I order them to give quarter to a man who
throws down his arms at the start. Some work their guns to the last
and cut us up and when they see the game is up, throw up hands and
peddle this Kamerad stuff to us. Well it's a case of "It don't get him
nothing."'[38]

Rage and a desire for revenge could sometimes overwhelm even
the most conscientious of men. A British soldier, A. J. Turner, who
was serving with 38th Division when it was trudging through the
Forest of Mormal, lost control when his best friend, Milligan, was
killed by a machine-gunner. It was a shattering moment. 'In the past,
deaths had saddened, sickened, or had merely left me unaffected;
Milligan's death roused me to a pitch of fury,' he admitted. 'This
mere kid, so full of life, so happy – blasted into eternity in the high
noon of his existence. The bastards. The utter bastards!' Turner's platoon fired their rifles in the direction of the enemy, pinning them
down, while they waited for support to arrive. Then Turner caught
sight of the enemy; a rare enough event those days when the only
glimpse of their elusive quarry was 'of figures skulking behind distant hedges or on a far-off road'.

> A figure was seen to scramble up and poise momentarily unbalanced
> whilst silhouetted against the sky; rifles cracked, I fired carefully – the
> figure fell. I felt savagely exultant . . . I climbed the bluff. Spread-
> eagled and face down was a very young German, younger than
> Milligan. His helmet had rolled off, his scalp was close-cropped, his
> uniform looked absurdly big, his hands clutched grass where he had
> clawed the earth in his last moment of agony, and his childish face was
> distorted with pain. Poor kid! And it was such a beautiful day.

Turner remembered that for most of his time as a soldier 'the only
Germans with whom I came into contact were dead, wounded, or
prisoners'. 'Jerry', as they called him, 'was more of a nebulous geo-
graphical position than a person: a group name covering the opposing
forces or even the entire German race. With the exception of the

Milligan episode my emotions were centred more on the preservation of my own skin than directed to any hate complex.'[39] But, as that incident had shown, beneath the veneer of civilization and reason were forces that few could restrain; forces that threatened to spiral out of control as the war inched, as bloodily as ever, towards its pitiless end.

14.   'Cowards die many times'

*We keep shooting at different targets: at batteries, bridges, street crossings.
We are trying to do to him what he loves to do to us.*

Ernst Kielmayer[1]

26 October–4 November 1918

German patience with their brilliant, if erratic, First Quartermaster-General finally ran out on 26 October, in the grounds of the Bellevue Palace in Berlin. The Kaiser met Hindenburg and Ludendorff that morning. Ludendorff began by launching into his familiar 'brusque tone', making 'serious allegations against the government because they did not back the army command and left egregious insults against the military staff unanswered'. The Kaiser, having finally been prodded into action by Prince Max, told him that the order of 24 October had been unacceptable and gone against both his and the Chancellor's authority. With his hands shaking and his voice trembling, Wilhelm tried to make it clear to Ludendorff that 'this difficult political situation was ultimately created by the military situation'. As he later told an aide, 'I made him aware how distressing the demand for an immediate ceasefire was.' He tried to reassure Ludendorff, repeatedly emphasizing the general's 'tremendous military achievements . . . It was a misfortune, however, that he was too over-burdened. The military task was so large that it required the commitment of his entire character.'[2]

As might have been expected Ludendorff was stunned by the Kaiser's change of heart and immediately offered his resignation. Because he no longer commanded the confidence of the Emperor, he no longer wished to bear the responsibility of command, he said. The Kaiser, with a heavy heart, nodded and replied, 'Good, then you can have it.' At that moment, Hindenburg – who had stood silently by – also tendered his resignation, saying that he could not continue without the support of his 'loyal' and 'irreplaceable' companion, but Wilhelm refused, telling him that the German people could not do without him in this hour of extreme need. For the All-Highest War Lord, the meeting had been exhausting. He later told Major Alfred Niemann, one of his closest members of staff, that 'I stood before the ruins of genuine efforts and shattered hopes; I had not lived up to the expectations that had been placed upon me.'

Ludendorff returned to his apartment in Berlin shortly after eleven o'clock that morning. His wife, Margarethe, was standing by the window when his car pulled up and her husband got out. She was surprised at his return so early and immediately felt 'a strange sense of depression'. When Ludendorff came into the room, slumping down in a chair, his face as 'pale as death', her worst fears were confirmed.

'The Kaiser has sacked me. I have been dismissed.'

'Who is to be your successor?' she asked.

'I have suggested Kuhl,' he replied. His words were 'spoken almost without expression', his face inscrutable, his eyes staring straight ahead.

'Why not Seeckt?'

'I never thought of him.'

A moment later Ludendorff got up and snapped back: 'In a fortnight we shall have no Empire and no Emperor left. You will see.'³

The news of Ludendorff's resignation was met with mixed feelings in the German Army. For many socialists Ludendorff was the epitome of brutal, unthinking militarism and there was open rejoicing in the cabinet in Berlin. When his departure was reported in one cinema, many soldiers cheered.⁴ From sections of the Army, particularly Bavarians and Württembergers, Poles and Austrians, there seems to have been indifference rather than anger, exhaustion rather than frustration.⁵ For many, the time for caring about Germany's future had long since passed. What mattered, most of all, was peace, and doing whatever was necessary to get away from the front and its daily, horrific carnage. But for those who still believed in the war and felt that Germany must continue to fight on, the loss of such an esteemed commander was devastating. One such officer, Karl Urmacher, wrote to his father on 28 October after his company had got their hands on recent newspapers. 'Up until now I haven't seen our soldiers taking such a great interest in our offensive in the newspapers as they do now,' he wrote. 'But the pages are read in silence. The once lively debates that took place are rarely heard now. The goings-on at home are too unbelievable and the not knowing of how this is all going to turn out is too great.' He was disgusted by the news about the Quartermaster-General.

> When Ludendorff came, there was a real drive in the whole military service, he was a man who used every good experience at the front in a swift and practical way for the general good and who had a real empathy with the front . . . Where politics is concerned, we can only hope that his tireless devotion to duty in the army will be kept as a living example. There are very few men who devoted themselves to work as much as Ludendorff did. When he left, a star disappeared from Germany.[6]

Others agreed. Despite their recent clashes and frequent differences of opinion, Fritz von Lossberg retained a great respect for his former chief and deeply regretted his departure. Alongside Helmuth von Moltke and Count von Schlieffen, Lossberg counted Ludendorff as the greatest strategist the German Army ever produced and called his achievement as First Quartermaster-General simply 'magnificent'. After Amiens, however, Lossberg felt that Ludendorff's decisions were founded upon 'inappropriate conclusions', having overestimated the people's support for the war and miscalculated the strength of the Army. 'Given his extreme self-assurance, Ludendorff held fast to his – in the event incorrect – inner conviction that the assaults of the enemy could be repulsed. This is the only ultimate explanation for what was in fact the utter collapse of the German Army. Ludendorff was the author of his own downfall and he overstretched the might of the German Army. It was a tragic fate for both.'[7]

Ludendorff's replacement was not Max von Gallwitz (who had been tipped to take the post) or Hermann von Kuhl (whom Ludendorff had suggested), but the Chief of Staff of Army Group Kiev, General Wilhelm Groener. Recalled from his mission in the east, where he had been working out how best to exploit the Ukraine for Germany, Groener was ordered to Spa. On the face of it, Groener's appointment seemed odd. He was fifty years old and not widely known, certainly not the 'star' that Ludendorff had been. He was not the kind of man who would achieve victory against overwhelming odds or galvanize a great popular revolt against the Entente. As soon as the Crown Prince heard the news, he immediately telephoned Hindenburg and 'begged him not to choose this man in whom there was no trace of the spirit that was now our only hope of salvation'.[8] Groener originally hailed from Württemberg in south Germany – not Prussia – and had spent most of the war on the home front, organizing and running Germany's railway network to meet the demands of a war on two fronts. Nevertheless, his appointment was sensible one; indeed it is doubtful whether the socialists and independents in Berlin would have dealt with anyone else, certainly not a firebrand like Gallwitz or Kuhl. Now they needed a man who knew how to arrange a strategic retreat and a man who had dealt with the politicians and trade unionists in Berlin. Groener, with short, grey hair parted in the middle, and a thin white moustache, was the new face of the German Army.

Groener did what he could. He lacked the manic energy of his predecessor, but was a calm, organized and realistic presence. He understood the degree to which the German Army had been exhausted and the difficulty of securing its lines of communication as it fell back. He arrived at Spa on 30 October and was met by Hindenburg, who told him what had happened. They spent the day in discussions over the state of the Army, the amount of materiel that would need to be pulled back, as well as the difficulty of evacuating the scores of wounded from the front. On the evening of 1 November, Groener left Spa and travelled on to Brussels, Charleville and Charleroi to meet his Army Group commanders. Groener found Crown Prince Rupprecht in a serious mood and well aware of the dangers facing the monarchy. At Charleville – the headquarters of Crown Prince Wilhelm – there was less clarity. 'Here,' he wrote, 'one simply lived in the war, all the other considerations played no role, and Berlin was a frightful lair in which the politicians chatted and did useless things'; an attitude particularly noticeable in the Chief of Staff, Count Schulenburg. Groener soon realized that – contrary to the mood prevailing at Spa – the retreat to the Antwerp–Meuse Line could no longer be delayed. According to Rupprecht, they could wait for eight days, but most of his army commanders believed that they could not sustain more than one day of heavy fighting. At Charleroi, Gallwitz informed him that Fifth Army was no longer capable of maintaining 'sustainable resistance' and advocated retreating behind the Meuse as soon as possible. Therefore, it was agreed that Crown Prince Wilhelm's armies should fall back along the line Hirson–Mézières–the Meuse, in conjunction with the embattled Fifth Army north of the Argonne. On the evening of 4 November, with the German Armies buckling under renewed Allied attacks, Groener finally gave the order to begin the retreat.[9]

The Kaiser may have acted against Ludendorff, but after Wilson's third note, which had demanded constitutional change to the role of the 'King of Prussia', his own position was becoming increasingly precarious. The cabinet member Philip Scheidemann remembered how 'The number of letters reaching me at the time, saying that the Kaiser must be got rid of, was legion. I had calls from every class of the population: officials and soldiers told me plainly that the Kaiser could not remain.'[10] Even so, Prince Max was loath to press the Emperor to make such a step and preferred to wait in the hope that a decision would be taken out of his hands. For his part, the Kaiser tried to be bullish and was convinced that he was beloved by the German people. He was buoyed by the somewhat ridiculous hope that the British and Americans were 'at loggerheads' with each other and that it would be possible to make an agreement with Japan to ship her troops over to the Western Front and join the English in a grand coalition against America.[11] On 29 October he went to Spa – without Prince Max's knowledge – and toured the front in his Royal Train, spending his evenings waxing lyrical about life and death and how his soldiers adored him. On one occasion, when some bombs had fallen near the train, the Kaiser apparently quoted some lines from William Shakespeare's *Julius Caesar*:

> Cowards die many times before their deaths;
> The valiant never taste of death but once.
> Of all the wonders that I yet have heard,
> It seems to me most strange that men should fear;
> Seeing that death, a necessary end,
> Will come when it will come.[12]

But in Berlin there was no question of simply waiting for events to take their course. On Prince Max's orders, Dr Drews, the Prussian Minister of the Interior, was sent to Spa on 1 November to tell the Kaiser (gently) of the growing demands for his departure and of the potential difficulties that would arise if he remained on the throne. The Kaiser was nonplussed.

'How comes it that you, a Prussian official, one of my subjects who have taken an oath of allegiance to me, have the insolence and effrontery to appear before me with a request like this?'

Dr Drews said nothing, just bowed slightly and stared at His Majesty.

'Very well then, supposing I did,' continued the Kaiser. 'What do you suppose would happen next, you, an administrative official? My sons have assured me that none of them will take my place. So the whole house of Hohenzollern would go along with me.'

Drews made another bow.

'All right then, let me tell you the form chaos would take. I abdicate. All the dynasties fall along with me, the army is left leaderless, the front-line troops disband and stream over the Rhine. The disaffected gang up together, hang, murder and plunder – assisted by the enemy. That is why I have no intention of abdicating. The King of Prussia cannot betray Germany.'[13]

The Kaiser would repeat the substance of this conversation many times. His aides would repeat it back to him and assure him of the esteem in which he was held. It was a perfect, circular argument that comforted Wilhelm as October turned to November. The argument depended upon one thing, however: that the Army remained loyal to him and would desert if he abdicated, and this assumption would come under increasing pressure as the German Army fell back from the Western Front and as the fires of revolution took hold in the Fatherland, from Kiel to Munich, from Hamburg to Berlin. If the Kaiser had felt that his staunch rebuttal of Dr Drews would be the end of the matter, he was to be disappointed because the question would be asked again and again. Prince Max caught a punishing bout of influenza in late October and was increasingly unable to control the situation in Berlin and the growing clamour for the Kaiser to go. As Drews had said to the Chancellor before he set out for Spa, what slogan at the moment could be more effective against their efforts than 'The war must go on because the Kaiser will not sacrifice his personal interests in the cause of peace'?[14]

Rumours of an armistice passed through all the armies on the Western Front with remarkable speed, but they were not always greeted with relief and happiness. On the contrary, the US Marine Elton Mackin remembered that whenever talk of peace came, 'You saw men take a deep, full breath at the thought of it. You watched them look away beyond the front and picture hope. You watched men curl their lips in bitter disbelief, remembering the promises of rest camps, winter quarters, and other things. You heard them curse disinterestedly at men who dared to dream, and call them fools.'[15] It was not uncommon for the British, who had long specialized in dry, graveyard humour, to dismiss the whole thing as a conspiracy to undermine their morale. They knew how dangerous it was to think too much of peace. When the men of A. J. Turner's battalion heard that an armistice would probably be signed the following day, they received it, he wrote, 'with the usual scepticism'; one man quipping that 'of course' it would happen, 'and Lloyd George will be bringing each of us a nice hot steak and kidney pie'.[16]

The increasing likelihood of peace, or at least some form of temporary ceasefire, weighed heavily upon Allied commanders. They knew that their armies, drawn from every corner of their societies, many of whom were wartime volunteers or conscripts, would only keep going for so long. The French had already mutinied in 1917 so there was little chance that Pétain could push them much harder, no matter how many times Foch pestered him. By the last weeks of the war the length of active front held by the French Army had narrowed dramatically – down to just forty kilometres – in part owing to the convergent advances of the British and Americans on either wing, but also because it was rapidly running out of manpower.[17] As for the BEF, it was, as Haig had told Lloyd George on 19 October, 'never more efficient, but has fought hard, and it lacks reinforcements'.[18] Even the Americans, who had no shortage of men, were beginning to tire. When Hunter Liggett took command of the US First Army in late October (Pershing having been elevated to the same authority as Haig and Pétain), he found, to his despair, that 'some signs of discouragement were beginning to appear among both men and officers, the most conspicuous evidence of which was the great number of stragglers', which he estimated to be as high as 100,000 men. Because American casualties had been so heavy, and because so many divisions were filled with raw recruits, a loss of cohesion and discipline was probably inevitable, but it was shocking nonetheless.[19] There was only one thing to do: continue to push on and ensure that operations were conducted with as much care and attention to detail as possible.

Heavy fighting continued in the Franco-American sector in the south. By the last days of October, First Army had chewed its way through twenty-one kilometres of some of the worst ground on the Western Front, and had secured a good jump-off line for what Pershing hoped would be the final, decisive push. On 1 November, in conjunction with Gouraud's forces on the left, three American corps launched a major offensive to secure the third German position on the Barricourt Heights. Once this had been achieved, the Americans would then be able to cross the Meuse and head up to the city of Sedan, severing the German rail links that supplied the rest of the front. The Americans may have tried to do too much too soon in earlier offensives, but they had learnt remarkably quickly, and the November offensive was noticeable for the care and attention to detail that preceded it. It was also helped by the disastrous state of the German defences. Along an eighteen-kilometre front there were barely seven divisions in the line, and they had long been worn out.

There were a handful of reserve units, but they were unable to move up because of the shelling of the road network, and the collapse of the telephone system (also due to shelling) meant that their commanders were cut off.[20] At Fifth Army headquarters, General von der Marwitz wanted to pull back behind the Meuse; a sensible and prudent manoeuvre that would have given his tired men a breathing space and allowed them to hold the river line. Instead OHL had forbidden any retirement because of its effect on the negotiations and compelled Marwitz to stand and fight where he was.[21]

At 3.30 a.m. the preliminary shelling began, an agonizing two-hour 'hurricane' bombardment that pulverized the German defenders in their shell holes and trenches. Herbert L. McHenry, serving with 1st US Division, and in reserve that day, remembered watching the guns open fire – what he called 'the real roaring sound of war'. 'Then each of those "big babies" let go, it shook the earth, and as the "letting go" was continuous the earth was in a constant state of tremble.' By noon the first lines of German prisoners were filing past their positions, the usual cowed young boys and stumbling old men.[22] The Americans achieved remarkable success that day. Although some enemy regiments resisted stubbornly, most did not and US troops swept over the German lines, secured the high ground, and mauled whatever units they engaged. Hunter Liggett was mightily pleased with the results of the day's fighting. 'We had caught Von der Marwitz as I expected to – braced for the attack on his right. His weakened centre broke before the Fifth and Third Corps and these corps drove through to the Barricourt Ridge, as ordered, overrunning his entire defensive system . . .'[23]

On the same day that Pershing's corps had reached the Meuse, the Canadian Corps was in action on the outskirts of Valenciennes, attacking a fortified hill called Mont Houy that commanded the town. Furious attacks by British forces in the last days of October had come to nothing, so Arthur Currie had agreed to mount an operation to secure it. In what was a masterpiece of preparation and care, Currie's gunners, led by the tireless Andrew McNaughton, went to work. 'Owing to the fact that the German Army was approaching a defeat on a grand scale and that there was much peace talk in the air,' a report on the operation stated, 'it was decided that all restrictions concerning the economical use of supporting arms . . . were now out of place, and it was therefore the proper time to neglect economy.' Six brigades of field artillery and 104 heavy guns, supported by nine batteries of heavy machine-guns (totalling seventy-two barrels), were brought up to the front. They were to launch a massive creeping barrage on the German positions at Zero Hour. Because of the layout of the ground, it was possible to deploy a great deal of artillery forward and allow a combination of not only frontal artillery fire, but also oblique, enfilade and, incredibly, reverse fire. It would not only be a startling demonstration of the effectiveness of Currie's policy of 'neglect nothing', but a brutal illustration of the sheer weight and accuracy of firepower that the British and French Armies could wield in the closing months of the war.[24]

On the cold, wet morning of 1 November, just one Canadian brigade, the 10th, went forward, supported by what historians have judged to be one of the most intensive fire plans of the war. During the attack seven tonnes of high explosive were fired *every minute* on a front of less than two miles, completely pulverizing the dazed defenders and tearing apart any defences they had made.[25] If anywhere on the Western Front epitomized the Dante's *Inferno*-like conditions faced by the German soldier in this period then it was Mont Houy. When Andrew McNaughton examined the cratered, smoking ground after the battle he noted that enemy dead were everywhere, 'in rifle and machine gun pits, in trenches and sunken roads, in the open, in the rows of houses demolished by the siege howitzers; the concentrations, particularly those in enfilade on railway cuttings and other defiles, had left a shambles . . .' In total the Germans had suffered 800 dead. Another 1,400 prisoners were being shepherded to the rear. The Canadians had suffered only 420 casualties, with just 60 fatalities, an astonishingly light figure given the strength of the enemy defences and the limited numbers of attackers.[26] The German Army had no answer to this kind of punishment. Its soldiers, many still bravely led and well-trained, always took a toll on the attacking forces, but under such fire they could do little but retreat or die. If they decided to hold any position, they did so at a terrible risk and in the knowledge that it would only take a matter of days – sometimes hours – before the Allies pushed them off.

By the first week of November the German Army was in full retreat across the Western Front. From the air 'we saw all the roads crowded with columns of men marching back,' wrote one German pilot.[27] Endless lines of weary troops splashed and shuffled their way eastwards, bowed down with their equipment, looking over their shoulders in fear, half expecting to see Allied aircraft or cavalry squadrons ready to scatter them again. It was an awful sight: the faces of young boys overshadowed by the steel helmets that were too big for them, or hobbling along in boots that had been worn away long ago; old veterans who had seen too many battles marching along with glassy eyes and a grim acceptance of death or wounding. It was by now a motley army; the exact opposite of the legions of proud *feldgrau* that had marched across Europe in the summer of 1914 on their way to enact Count von Schlieffen's great war plan. The German Army had reached its end; worn down by four years of merciless slaughter and pounded into dust by the brutal Allied artillery bombardments. Some still believed in victory, in some divine intervention – a catastrophic outbreak of flu in Paris or London; a devastating fallout between the English and Americans perhaps – but most realized there was little they could do. How could they defeat the endless power of the Allied guns or their swarms of tanks? How many Americans would they have to kill before they too gave in? And in any case, was it really worth fighting and dying for any more? Did anyone really care whether Alsace-Lorraine was French or German?

Casualties were nothing short of catastrophic. Fritz von Lossberg estimated that by the time the German Army reached the Antwerp–Meuse Line it had lost over 400,000 men and 6,000 guns.[28] Other authorities put it higher, and it is possible that between 18 July and 11 November the Army suffered 420,000 dead and wounded with another 385,000 men being taken prisoner. Such a magnitude of loss was simply unsustainable, and when this was combined with the thousands of casualties from Germany's spring offensives earlier in the year – perhaps as high as a million – it meant that her army was bleeding to death.[29] The strength of many units was now a fraction of their full establishments. According to Major-General von Kuhl, by the end of October most German battalions could muster only 450 men, and of them barely half were fighting troops, and this was almost certainly an overestimation.[30] There were not enough men to man the trenches, not enough men to bring up the guns, and fewer and fewer reliable NCOs. For example, against the British Third Army, 111th Division registered company strengths of between fifty and sixty men. Likewise in 21st Reserve Division, one of its regiments was now down to three companies, each numbering around sixty soldiers, and this seems to have been entirely typical of the German Army in the West by this point, its ranks ravaged by the endless Allied attacks and stalked by the merciless influenza pandemic.[31]

Given the chronic shortages of manpower, morale quickly declined. When rumours spread through units of the increasing rate of desertion, of how more and more men were simply giving up and heading for home, those at the front understandably asked why they should continue to suffer when others declined to do the same. Reinforcements would occasionally turn up, but they were always far fewer than had been promised and often surly and unhappy, always muttering about 'war prolongers' and doing nothing for unit cohesion. Adolf Hitler later complained that the arrival of recruits from home meant not a reinforcement but 'a weakening of our fighting strength', with the young ones being 'mostly worthless'.[32] Such was the toxic mixture of exhaustion and ill-discipline that was crippling the German Army. It was now nothing more than a collection of units, some good, mostly bad, but all lacking organization and structure. Commanders tried their best to explain to their men the importance of continuing to resist, but it was an almost hopeless task. Tales would be spread of the horrific consequences of peace with the Allies; of how the land would be exhausted and the people taxed beyond anything they had ever known. Second Army even issued a message to its troops in late October warning them that any peace would bring worse devastation to Germany than the struggle against Napoleon had in the last century. 'Only when the enemy's guns are silent forever is peace in sight,' it read. 'Until that happens we HAVE GOT TO FIGHT ON. Every man has got to do his duty, unless the enemy is to snatch victory at the eleventh hour. Only by setting our teeth and holding on to the end are we to get peace. THE FATHER-LAND FOREVER.'[33]

In spite of the increasingly shrill exhortations from its leaders, the Army gradually ceased to function. Orders would go missing; supporting artillery fire would never come; reports would not be written; supplies would never turn up. Alfred Mahncke, a staff officer with the German Air Force at Verviers, was tasked with organizing supplies to the front-line squadrons. 'Considering the many shortages at this late stage of war,' he wrote, 'it was a thorny and almost hopeless task which could not be solved to everyone's satisfaction.' Lack of coal and strikes in the factories had a devastating effect on the number of engines, guns and ammunition he received, but getting enough fuel to the squadrons was his greatest challenge. By November, fighter squadrons were limping by on just 150 litres of aviation fuel a day – barely enough for a handful of individual sorties – which meant that the Air Force could no longer contest control of the skies. 'I toiled at the centre of it all – compromising, balancing, reconciling and pacifying.' The disintegration was noticeable even at OHL. Mahncke went to Spa for a meeting in early November and noticed that the atmosphere at the Hôtel Britannique was 'tense and charged; nervous individuals rushed around, seemingly without purpose'.[34]

Fritz von Lossberg was glad to leave Spa on 1 November. He had been shocked by the decline in efficiency and order. 'Under Ludendorff there was a regime of strict discipline and deference,' he wrote. 'Now strong leadership was lacking. Now all the many self-important people were bragging. Everyone had his own opinion and liked to air it.' As he was climbing into his car that morning, intending to travel to Strasbourg to take up his position as Chief of Staff to the Duke Albrecht of Württemberg (who commanded the southern sector of the German line in France), he was handed a telegram from the senior doctor of a military hospital in Antwerp. 'Your son is ill with an infection in both lungs,' it read. 'His life is in grave danger.' Lossberg's son had already been wounded four times and had been employed as a desk officer at the Supreme Command until his fitness improved. Now, it seemed, his health had failed him again. Lossberg travelled on to Strasbourg, but as soon as he arrived he telephoned his wife and asked her to go to Antwerp. Unfortunately, by the time she reached Holland, mutiny had broken out and was spreading quickly behind the lines. 'In order to return to Stuttgart she had to travel for five days in trains crammed with riotous soldiers,' he remembered. 'The transportation of our son from Antwerp ran into difficulties because the hospital trains were stormed and occupied by lawless people from behind the lines. It was not possible to evacuate the sick and wounded in an organised manner.' Fortunately they managed to get on another hospital train that took them to safety in Germany.[35]

By the last days of October the German Seventeenth, Second and Eighteenth Armies — those that had borne the brunt of British and French attacks since August — had occupied the line of the Sambre–Oise canal that ran from La Fère northeastwards up past Guise and Le Cateau. On 4 November the Allies would attack this line in what became one of the last great offensives on the Western Front: the Battle of the Sambre. Three British armies attacked along a twenty-mile front; pushing towards Avesnes and Mons, marching through difficult wooded terrain, hedgerows and orchards, and over numerous water obstacles ranging from canals and streams to irrigation ditches. To the south, the French were also on the move, extending the frontage of attack for another twenty miles, with Debeney's First Army aiming for the town of La Capelle.[36] Against them was an assorted collection of divisions from the battered Army Group of General von Boehn. The German positions were just hastily dug foxholes or rifle pits. There was not the time or the manpower to convert them into something more substantial, leaving the men in the open to face the oncoming storm. The history of 3rd Westphalian Regiment (holding the line at Raucourt near the Forest of Mormal) complained that:

The whole position consisted of rifle-pits connected up irregularly. There were no dug outs. There was no field of view owing to hedges, houses, walls and gardens. The battle headquarters were in small cellars, hardly splinter proof. In these inadequate positions weakened and used up troops awaited the attack of an overwhelming enemy.[37]

The feelings of those soldiers can well be imagined as they crouched in the dirt under their steel helmets, clutching their rifles and breathing heavily through their foul-smelling rubber gas masks, waiting nervously for the bombardments to begin or the tanks to rumble forward.

Wilfred Owen would write what would turn out to be the final letter to his mother on 31 October, just after six in the evening. His battalion had moved up to the front several days earlier, taking up a position on the heavily wooded west bank of the Sambre canal, north of the village of Ors. Owen had been billeted in a stone cottage known as the 'Forester's House'. 'So thick is the smoke in this cellar that I can hardly see by a candle 12 inches away, and so thick are the inmates that I can hardly write for pokes, nudges and jolts. On my left the Company Commander snores on a bench: other officers on wire beds behind me.' Despite the discomfort, Owen seemed more content than he had been for many months. He ended by saying that he was perfectly safe and that 'I hope you are as warm as I am; as serene in your room as I am here . . . you could not be visited by a band of friends half so fine as surround me here.'38 Owen may not have said much about the forthcoming attack, but it must have weighed heavily on his men. All the bridges had been demolished by the retreating Germans, leaving the British with little option other than to swim the seventy-foot canal or improvise boats or bridges. On the far bank, the ground rose steadily away, giving enemy observers a clear view of the British lines. It was just like Bellenglise again, and many men shivered in apprehension at going over the top here, particularly when peace seemed so tantalizingly close.

The battalion attacked at 5.45 in the foggy, dew-stained morning of 4 November. Owen was in one of the assaulting companies. They went forward after a five-minute 'hurricane' bombardment fell on the far bank, before lifting 300 yards into the enemy defences, where it would remain for a further half an hour; more than enough time, staff officers had said, for the men to establish themselves across the canal, and push on eastwards. Unfortunately, as at Gouzeaucourt and at scattered places across the front throughout the Hundred Days, here the Germans were determined to stay put, and greeted the attackers with heavy machine-gun and rifle fire, pounding shells and mortar rounds that dug into the damp earth or splashed into the murky waters of the canal. The engineers and bridging specialists who had been called in to get the Manchesters over the obstacle could make little progress against such lethal fire. Thirty of the forty-two engineers tasked with putting pontoon bridges into place were killed or wounded, which left the battalion's junior officers with no choice but to secure the bridges as best they could.[39]

One of those who fought in this sector was Leutnant Erich Alenfeld, serving with 280th Field Artillery Regiment, whose batteries were dug in about 600 metres from the far bank. They were woken shortly before 6 a.m. when a heavy bombardment opened on their position. They immediately fired off flares to warn the other batteries and commenced firing 'like the devil'. 'The battle has broken out,' he remembered. 'We continuously shoot protective barrages in waves, that is, allowing the artillery to increase and decrease. The enemy is no less active. There are howls and crashes, a grey wall spreads out before us, and the enemy shrouds us in smoke. Machine gun fire can be heard from close by.' News reached Alenfeld that the British were coming.

> I know what this means; there's a reason we are here. I fasten on my sling and pistol, bag and water, give my luggage to my batman and just want to give the new order, when I'm told that I should engage the enemy on the banks of the canal. I call Jacoby to my side, explain the situation to him, leave the third gun to him (on the left flank), say goodbye with a handshake and assume command of the right column, gunners at the ready! I tell them what is going on in a few words, and ask them to hold on with me until the end.[40]

Alenfeld fought along the canal all morning, beating off attacks and organizing protective fire from his guns, before eventually being wounded. 'I am the first to be hit in the left thigh and the right upper arm – I throw myself on the ground; next to me the brave telephone operator Herten falls to the ground screaming.' Alenfeld could now see British troops about 300 metres from where he was lying, but fortunately one of his gunners dragged him back to the battery, where he was attended by a medical orderly. 'The arm wound is nothing, a scrape on my skin, the leg is bleeding quite a bit.' Alenfeld then had to make a decision, whether to hold on until reinforcements arrived or retreat. In the end, seeing that the main road to Landrecies was already in British hands he ordered his men to fall back.

The Manchesters suffered heavily that day. One of their most promising officers, Second-Lieutenant James Kirk, was killed operating a Lewis gun on the far bank of the canal, after having paddled a raft across under heavy fire. He kept up a constant fire, vainly attempting to suppress the incoming machine-gun rounds so that his men could survive. He would later be awarded a posthumous Victoria Cross, his citation commending his 'supreme contempt for danger and magnificent self-sacrifice' that he showed that day.[41] It was an awful scene: heavy machine-gun bullets scything through the dark waters and shredding the thin lines of infantry; artillery fire on the banks; smoke; confusion. His fellow officer, Wilfred Owen, was last seen on a raft in the water with some of his men when he came under murderous machine-gun fire. At one point he comforted two members of his platoon – green young boys – telling them 'well done' and 'you're doing well', hoping to instil some courage into them, even as it became clear that the battalion would not be able to cross here. Shortly afterwards Owen was shot and killed. Thus, on 4 November, seven days before the Armistice, ended the life of the most promising English poet since Keats.

Despite the carnage at Ors, 4 November had been a day of good returns for the Allies with most divisions taking their objectives on time without running into heavy resistance. Rawlinson's Fourth Army had crossed the Sambre–Oise canal across a fifteen-mile front and taken over 4,000 prisoners.[42] To the south, Debeney's French troops had also encountered 'energetic resistance' in getting over the canal – footbridges could not be secured and the troops had to raft themselves across – but they would march into the village of Guise the following day.[43] For the Germans, however, it was the same dispiriting story of crushing bombardments, heavy attacks and panicked retreats. Leutnant Alenfeld and his men fell back at 2.30 p.m., marching away from the fighting with their wounded on stretchers, trying

to escape the attention of passing aircraft. Although British shellfire
continually harassed them, it was the aircraft that they really hated;
flying low, shooting and throwing bombs and grenades at anything
they saw. By the time darkness fell they were in Maroilles, four miles
from the canal, getting their wounded treated while they snatched
quick mugs of coffee. There were no horses or trucks available, so
they spent the next six hours continuing the retreat, marching on
dead feet towards Avesnes ('countless columns march beside us'),
which only two months before had housed the Advanced Headquarters of the Supreme Command. Alenfeld's battery had lost two dead,
seventeen wounded, five missing, and a number of guns and horses.
When they reached their destination, they could rest for the time
being and reflect upon what had happened. 'Since the Englishman is
cowardly,' he raged, 'he attacks only if he finds no opposition. His
artillery shoots well. The airmen are too many for us to deal with.
They have absolute control of the air, they simply go for a flight and
do a lot of damage . . . Germany is defeated and the conditions of
peace are dreadful. With Austria's collapse everything becomes much
worse still . . .'[44]

A question was on everyone's lips: how long could this go on?

15. Armistice at Compiègne

A successor of Frederick the Great does not abdicate.

Kaiser Wilhelm II[1]

5–11 November 1918

Shortly after 7 a.m. on 8 November, Foch's Chief of Staff, Maxime Weygand, noticed a red light moving slowly through the mist. It was all he could see of the train that was carrying the German Armistice Commission, and thus the fate of Germany, to the small station of Rethondes in the forest of Compiègne.[2] The delegation had been hastily cobbled together by Prince Max two days earlier after he had received a note from President Wilson confirming that he was willing to make peace. Because the Allies had accepted the Fourteen Points (apart from reservations on the clause relating to freedom of the seas and over reparations), Foch was now authorized to communicate those terms with any German delegates.[3] Groener told Max that they could no longer delay direct armistice talks and, with the Army threatening to collapse at any moment, they would have to cross the lines with a white flag. Prince Max baulked at doing this so soon, fearing that any terms would be too severe, but in the end he agreed, managing to persuade the leader of the Catholic Party in the Reichstag, the Secretary of State, Matthias Erzberger, to lead the delegation. He hoped that by sending Erzberger, a man of courage and integrity with a track record of working for peace, the terms could be softened.

Gradually the train came into view and then stopped with a hiss of steam. Shortly afterwards Weygand saw them. There were six of them in total, led by Erzberger, who was dressed in a long black coat. He was accompanied by a military representative, Major-General Hans von Winterfeldt, a diplomat, Count Oberndorff, and three military advisers.[4] The men were already exhausted, but knew that hours of tense and detailed negotiation lay ahead of them. They had spent the night travelling and had been much delayed, such was the traffic on the roads leading to and from the front. They had crossed no-man's-land under a white flag the previous evening and been picked up by a French patrol outside La Capelle in General Debeney's sector. From there they had driven through the town of Guise, avoiding the shell holes and dead horses, and past the columns of troops – the grey-faced *poilus* – and trucks moving up to the front ready to continue the offensive. At the appointed time a guard showed them the way, along a boardwalk through a grove of trees, to the Marshal's personal train, where they boarded and prepared to see what was on offer, to see whether Germany would receive her 'peace of justice' or not. The German Armistice Commission had arrived.

Foch was waiting for them. He was dressed in a long *horizon-bleu* coat and *képi*, leaning heavily on a cane, with a stern look upon his face. Beside him was Weygand, his loyal, attentive ghost, followed by Admiral Rosslyn Wemyss, Chief of the British naval detachment (who was accompanied by two other Royal Navy officers) and their interpreters. When they were settled, the *Generalissimo* began. His tone was sharp, his manner severe. He asked, what was the purpose of their visit? Erzberger looked across at Foch and replied that they had come 'to receive the proposals of the Allied Powers looking to an armistice on land, on sea and in the air on all fronts'. Foch replied that he had no proposals to make and when Count Oberndorff queried this, with a confused look on his face, the *Generalissimo* snapped back.

'Do you ask for an armistice? If you do, I can inform you of the conditions subject to which it can be obtained.'

Yes, Erzberger and Oberndorff nodded, they asked for an armistice.

Foch ordered the terms, which had been agreed at Versailles four days earlier, to be read aloud. Although the reading only included the principal clauses, this took some time. The Allies demanded the cessation of hostilities within six hours of any agreement, the evacuation of occupied France and Belgium (including Alsace-Lorraine) within

two weeks, and the surrender of thousands of machine-guns, artillery pieces and aircraft, as well as rolling stock and military stores.
Weygand, who read these terms aloud, found this the most emotional
part of the proceedings. When he explained that the Allies would
also march into the left bank of the Rhine and occupy Mainz,
Coblenz and Cologne, he noticed that General von Winterfeldt's face
turned 'deathly pale' and Captain Helldorf's eyes filled with tears.[5]
Once the conditions had been read, Erzberger asked for an immediate suspension of military operations. He cited the growth of
revolutionary spirit in Germany and the urgent need to prevent more
people from suffering in these final hours. If the fighting could stop,
he pleaded, the German Army could reform and re-establish discipline in the Fatherland. But Foch was unimpressed. Bolshevism
was, he said, 'the usual disease prevailing in beaten armies' and Western Europe would look after itself. Therefore, there would be no
suspension of military activity, no let-up in the offensives, until Germany had accepted the Allied demands. One of the German
delegation, Captain Helldorf, was handed a copy of the armistice
conditions, and then set out, on the long road back to Spa, to deliver
them in person to the Supreme Command.[6]

As Erzberger's team were getting to grips with the Allied demands,
the German war effort began to collapse with alarming speed. In Berlin, Philip Scheidemann noted that 'If hitherto one had only heard
the cracking of the main joints of the Empire, now a cracking of the
smaller ones was distinctly audible.'[7] On 4 November, the day Wilfred Owen was killed, sailors mutinied at Kiel. Revolution then
began to spread across Germany's northern coast and within days
Lübeck, Cuxhaven, Hanover and Hamburg fell to sailors flying the
red flag of Bolshevism, demanding an immediate armistice and an
end to military dictatorship. What troops there were on hand
remained sullen and immobile, unwilling to fire upon their fellow
Germans and waiting, uneasily, for the response from Berlin. On 8
November, as Prince Max tried desperately to hold the country
together at the end of telegraph and telephone lines that flickered and
failed like the struggles of a dying man, the Social Democrats issued
their ultimatum. Unless the Kaiser and the Crown Prince went, they

would walk out of the Government. That night Prince Max received word that the revolution was continuing to spread. Brunswick and Munich had already gone. The authorities in Stuttgart had handed over power to Workers' and Soldiers' Councils and Cologne was expected to fall into revolutionary hands that night. It was even rumoured that sailors were marching on Berlin.

That evening, Prince Max, carrying the burden of an empire on his shoulders, spoke to the Kaiser, through a crackly telephone line. His abdication had become necessary to save Germany, he said.

'We are steering straight for civil war,' he warned. 'I have struggled against admitting it, but the position is today untenable; the abdication would be received with universal relief and hailed as a liberating and a healing act.'

But the Kaiser refused to listen. He would remain at the head of his army and utterly rejected all calls for his abdication. When Prince Max offered his resignation, saying that he did not command the confidence of the Kaiser, Wilhelm refused.

'You sent out the armistice offer,' he raged, 'you will have to put your name to the conditions!'

The Chancellor backed down, chastened and heavy with remorse. He would remain in office until the Armistice was signed.[8]

At Compiègne, the discussions continued into the following day, 9 November. Erzberger handed Foch a paper on the armistice conditions that had been drafted by his team. It contained a series of complaints and counter-arguments to Foch's terms, warning of the danger that the Allied demands were too severe, and again stressing the urgent need to give the German Army a break so that it could return home and restore order. This would become a familiar German refrain, one that they would repeat with ever more desperation, but it impressed no one. Foch brushed it aside with his customary disdain, and kept asking Erzberger whether he had received an answer from Berlin and whether he had been empowered to sign the Armistice or not. Erzberger would look depressed and shake his head; no, he would reply, he had not heard anything. In the German capital the atmosphere was 'oppressive and sultry', like the moments before a storm. Scheidemann remembered how the big factories were 'seething with excitement. The machines seemed to be working faster and the wheels grating louder. The shouts of the workers sounded angrier; the curses of the Spartacists and Communists against the Majority Socialists were more bitter; the furnaces grew hotter.' Large meetings had been held across the city over the last few days and at the Reichstag the discussions over when the Kaiser would resign continued with ever greater urgency. Scheidemann even rang up the Chancellery that morning and asked if the Kaiser had gone. 'Not yet,' came the reply, 'but we expect to hear at any moment.'[9]

9 November was the Kaiser's last day at Spa. At midday his son, Crown Prince Wilhelm, arrived after having made the journey from his headquarters during the night. He was received by the Court Marshal, General von Gontard, whose face 'wore a serious and very anxious look'. The Crown Prince immediately began asking questions about the situation, but all the general did was 'to raise his hands helplessly', a gesture that seemed to say far more than words could. He eventually found his father in the garden of his villa surrounded by a group of officers. 'Never shall I forget the picture of that half-score of men in their grey uniforms, thrown into relief by the withered and faded flower-beds of ending autumn, and framed by the surrounding mist-mantled hills with their glorious foliages . . .'

> The Kaiser stood there as though he had suddenly halted with them in the midst of a nervous pacing up and down. He was passionately excited, and addressing himself to those near him with violently expressive gestures. His eyes were upon General Groener and His Excellency von Hintze; but a glance was cast now and then at the Field Marshal General [Hindenburg], who, with his gaze fixed in the distance, nodded silently.[10]

The Kaiser seemed to have aged; his face was emaciated and sallow. As Ludendorff had done before him, he raged at the situation he was now in, seeking a way out only to find that the maze was now closed, the doors bolted; the only option was to abdicate. Telegrams from Germany and Austria added to the sense of urgency and panic at Spa. That morning Prince Max had informed him that the King of Bavaria and the Duke of Brunswick had renounced their thrones, and that

Beckton Globe Library
24 hr Tel: 0333 370 4700

Renewed Items 09/01/2020 20:01
XXXX7758

Item Title	Due Date
* New GCSE Spanish Revision Guide - For the Grade 9-1 Course (with Onlin e Edition)	30/01/2020
* In the midst of winter	30/01/2020
* The Red-Haired Woman	30/01/2020
* The vanquished : why the First World War failed to end, 1917-1923	30/01/2020
* Hundred days : the end of the Great War	30/01/2020

* Renewed today
Thank you for renewing

www.newham.gov.uk
BecktonGlobeLibrary@newham.gov.uk
From 2 April 2013 notification charges will apply. To register for the free email Pre-overdue service please see a staff member

Beckton Globe Library

24 hr Tel: 0333 370 4700

Renewed Items 09/01/2020 20:01

XXXX7758

Item Title	Due Date
* New GCSE Spanish Revision Guide - For the Grade 9-1 Course (with Onlin e Edition)	30/01/2020
* In the midst of winter	30/01/2020
* The Red-Haired Woman	30/01/2020
* The vanquished : why the First World War failed to end, 1917-1923	30/01/2020
Hundred days : the end of the Great War	30/01/2020

* Renewed today
Thank you for renewing
www.newham.gov.uk
BecktonGlobeLibrary@newham.gov.uk
From 2 April 2013 notification charges will apply. To register for the free email
Pre-overdue service please see a staff member.

the 'overwhelming majority' of the cabinet believed abdication was the only way of avoiding civil war.[11]

Discussions over what should be done had been raging at both the Kaiser's villa and the Hôtel Britannique all morning. All of Prussia's great warrior caste were there; the surviving remnants of an empire that stood on the brink of collapse, including Hindenburg and Groener, Paul von Hintze, Colonel Heye, and the Crown Prince's Chief of Staff, Count Schulenberg; all airing their views and arguing over whether the Army would stand firm or not. The sense of time and history hung heavily upon them, like the thick fog that blanketed the forested hills around Spa. Some talked of the Kaiser leading the Army back to Germany in person, a kind of *reconquista*, purging the Fatherland of socialists and anarchists and restoring discipline and honour. Others suggested that he should go to the front, join his men in the trenches and die fighting, although it was pointed out that not only would this be highly dangerous, but also that suicide was un-Christian and might bring the accusation that the Emperor had taken an easy route out of his difficulties. It was left to Groener to introduce a sense of realism into the proceedings. He talked at length, calmly and firmly, saying that any kind of campaign into Germany would not be possible given the unreliability of the troops and the fact that most of the bridges and railway stations were now in the hands of rebels. If it were done then civil war would almost certainly be the result.[12]

Groener knew the game was up. He may have been outshone by the dazzling brilliance of Ludendorff, but he had a much greater, earthier understanding of what the German Army was really going through. While many units would probably continue to fight, at least for now, he believed that they would never raise arms against their fellow countrymen, let alone if the Kaiser remained on the throne. On 5 November he had received a letter from the commander of 192nd Infantry Division, Major-General Löffler, who wrote to him not as the Quartermaster-General, but as an old friend.

My dear Groener, I am writing to you because, from the General Headquarters, insight into the troops doesn't penetrate deeply enough to measure combat strength by its actual value. As a result, a tone or a shade of vital importance can be missing or not distinct enough in the overall general impression. The strength of the troops is running out. You know me well enough to know that I am not a pessimist. My division hasn't had a single day of rest since the beginning of May. For weeks and months on end only bivouacs have been possible. There has been no talk of proper sanitizing, delousing, and the like for just as long. At the same time, the troops have been taking part in the fighting and battles along the Aire River for three months; from there they stumbled into the Saint-Mihiel sweep shortly before the crisis there, and for the past eleven days they have been in sustained combat just east of the Meuse. Every man has been committed for the duration, almost without exception. The combat situation or the weakness of the troops after losses has not afforded the retreat of even the smaller companies. As a result of bloody losses of about 7,000 men since the middle of May, particularly in the ranks and in the infantry, the units are no longer as well-formed as before.

Löffler warned Groener that the end was near:

From what I have been able to gather, it has been the same with every other division. Yet we've done our part. Every day brings proof of that. The moment of overturning is, however, no doubt approaching. It is no longer a matter of weeks. Eventually there comes a time when every action fails due to fatigue. It is into this state that we are now entering.[13]

Groener would never be forgiven for what many diehards saw as his treachery on 9 November. They claimed that his pessimism, his defeatism, meant that the Kaiser received an incorrect view of the army's capabilities and gave in when it should have fought on. General Count Friedrich von der Schulenburg, the Crown Prince's ultra-loyal Chief of Staff and a former member of the *Corps de Garde* – a man who had clashed with Groener before – spoke for the diehards. He rubbished Groener's claims and argued that the Army was holding and only needed rest. If it could be given an opportunity to refresh, to have 'a good night's sleep', to reform its shattered ranks, then it would continue to fight, particularly once it had been told how shamelessly it was being betrayed by traitors and Bolsheviks at home. However, if an armistice was signed, he warned them that it would be very difficult to rouse the men to fight again.[14] The Kaiser, as befitted his notoriously fragile character, was unsure. He was buoyed by Schulenberg's staunch defence of the imperial throne and his words about the Army remaining loyal, but knew Groener was not a man to be taken lightly. For his part, the Quartermaster-General explained at length, again and again, that it was too late to restore order at home, that it would be hopeless to take up the fight against the rebels and that, in any case, the Army was no longer loyal to His Majesty.

At one point, when Groener had, once again, reaffirmed his belief that Schulenberg did not understand the difficulties of the situation and that the army's loyalty had gone, Wilhelm lost his temper. He walked up to Groener – 'his eyes blazing with anger' – and said that he must prove his statement by asking the army commanders.[15]

'The army,' said Groener, now also becoming angry, 'will march back to Germany, peacefully and orderly, under its commanders and commanding generals, but not at the command of Your Majesty because it no longer supports Your Majesty.'

Groener's stand took courage; more courage than he was ever given credit for. He later admitted that he spoke 'rather more sharply' than he should have done; his patience failing him 'in the face of such unrealistic notions'. 'Even this brusque word from me was no more than a warning from the bottom of my heart to the Kaiser not to clutch at straws,' he wrote. 'If one of the men present had gunned me down at that moment, it wouldn't have come as any surprise to me, since these words were a monstrosity in a circle such as this, in which only old Hindenburg (and only with the greatest of difficulty) mustered up the levelheadedness to see things as they really were.' It may have been more prudent for Groener to have kept quiet, but his words were necessary to banish what he called the 'political fantasy world' that the Kaiser and his staff, as well as loyalists like Schulenberg, inhabited. Groener's dour realism, combined with his understanding of what it was really like at the front, may not have won him any friends at Spa, but the thousands of German soldiers in the trenches had cause to thank him. Finally, after all the dreams and illusions of Hindenburg and Ludendorff, the German Army had found a sense of reality and objectivity. The man from Württemberg had delivered the *coup de grâce*.[16]

The Kaiser was understandably shaken by what Groener had said. He muttered something about getting this in writing from his generals, but it never came to that. Instead a group of chosen officers who had arrived at Spa that morning were consulted. It had originally been intended that fifty soldiers from the three main army groups should attend meetings on the state of the Army, but only thirty-nine had made it, with many being delayed on the roads, itself an indication of the crumbling supply lines behind the front. Wilhelm Heye, the Chief of Operations at OHL, was given the delicate task of speaking to them. After they had assembled, some still in their muddy uniforms, almost all exhausted, he asked them a series of questions. Whether they realized it or not, the future of the empire rested on their answers. What was their attitude to the Emperor and to Bolshevism? Were they willing to march back behind the Kaiser and re-conquer the homeland? Amid a stunned, uncomprehending silence, a vote was held. On the question of whether it would be possible to regain control of Germany alongside the Kaiser, only one officer said yes, a Major von Kretschmann, Adjutant of 36th Infantry Division in Sixth Army. But his was a lone voice. Twenty-three officers were against it, while 15 were unsure. On the second question, of whether they would be willing to fight against the Bolsheviks, 8 officers thought not, 19 were doubtful, but 12 thought that a period of rest was essential before any further campaign was begun.[17] Heye took their replies and reported to the Kaiser. An immediate armistice was essential, he said. 'The troops remain loyal to His Majesty, but they are tired and indifferent and want nothing except rest and peace. At the present moment they would not march against Germany, even with Your Majesty at their head. They would not march against Bolshevism. They want one thing only – an armistice at the earliest possible moment.'[18]

Sometime around 1 p.m. the Kaiser finally agreed to abdicate from the imperial throne, but *not* as the King of Prussia; a constitutional nonsense, but one which salvaged some of his pride. He sent a short telegram to Berlin and told them that the Armistice Commission was now empowered to conclude an agreement with the Allies immediately. He offered to resign from the imperial throne, but would remain as King of Prussia with Hindenburg taking over as Supreme Commander. 'The Army Commanders and the Supreme Command,' he stated, 'are of the opinion that the abdication of the German Kaiser and Supreme War Lord at this moment will provoke the gravest convulsions in the army, and they can therefore no longer assume responsibility for the Army holding together.'[19] As the telegram was being drafted, the Kaiser and his staff had lunch, although, as the Crown Prince later noted, it was not a happy one.

> That silent meal, in a bright, white room whose table was decked with flowers but surrounded only by bitter anguish and despairing grief, is among the most horrible of my recollections. Not one of us but masked his face, not one who did not make fitful attempts, for that half-hour, to hide his uneasiness and not to talk of the phantom that lurked behind him and could not for a single moment be forgotten. Every mouthful seemed to swell and threaten to choke the eater. The whole meal resembled some dismal funeral repast.[20]

If the Kaiser felt some pride in remaining stubborn to the end, in never giving in completely to his opponents, and ensuring that he would stay with his army, it was to be short-lived. Just after 2 p.m., as the Kaiser's last supper was being cleared up, General von Plessen, the General-Adjutant, called His Majesty away. An urgent communiqué had been received from Berlin. The abdication of His Majesty *both* from the imperial throne *and* as the King of Prussia (as well as that of his son) had just been announced by Prince Max. Scheidemann had even proclaimed the republic from the Chancellery.

There was a moment of stunned, disbelieving silence, which soon gave way to panic and loud protests as the news got around. There had been some great mix-up, some foul play, some horrific accident, that meant the wrong information had got out. Furious telegrams and phone calls began issuing from Spa as the Kaiser and his staff desperately tried to clarify his position and ensure that the correct information was passed on. The Kaiser was *not* abdicating from the throne of Prussia, they stated, and he *would* remain with the Army. Groener, as unruffled as ever, pointed out that there was little they could do in this situation. They sent a formal protest, but the news could not be reined in, no one was listening any more. The Kaiser, now broken in heart and spirit, was then told that there were increasing concerns for his personal safety. There were fears that groups of soldiers were making their way to Spa and rumours that the troops defending him were shaky in their loyalty. Heavy-hearted, and now recognizing that there was no way out, the Kaiser agreed to enter exile in Holland. It was arranged that he would head for the border at five o'clock the following morning. As he was leaving, he bid farewell to Groener, curtly and angrily.

'You are a Württemberg general; when I am no longer Kaiser, I will have nothing more to do with you.'[21]

The reign of the Hohenzollerns, once the most feared throne in Europe, had come to an end, not under a great wave of blood and revolution, but fitfully, in confusion, with a whimper.

As Foch had made clear, until the German delegation signed the Armistice, the war would go on, and so it did. For the British and French Armies in the north, progress was steady, but becoming ever more difficult. Wet weather made the roads difficult to pass and the extensive destruction left by the retreating German Army only added to the problems facing Haig and Pétain's forces. Almost everywhere soldiers got used to the sight of lorries lying helplessly in deep shell holes or stacked up behind the lines unable to move along the sodden roads. Walter Guinness, a staff officer with 66th Division, noted with resigned fatalism the 'downpours of rain' they had on 6 November as they were getting ready to cross the Sambre. On one march to the front, with his uniform wet through and water pattering on his tin helmet, Guinness found 'much difficulty in distinguishing between the shallow puddle and the shellholes four or five feet deep and it was quite impossible even to ride at more than a walk'. Getting food up to the front was a constant worry. The night before they had had to wait four hours at divisional HQ for a sober meal of bully beef and dried bread as the mess lorry had taken six hours to cover the six miles from their supply dump. 'Everyone in the battle is soaked to the skin,' he admitted, 'which of course stops things even quicker than bullets.'[22]

The weather was a constant annoyance, but it was the extensive destruction which the Germans had meted out to French villages, roads and railway tracks in their efforts to impede their pursuers that slowed the Allies down more than anything. A report by the British First Army complained that:

> The roads on the whole front of the Army, although numerous on the map, are seldom fit for heavy traffic under the most favourable conditions, and the enemy had destroyed both roads and railways very thoroughly. There was scarcely a bridge over a stream or canal which had not been destroyed and few cross-roads at which a crater had not been blown.[23]

The following day, Guinness complained about the number of wrecked bridges and railway crossings they came across, as well as delayed-action mines that exploded, which again cut their supply lines, and in some places threatened to sever the delivery of food up to the troops in the lead; a situation exacerbated by the need to feed the thousands of destitute civilians they had liberated. The amount of labour that it took to repair the destruction caused during the German retreat was remarkable. It was dangerous, backbreaking and exhausting work. William Woods, serving with the Canadian Corps, remembered one railway where every second rail joint had been blown up. 'This time, the railroad troops took over and cut the rail ends with hand hack saws, a man on each end of the saw. Another crew came along with two man-power drills and drilled the new rail ends . . . There was one dud still in place as we passed. They had used *Minenwerfer* trench mortar shells apparently exploded electronically.'[24]

9 November may have been a day of high drama in Berlin and Spa, but along the Western Front it was relatively quiet. The German armies were now in headlong retreat, still demolishing bridges and mining towns, still blowing up wells and firing off thousands of gas shells, but now with no hope of reversing the great tide of the war.

That morning Major Carl Degelow, decorated hero of the Fatherland and renowned fighter ace, was awarded the *Pour le Mérite*. He had been summoned to the headquarters of Fourth Army by its commander, General der Infanterie Sixt von Armin. Degelow had claimed his last kill on 30 October, but by then the German Air Force was on its knees, lacking spare parts and ammunition, and suffering from a chronic lack of fuel, the few surviving pilots unable to contest the skies any more. 'All around us we could see the war effort collapsing,' he wrote sadly. 'Although our ever-eastward trek was officially designated a "regroupment", we knew the end was coming. The first rumours of communist-inspired take-overs of other units had already infiltrated our ranks. Horror stories of "soldiers' councils" that condemned their officers to death made the blood run cold. It was therefore a time when strict discipline *had* to be enforced. When Headquarters issued an order, unit commanders such as myself were responsible for carrying it out – or suffering the consequences of a court-martial.' Degelow later realized that he had been bestowed with the last *Pour le Mérite* 'before the monarchy and all the pageantry of the once great German Empire passed into history'.[25]

More and more German soldiers were now giving in, packing up their equipment and heading to the rear, or surrendering in droves to Allied patrols. Increasing numbers of them were also on the verge of mutiny, forming local soldiers' committees and negotiating conditions with their officers. On the Meuse, General von der Marwitz went to see Gallwitz on 10 November and told him that an armistice must be signed as soon as possible. The loss of the Barricourt Heights and the collapse of his divisions a week earlier had been an alarming portent of what was to come. His troops were no longer reliable and he had received news that a number of companies had refused to go into the line.[26] He had good reason to be concerned. US divisions had reached Sedan on the night of 6–7 November, thus severing one of Germany's two 'arteries' on the Western Front and making a major retreat now inevitable. On most sectors, there was no organized resistance as such to hold up forward patrols, only a handful of machine-gunners and snipers, and of course the usual smattering of mines and booby-traps. In any case, the Allies had enough problems clearing up the vast array of materiel – trucks, supplies and ammunition – that had been dumped in their path. The day after Captain Helldorf had come back through French lines on his way to Spa, Debeney's First Army gained sixteen kilometres of ground. Its war diary recorded that there were 'Numerous fires behind the enemy lines. The Germans beat a retreat in a great hurry throughout the day; their rearguards only gave weak resistance, and left behind considerable equipment.'[27]

The final hours witnessed more of the same, familiar struggles to get forward, more bad weather, endemic shelling that periodically swept across the front, and yet more terrifying moments of combat that could change a man for ever. A Marine, John Ausland, serving with 2nd US Division, came face to face with the enemy during a patrol on 10 November. His men were part of a number of American units that had been ordered to begin crossing the Meuse, which snaked its way northwest of the Argonne, before striking into Germany's coal-producing areas. As their platoon was forming a skirmish line, they were shaken by the clatter of machine-gun fire coming from somewhere up ahead. Ausland's men started running towards the sound, firing their rifles and Chauchats at the hip, when one of their men was shot. 'The skirmish line was moving steadily to my right,' he remembered, 'so I kept right on going abreast of them . . . About 200 feet past the machine gun I saw a pair of hands come up out of the weeds then the head and then the whole German.' Ausland was determined to kill him.

> I suppose it was only a man or two, surely not the whole battalion, but the idea was firmly in my mind that I had to kill him, and as I walked toward him I aimed my rifle at him. When I got so close that the rifle was only 18 inches from his face I stopped. I don't know why, but I was going to pull the trigger, and he knew I was, and he knew his hour had come. His hands came down and he mumbled something in German, and the look that came into his eyes I will remember forever.

But Ausland did not fire. One of his platoon ran up, out of breath, and told him to shoot, but he did not; he just grabbed the prisoner by the arm and pushed him to the rear, swearing at him in German. Through a thick fog they eventually reached their objective, a farmhouse, and dug in for the night. Ausland was exhausted and slept so soundly that he woke at noon the following day, thus missing – to his eternal frustration – what he called 'the greatest moment in the world, to date, since that first Easter morning'.[28]

11 November dawned fine and cold, with a white frost covering everything. Wild rumours were doing the rounds at the front. Leutnant Karl Urmacher, retreating with his artillery battery, heard from a soldiers' council that Foch had been assassinated, that Bolshevism had triumphed in England and France, and that Raymond Poincaré and Albert, the King of Belgium, had also been killed.[29] None of this was true, but it lent a sinister air to the feelings of despair, depression and fear that were running through the German Army. At Foch's railway carriage at Rethondes, Matthias Erzberger had received word from the German Government between seven and eight o'clock the previous evening. The new Chancellor, Friedrich Ebert – the leader of the majority Socialist Party – had taken over from Prince Max and acted immediately, informing Erzberger that he was empowered to sign the Armistice as soon as possible. Erzberger's team spent an exhausting night with Foch and Weygand drawing up a definitive text of the Armistice agreement and then, once they were satisfied, agreed that it would come into force at 11 a.m. French time. This was only completed around five o'clock in the morning, which meant that there were only six hours to telegraph the news to the front and ensure that the fighting stopped.

In places the killing and maiming continued with seconds to go. The American Captain T. F. Grady was met by a runner at 10.30 that morning who told him that hostilities would cease in half an hour. At 10.55, with just five minutes left, a company on his right flank was hit by a high-explosive shell that killed twelve men.[30] One of the last Allied soldiers to die was Private George Lawrence Price, serving with 2nd Canadian Division on the outskirts of the Belgian city of Mons. His detachment of 28th Battalion, led by Major B. Ross, was advancing through the streets, occasionally skirmishing with groups of German soldiers who would fire a few rounds and then scatter.

Because they were so far forward, news that hostilities would cease that morning had not reached them. Shortly before eleven o'clock, they arrived at their objective for the day (the canal) when Private Price, who was a runner, asked one of his friends, Private Arthur Goodmurphy, whether he would be interested in investigating a number of brick houses further up ahead. 'They looked like a wonderful place to stick a machine gun out of, you know,' said Price, 'or a sniper or a rifle or anything like that.' Initially, Goodmurphy was not keen, but Price eventually persuaded him and they crossed the bridge without coming under fire, accompanied by three other men from their section.

Once they were on the other side of the canal, however, a German machine-gun opened up on them, forcing them to take cover. With one way totally impassable owing to the gunfire (which 'knocked bricks off the house'), Price and Goodmurphy retraced their steps to see if there was another route out. Price had just muttered something about 'how the Hell they were going to get back' when a single rifle shot rang out. Goodmurphy wrote:

> All of a sudden, bang, one shot came from one of these houses up on, way up the end of the street. It wasn't an accidental shot, it was a sniper like, you know, got him right through the back and through the heart. He fell dead right in my arms there. I laid him down behind the fence. If there had been two there, he'd have got both of us. There should have been two there you know. If he'd fired at me he'd have got me, there was no doubt about that, he hit what he shot at.

When Major Ross found out he 'blew a fuse'.

'The war's over . . . the war's over!' he shouted.

'Well I can't help that,' replied Goodmurphy.

'What the hell did you go across there for, you have no orders to go across there?'

'We went across to see what was in those brick houses there, they look like good spots for somebody to pick us off there.'

Price died at 10.58 a.m., two minutes before the Armistice, leaving Goodmurphy distraught. 'We never even thought about the war being over then you know. What we thought about was getting back to join our unit, you know, in case these guys pulled off an attack on us or something. We wanted to be on the other side of that river. Oh they said there was a rumour that the war was going to be over that day, just a rumour you know like, we had them before you know ... we didn't even think that the rumour was even a decent rumour you know, because we had heard it before.' In the end, Price had been correct; it was a good spot for a sniper.[31]

On certain sectors of the front, it is possible that fighting continued for several hours after the Armistice − American accounts sometimes refer to combat up to 12.30 p.m.[32] − but along most of the front eleven o'clock saw the end of hostilities. In the final few minutes, as furious runners and overworked wireless operators spread the word, the guns of both sides blasted away into the morning, shells shrieking through the sky and pounding into roads and tracks, trenches and dug-outs, villages and towns, as they had done for four years. And then it came, the Armistice; silent and hollow, strange and mysterious. The front-line soldiers, crouching in their shell holes or sheltering in ruined buildings, looked at each other from beneath their helmets as the firing ceased and the roar of shellfire abated. For many, they remained where they were, unsure of what would happen next, convinced perhaps that it was all some kind of treacherous ruse and that soon the shelling would resume and the killing would begin all over again. As a doughboy, Private Frank Groves, recalled:

> At the front our days and nights were filled with the sounds and smells of the bombardment. Never were we free of it and we had learned to live with it. On November 11 at 11.00 a.m. those sounds and vibrations abruptly stopped. The quietness that followed was awesome; you could feel it − almost smell and taste it. There was no singing, no shouting, no laughter; we just stood around and looked and listened.[33]

Behind the lines, the news rarely provoked outright celebration. When the battery commander, Major F. J. Rice, got up that morning and was on his way to the regimental mess for breakfast, one of his men told him that 'it was all over sir'. Orders had come in that hostilities would cease at 11 a.m. 'All the officers took it very calmly,' he recalled. After breakfast they managed to get their hands on a bottle of port and shared it with their NCOs. When they saw one of the sergeants walking across the gun park, they shouted out the news. The man merely halted, saluted, and said 'very good, sir', before continuing on, seemingly as unconcerned as ever.[34]

The American First-Lieutenant Clair Groover of 313th Infantry Regiment – the junior officer who had survived the assault on Montfaucon – remembered how the quietness that followed the Armistice 'got to you'. 'It was so unreal, that it disturbed you emotionally,' he admitted. 'Some of the hardest officers wept. It was so unusual that you would walk around without being shot at.' Within moments he noticed German soldiers getting up out of their positions and moving out into the open. One of them came over and told him, with tears in his eyes, that his brother had been killed the day before and that he would like permission to locate and bury the body. Groover agreed. That night 'all the troops along the line were treated to the greatest display of fireworks ever set off. Both sides were setting off their entire pyrotechnic supply of rockets, Very candles, red, blue, green, were sparkling in the air. The first few scared you and you would flatten out on the ground, forgetting that it was all over. That night there were camp fires all along the lines.' That was it; it was over. 'It was the end of the shooting war.'[35]

For Allied commanders, 11 November would be a memorable day, when the realization of what they had achieved began to sink in. Douglas Haig held a meeting in Cambrai with his army commanders and they discussed the importance of continuing the advance towards the German frontier, as well as the difficulties that might now arise with the troops. 'Very often the best fighters are the most difficult to deal with in periods of quiet!' said Haig. He suggested that it was the duty of all officers to keep their men occupied and to maintain training schedules. Afterwards the men were taken outside and filmed by a moving picture company, which the generals found very amusing. Haig told General Plumer, Second Army commander and his most senior officer, to 'go off and be cinema'd', which he did obediently, standing before the camera 'trying to look his best, while Byng and others near him were chaffing the old man and trying to make him laugh'.[36] The French Commander-in-Chief, Philippe Pétain, spent the day at the *Grand Quartier Général* in Provins, where he joined his commanders and staff officers in the local theatre, a 'tiny and shabby, bare and cold' building. Local soldiers and civilians had improvised a performance, and afterwards Pétain read out the victory communiqué, while a soldier 'declaimed heroic poetry from the stage'.[37]

Ferdinand Foch, the Allied *Generalissimo* and man who had masterminded the campaign on the Western Front since the spring, left Rethondes for Paris at 7 a.m., with the Armistice conditions in his pocket. He handed them personally to Clemenceau later that morning before returning to his home, an apartment along the Avenue de Saxe, where joyous, victorious crowds awaited him. He was not, however, in the mood for celebration. He had sent Weygand to bed earlier, after being exhausted from thirty-six hours of continuous work, and spent the night sitting in his rocking chair, a rug across his knees, a lit cigarette between his fingers; deep in thought. He greeted Clemenceau with the prophetic words:

'My work is finished. Your work begins.'[38]

It was a task that would remain with France for the next twenty-two years.

Epilogue

*No more slaughter, no more maiming, no more mud and blood and no more killing
and disembowelling of horses and mules — which was what I found most difficult to
bear. No more of those hopeless dawns with the rain chilling the spirits, no more
crouching in inadequate dug-outs scooped out of trench walls, no more dodging of
snipers' bullets, no more of that terrible shell-fire. No more shovelling up bits of men's
bodies and dumping them into sandbags; no more cries of 'Stretcher-bear-ERS!',
and no more of those beastly gas-masks and the odious smell of pear-drops which was
deadly to the lumps, and no more writing of those dreadfully difficult letters to the
next-of-kin of the dead.*

Lieutenant R. G. Dixon[1]

The Armistice brought forth mixed feelings. Of course there was joy
— joy that one had survived — but the immensity of the war with its
endless slaughter and waste brought only a kind of numbness, like
the unearthly wall of silence that broke out along the Western Front
at eleven o'clock on that fateful November morning. For four and a
half years, Europe had been ablaze. At least ten million soldiers had
died. Perhaps another twenty million had been wounded or scarred
for ever. Large parts of Poland, the Balkans and Western Europe had
been utterly wrecked. The devastation was probably worse in northeastern France, where the German retreat had left a ghostly zone of
razed villages and burning towns. Roads and tracks had been torn
up; bridges had been felled; mines had been flooded; factories had
been stripped down and transported to Germany. But perhaps more
lasting than the physical destruction and human carnage produced by
the war was the destruction of the certainties of an earlier age. Four
empires — Tsarist Russia, Ottoman Turkey, the Kaiser's Germany and
Austro-Hungary — had collapsed into a sea of conflicting nationalities and ethnic groups all vying for power and influence. The

Armistice may have brought the fighting to an end, but, in one form or another, the war would go on.

For many it was, initially at least, hard to grasp that the fighting was actually over. One British soldier remembered that:

> The full impact of the cease-fire took a long time to sink in. The War had become so much a part of our lives that it seemed impossible there would from now on be no need to carry a tin hat and a gas mask everywhere, nor a rifle, nor to walk about slightly bent ready to fall flat at the whine of an approaching shell. The mind was incapable of immediately grasping the tremendous single fact that the fighting was over . . .[2]

Frank Clifton Teskey, serving with the Canadian Corps, reached Mons on Armistice day. The civilians were wild with joy. 'They decorate us with colours and flowers but best of all the young maidens are right there with beaucoup kisses,' he wrote. 'We only captured the town the day before yesterday and a man told me that the civilians cannot realize that they are free once more and that all is over. In Canada you can't imagine what it means to them to be rid of the terror of German rule and also of the danger of having their houses blown down about their ears.' After making a formal procession, they lined up outside the city hall with 'bands playing and colours flying'. 'Talk about receptions,' he wrote. 'Thousands of people lined the streets. Old women cried as we went by.' When they played the Belgian National Anthem – heard in Mons for the first time in over four years – a man 'rushed out and threw his arms right around the bandmaster and kissed him. The chimes in the cathedral played all of the allied national anthems. Aeroplanes flew low throwing up coloured flares.'[3]

In Paris, there were unforgettable scenes as huge cheering crowds thronged the streets to celebrate the victory over Germany. Elise Bidet, the daughter to a family of wine-growers, was in the capital on Armistice day and wrote to her brother, Edmond. 'At last it's all over,' she cried.

> No more fighting! We can't believe it and yet it's true! Here in Paris we knew at eleven o'clock because of the guns and the bells; immediately

everyone everywhere was let off work; immediately the streets were swarming with people. All the windows are decked out with flags. I have never seen so many flags and they are all in the colours of the Allies, the view is magnificent. Everybody has a cockade, women have red, white and blue ribbons in their hair; all the people from the workshops in groups, men and women arm in arm, flags at the front, singing as they walk up and down the boulevards and the main avenues.

The Place de la Concorde was packed with large guns, aeroplanes, tanks, 'mountains of Kraut helmets', even anti-aircraft balloons, while the streets were jammed with thousands of people. Children crawled on the guns and dragged them away – some even ending up as far away as Montmartre – but no one seemed to mind. French soldiers were cheered and hugged. Americans drove up and down the boulevards in lorries giving lifts to the young girls. Everybody seemed to be either kissing or singing.[4]

For German officers and men there was little time for celebration when the war ended at noon Berlin time. Those who were with their units had to keep moving as quickly as possible to avoid the pursuing Allied forces; limping along in bedraggled columns, eastwards, back towards the Fatherland. That day Leutnant Karl Urmacher was in Belgium with his regiment when they received orders from Hindenburg stating that a new government was now in place and that the Supreme Command wanted to speed up the ceasefire and avoid further bloodshed. They were to maintain peace and only use their weapons on civilians in an emergency. 'So this *is* the revolution,' he wrote bitterly as he was told the news of the Armistice. The slaughter may have ended, but officers and men could not relax until they crossed the Rhine and re-entered Germany. Urmacher's unit moved off in the moonlight at 5 a.m. 'Behind us was the crashing sound of the bridges and railways being blown up,' he noted. By one o'clock the following morning they had reached Dendermonde, north of Brussels, where they ran into Belgian forces being repatriated. They came towards them, he remembered, 'singing and flying flags'. One soldier, thoroughly drunk, even assaulted Urmacher's Commanding Officer with a knife.[5]

Over the next month Germany's battered armies would make their way back home, leaving the desolate battlefields of France and Belgium, and returning to a land that may have escaped the physical scars of war, but was far from untouched by it. Germany was now a country on the verge of revolution. In Berlin street-fighting had broken out between groups of socialists and communists, and bands of soldiers and nationalists still loyal to the war effort. The politician Philip Scheidemann recalled how 'Machine-guns rattled day and night in the Wilhelmstrasse' and 'deputations holding hand grenades' hammered on the doors of the Chancellery, demanding to be heard.[6] The monarchy had been overthrown and a new, more representative government put in place, but Germany would suffer instability and economic ruin for years to come. The tragedy of 1918 and the extinction of her hopes of victory would haunt Germany, and German politicians, for the next two decades. The Weimar Republic, which Friedrich Ebert would found in August 1919, lasted for fourteen years until it was overthrown by Adolf Hitler's Nazi Party, having never been able to shake off the original sin of parliamentary government, the collapse and armistice at the end of the Great War.

Was the German Army defeated in November 1918? Could the war have continued? Should the Allies have pressed on and taken the war into Germany? These questions, alongside many others, continue to reverberate down the years, demanding to be answered; echoing through history like the aftershocks of a great earthquake. Many Germans, particularly fervent nationalists and ardent patriots, were left reeling by the resignation of the Kaiser on 9 November and the coming of the Armistice two days later. News of what was really going on at the front had been hidden from the vast majority of Germans so the sudden collapse was deeply shocking. Therefore, it was probably unsurprising that within months a 'stab in the back' myth had been created that proved remarkably successful and enduring. The Fatherland was blamed for betraying an army still fighting bravely on foreign soil. Socialists and Bolsheviks, Jews and Slavs, were really responsible for the fate of the Imperial German Army that returned home, so it was said, 'undefeated in the field'.[7] For many, the idea of a 'stab in the back' was almost comforting, confirming to them what they had always known: that the German Army had not really been defeated, only succumbed to treachery at home. If Germany was ever to rise again, the nationalists now claimed, she would have to be cleansed of undesirables and those who could pose a threat in any future war, and during the rise of Nazism this narrative of cloaked, murderous betrayal was never far from the surface. Adolf Hitler would later call what happened 'the greatest villainy of the century' and dedicate his life to righting the 'betrayal' of 1918.[8]

The 'stab in the back' legend was only part of a wider misunderstanding about what happened in the last phase of the Great War. The myth of German military infallibility, which was enshrined after their stunning victory in 1940, meant that many writers were loath to give more than grudging acceptance to the Allied achievement of 1918. It has sometimes been claimed that the German Army defeated itself; that the cream of its manpower was squandered in the great offensives of March, April and May, thus leaving the rest of the Army weakened and without enough experienced soldiers to hold on. Because it had been so worn down by previous operations, or decimated by flu, the Allied victory was not only inevitable, but in some ways not a real victory at all. It is certainly true that the German Army of late 1918 was not the great, cohesive and professional force it had been in earlier years, particularly after the murderous attrition of the Kaiser's offensives, but this should not detract from what the Allies managed to do. If the German Army was no longer what it had been, then the same, equally, could be said for both the British and French. The French were, quite literally, a pale, gaunt shadow of their former selves and only capable of very limited operations, while the BEF had been fighting continuously since the spring of 1917 and by the following year was composed mainly of youthful conscripts – the 'men of 18 in 1918' – some of whom, according to contemporary accounts, could barely lift their rifles.[9] Yet it was these men, assisted by their inexperienced but brave American counterparts, who stormed some of the toughest defensive positions ever constructed and forced their opponents back time after time.

The Armistice of 1918 was not a total victory for the Allies, only a

partial one; a reflection of the precarious balance of power at the
front. But it could only happen because the German war effort was
collapsing. The remaining elements of her military power were no
more, including the Kaiser's 'luxury' High Seas Fleet, which was
interned on 11 November after the largest surrender at sea in naval
history. Her army may not have been completely annihilated, but it
was rapidly getting to that point. Officers and men were either
deserting, simply heading home, or dodging military police in railway stations in increasing numbers — numbers that, had the war gone
on much longer, would have become insupportable. It is true that
elements continued to resist with considerable skill and determination, but these were the exception rather than the rule. Indeed, the
decision to ask for an armistice during those frantic, final months was
one of the most sensible decisions ever made by the German Supreme
Command because — finally — it explicitly recognized the hopeless-
ness of their situation and tried to make the best of it, in the full
knowledge that with each passing day things got inexorably worse.

Three months before the Armistice, Crown Prince Rupprecht,
one of the more realistic and responsible of the German Army Group
commanders, wrote to the future Imperial Chancellor, Prince Max,
and explained his thoughts on the war. 'What we must therefore do,'
he wrote, 'if we are to avoid a military catastrophe which will destroy
our whole future as a nation, is to make haste and approach our
enemies, and especially England, with peace offers, and peace offers
which both can be accepted and in view of the temper of the English
people must be accepted.' Rupprecht knew the war was lost. The
only question was whether they could save enough of the Army for
the greater battle that they could see looming: the fight against the
Spartacists and Bolsheviks at home, and the struggle for the German
soul. If the Army was destroyed and the Allies marched into the
Fatherland, then more than a war would have been lost. There was an
urgent need to ward off something that was — in the words of Rupprecht — 'far worse'.[10] Had the German Army continued to fight after
11 November, it would have done more damage to the Allies, but it
would, in all probability, have collapsed at some point, perhaps during the spring. That was why Germany agreed to the Armistice in

November 1918: the Army could do no more at the front, but it might be able to tip the balance at home against the revolution. There was, as Rupprecht could see, something left to save.

Could the Allies have continued to fight? Many commanders, including Pershing and Hunter Liggett, were convinced that the Armistice was premature, and had the Allies kept up the pressure – perhaps only for another month – then it would have resulted in the complete collapse of German resistance across the Western Front. This was all well and good, but the British and French Armies were approaching total exhaustion (not to mention logistical overstretch) by early November. The spearhead of the BEF, Rawlinson's Fourth Army, was over fifty miles from its railheads by the Armistice and was only kept supplied via a handful of narrow, thinly cobbled roads.[11] Many units were lacking reinforcements, increasingly unhappy at being asked to keep going, and, perhaps most importantly, approaching the limit of their physical capability. There can be no definitive answer to what would have happened had the war gone on, but a complete collapse of German resistance in 1918 is unlikely. Large sections of the Army would probably have escaped their pursuers and slipped across the Rhine (even if many units could not), particularly given the difficulty the Allies were having in keeping up, which became harder with every mile they covered, every village they liberated, and every river they crossed. More than likely, a new offensive in early spring would have been necessary to finish off the Germans, which might have been militarily possible, but would have put both the British and French governments under intense domestic pressure to stop the war.

In the end, for both sides, it came down to a question of whether it was worth it; whether the German Army should continue to fight what was now an unwinnable and fruitless war, with the promise only of defeat in detail and yet more casualties in the near future. In any case, the Army was needed for the fight at home, in the struggle against the Bolsheviks and the need to rescue the Fatherland from chaos and destitution. For the Allies, there was also a choice: whether they should maintain their offensive in the hope of better terms or with the goal of completely annihilating the enemy. As it was, they got most of what they wanted: the liberation of their territory, the occupation of the left bank of the Rhine, a great deal of war materiel, and the promise of reparations. As Foch had told Colonel House in late October, once they had secured what they wanted, no one had a right to shed another drop of blood. Clearly there was a desire for total victory, for the complete destruction of Germany's armies, the occupation of her soil, the kind of *Endkampf* that had vanquished Napoleon at Waterloo, but given the slaughter of the previous four years, it is difficult to be too critical of the men who said, finally, that enough was enough.

For years what happened at the end of 1918 has been forgotten, overshadowed by the great trench battles of 1916–17 and the controversies that still swirl around Germany's treatment at the Treaty of Versailles in the summer of 1919. The Armistice has thus been seen as the last pointless and ultimately futile act of an apparently pointless and futile war. Yet it should be considered afresh. Few were predicting an early end to the war in the summer of 1918, yet between July and November the Allied armies were able to make remarkable gains, having finally mastered a tactical and operational system that could achieve victory on the battlefield. With hindsight, however, Pershing and Hunter Liggett were probably right. The Allies should not have signed an armistice, but carried on, fought the war into 1919 and occupied large parts of Germany. Only through the systematic breaking up of the Fatherland and the reversal of the unification of 1871 could France's long-term security be assured. Yet the partial victory of 1918, which left Germany weakened and constrained, but not crushed, meant there was always a possibility that she would rise again. Regrettably, the leaders of Britain and her Empire, France and America shied away from taking such drastic measures. War weariness, combined with Woodrow Wilson's opposition to too much interference in Germany, meant that there would be no radical reshaping of the Fatherland and no military occupation (except for the Rhineland). Thus began the long and sad progress of two decades of missed opportunities and appeasement, when the Allies collectively let slip the priceless advantage they had gained after the Second Battle of the Marne in July 1918.

The battlefields of the Hundred Days are seldom visited. Some pilgrims may make their way to lay a rose on the grave of Wilfred Owen in the little village of Ors, close to where the poet was killed, but the Battles of Amiens and Montdidier, the Scarpe, the Third Battle of Picardy, the Meuse–Argonne, the Sambre, and others, remain forgotten and unrecognized. Perhaps it is understandable why the trench offensives of earlier years, at the Somme, Verdun or Ypres, have so captured the imagination (or nightmares) of generations of Europeans, but the fighting at the end of the Great War deserves to be remembered and commemorated too. In one of Wilfred Owen's last letters, written to his mother on 4 or 5 October 1918, he talked about coming back out to France 'in order to help these boys – directly by leading them as well as an officer can; indirectly, by watching their sufferings that I may speak of them as well as a pleader can'.[12] For too long their tale has been overlooked. What happened in those final Hundred Days is an incredible story of shot and shell, of battles on a scale unimaginable to modern generations used to wars of almost surgical precision. We should never forget those *poilus*, those *Frontschwein*, those doughboys, those Tommies, who fought in the last days of the Great War, and who fell within sight of the finishing line; those who died when you could almost hear the bells of the Armistice ringing out over the towns and villages of Europe, signalling the end of the greatest tragedy in European history, and the beginning of a new world, utterly changed.

Acknowledgements

This book would not have been possible without the help of a number of family members, friends and colleagues who have graciously assisted me in my research. Firstly, thanks to my agent, Peter Robinson, and my editor at Penguin, Eleo Gordon, for taking me on and for overseeing this project with their customary expertise, goodwill and trust.

During the course of writing and researching *Hundred Days*, I have been fortunate to visit Canada and the United States. In Ottawa, Dr Nathan Greenfield and his wife, Micheline, hosted me and made my time in the senior dominion most enjoyable and comfortable. While in the US, Dr Richard Sommers and the staff at the Military History Institute, US Army War College, Carlisle, Pennsylvania, were extremely helpful and very friendly. Financial support was provided by King's College London (for German translations and a trip to the National Archives and Records Administration in Maryland) and the US Army War College (which awarded me a General and Mrs Matthew B. Ridgway research grant). In the UK I would like to record the generosity and assistance of Mrs Delia Bettaney (for various French translations); Mr Philip Cotterill (for showing me Tom Cotterill's surviving papers); Dr Tim Gale (for kindly sharing with me his extensive knowledge of the French Army and French language sources); Andrew Polkey (for material relating to 46th (North Midland) Division); Professor Peter Simkins (for his great support and unrivalled knowledge of the BEF); and Alan Tucker (for allowing me to quote from the diary of Captain Arthur Impey). Thanks also to Dr Tim Cook, Dr Gregor Dallas, Dr Oliver Haller, Dr Ben Jones and Dr William Philpott. At Shrivenham, I would like to salute my colleagues in the Defence Studies Department for their support and friendship, particularly Dr David Hall, Dr Mark Hilborne, Dr Saul Kelly and Dr Kate Utting.

My gratitude is due to the staff at the following libraries: the Bundesarchiv-Militärarchiv, Freiburg; the Canadian War Museum, Ottawa; the Imperial War Museum, London; the Joint Services Command and Staff College, Shrivenham; Library and Archives Canada, Ottawa; the Liddell Hart Centre for Military Archives, King's College London; the Maughan Library, London; the Military History Institute, US Army War College, Carlisle, Pennsylvania; the National Archives of the UK, Kew; and the National Archives and Records Administration, College Park, Maryland. As always, my family have been greatly supportive of the project and helped me out too many times to mention. My wife, Louise, deserves special thanks for accompanying me to America and enduring the frustration when the airline managed to lose our luggage on *both* legs of the journey! *Hundred Days* is dedicated to my great-uncle, Tom Cotterill, who was killed six weeks before the end of the war. Like most other families in Britain, the memory of loved ones lost in that awful conflict remains a source of pride and interest as well as sadness. It is unfortunate that my grandmother, Gladys, did not live to see the fruition of this project. She kept alive the memory of her late brother all her life, and I am sure she would be happy to know that in some small way, he has not been forgotten.

Cheltenham, England
December 2012

Select Bibliography

Archive sources

Bundesarchiv-Militärarchiv, Freiburg

Guido Hermann (Pers 9/1.1.97); Wilhelm Wilhöft (Pers 9/1.1.99); Cyrus Karl (Pers 9/1.7.93); Karl Passhaus (Pers 9/1.7.94); Anonymous letters 'Alfred' (MSG2/5792); Anonymous letters 'Josef' (MSG2/5548); Erich Alenfeld (MSG2/1291); Paul Ludwig (BIV21); Hans Mahler (MSG2/13746); Richard and Willy Schütt (MSG2/5710); Karl Urmacher (MSG2/10347); 41st Division War Diary (PH8I/385); 75th Reserve Division War Diary (PH8II/83); Feldpost Postüberwachung beim AOK 5 (RH61/1035)

Canadian War Museum, Ottawa

Clifford M. Johnston (58A 1 187.1); Keith Campbell MacGowan (58A 1 154.4); E. W. B. Morrison (58A 1 20.3); Frank C. Teskey (58A 1 237.6)

Imperial War Museum, London

T. Brookbank (99/13/1); C. W. Clarke (81/1/1); G. T. Coles (03/58/1 and Con Shelf); R. G. Dixon (92/36/1); R. C. Foot (86/57/1); T. F. Grady (06/62/1); T. H. Holmes (06/30/1); H. J. C. Marshall (84/11/2); T. G. Mohan (80/28/1); H. C. Rees (77/179/1); F. J. Rice (78/29/1); A. J. Turner (81/21/1)

Library and Archives Canada, Ottawa

Sir Arthur Currie (MG30 E100); Arthur J. Foster (MG30 E393); William Green (MG30 E430); Albert C. West (MG30 E32); William B. Woods (MG31 G30); interviews from CBS documentary In Flanders Fields (RG41, Volumes 7–21)

War diaries and unit reports of the Canadian Corps held online at:
http://www.collectionscanada.gc.ca/archivianet/02015202_e.html

Service Historique de la Défense, Vincennes

War diaries and unit reports of the French Army held online at:
http://www.memoiredeshommes.sga.defense.gouv.fr/jmo/cdc.html

The National Archives, London

HQ Tank Corps, June–September 1918 (WO 95/94); HQ Branches & Services, General Staff First Army, October 1918–March 1919 (WO 95/180); HQ Branches & Services, General Staff Third Army, August 1918 (WO 95/372); HQ Branches & Services, General Staff Fourth Army, July–September 1918 (WO 95/437-8); HQ Branches & Services, General Staff 5th Division, April 1918–February 1919 (WO 95/1516); 13 Infantry Brigade HQ, April 1918–May 1919 (WO 95/1551); 15/Royal Warwickshire Regiment War Diary, April–October 1918 (WO 95/1557); GHQ Summary of Intelligence, August 1918 (WO 157/34); Third Army Intelligence Summaries, October–November 1918 (WO 157/166-7); Fourth Army Intelligence Summaries, July–October 1918 (WO 157/196-9); Haig–Foch Correspondence (WO 158/29)

The United States Army Military History Institute, Carlisle, Pennsylvania

Hakon Anderson (WWI 6801); John E. Ausland (WWI 146); L. M. Beyer (WWI 2305); William T. Carpenter (WWI 8178); John D. Clarke (WWI 369); Frank L. Faulkner (WWI 246); Clair Groover (WWI 2450); Frank W. Groves (WWI 3345); Malcolm B. Helm (WWI 2487); Ernst Kielmayer (WWI 2832); Joseph D. Lawrence (WWI 561); Herbert L. McHenry (WWI 8188); James E. Meehan (WWI 380); Walter J. Strauss (WWI 1827); Ralph L. Williams (WWI 5499); Sophie G. Winton (WWI 6171); Harold Woehl (WWI 456)

Other archive material

Bertram Howard Cox (www.canadianletters.ca); Arthur Impey (http://

www.fylde.demon.co.uk/tucker/tuckerbiography.htm); C. H. Savage (www.canadianletters.ca); George Waters (private collection)

Secondary sources

Official histories and reports

T. von Bose, *Die Katastrophe des 8. August 1918* (Berlin: Stalling, 1930)

Bundesarchiv, *Der Weltkrieg 1914 bis 1918*, XIV: *Die Kriegführung an der Westfront im Jahre 1918* (Berlin: E. S. Mittler und Sohn, 1944)

Sir J. Edmonds (ed.), *Military Operations France and Belgium 1918*, III, *May–July: The German Diversion Offensives and the First Allied Counter-Offensive* (London: Macmillan & Co., 1939)

— (ed.), *Military Operations France and Belgium 1918*, IV, *8th August–26th September. The Franco-British Offensive* (London: HMSO, 1947)

Sir J. Edmonds and R. Maxwell-Hyslop (eds.), *Military Operations France and Belgium 1918*, V, *26th September–11th November. The Advance to Victory* (London: HMSO, 1947)

H. A. Jones, *The War in the Air. Being the Story of the Part Played in the Great War by the Royal Air Force* (6 vols., Oxford: Clarendon Press, 1922–37)

Sir W. G. Macpherson, *Medical Services. Diseases of the War*, I (London: HMSO, 1921)

—, *Medical Services General History*, III, *Medical Services during the Operations on the Western Front in 1916, 1917 and 1918; in Italy; and in Egypt and Palestine* (London: HMSO, 1924)

J. J. Pershing, *Final Report of Gen. John J. Pershing* (Washington, DC: Government Printing Office, 1919)

P. Pétain, *Report by the Field Marshal Commander-in-Chief of the French Armies of the North and Northeast on the Operations in 1918. The Offensive Campaign (18 July–11 November 1918)* (3 parts, trans. A. Woldike) (Part II: Château-Thierry–Soissons Counter-Offensive (18 July–6 August); Part III: Montdidier–Noyon Offensive and the Advance towards the Hindenburg Position (1st August–15th September)

Reichskriegsministerium Heeressanitätsinspektion, *Sanitätsbericht über das Deutsche Heer* (3 vols., Berlin: E. S. Mittler und Sohn, 1934–8)

A. Stenger, *Schicksalswende. Von der Marne bis zur Vesle 1918* (Berlin: Stalling, 1930)

US Department for the Army, Historical Division, *Histories of Two Hundred and Fifty-One Divisions of the German Army Which Participated in the War (1914–1918)* (Washington, DC: Government Printing Office, 1920)

—, *United States Army in the World War, 1917–1919* (17 vols., Washington, DC: Government Printing Office, 1948)

Biographical sources

Sir G. Aston, *The Biography of the Late Marshal Foch* (London: Hutchinson, 1932)

M. Balfour, *The Kaiser and His Times* (London: The Cresset Press, 1964)

W. Foerster, *Der Feldherr Ludendorff im Unglück* (Wiesbaden: Limes Verlag, 1952)

E. Greenhalgh, *Foch in Command. The Forging of a First World War General* (Cambridge: Cambridge University Press, 2011)

J. Grigg, *Lloyd George. War Leader 1916–1918* (London: Penguin, 2003; first publ. 2002)

J. P. Harris, *Douglas Haig and the First World War* (Cambridge: Cambridge University Press, 2008)

D. Hibberd, *Wilfred Owen. A New Biography* (London: Weidenfeld & Nicolson, 2002)

B. H. Liddell Hart, *Reputations* (London: John Murray, 1928)

C. Mangin, *Lettres de guerre 1914–1918*, ed. L. Eugène (Paris: Fayard, 1950)

A. Niemann, *Revolution von oben – Umsturz von unten* (Berlin: Verlag für Kulturpolitik, 1928)

W. Owen, *The Poems of Wilfred Owen*, ed. J. Stallworthy (London: Chatto & Windus, 1990)

—, *Selected Letters*, ed. J. Bell (Oxford: Oxford University Press, 1985)

R. Prior and T. Wilson, *Command on the Western Front. The Military Career of Sir Henry Rawlinson, 1914–1918* (Oxford: Blackwell, 1992)

G. Sheffield, *The Chief. Douglas Haig and the British Army* (London: Aurum Press, 2011)

J. Stallworthy, *Wilfred Owen. A Biography* (Oxford: Oxford University Press, 1977)

J. Terraine, *Douglas Haig. The Educated Soldier* (London: Cassell, 2000; first publ. 1963)

D. T. Zabeki (ed.), *Chief of Staff. The Principal Officers behind History's Great Commanders*, I (Annapolis, Md: Naval Institute Press, 2008)

Memoirs

Prince Max of Baden, *The Memoirs of Prince Max of Baden*, trans. W. M. Calder and C. W. H. Sutton (2 vols., London: Constable, 1928)

R. Binding, *A Fatalist at War*, trans. I. F. D. Morrow (London: George Allen & Unwin, 1929)

G. Bucher, *In the Line 1914–1918*, trans. Norman Gullick (Uckfield: Naval & Military Press, 2005; first publ. 1932)

C. M. Chenu, *Du képi rouge aux chars d'assaut* (Paris: Albin Michel, 1932)

M. E. Debeney, *La Guerre et les hommes. Réflexions d'après-guerre* (Paris: Librairie Plon, 1937)

C. Degelow, *Germany's Last Knight in the Air. The Memoirs of Major Carl Degelow*, trans and ed. P. Kilduff (London: William Kimber, 1979)

F. Foch, *The Memoirs of Marshal Foch*, trans. T. Bentley Mott (London: William Heinemann, 1931)

M. von Gallwitz, *Erleben im Westen 1916–1918* (Berlin: E. S. Mittler und Sohn, 1932)

J. Glubb, *Into Battle. A Soldier's Diary of the Great War* (London: Cassell, 1978)

W. Görlitz (ed.), *The Kaiser and His Court. The Diaries, Note Books and Letters of Admiral Georg Alexander von Müller, Chief of the Naval Cabinet, 1914–1918* (London: Macdonald & Co., 1961; first publ. 1959)

W. Groener, *Lebenserinnerungen. Jugend. Generalstab. Weltkrieg* (Göttingen: Vandenhoeck & Ruprecht, 1957)

Sir D. Haig, *War Diaries and Letters 1914–1918*, eds. G. Sheffield and J. Bourne (London: Weidenfeld & Nicolson, 2005)

P. von Hindenburg, *Out of My Life*, trans. F. A. Holt (London: Cassell & Company, 1920)

F. A. Holden, *War Memories* (Athens, Ga: Athens Book Company, 1922)

E. M. House, *The Intimate Papers of Colonel House*, ed. C. Seymour (4 vols., London: Ernest Benn, 1928)

D. von Kuhl, *Entstehung, Durchführung und Zusammenbruch der Offensive von 1918* (Berlin: Deutsche Verlagsgesellschaft für Politik und Geschichte, 1927)

H. Liggett, *Commanding an American Army* (Boston and New York: Houghton Mifflin, 1925)

—, *AEF. Ten Years Ago in France* (New York: Dodd, Mead and Co., 1928)

D. Lloyd George, *War Memoirs of David Lloyd George* (2 vols., London: Odhams Press, 1933–6)

F. von Lossberg, *Meine Tätigkeit im Weltkrieg 1914–1918* (Berlin: E. S. Mittler und Sohn, 1939)

E. von Ludendorff, *Concise Ludendorff Memoirs 1914–1918* (London: Hutchinson, 1933)

M. Ludendorff, *My Married Life with Ludendorff*, trans. R. Somerset (London: Hutchinson, 1930)

E. E. Mackin, *Suddenly We Didn't Want to Die. Memoirs of a World War I Marine* (Novato, Calif.: Presidio Press, 1993)

G. C. Marshall, *Memoirs of My Services in the World War 1917–1918* (Boston: Houghton Mifflin, 1976)

G. von der Marwitz, *Weltkriegsbriefe*, ed. E. von Tschischwitz (Berlin: Steiniger-Verlage, 1940)

P. Maze, *A Frenchman in Khaki* (Kingswood: William Heinemann, 1934)

Sir J. Monash, *The Australian Victories in France in 1918* (London: Hutchinson, 1920)

F. E. Noakes, *The Distant Drum. A Memoir of a Guardsman in the Great War* (Barnsley: Frontline Books, 2010)

Sir W. Orpen, *An Onlooker in France 1917–1919* (London: Williams & Norgate, 1921)

J. J. Pershing, *My Experiences in the World War* (2 vols., New York: Frederick A. Stokes, 1931)

Crown Prince Rupprecht, *Mein Kriegstagebuch* (3 vols., Berlin: E. S. Mittler und Sohn, 1929)

P. Scheidemann, *Memoirs of a Social Democrat*, trans. J. E. Michell (2 vols., London: Hodder & Stoughton, 1929)

R. Stark, *Wings of War. A German Airman's Diary of the Last Year of the Great War*, trans. C. W. Sykes (London: Greenhill Books, 1988)

H. Sulzbach, *With the German Guns. Four Years on the Western Front 1914–*

1918, trans. R. Thonger (London: Frederick Warne, 1981; first publ. 1973)

M. Weygand, *Mémoires. Idéal vécu* (Paris: Flammarion, 1953)

Crown Prince Wilhelm, *The Memoirs of the Crown Prince of Germany* (London: Thornton Butterworth, 1922)

Wilhelm II of Germany, *The Kaiser's Memoirs*, trans. T. R. Ybarra (New York and London: Harper & Brothers, 1922)

A. Williams, *Experiences of the Great War* (Roanoake, Va: Stone, 1919)

Unit histories

C. E. W. Bean, *The Official History of Australia in the War of 1914–1918* (12 vols., Sydney: Angus & Robertson, 1941–2)

C. A. Bill, *The 15th Battalion Royal Warwickshire Regiment (and Birmingham Battalion) in the Great War* (Birmingham: Cornish Brothers, 1932)

T. Carter, *Birmingham Pals. 14th, 15th & 16th (Service) Battalions of the Royal Warwickshire Regiment: A History of the Three City Battalions Raised in Birmingham in World War One* (Barnsley: Pen & Sword, 1997)

A. Grasset, *La Guerre en action, Montdidier. Le 8 août 1918 à la 42ème Division* (Paris: Éditions Berger-Levrault, 1930)

A. H. Hussey and D. S. Inman, *The Fifth Division in the Great War* (London: Nisbet & Co., 1921)

Sir A. Montgomery, *The Story of Fourth Army in the Battles of the Hundred Days, August 8th to November 11th, 1918* (London: Hodder & Stoughton, 1920)

R. E. Priestley, *Breaking the Hindenburg Line. The Story of the 46th (North Midland) Division* (London: T. Fisher Unwin, 1919)

General accounts

R. B. Asprey, *The German High Command at War. Hindenburg and Ludendorff and the First World War* (London: Warner Books, 1994; first publ. 1991)

M. Baumont, *The Fall of the Kaiser*, trans. E. I. James (London: George Allen & Unwin, 1931)

D. Blair, *The Battle of Bellicourt Tunnel. Tommies, Diggers and Doughboys on the Hindenburg Line, 1918* (Barnsley: Frontline Books, 2011)

J. Boff, *Winning and Losing on the Western Front. The British Third Army and the Defeat of Germany in 1918* (Cambridge: Cambridge University Press, 2012)

T. Cook, *No Place to Run. The Canadian Corps and Gas Warfare in the First World War* (Vancouver: UBC Press, 1999)

—, *Shock Troops. Canadians Fighting the Great War 1917–1918* (Toronto: Penguin Canada, 2008)

J. J. Cooke, *Pershing and His Generals. Command and Staff in the AEF* (Westport, Conn.: Praeger, 1997)

G. Dallas, *1918. War and Peace* (London: John Murray, 2000)

P. Dennis and J. Grey (eds.), *1918. Defining Victory* (Canberra: Army History Unit, 1999)

R. A. Doughty, *Pyrrhic Victory. French Strategy and Operations in the Great War* (Cambridge, Mass.: Harvard University Press, 2008; first publ. 2005)

A. Elkins (ed.), *1918. Year of Victory: The End of the Great War and the Shaping of Victory* (Auckland: Exisle Publishing, 2010)

J. F. C. Fuller, *Tanks in the Great War 1914–1918* (London: John Murray, 1920)

P. Griffith, *Battle Tactics of the Western Front. The British Army's Art of Attack 1916–1918* (New Haven and London: Yale University Press, 1994)

— (ed.), *British Fighting Methods in the Great War* (London: Frank Cass, 1996)

M. E. Grotelueschen, *The AEF Way of War. The American Army and Combat in World War I* (Cambridge: Cambridge University Press, 2007)

J. P. Guéno and Y. Laplume (eds.), *Paroles de poilus. Lettres et carnets du front 1914–1918* (Paris: Radio France, 1998)

J. H. Hallas, *Squandered Victory. The American First Army at St Mihiel* (Westport, Conn.: Praeger, 1995)

— (ed.), *Doughboy War. The American Expeditionary Force in World War I* (London and Boulder, Colo.: Lynne Rienner, 2000)

J. P. Harris and N. Barr, *Amiens to the Armistice* (London: Brassey's, 1998)

H. Herwig, *The First World War. Germany and Austria-Hungary 1914–1918* (London: Arnold, 1997)

I. V. Hull, *Absolute Destruction. Military Culture and Practices of War in Imperial Germany* (London and Ithaca, NY: Cornell University Press, 2005)

R. Jackson, *Aces' Twilight. The War in the Air, 1918* (London: Sphere, 1988)

M. Kitchen, *The Silent Dictatorship. The Politics of the German High Command under Hindenburg and Ludendorff, 1916–1918* (London: Croom Helm, 1976)

E. G. Lengel, *To Conquer Hell. The Battle of Meuse–Argonne* (New York: Henry Holt, 2009)

B. Lowry, *Armistice 1918* (Kent, Ohio: Kent State University Press, 1996)

G. Mead, *Doughboys. America and the First World War* (London: Penguin Books, 2001)

C. Messenger, *The Day We Won the War. Turning Point at Amiens 8th August 1918* (London: Phoenix, 2009; first publ. 2008)

J. McWilliams and R. J. Steel, *Amiens. Dawn of Victory* (Toronto: Dundurn Press, 2001)

M. S. Neiberg, *The Second Battle of the Marne* (Bloomington, Ind.: Indiana University Press, 2008)

E. Otto, *The Battle at Blanc Mont (October 2 to October 10, 1918),* trans. Martin Lichtenberg (Annapolis, Md: United States Naval Institute, 1930)

R. Paschall, *The Defeat of Imperial Germany 1917–1918* (Chapel Hill, NC: Algonquin Books, 1989)

S. B. Schreiber, *Shock Army of the British Empire. The Canadian Corps in the Last 100 Days of the Great War* (Westport, Conn.: Praeger, 1997)

R. Slotkin, *Lost Battalions. The Great War and the Crisis of American Nationality* (New York: Henry Holt, 2005)

S. Stephenson, *The Final Battle. Soldiers of the Western Front and the German Revolution of 1918* (Cambridge: Cambridge University Press, 2009)

D. Stevenson, *With Our Backs to the Wall. Victory and Defeat in 1918* (London: Allen Lane, 2011)

J. Terraine, *To Win a War. 1918: The Year of Victory* (London: Cassell, 2000; first publ. 1978)

D. F. Trask, *The AEF and Coalition Warmaking, 1917–1918* (Lawrence, Kan.: University of Kansas, 1993)

T. Travers, *How the War was Won. Command and Technology in the British Army on the Western Front, 1917–1918* (Barnsley: Pen & Sword, 2005; first publ., 1992)

G. S. Viereck (ed.), *As They Saw Us. Foch, Ludendorff and Other Leaders Write Our War History* (Cranbury, NJ: Scholar's Bookshelf, 2005; first publ. 1929)

A. Watson, *Enduring the Great War. Combat, Morale and Collapse in the German and British Armies, 1914–1918* (Cambridge: Cambridge University Press, 2008)

M. A. Yockelson, *Borrowed Soldiers. Americans under British Command, 1918* (Norman, Ohio: University of Oklahoma Press, 2008)

D. Zabecki, *The German 1918 Offensives. A Case Study in the Operational Level of War* (London and New York: Routledge, 2006)

Articles

W. H. Anderson, 'The Breaking of the Quéant–Drocourt Line by the Canadian Corps, First Army 2nd–4th September, 1918', *Canadian Defence Quarterly*, Vol. 4, No. 1 (January 1926), pp. 120–27

J. Boff, 'Air/Land Integration in the 100 Days: The Case of Third Army', *RAF Air Power Review*, Vol. 12, No. 3 (Autumn 2009), pp. 77–88

W. Deist, 'The Military Collapse of the German Empire: The Reality behind the Stab-in-the-Back Myth', *War in History*, Vol. 3, No. 2 (April 1996), pp. 186–207

M. Geyer, 'Insurrectionary Warfare: The German Debate about a Levée en Masse in October 1918', *Journal of Modern History*, Vol. 73, No. 3 (September 2001), pp. 459–527

D. Jordan, 'The Royal Air Force and Air/Land Integration in the 100 Days', *RAF Air Power Review*, Vol. 11, No. 2 (Summer 2008), pp. 12–29

A. G. L. McNaughton, 'The Development of Artillery in the Great War', *Canadian Defence Quarterly*, Vol. 6, No. 2 (January 1929), pp. 160–71

—, 'The Capture of Valenciennes: A Study in Coordination', *Canadian Defence Quarterly*, Vol. 10, No. 3 (April 1933), pp. 279–94

J. McRandle and J. Quirk, 'The Blood Test Revisited: A New Look at German Casualty Counts in World War I', *Journal of Military History*, Vol. 70, No. 3 (July 2006), pp. 667–701

G. C. Wynne, 'The Hindenburg Line', *Army Quarterly*, Vol. XXXVII (October 1938 and January 1939), pp. 205–28

Unpublished theses

T. Gale, 'La Salamandre: The French Army's *Artillerie Spéciale* and the Development of Armoured Warfare in the First World War' (Ph.D., King's College London, 2010)

References

BA-MA	Bundesarchiv-Militärarchiv, Freiburg
CLIP	Canadian Letters and Images Project [www.canadianletters.ca]
CWM	Canadian War Museum, Ottawa
IWM	Imperial War Museum, London
JMO	*Journal de Marche et d'Opérations* (French Army war diaries) [http://www.memoiredeshommes.sga.defense.gouv.fr/jmo/cdc.html]
LAC	Library and Archives Canada, Ottawa
MHI	Military History Institute, US Army War College, Carlisle Pennsylvania
TNA	The National Archives of the UK, Kew
USAWW	*United States Army in the World War, 1917–1919*

Preface: Death at Gouzeaucourt

1 E. Blunden, *Undertones of War* (London: Penguin Books, 2010; first publ. 1928), p. 214.

2 Ibid., pp. 186 and 188.

3 C. A. Bill, *The 15th Battalion Royal Warwickshire Regiment (and Birmingham Battalion) in the Great War* (Birmingham: Cornish Brothers, 1932), p. 119.

4 Army records show that Tom enlisted at Shotton and was originally posted to the Cheshire Regiment, before being transferred to the Warwicks. The reason why Tom found himself in a Warwickshire battalion was because he had been born in Willenhall in the Black Country (on 18 March 1899), which was a traditional recruiting ground for the Warwickshire Regiment. His army file seems to have been one of many that were destroyed by German bombing raids on the Public Record Office in the Second World War (the 'burnt documents'), so it is impossible to delve any deeper.

5 T. Carter, *Birmingham Pals. 14th, 15th & 16th (Service) Battalions of the Royal Warwickshire Regiment: A History of the Three City Battalions*

Raised in Birmingham in World War One (Barnsley: Pen and Sword, 1997), p. 139.

6 Bill, *The 15th Battalion Royal Warwickshire Regiment*, pp. 147–8.

7 The term 'Hundred Days' has been criticized for being Anglocentric and for missing the role that the French and American forces played in the turning point of the war on the Western Front, the Second Battle of the Marne that began on 15 July. This book begins at the Marne, but uses the term 'Hundred Days' in its wider sense to refer to the series of remarkable triumphs won by the Allied armies that began on 18 July and continued until the Armistice.

8 J. Terraine, *To Win a War. 1918: The Year of Victory* (London: Cassell, 2000; first publ. 1978), p. 13.

9 D. Stevenson, *With Our Backs to the Wall. Victory and Defeat in 1918* (London: Allen Lane, 2011), p. xvii.

10 It is impossible to find precise casualty figures for this period. British casualties between 7 August and 12 November 1918 were 298,125, including over 13,000 officers. French casualties between 1 July and 15 September were approximately 279,000. Total American losses were 130,000 with the vast majority being sustained between July and November 1918. See Sir J. Edmonds and R. Maxwell-Hyslop (eds.), *Military Operations France and Belgium 1918*, V, *26th September–11th November. The Advance to Victory* (London: HMSO, 1947), p. 562; Terraine, *To Win a War*, p. 202; and G. Mead, *Doughboys. America and the First World War* (London: Penguin Books, 2001), p. 353. German losses are even more difficult to ascertain. The German Medical History only covers the war up to the end of July 1918, thus missing out the heavy losses throughout August to November. According to Wilhelm Deist, German dead and wounded may have been as high as 420,000 in the final phase of the war (plus upwards of 340,000 prisoners). See Reichskriegsministerium Heeressanitätsinspektion, *Sanitätsbericht über das Deutsche Heer* (3 vols., Berlin: E. S. Mittler und Sohn, 1934–8); W. Deist, 'The Military Collapse of the German Empire: The Reality behind the Stab-in-the-Back Myth', *War in History*, Vol. 3, No. 2 (April 1996), pp. 186–207 (p. 203), and J. McRandle and J. Quirk, 'The Blood Test Revisited: A New Look at German Casualty Counts in World War I', *Journal of Military History*, Vol. 70, No. 3 (July 2006), pp. 667–701.

Prologue: 'Surprise was complete'

1 J. de Pierrefeu, *French Headquarters 1915–1918*, trans. Major C. J. C. Street (London: Geoffrey Bles, 1924), p. 277.

2 MHI: WWI 246, Corporal F. L. Faulkner, letter, 1 February 1919.

3 M. S. Neiberg, *The Second Battle of the Marne* (Bloomington, Ind: Indiana University Press, 2008), p. 100.

4 T. Gale, 'La Salamandre: The French Army's *Artillerie Spéciale* and the Development of Armoured Warfare in the First World War' (Ph.D., King's College London, 2010), p. 202.

5 C. M. Chenu, *Du képi rouge aux chars d'assaut* (Paris: Albin Michel, 1932), p. 289.

6 Bundesarchiv, *Der Weltkrieg 1914 bis 1918*, XIV, *Die Kriegführung an der Westfront im Jahre 1918* (Berlin: E. S. Mittler und Sohn, 1944), p. 478.

7 D. Zabecki, *The German 1918 Offensives. A Case Study in the Operational Level of War* (London and New York: Routledge, 2006), pp. 273–5.

8 Chenu, *Du képi rouge*, p. 290.

9 E. E. Mackin, *Suddenly We Didn't Want to Die. Memoirs of a World War I Marine* (Novato, Calif.: Presidio Press, 1993), p. 92.

10 MHI: WWI 5499 (Folder 3), 'The Luck of a Buck', by Private R. L. Williams, pp. 147–8.

11 MHI: WWI 2487, 'My Memories of World War I', by Captain M. B. Helm, p. 12.

12 Chenu, *Du képi rouge*, p. 290.

13 JMO: 26 N 18/1, Groupe d'Armées de Réserve, 'Journal de Marche période du 18 février au 11 novembre 1918', p. 94.

14 JMO: 26 N 39/7, VI Armée, 'Journal des marches et opérations du 29 juin au 10 septembre 1918'.

15 Reinhardt cited in G. S. Viereck (ed.), *As They Saw Us. Foch, Ludendorff and Other Leaders Write Our War History* (Cranbury, NJ: Scholar's Bookshelf, 2005; first publ. 1929), pp. 112–13.

16 E. von Ludendorff, *Concise Ludendorff Memoirs 1914–1918* (London: Hutchinson, 1933), p. 283.

17 H. Sulzbach, *With the German Guns. Four Years on the Western Front 1914–1918*, trans. R. Thonger (London: Frederick Warne, 1981; first publ. 1973), p. 209.

1. Decision on the Marne

1 Speech of 4 June 1918 cited in G. Clemenceau, *Grandeur and Misery of Victory* (London: George G. Harrap & Co., 1930), p. 54.

2 R. Binding, *A Fatalist at War*, trans. I. F. D. Morrow (London: George Allen & Unwin, 1929), pp. 238–9.

3 TNA: WO 157/197, Fourth Army Summary of Information, 3 July 1918.

4 G. Bucher, *In the Line 1914–1918*, trans. Norman Gullick (Uckfield: Naval & Military Press, 2005; first publ. 1932), pp. 265–6.

5 Crown Prince Wilhelm, *The Memoirs of the Crown Prince of Germany* (London: Thornton Butterworth, 1922), p. 197.

6 TNA: WO 157/196, Fourth Army Weekly Appreciation, 13 July 1918, and A. Watson, *Enduring the Great War. Combat, Morale and Collapse in the German and British Armies, 1914–1918* (Cambridge: Cambridge University Press, 2008), pp. 179–81 and 187.

7 F. von Lossberg, *Meine Tätigkeit im Weltkrieg 1914–1918* (Berlin: E. S. Mittler und Sohn, 1939), p. 352.

8 Crown Prince Wilhelm, *Memoirs*, pp. 195–6.

9 Ibid., pp. 25–6.

10 Ibid., pp. 154–5.

11 M. Ludendorff, *My Married Life with Ludendorff*, trans. R. Somerset (London: Hutchinson, 1930), pp. 19 and 232.

12 E. von Ludendorff, *Concise Ludendorff Memoirs 1914–1918* (London: Hutchinson, 1933), p. 16.

13 See W. J. Astore and D. E. Showalter, *Hindenburg. Icon of German Militarism* (Washington, DC: Potomac Books, 2005), p. 66.

14 See D. Zabecki, *The German 1918 Offensives. A Case Study in the Operational Level of War* (London and New York: Routledge, 2006), ch. 11.

15 TNA: WO 157/34, GHQ Summary of Intelligence, 9 August 1918.

16 BA-MA: MSG2/5710, Leutnant Richard Schütt, letter, 12 August 1918.

17 Cited in Prince Max of Baden, *The Memoirs of Prince Max of Baden*, trans. W. M. Calder and C. W. H. Sutton (2 vols., London: Constable, 1928), I, p. 307.

18 J. P. Guéno and Y. Laplume (eds.), *Paroles de poilus. Lettres et carnets du front 1914–1918* (Paris: Radio France, 1998), p. 476.

19 Sir J. Edmonds (ed.), *Military Operations France and Belgium 1918*, III,

May–July. The German Diversion Offensives and the First Allied Counter-Offensive (London: Macmillan & Co., 1939), p. 305.

20 A. Stenger, *Schicksalswende. Von der Marne bis zur Vesle 1918* (Berlin: Stalling, 1930), p. 219.

21 J. McRandle and J. Quirk, 'The Blood Test Revisited: A New Look at German Casualty Counts in World War I', *Journal of Military History*, Vol. 70, No. 3 (July 2006), pp. 667–701 (p. 683), Table 6.

22 MHI: WWI 5499 (Folder 3), 'The Luck of a Buck', by Private R. L. Williams, pp. 153–4.

23 N. Johnson, *Britain and the 1918–19 Influenza Pandemic. A Dark Epilogue* (London: Routledge, 2006), p. 82.

24 Sir W. G. Macpherson, *Medical Services. Diseases of the War* (London: HMSO, 1921), I, pp. 174–7 and 179–81.

25 Reichskriegsministerium Heeressanitätsinspektion, *Sanitätsbericht über das Deutsche Heer* (3 vols., Berlin: E. S. Mittler und Sohn, 1934–8), III, p. 123.

26 S. Weintraub, *A Stillness Heard Round the World. The End of the Great War: November 1918* (London: Allen & Unwin, 1985), p. 9.

27 One contemporary described Clemenceau's words as being 'like cold, sharp, well-tempered steel'. 'No more pacifist campaigns, no more German intrigues', he had said before the Chamber of Deputies on 20 November 1917 in what would become one of his most famous speeches. 'Neither treason, nor semi-treason: the war. Nothing but the war. Our armies will not be caught between fire from two sides. Justice will be done. The country will know that it is defended.' Clemenceau cited in D.R. Watson, *Georges Clemenceau. A Political Biography* (London: Eyre Methuen, 1974), p. 271. The 'well-tempered steel' reference was from an early biographical sketch written in 1883, cited p. 72.

28 B. H. Liddell Hart, *Reputations* (London: John Murray, 1928), p. 176.

29 Colonel C. J. C. Grant cited in Sir G. Aston, *The Biography of the Late Marshal Foch* (London: Hutchinson, 1932), pp. 128–9.

30 Aston, *Biography of the Late Marshal Foch*, p. 116.

31 See E. Greenhalgh, *Foch in Command. The Forging of a First World War General* (Cambridge: Cambridge University Press, 2011), pp. 301–9.

32 J. de Pierrefeu, *French Headquarters 1915–1918*, trans. Major C. J. C. Street (London: Geoffrey Bles, 1924), p. 284.

33 Liddell Hart, *Reputations*, p. 215.

34 Hellé cited in G. S. Viereck (ed.), *As They Saw Us. Foch, Ludendorff and Other Leaders Write Our War History* (Cranbury, NJ: Scholar's Bookshelf, 2005; first publ. 1929), p. 127.

35 D. Lloyd George, *War Memoirs of David Lloyd George* (2 vols., London: Odhams Press, 1933–6).

36 G. S. Duncan, *Douglas Haig as I Knew Him* (London: George Allen & Unwin, 1966), p. 23.

37 Details of the meeting on 24 July 1918 taken from F. Foch, *The Memoirs of Marshal Foch*, trans. T. Bentley Mott (London: William Heinemann, 1931), pp. 425–30.

38 B. H. Liddell Hart, *Foch. The Man of Orleans* (London: Eyre & Spottiswoode, 1931), p. 342.

39 R. L. Bullard, *Personalities and Reminiscences of the War* (New York: Doubleday, 1925), p. 42.

40 Haig to Sir Henry Wilson (Chief of the Imperial General Staff), 24 July 1918, in D. Haig, *War Diaries and Letters 1914–1918*, eds. G. Sheffield and J. Bourne (London: Weidenfeld & Nicolson, 2005), p. 430.

2. 'Neglect nothing'

1 Sir J. Monash, *The Australian Victories in France in 1918* (London: Hutchinson, 1920), p. 105.

2 C. Vince and S. R. Jones, *England in France. Sketches Mainly with the 59th Division* (New York: E. P. Dutton, 1919), pp. 47 and 55.

3 Sir A. Montgomery, *The Story of Fourth Army in the Battles of the Hundred Days, August 8th to November 11th, 1918* (London: Hodder & Stoughton, 1920), p. 11.

4 TNA: WO 95/437, Rawlinson to Haig, 17 July 1918.

5 Field Marshal Sir D. Haig, diary, 26 July 1918, in D. Haig, *War Diaries and Letters 1914–1918*, eds. G. Sheffield and J. Bourne (London: Weidenfeld & Nicolson, 2005), p. 435.

6 Montgomery, *The Story of Fourth Army*, p. 18.

7 'Organization of the Attacks of the 1st Army', in P. Pétain, *Report by the Field Marshal Commander-in-Chief of the French Armies of the North and Northeast on the Operations in 1918. The Offensive Campaign (18 July–11 November 1918)* (3 parts, trans. A. Woldike), III, pp. 11–14; JMO: 26 N

20/1, 'Journal de Marche de la 1ère Armée à partir du 1er janvier 1918 au 31 octobre 1918', p. 479.

8 See S. B. Schreiber, *Shock Army of the British Empire. The Canadian Corps in the Last 100 Days of the Great War* (Westport, Conn.: Praeger, 1997).

9 LAC: MG30 E100, Sir Arthur Currie Papers, Vol. 43, File 191, Notebook entitled 'Things Worth Remembering', and Monash, *Australian Victories*, p. 96.

10 Haig, diary, 31 July 1918, in Haig, *War Diaries and Letters*, p. 436.

11 Mark Vs were powered by a 150 horsepower Ricardo engine that could reach a maximum speed of 4.6 mph, but with an average speed of 3 mph. It had a nine-hour endurance that could take it up to twenty-five miles. It was crewed by one officer and seven other ranks.

12 For the different characteristics of British tanks see the table in J. F. C. Fuller, *Tanks in the Great War 1914–1918* (London: John Murray, 1920), p. 44. The Mark V Star was a good idea, but let down by its extremely poor conditions for passengers, who were exposed to potentially lethal engine fumes.

13 A. G. L. McNaughton, 'The Development of Artillery in the Great War', *Canadian Defence Quarterly*, Vol. 6, No. 2 (January 1929), pp. 160–61.

14 C. E. W. Bean, *The Official History of Australia in the War of 1914–1918* (12 vols., Sydney: Angus & Robertson, 1941–2), VI, p. 499.

15 Monash, *Australian Victories*, pp. 102–3.

16 J. H. Morrow, Jr, *The Great War in the Air. Military Aviation from 1909 to 1921* (Washington, DC: Smithsonian Institute Press, 1993), p. 294.

17 H. A. Jones, *The War in the Air. Being the Story of the Part Played in the Great War by the Royal Air Force* (6 vols., Oxford: Clarendon Press, 1922–37), VI, pp. 433–6.

18 CLIP: Memoirs of C. H. Savage.

19 IWM: 78/29/1, 'A Field Artillery Officer, 1914–1919', by Colonel F. J. Rice, p. 88.

20 CLIP: Memoirs of C. H. Savage.

21 TNA: WO 95/94, 'Summary of Tank Actions from August 8th to October 20th', by H. J. Elles, 29 October 1918.

22 Various commanders compared the orchestration of military power in the Great War to pieces of music, to great symphonies, including

Monash, who stated that 'A perfected modern battle plan is like nothing so much as a score for orchestral composition, where the various arms and units are the instruments, and the tasks they perform are their respective musical phrases.': Monash, *Australian Victories*, p. 56.

23 Sir J. Edmonds (ed.), *Military Operations France and Belgium 1918,* IV, *8th August–26th September. The Franco-British Offensive* (London: HMSO, 1947), p. 11.

24 US Department for the Army, Historical Division, *Histories of Two Hundred and Fifty-One Divisions of the German Army Which Participated in the War (1914–1918)* (Washington, DC: Government Printing Office, 1920), pp. 449, 457, 594, 596, 635, 709 and 743.

25 T. von Bose, *Die Katastrophe des 8. August 1918* (Berlin: Stalling, 1930), p. 47.

26 TNA: WO 157/196, Fourth Army Summary of Information, 29 July 1918.

27 Edmonds (ed.), *Military Operations France and Belgium 1918,* IV, p. 37.

28 JMO: 26 N 202/1, 'Compte-rendu des opérations du 8 au 14 août 1918: 31 Corps d'Armée', p. 7.

29 See Edmonds (ed.), *Military Operations France and Belgium 1918,* IV, pp. 22–4, and Bean, *Official History of Australia in the War of 1914–1918,* VI, p. 512.

30 P. Maze, *A Frenchman in Khaki* (Kingswood: William Heinemann, 1934), pp. 325–7.

31 A. Grasset, *La Guerre en action, Montdidier. Le 8 août 1918 à la 42ème Division* (Paris: Éditions Berger-Levrault, 1930), p. 67.

32 IWM: 80/28/1, Account of T. G. Mohan, p. 117.

33 Monash, *Australian Victories*, pp. 120–21.

3. 'Death will have a rich harvest'

1 T. von Bose, *Die Katastrophe des 8. August 1918* (Berlin: Stalling, 1930), p. 110.

2 LAC: RG41, Vol. 8, Testimony of W. E. Curtis.

3 Bose, *Katastrophe*, p. 140.

4 Ibid., pp. 49–50.

5 A. Grasset, *La Guerre en action, Montdidier. Le 8 août 1918 à la 42ème Division* (Paris: Éditions Berger-Levrault, 1930), p. 126.

6 Bose, *Katastrophe*, p. 158.

7 CLIP: Bertram Howard Cox to his brothers (Carl, Herbert and Murrill), 13 August 1918.

8 J. F. B. Livesay, *Canada's Hundred Days. With the Canadian Corps from Amiens to Mons, Aug. 8–Nov. 11, 1918* (Toronto: Thomas Allen, 1919), p. 28.

9 W. H. Downing, *To the Last Ridge. The World War One Experiences of W. H. Downing* (London: Grub Street, 2002; first publ. 1920), pp. 143 and 145. Original emphasis.

10 TNA: WO 95/437, Fourth Army Summary of Operations, 8 August 1918; Sir J. Edmonds (ed.), *Military Operations France and Belgium 1918, IV, 8th August–26th September. The Franco-British Offensive* (London: HMSO, 1947), pp. 51 and 73.

11 *Les Armées françaises dans la Grande Guerre* (11 vols., Paris: Ministère de la Guerre, 1923), VII, p. 177.

12 Edmonds (ed.), *Military Operations France and Belgium 1918,* IV, pp. 90–92.

13 G. von der Marwitz, *Weltkriegsbriefe*, ed. E. von Tschischwitz (Berlin: Steiniger-Verlage, 1940), pp. 303 and 306.

14 TNA: WO 95/94, 'Summary of Tank Actions from August 8th to October 20th', by H. J. Elles, 29 October 1918.

15 LAC: '1st Canadian Division. Report on Amiens Operations August 8th–20th Inclusive 1918', p. 3.

16 Bose, *Katastrophe*, pp. 109–10.

17 BA-MA: PH8I/385, 'Erfahrungen bei dem englischen Angriff am 8.8.18', 16 August 1918.

18 P. Maze, *A Frenchman in Khaki* (Kingswood: William Heinemann, 1934), p. 331.

19 Bose, *Katastrophe*, p. 61.

20 LAC: '4th Canadian Division Narrative of Operations, Battle of Amiens, August 8th to August 13th, 1918', pp. 7 and 20.

21 Maze, *Frenchman in Khaki*, p. 332.

22 Bose, *Katastrophe*, p. 127.

23 Bundesarchiv, *Der Weltkrieg 1914 bis 1918,* XIV, *Die Kriegführung an der Westfront im Jahre 1918* (Berlin: E. S. Mittler und Sohn, 1944), p. 567.

24 Edmonds (ed.), *Military Operations France and Belgium 1918,* IV, pp. 89–90.

25 LAC: RG41, Vol. 10, Testimony of R. H. Camp.

26 R. Stark, *Wings of War. A German Airman's Diary of the Last Year of the Great War*, trans. C. W. Sykes (London: Greenhill Books, 1988), pp. 115–16.

27 Maze, *A Frenchman in Khaki*, pp. 335–6.

28 Edmonds (ed.), *Military Operations France and Belgium 1918,* IV, p. 93.

29 TNA: WO 95/437, Fourth Army Summary of Operations, 9 August 1918.

30 TNA: WO 95/94, 'Summary of Tank Actions from August 8th to October 20th', by H. J. Elles, 29 October 1918.

31 Crown Prince Rupprecht, *Mein Kriegstagebuch* (3 vols., Berlin: E. S. Mittler und Sohn, 1929), II, p. 434.

32 Edmonds (ed.), *Military Operations France and Belgium 1918,* IV, pp. 88–92, 117 and 139.

33 E. P. F. Lynch, *Somme Mud. The Experiences of an Infantryman in France, 1916–1919*, ed. W. Davies (London: Bantam, 2008; first publ. 2006), pp. 341 and 343–4.

34 LAC: RG41, Vol. 21, Testimony of Brigadier-General A. Ross.

35 R. Prior and T. Wilson, *Command on the Western Front. The Military Career of Sir Henry Rawlinson, 1914–1918* (Oxford: Blackwell, 1992), pp. 327–33; Edmonds (ed.), *Military Operations France and Belgium 1918,* IV, pp. 116 and 138.

36 JMO: 26 N 20/1, 'Journal de Marche de la 1ère Armée à partir du 1er janvier 1918 au 31 octobre 1918', p. 485.

37 Maze, *A Frenchman in Khaki*, p. 338.

38 Edmonds (ed.), *Military Operations France and Belgium 1918,* IV, p. 138.

39 TNA: WO 95/94, 'Summary of Tank Actions from August 8th to October 20th', by H. J. Elles, 29 October 1918.

40 LAC: '4th Canadian Division Narrative of Operations, Battle of Amiens, August 8th to August 13th, 1918', p. 13.

4. 'Another black day'

1 G. von der Marwitz, *Weltkriegsbriefe*, ed. E. von Tschischwitz (Berlin: Steiniger-Verlage, 1940), p. 304.

2 Sir G. Aston, *The Biography of the Late Marshal Foch* (London: Hutchinson, 1932), p. 256.

3 Sir W. Orpen, *An Onlooker in France 1917–1919* (London: Williams & Norgate, 1921), pp. 77–9.

4 F. Foch, *The Memoirs of Marshal Foch*, trans. T. Bentley Mott (London: William Heinemann, 1931), pp. 438 and 439. Original emphasis.

5 Foch to Haig and Pétain, 12 August 1918, in Sir J. Edmonds (ed.), *Military Operations France and Belgium 1918, IV, 8th August–26th September. The Franco-British Offensive* (London: HMSO, 1947), pp. 583–4.

6 LAC: RG41, Vol. 21, Testimony of Brigadier-General J. A. Clark, p. 8.

7 TNA: WO 95/437, 'Notes of Conference Held at 2nd Australian Division Hdqrs., Villers-Bretonneux, at 3 p.m., 11th August, 1918'.

8 See M. Daille, *La Bataille de Montdidier* (Paris: Éditions Berger-Levrault, 1924).

9 *Les Armées françaises dans la Grande Guerre* (11 vols., Paris: Ministère de la Guerre, 1923), VII, p. 195; JMO: 26 N 20/1, 'Journal de Marche de la 1ère Armée à partir du 1er janvier 1918 au 31 octobre 1918', p. 485.

10 'General Operations Order No. 606', 11 August 1918, in P. Pétain, *Report by the Field Marshal Commander-in-Chief of the French Armies of the North and Northeast on the Operations in 1918. The Offensive Campaign (18 July–11 November 1918)* (3 parts, trans. A. Woldike), III, p. 154.

11 Edmonds (ed.), *Military Operations France and Belgium 1918, IV*, pp. 167–8.

12 TNA: WO 158/29, Haig to Foch, 14 August 1918.

13 Ibid., 15 August 1918.

14 Field Marshal Sir D. Haig, diary, 15 August 1918, in D. Haig, *War Diaries and Letters 1914–1918*, eds. G. Sheffield and J. Bourne (London: Weidenfeld & Nicolson, 2005), pp. 445–6.

15 E. von Ludendorff, *Concise Ludendorff Memoirs 1914–1918* (London: Hutchinson, 1933), pp. 290–91.

16 Crown Prince Rupprecht, *Mein Kriegstagebuch* (3 vols., Berlin: E. S. Mittler und Sohn, 1929), II, p. 435.

17 TNA: WO 95/94, Tank Corps Summary of Information, 10 September 1918.

18 F. von Lossberg, *Meine Tätigkeit im Weltkrieg 1914–1918* (Berlin: E. S. Mittler und Sohn, 1939), pp. 352, 354 and 355.

19 P. von Hindenburg, *Out of My Life*, trans. F. A. Holt (London: Cassell & Company, 1920), pp. 394 and 395.

20 Hindenburg, *Out of My Life*, p. 396.

21 Prince Max of Baden, *The Memoirs of Prince Max of Baden*, trans. W. M. Calder and C. W. H. Sutton (2 vols., London: Constable, 1928), I, p. 315.

22 Ludendorff, *Memoirs*, pp. 294 and 295.

23 W. Görlitz (ed.), *The Kaiser and His Court. The Diaries, Note Books and*

Letters of Admiral Georg Alexander von Müller, Chief of the Naval Cabinet, 1914–1918 (London: Macdonald & Co., 1961; first publ. 1959), p. 42.

24 W. Foerster, *Der Feldherr Ludendorff im Unglück* (Wiesbaden: Limes Verlag, 1952), pp. 76–7.

25 'Occupation of the Plateaux to the North of the Aisne and the Advance as Far as the Oise (20th–23rd August)', in Pétain, *Report*, III, p. 47.

26 Ludendorff, *Memoirs*, p. 300.

27 'Special Order No. 410', 19 August 1918, in Pétain, *Report*, III, p. 211.

28 'Instruction for the Attack', 15 August 1918, in Pétain, *Report*, III, p. 185.

29 C. Mangin, *Lettres de guerre 1914–1918*, ed. L. Eugène (Paris: Fayard, 1950), pp. 294–5.

30 R. L. Bullard, *Personalities and Reminiscences of the War* (New York: Doubleday, 1925), p. 200.

31 Mangin, *Lettres de guerre*, pp. 299–301.

32 'General Operations Orders No. 648', 17 August 1918, in Pétain, *Report*, III, pp. 199–200.

33 'Making Contact with the Hindenburg Position (4th–15th September)', in Pétain, *Report*, III, p. 65.

5. *'The incredible roar of massed guns'*

1 E. P. F. Lynch, *Somme Mud. The Experiences of an Infantryman in France, 1916–1919*, ed. W. Davies (London: Bantam, 2008; first publ. 2006), p. 357.

2 M. E. Debeney, *La Guerre et les hommes. Réflexions d'après-guerre* (Paris: Librairie Plon, 1937), pp. 38–9.

3 R. L. Bullard, *Personalities and Reminiscences of the War* (New York: Doubleday, 1925), p. 130.

4 Field Marshal Sir D. Haig, diary, 19 August 1918, in D. Haig, *War Diaries and Letters 1914–1918*, eds. G. Sheffield and J. Bourne (London: Weidenfeld & Nicolson, 2005), p. 447. Original emphasis.

5 TNA: WO 95/372, 'Notes for Operation GZ (Bucquoy–Moyenneville)', 14 August 1918.

6 Sir James Edmonds (ed.), *Military Operations France and Belgium 1918*, IV, *8th August–26th September. The Franco-British Offensive* (London: HMSO, 1947), pp. 186 and 192.

7 A. H. Hussey and D. S. Inman, *The Fifth Division in the Great War* (London: Nisbet & Co., 1921), pp. 231, 232 and 238.

8 TNA: WO 95/1516, 'Resume of Reports on Operations of 95th, 15th and 13th Infantry Brigades.'

9 TNA: WO 95/1557, 15/Royal Warwickshire Regiment War Diary, 23 August 1918.

10 IWM: 86/57/1, 'Once a Gunner', by Brigadier R. C. Foot, pp. 96–8.

11 IWM: 81/21/1, Account of A. J. Turner, p. 44.

12 IWM: 92/36/1, 'The Wheels of Darkness', by Lieutenant R. G. Dixon, p. 26.

13 IWM: 80/28/1, Memoirs of T. G. Mohan, p. 119.

14 IWM: 06/30/1, Account of T. H. Holmes.

15 Edmonds (ed.), *Military Operations France and Belgium 1918,* IV, p. 18n.

16 J. M. A. Durrant, 'Some Aspects of the Operations of the 2nd Australian Division from the 27th of August to the 2nd of September, 1918', *Army Quarterly*, Vol. XXXI (October 1935 and January 1936), p. 19.

17 W. H. Downing, *To the Last Ridge. The World War One Experiences of W. H. Downing* (London: Grub Street, 2002; first publ. 1920), pp. 157–8.

18 Sir J. Monash, *The Australian Victories in France in 1918* (London: Hutchinson, 1920), p. 177.

19 Lynch, *Somme Mud*, p. 361.

20 Details taken from C. E. W. Bean, *The Official History of Australia in the War of 1914–1918* (12 vols., Sydney: Angus & Robertson, 1941–2), VI, pp. 816–17.

21 Sir A. Montgomery, *The Story of Fourth Army in the Battles of the Hundred Days, August 8th to November 11th, 1918* (London: Hodder & Stoughton, 1920), p. 101.

22 G. von der Marwitz, *Weltkriegsbriefe*, ed. E. von Tschischwitz (Berlin: Steiniger-Verlage, 1940), p. 309.

23 F. von Lossberg, *Meine Tätigkeit im Weltkrieg 1914–1918* (Berlin: E. S. Mittler und Sohn, 1939), pp. 355–6.

24 Edmonds (ed.), *Military Operations France and Belgium 1918,* IV, p. 236.

25 Hauptman Poetter, *Infanterie-Regiment Nr. 55* (Oldenburg: Stalling, 1922), p. 54.

26 Marwitz, *Weltkriegsbriefe*, p. 307.

27 G. Bucher, *In the Line 1914–1918* (Uckfield: Naval & Military Press, 2005; first publ. 1932), p. 294.

28 TNA: WO 95/94, Tank Corps Summary of Information, 16 September 1918.

29 R. Stark, *Wings of War. A German Airman's Diary of the Last Year of the Great War*, trans. C. W. Sykes (London: Greenhill Books, 1988), pp. 135–7.

30 Lossberg, *Meine Tätigkeit im Weltkrieg*, p. 356.

31 TNA: WO 95/94, Tank Corps Summary of Information, 26 September 1918.

32 BA-MA: MSG2/5710, Leutnant Richard Schütt, letter, 17 August 1918, and Kanonier Willy Schütt, letter, 24 August 1918.

33 BA-MA: RH61/1035, 'Feldpost Postüberwachung beim AOK 5', 31 August 1918.

34 Marwitz, *Weltkriegsbriefe*, p. 308.

35 R. Binding, *A Fatalist at War*, trans. I. F. D. Morrow (London: George Allen & Unwin, 1929), pp. 241 and 242.

36 For the effect of RAF bombing and strafing attacks see J. Boff, 'Air/Land Integration in the 100 Days: The Case of Third Army', *RAF Air Power Review*, Vol. 12, No. 3 (Autumn 2009), pp. 84–5.

37 Marwitz, *Weltkriegsbriefe*, pp. 304–5 and 307.

38 L. A. Strange, *Recollections of an Airman* (London: Greenhill Books, 1989), pp. 190–91.

39 C. Degelow, *Germany's Last Knight in the Air. The Memoirs of Major Carl Degelow*, trans. and ed. P. Kilduff (London: William Kimber, 1979), p. 145.

40 Edmonds (ed.), *Military Operations France and Belgium 1918*, IV, p. 351.

41 F. Foch, *The Memoirs of Marshal Foch*, trans. T. Bentley Mott (London: William Heinemann, 1931), pp. 456–7.

6. 'The whole thing was simply magnificent'

1 Crown Prince Rupprecht, *Mein Kriegstagebuch* (3 vols., Berlin: E. S. Mittler und Sohn, 1929), II, p. 158.

2 Anonymous, 'A German Account of the British Offensive of August, 1918', *Army Quarterly*, Vol. VI (April/July 1923), p. 16.

3 BA-MA: MSG2/5710, Kanonier Willy Schütt, letter, 6 September 1918.

4 R. Stark, *Wings of War. A German Airman's Diary of the Last Year of the Great War*, trans. C. W. Sykes (London: Greenhill Books, 1988), pp. 151–4.

5 Sir J. Edmonds (ed.), *Military Operations France and Belgium 1918*, IV, *8th August–26th September. The Franco-British Offensive* (London: HMSO, 1947), pp. 413–14.

6 LAC: MG30 E100, Sir Arthur Currie Papers, Vol. 43, File 1914, diary, 3 September 1918.

7 S. B. Schreiber, *Shock Army of the British Empire. The Canadian Corps in the Last 100 Days of the Great War* (Westport, Conn.: Praeger, 1997), p. 79.

8 TNA: WO 95/94, 'Summary of Tank Actions from August 8th to October 20th', by H. J. Elles, 29 October 1918.

9 J. F. B. Livesay, *Canada's Hundred Days. With the Canadian Corps from Amiens to Mons, Aug. 8–Nov. 11, 1918* (Toronto: Thomas Allen, 1919), p. 162.

10 LAC: MG30 E393, Account of Private A. J. Foster, pp. 27 and 29.

11 W. H. Anderson, 'The Breaking of the Quéant–Drocourt Line by the Canadian Corps, First Army 2nd–4th September, 1918', *Canadian Defence Quarterly*, Vol. 4, No. 1 (January 1926), p. 126.

12 Captain A. Impey, diary, 30 September 1918, in http://www.fylde. demon.co.uk/tucker/tuckerbiography.htm.

13 Sir A. Macdonell, 'The Old Red Patch at the Breaking of the Drocourt–Quéant Line, the Crossing of the Canal du Nord and the Advance on Cambrai, 30th Aug–2nd Oct 1918', *Canadian Defence Quarterly*, Vol. 6 (October 1928), pp. 17–18.

14 Field Marshal Sir D. Haig, diary, 1 September 1918, in D. Haig, *War Diaries and Letters 1914–1918*, eds. G. Sheffield and J. Bourne (London: Weidenfeld and Nicolson, 2005), pp. 452–3.

15 T. Cook, *No Place to Run. The Canadian Corps and Gas Warfare in the First World War* (Vancouver: UBC Press, 1999), p. 200.

16 IWM: 06/30/1, Account of T. H. Holmes.

17 Cook, *No Place to Run*, p. 200.

18 F. A. Holden, *War Memories* (Athens, Ga: Athens Book Company, 1922), pp. 128–31.

19 IWM: 86/57/1, 'Once a Gunner', by Brigadier R. C. Foot, pp. 98 and 120.

20 CWM: 58A 1 187.1, 'The Life History of Clifford M. Johnston 1896–1951' (2 vols.), II, pp. 592, 593 and 598.

21 Sir J. Monash, *The Australian Victories in France in 1918* (London: Hutchinson, 1920), pp. 194–7.

22 Anonymous, 'The Work of the Royal Engineers in the European War, 1914–1919 – Bridging', *The Royal Engineers Journal*, Vol. XXX (July–December 1919), p. 261.

23 A. H. Hussey and D. S. Inman, *The Fifth Division in the Great War* (London: Nisbet & Co., 1921), p. 289.

24 Monash, *Australian Victories*, p. 207.

25 Stark, *Wings of War*, pp. 138–9.

26 F. von Lossberg, *Meine Tätigkeit im Weltkrieg 1914–1918* (Berlin: E. S. Mittler und Sohn, 1939), p. 358.

27 R. Binding, *A Fatalist at War*, trans. I. F. D. Morrow (London: George Allen & Unwin, 1929), pp. 227 and 229.

28 Crown Prince Wilhelm, *The Memoirs of the Crown Prince of Germany* (London: Thornton Butterworth, 1922), p. 203.

29 S. Stephenson, *The Final Battle. Soldiers of the Western Front and the German Revolution of 1918* (Cambridge: Cambridge University Press, 2009), p. 21.

30 BA-MA: Patient Files of Guido Hermann (Pers 9/1.1.97) and Cyrus Karl (Pers 9/1.7.93).

31 BA-MA: Patient Files of Wilhelm Wilhöft (Pers 9/1.1.99) and Karl Passhaus (Pers 9/1.7.94).

32 Lossberg, *Meine Tätigkeit im Weltkrieg*, pp. 356–8.

33 Edmonds (ed.), *Military Operations France and Belgium 1918*, IV, pp. 467–8; M. Kitchen, *The Silent Dictatorship. The Politics of the German High Command under Hindenburg and Ludendorff, 1916–1918* (London: Croom Helm, 1976), p. 252.

34 Rupprecht, *Mein Kriegstagebuch*, II, p. 443.

7. Enter the Americans

1 Crown Prince Rupprecht cited in a letter to Prince Max, 15 August 1918, in Prince Max of Baden, *The Memoirs of Prince Max of Baden*, trans. W. M. Calder and C. W. H. Sutton (2 vols., London: Constable, 1928), I, p. 320.

2 E. E. Mackin, *Suddenly We Didn't Want to Die. Memoirs of a World War I Marine* (Novato, Calif.: Presidio Press, 1993), pp. 19–20.

3 G. Mead, *Doughboys. America and the First World War* (London: Penguin Books, 2001), p. 92.

4 J. J. Pershing, *My Experiences in the World War* (2 vols., New York: Frederick A. Stokes, 1931), I, p. 159.

5 Ibid., pp. 30–33.

6 D. Trask, *The AEF and Coalition Warmaking, 1917–1918* (Lawrence, Kan.: University of Kansas, 1993), pp. 53–5.

7 IWM: 92/36/1, 'The Wheels of Darkness', by Lieutenant R. G. Dixon, pp. 64–6.

8 C. M. Chenu, *Du képi rouge aux chars d'assaut* (Paris: Albin Michel, 1932), p. 284.

9 According to Savatier, 'Nothing disconcerted us Frenchmen quite so much as the attitude of the white American officers towards the coloured men in the American forces.' Cited in G. S. Viereck (ed.), *As They Saw Us. Foch, Ludendorff and Other Leaders Write Our War History* (Cranbury, NJ: Scholar's Bookshelf, 2005; first publ. 1929), pp. 295 and 303.

10 IWM: 06/62/1, Captain T. F. Grady, diary, 8–11 April 1918.

11 See Mead, *Doughboys*, pp. 66–8.

12 MHI: WWI 8178, 'A Peace Lover Goes to War', by Lieutenant W. T. Carpenter, p. 26.

13 MHI: WWI 8188 (Folder 8), 'A Private Saw It. My Memoirs of the First Division World War I', by H. L. McHenry, p. 36.

14 F. A. Holden, *War Memories* (Athens, Ga: Athens Book Company, 1922), p. 45.

15 A. Williams, *Experiences of the Great War* (Roanoake, Va: Stone, 1919), p. 16.

16 Ibid., pp. 16–17.

17 Holden, *War Memories*, pp. 79 and 80.

18 Mead, *Doughboys*, p. 67.

19 Pershing, *My Experiences in the World War*, I, p. 152.

20 M. E. Grotelueschen, *The AEF Way of War. The American Army and Combat in World War I* (Cambridge: Cambridge University Press, 2007), pp. 214–15, 258–9 and 277–8.

21 Pershing, *My Experiences in the World War*, II, p. 144.

22 Haig to Pershing, 27 August 1918, in D. Haig, *War Diaries and Letters 1914–1918*, eds. G. Sheffield and J. Bourne (London: Weidenfeld and Nicolson, 2005), p. 451.

23　Grotelueschen, *The AEF Way of War*, p. 109.

24　'Indications of Impending American Attack', 9 September 1918, in US Department for the Army, Historical Division, *United States Army in the World War, 1917–1919* (17 vols., Washington, DC: Government Printing Office, 1948 [hereafter *USAWW*]), VIII, pp. 291–3.

25　See Grotelueschen, *The AEF Way of War*, p. 111n.

26　US Department for the Army, Historical Division, *Histories of Two Hundred and Fifty-One Divisions of the German Army Which Participated in the War (1914–1918)* (Washington, DC: Government Printing Office, 1920), pp. 119, 161, 183, 235, 398, 533, 568, 622, 635 and 745.

27　Ludendorff to Group of Armies von Gallwitz, 10 September 1918, in *USAWW*, VIII, p. 294.

28　Pershing, *My Experiences in the World War*, II, p. 267.

29　Corporal E. B. Searcy cited in J. H. Hallas (ed.), *Doughboy War. The American Expeditionary Force in World War I* (London and Boulder, Colo.: Lynne Rienner, 2000), p. 227.

30　J. J. Pershing, *Final Report of Gen. John J. Pershing* (Washington, DC: Government Printing Office, 1919), p. 42.

31　Sergeant W. Brown cited in Hallas, *Doughboy War*, p. 229.

32　D. MacArthur, *Reminiscences* (London: Heinemann, 1964), p. 63.

33　Viereck (ed.), *As They Saw Us*, pp. 196–201.

34　Pershing, *Final Report*, p. 43.

35　Hindenburg to Group of Armies von Gallwitz, 17 September 1918, in *USAWW*, VIII, p. 312. For a discussion of the German view of Saint-Mihiel see Grotelueschen, *The AEF Way of War*, p. 120n.

36　Group of Armies von Gallwitz to Composite Army C, 20 September 1918, in *USAWW*, VIII, p. 320.

37　Gallwitz cited in J. Toland, *No Man's Land. 1918. The Last Year of the Great War* (Garden City, NY: Doubleday, 1980), p. 424.

8. 'A country of horror and desolation'

1　W. Owen, *The Poems of Wilfred Owen*, ed. J. Stallworthy (London: Chatto and Windus, 1990), p. 196.

2　IWM: 84/11/2, Memoirs of Major H. J. C. Marshall (6 vols.), VI, pp. 1–2.

3　IWM: 06/30/1, Account of T. H. Holmes.

4 Wilfred Owen to Susan Owen, 28 March 1917, in W. Owen, *Selected Letters*, ed. J. Bell (Oxford: Oxford University Press, 1985), p. 499.

5 C. Stone, *From Vimy Ridge to the Rhine*, eds. G. D. Sheffield and G. Inglis (Marlborough: Crowood Press, 1989), p. 133.

6 P. Maze, *A Frenchman in Khaki* (Kingswood: William Heinemann, 1934), p. 348.

7 Wilfred Owen to Siegfried Sassoon, 22 September 1918, in Owen, *Selected Letters*, p. 349.

8 Sir J. Edmonds (ed.), *Military Operations France and Belgium 1918, IV, 8th August–26th September. The Franco-British Offensive* (London: HMSO, 1947), p. 453.

9 TNA: WO 95/1557, 15/Royal Warwickshire Regiment War Diary, September 1918.

10 For conflicting views on whether Saint-Mihiel could have been more successful (had it been conducted according to its original design) see Douglas MacArthur's damning criticism in *Reminiscences* (London: Heinemann, 1964), p. 64. For a more sober appreciation see H. Liggett, *AEF. Ten Years Ago in France* (New York: Dodd, Mead & Co., 1928), p. 159.

11 J. J. Pershing, *My Experiences in the World War* (2 vols., New York: Frederick A. Stokes, 1931), II, p. 244.

12 Pershing to Foch, 31 August 1918, and 'Decision Concerning Allied Attacks at St Mihiel and West of the Meuse', 2 September 1918, in US Department for the Army, Historical Division, *United States Army in the World War, 1917–1919* (17 vols., Washington, DC: Government Printing Office, 1948 [hereafter *USAWW*]), VIII, pp. 43–4 and 47.

13 F. Foch, *The Memoirs of Marshal Foch*, trans. T. Bentley Mott (London: William Heinemann, 1931), p. 462.

14 Field Marshal Sir D. Haig, diary, 21 September 1918, in D. Haig, *War Diaries and Letters 1914–1918*, eds. G. Sheffield and J. Bourne (London: Weidenfeld and Nicolson, 2005), p. 463. Original emphasis.

15 Edmonds (ed.), *Military Operations France and Belgium 1918, IV*, Appendix V, p. 534.

16 R. A. Doughty, *Pyrrhic Victory. French Strategy and Operations in the Great War* (Cambridge, Mass.: Harvard University Press, 2008; first publ. 2005), pp. 486–7.

17 Pershing, *My Experiences in the World War*, II, p. 279.

18 W. Foerster, *Der Feldherr Ludendorff im Unglück* (Wiesbaden: Limes Verlag, 1952), pp. 76–8. Original emphasis.

19 Crown Prince Rupprecht, *Mein Kriegstagebuch* (3 vols., Berlin: E. S. Mittler und Sohn, 1929), II, p. 435.

20 E. von Ludendorff, *Concise Ludendorff Memoirs 1914–1918* (London: Hutchinson, 1933), pp. 307–9. Original emphasis. See also P. von Hindenburg, *Out of My Life*, trans. F. A. Holt (London: Cassell & Company, 1920), p. 399.

21 Ludendorff, *Memoirs*, p. 311.

22 *Frankfurter Zeitung*, 22 September 1918.

23 G. C. Wynne, 'The Hindenburg Line', *Army Quarterly*, Vol. XXXVII (October 1938/January 1939), pp. 205–8. To avoid confusion, it should be noted that there were a number of other names for sections of the Hindenburg Line, including *Freya Stellung* (an unfinished reserve line behind the Hermann Line), *Alberich Stellung* (at the southern end of the Siegfried Line) and *Kriemhilde Stellung* (among others) in the Argonne.

24 Sir J. Monash, *The Australian Victories in France in 1918* (London: Hutchinson, 1920), pp. 217 and 218.

25 They were commanded by Duke Albrecht of Württemberg (from the Swiss border to Metz), Max von Gallwitz (from the Meuse to Rheims), Crown Prince Wilhelm (between Rheims and La Fère), General von Boehn (from La Fère to Douai), and Crown Prince Rupprecht (from Lens to the North Sea).

26 Sir J. Edmonds and R. Maxwell-Hyslop (eds.), *Military Operations France and Belgium 1918*, V, *26th September–11th November. The Advance to Victory* (London: HMSO, 1947), pp. 10–11.

27 D. von Kuhl, *Entstehung, Durchführung und Zusammenbruch der Offensive von 1918* (Berlin: Deutsche Verlagsgesellschaft für Politik und Geschichte, 1927), p. 210.

28 Bundesarchiv, *Der Weltkrieg 1914 bis 1918*, XIV, *Die Kriegführung an der Westfront im Jahre 1918* (Berlin: E. S. Mittler und Sohn, 1944), p. 621.

29 TNA: WO 157/199, Fourth Army Summary of Information, 1 October 1918.

30 TNA: WO 95/94, Tank Corps Summary of Information, 10 September 1918.

31 TNA: WO 95/94, Tank Corps Summary of Information, 18 and 27 September 1918.

32 Rupprecht, *Mein Kriegstagebuch*, II, p. 439.

33 G. von der Marwitz, *Weltkriegsbriefe*, ed. E. von Tschischwitz (Berlin: Steiniger-Verlage, 1940), p. 308.

34 R. Binding, *A Fatalist at War*, trans. I. F. D. Morrow (London: George Allen & Unwin, 1929), pp. 237 and 242.

35 Marwitz, *Weltkriegsbriefe*, pp. 317–18.

9. *Return to the Wilderness*

1 H. Liggett, *AEF. Ten Years Ago in France* (New York: Dodd, Mead & Co., 1928), pp. 208–9.

2 Gallwitz cited in G. S. Viereck (ed.), *As They Saw Us. Foch, Ludendorff and Other Leaders Write Our War History* (Cranbury, NJ: Scholar's Bookshelf, 2005; first publ. 1929), pp. 234–7. Pershing had mounted an extensive deception programme to convince the enemy that a future American attack would go into Lorraine. General von der Marwitz also believed the American artillery fire on 25–26 September was probably just a large demonstration. G. von der Marwitz, *Weltkriegsbriefe*, ed. E. von Tschischwitz (Berlin: Steiniger-Verlage, 1940), p. 322.

3 Gallwitz cited in Viereck (ed.), *As They Saw Us*, pp. 231 and 236–7.

4 Fifth Army Order, 1 October 1918, in US Department for the Army, Historical Division, *United States Army in the World War, 1917–1919* (17 vols., Washington, DC: Government Printing Office, 1948 [hereafter *USAWW*]), IX, p. 531; J. J. Pershing, *Final Report of Gen. John J. Pershing* (Washington, DC: Government Printing Office, 1919), p. 44.

5 MHI: WWI 8188 (Folder 8), 'A Private Saw It. My Memoirs of the First Division World War I', by H. L. McHenry, p. 46.

6 First Army Field Orders No. 20, 20 September 1918, in *USAWW*, IX, p. 82.

7 G. C. Marshall, *Memoirs of My Services in the World War 1917–1918* (Boston: Houghton Mifflin, 1976), p. 137.

8 Ibid., p. 149.

9 R. Slotkin, *Lost Battalions. The Great War and the Crisis of American Nationality* (New York: Henry Holt, 2005), pp. 263–4.

10 Chief of Staff, First Army to Commanding General I Corps, 22 September 1918, in *USAWW*, IX, p. 119.

11 Liggett, *AEF*, p. 171.

12 A. Williams, *Experiences of the Great War* (Roanoake, Va: Stone, 1919), p. 127.

13 Liggett, *AEF*, pp. 174–5.

14 R. A. Doughty, *Pyrrhic Victory. French Strategy and Operations in the Great War* (Cambridge, Mass.: Harvard University Press, 2008; first publ. 2005), pp. 489–90.

15 MHI: WWI 2450 (Folder 1), 'Memoirs of Clair Groover of Service in the US Army', pp. 18–22 and 28.

16 MHI: WWI 380, 'My Diary' by Sergeant J. E. Meehan, pp. 7–8.

17 IWM: 06/62/1, Captain T. F. Grady, diary, 26–30 September 1918.

18 IWM: 81/1/1, Account of Miss C. W. Clarke, pp. 19, 20, 30 and 55.

19 M. Blumenson, *The Patton Papers, 1885–1940* (New York: Da Capo Press, 1998; first publ. 1972), pp. 616–17 and 622.

20 Chief of Staff First Army to Commanding General, I, III, IV and V Corps, 27 September 1918, in *USAWW*, IX, pp. 138–40.

21 J. J. Cooke, *Pershing and His Generals. Command and Staff in the AEF* (Westport, Conn.: Praeger, 1997), p. 132.

22 Viereck (ed.), *As They Saw Us*, pp. 239–41.

23 BA-MA: BIV21, P. Ludwig, letter, 13 October 1918.

24 M. von Gallwitz, *Erleben im Westen 1916–1918* (Berlin: E. S. Mittler und Sohn, 1932), p. 405.

25 E. Otto, *The Battle at Blanc Mont (October 2 to October 10, 1918),* trans. M. Lichtenberg (Annapolis, Md: United States Naval Institute, 1930), p. 19.

26 Crown Prince Wilhelm, *The Memoirs of the Crown Prince of Germany* (London: Thornton Butterworth, 1922), pp. 205–6.

27 Marwitz, *Weltkriegsbriefe*, p. 324.

28 Pershing, *Final Report*, p. 46.

29 MHI: WWI 2450 (Folder 1), 'Memoirs of Clair Groover of Service in the US Army', p. 25.

30 G. Mead, *Doughboys. America and the First World War* (London: Penguin Books, 2001), p. 307.

31 Liggett, *AEF*, p. 178.

32 MHI: WWI 6801, 'My Life in the Army of World War I' by Sergeant H. Anderson, p. 16.

33 Mead, *Doughboys*, p. 309.

10. *'Just one panorama of hell'*

1 F. E. Noakes, *The Distant Drum. A Memoir of a Guardsman in the Great War* (Barnsley: Frontline Books, 2010), p. 171.

2 Crown Prince Wilhelm, *The Memoirs of the Crown Prince of Germany* (London: Thornton Butterworth, 1922), p. 204.

3 LAC: MG30 E100, Sir Arthur Currie Papers, Vol. 43, File 1914, diary, 4 September 1918.

4 Byng cited in S. B. Schreiber, *Shock Army of the British Empire. The Canadian Corps in the Last 100 Days of the Great War* (Westport, Conn.: Praeger, 1997), p. 98.

5 LAC: MG30 E430, 'An Autobiography of World War I', by W. Green, p. 11.

6 LAC: RG41, Vol. 7, Testimony of G. Mills.

7 LAC: RG41, Vol. 7, Testimony of Lieutenant-Colonel J. W. H. Joliffe.

8 T. Cook, *Shock Troops. Canadians Fighting the Great War 1917–1918* (Toronto: Penguin Canada, 2008), p. 513.

9 TNA: WO 95/180, 'Report on First Army Operations: 26th August–11 November, 1918', p. 31.

10 Sir J. Edmonds and R. Maxwell-Hyslop (eds.), *Military Operations France and Belgium 1918,* V, *26th September–11th November. The Advance to Victory* (London: HMSO, 1947), p. 33.

11 G. Gliddon, *VCs of the First World War. The Final Days: 1918* (Stroud: Sutton, 2000), p. 1.

12 TNA: WO 95/1516, '5th Division: Report on Operations from 13th September to 1st October 1918', p. 2.

13 TNA: WO 95/1551, 13 Brigade War Diary, 'Operations – 27 September 1918'.

14 Ibid.

15 Edmonds and Maxwell-Hyslop (eds.), *Military Operations France and Belgium 1918,* V, pp. 36–7.

16 TNA: WO 95/1516, '5th Division. Report on Operations from 13th September to 1st October 1918', pp. 9–11.

17 C. T. Atkinson, *The Queen's Own Royal West Kent Regiment, 1914–1919* (London: Simkin, Marshall, Hamilton, Kent & Co., 1924), p. 431.

18 Captain A. Impey, diary, 27 September 1918, in http://www.fylde.demon.co.uk/tucker/tuckerbiography.htm.

19 TNA: WO 95/1557, 15/Royal Warwickshire Regiment War Diary, 27 September 1918.

20 C. A. Bill, *The 15th Battalion Royal Warwickshire Regiment (and Birmingham Battalion) in the Great War* (Birmingham: Cornish Brothers, 1932), p. 146.

21 MHI: WWI 2832, 'Morgen Rot', by E. Kielmayer, diary, 30 September and 1 October 1918.

22 'Estimate of the Situation', 27 September 1918, in US Department for the Army, Historical Division, *United States Army in the World War, 1917–1919* (17 vols., Washington, DC: Government Printing Office, 1948 [hereafter *USAWW*]), VII, pp. 835–6.

23 'Army Order', Second Army, 27 September 1918, in *USAWW*, VII, p. 837.

24 Edmonds and Maxwell-Hyslop (eds.), *Military Operations France and Belgium 1918*, V, p. 64.

25 JMO: 26 N 18/6, Groupe d'Armées des Flandres, 'Journal des marches et opérations du 1 septembre au 19 novembre 1918'.

26 C. Degelow, *Germany's Last Knight in the Air. The Memoirs of Major Carl Degelow*, trans. and ed. P. Kilduff (London: William Kimber, 1979), pp. 166–7.

27 W. Görlitz (ed.), *The Kaiser and His Court. The Diaries, Note Books and Letters of Admiral Georg Alexander von Müller, Chief of the Naval Cabinet, 1914–1918* (London: Macdonald & Co., 1961; first publ. 1959), p. 400.

28 P. von Hindenburg, *Out of My Life*, trans. F. A. Holt (London: Cassell & Company, 1920), pp. 428–9.

29 E. von Ludendorff, *Concise Ludendorff Memoirs 1914–1918* (London: Hutchinson, 1933), p. 311. It may have been a gradual realization that defeat was inevitable. Five days earlier, on 23 September, he had cancelled a series of long-awaited incendiary raids by German bombers on London because of fears of reprisals. See N. Hanson, *First Blitz. The Secret German Plan to Raze London to the Ground in 1918* (London: Doubleday, 2008), pp. 330–31.

30 W. Foerster, *Der Feldherr Ludendorff im Unglück* (Wiesbaden: Limes Verlag, 1952), p. 79.

31 Ludendorff, *Memoirs*, pp. 312–13.

32 Hindenburg, *Out of My Life*, p. 429.

33 Görlitz (ed.), *The Kaiser and His Court*, p. 397.

11. The Tomb of the German World Empire

1 Crown Prince Rupprecht, *Mein Kriegstagebuch* (3 vols., Berlin: E. S. Mittler und Sohn, 1929), II, p. 453.

2 See the postscript to C. Messenger, *The Day We Won the War. Turning Point at Amiens 8th August 1918* (London: Phoenix, 2009; first publ. 2008), pp. 234–9. Some confusion still exists as to which headquarters the documents were stored in as no German corps had its headquarters at Framerville.

3 Sir A. Montgomery, *The Story of Fourth Army in the Battles of the Hundred Days, August 8th to November 11th, 1918* (London: Hodder & Stoughton, 1920), p. 147n.

4 'Evening Report', Bavarian I Army Corps, 28 September 1918, in US Department for the Army, Historical Division, *United States Army in the World War, 1917–1919* (17 vols., Washington, DC: Government Printing Office, 1948 [hereafter *USAWW*]), VII, p. 842.

5 MHI: WWI 2305, Mechanic L. M. Beyer, Army Service Experiences Questionnaire.

6 The traditional explanation for this failure is that the Americans did not properly consolidate their gains. Rawlinson believed that the failure to 'mop up' the deep dug-outs in the German line allowed the enemy to infiltrate back and prevent reinforcements from pushing on. See TNA: WO 95/438, 'Report on 2nd American Division during the Operations of 29th September 1918', 30 September 1918. This interpretation has been contested by D. Blair, *The Battle of Bellicourt Tunnel. Tommies, Diggers and Doughboys on the Hindenburg Line, 1918* (Barnsley: Frontline Books, 2011).

7 MHI: WWI 1827, 'Reminiscences and Diary of a Private in World War I', by W. J. Strauss, pp. 54, 56 and 57.

8 P. Maze, *A Frenchman in Khaki* (Kingswood: William Heinemann, 1934), pp. 349–50.

9 IWM: 84/11/2, Memoirs of Major H. J. C. Marshall (6 vols.), VI, pp. 2 and 4.

10 IWM: 84/11/2, Memoirs of Major Marshall, VI, pp. 7 and 8.

11 Account of Private G. Waters (personal collection).

12 Sir J. Edmonds and R. Maxwell-Hyslop (eds.), *Military Operations France*

and Belgium 1918, V, *26th September–11th November. The Advance to Victory* (London: HMSO, 1947), p. 106.

13 BA-MA: PH8II/83, 'Gefechtsbericht über den 29.9 u. 30.9.18'.

14 IWM: 84/11/2, Memoirs of Major Marshall, VI, pp. 5 and 11.

15 These included Hulluch on 13 October 1915, where the division had sustained over 3,500 casualties in a matter of hours, and 1 July 1916, when it had left most of its personnel lying dead or wounded on the open fields of Gommecourt north of the Somme.

16 IWM: 84/11/2, Memoirs of Major Marshall, VI, pp. 10–11.

17 LAC: MG30 E100, Sir Arthur Currie Papers, Vol. 43, File 1914, diary, 1 October 1918.

18 D. Hibberd, *Wilfred Owen. A New Biography* (London: Weidenfeld & Nicolson, 2002), pp. 344–53.

19 Wilfred Owen to Susan Owen, 4 or 5 and 8 October 1918, in W. Owen, *Selected Letters*, ed. J. Bell (Oxford: Oxford University Press, 1985), pp. 351 and 352.

20 C. A. Bill, *The 15th Battalion Royal Warwickshire Regiment (and Birmingham Battalion) in the Great War* (Birmingham: Cornish Brothers, 1932), pp. 147–9. British divisions in France had been reduced from twelve to nine battalions in early 1918, but because 5th Division had been in Italy, it had been spared this change.

21 JMO: 26 N 20/1, 'Journal de Marche de la 1ère Armée à partir du 1er janvier 1918 au 31 octobre 1918', p. 514.

22 Foch cited in R. A. Doughty, *Pyrrhic Victory. French Strategy and Operations in the Great War* (Cambridge, Mass.: Harvard University Press, 2008; first publ. 2005), p. 490.

23 BA-MA: MSG2/5792, 'Alfred', letter, 29 September 1918.

24 TNA: WO 157/199, Fourth Army Summary of Information, 6 and 7 October 1918.

25 TNA: WO 157/166, Third Army Summary of Information, 6 and 7 October 1918.

26 Rupprecht, *Mein Kriegstagebuch*, II, p. 453.

27 Operations Section to Group of Armies German Crown Prince, 30 September 1918, in *USAWW*, VI, p. 272.

28 General von Hutier to Group of Armies Boehn, 2 October 1918, in *USAWW*, VII, pp. 863–4.

29 Second Army to Group of Armies Boehn, 3 October 1918, in *USAWW*, VII, pp. 864–5.

30 Rupprecht, *Mein Kriegstagebuch* , II, p. 453, 455.

31 MHI: WWI 2832, 'Morgen Rot', by E. Kielmayer, diary, 1 October 1918.

32 BA-MA: MSG2/10347, Leutnant K. Urmacher, letter, 5 October 1918.

33 H. Sulzbach, *With the German Guns. Four Years on the Western Front 1914–1918*, trans. R. Thonger (London: Frederick Warne, 1981; first publ. 1973), p. 229.

34 W. Görlitz (ed.), *The Kaiser and His Court. The Diaries, Note Books and Letters of Admiral Georg Alexander von Müller, Chief of the Naval Cabinet, 1914–1918* (London: Macdonald & Co., 1961; first publ. 1959), p. 399.

35 Prince Max of Baden, *The Memoirs of Prince Max of Baden*, trans. W. M. Calder and C. W. H. Sutton (2 vols., London: Constable, 1928), II, p. 3.

36 Ibid., pp. 7–8.

37 Ibid., pp. 15–16.

38 Görlitz (ed.), *The Kaiser and His Court*, pp. 399–403.

39 Prince Max, *Memoirs*, II, pp. 18–19.

40 'First German Note to President Wilson', 3 October 1918, in *USAWW*, X, p. 3.

12. *'The most desperate battle of our history'*

1 MHI: WWI 456, Second-Lieutenant H. Woehl, diary, 9 October 1918.

2 W. Wilson, 'The War to Complete the Work Begun by Washington and His Associates', in *America Joins the World. Selections from the Speeches and State Papers of President Wilson, 1914–1918* (New York: Association Press, 1919), pp. 80–84.

3 Wilson's Fourteen Points were: 'open covenants of peace, openly arrived at'; 'absolute freedom of navigation upon the seas'; the establishment of 'an equality of trade conditions among all nations'; a 'free, open-minded, and absolutely impartial adjustment of all colonial claims' based upon self-determination; the 'evacuation of all Russian territory'; the evacuation of Belgium; the evacuation of French territory, including Alsace-Lorraine; a 'readjustment of the frontiers of Italy' based on nationality; the 'freest opportunity of autonomous development' by the 'peoples of Austria-Hungary'; the evacuation of

Romania, Serbia and Montenegro; the sovereignty of the Turkish portions of the Ottoman Empire and the 'autonomous development' of other nationalities in the empire; an independent Polish state; and the formation of a 'general association of nations'. See Woodrow Wilson, 'Address to Congress Stating the Peace Terms of the United States', in *America Joins the World*, pp. 70–79.

4 E. M. House, *The Intimate Papers of Colonel House*, ed. C. Seymour (4 vols., London: Ernest Benn, 1928), IV, pp. 78–9.

5 'Answer to German Peace Proposal', 8 October 1918, in US Department for the Army, Historical Division, *United States Army in the World War, 1917–1919* (17 vols., Washington, DC: Government Printing Office, 1948 [hereafter *USAWW*]), X, pp. 7–8.

6 Prince Max of Baden, *The Memoirs of Prince Max of Baden*, trans. W. M. Calder and C. W. H. Sutton (2 vols., London: Constable, 1928), II, pp. 65–9; E. von Ludendorff, *Concise Ludendorff Memoirs 1914–1918* (London: Hutchinson, 1933), p. 316.

7 'German Reply to President Wilson's Note', 12 October 1918, in *USAWW*, X, p. 9. It was signed by the Secretary of State for the Foreign Office, Wilhelm von Solf, because of a leaked letter Prince Max had written in January 1918 to Prince Alexander Hohenlohe and a group of pacifists in Switzerland. This had caused a domestic scandal and nearly cost Prince Max his position.

8 Prince Max, *Memoirs*, II, p. 75.

9 P. Scheidemann, *Memoirs of a Social Democrat*, trans. J. E. Michell (2 vols., London: Hodder & Stoughton, 1929), II, p. 501.

10 F. A. Holden, *War Memories* (Athens, Ga: Athens Book Company, 1922), pp. 145–6 and 149.

11 E. E. Mackin, *Suddenly We Didn't Want to Die. Memoirs of a World War I Marine* (Novato, Calif.: Presidio Press, 1993), pp. 182–3.

12 See R. Slotkin, *Lost Battalions. The Great War and the Crisis of American Nationality* (New York: Henry Holt, 2005). The term 'lost battalion' is somewhat misleading. The men were not in any sense 'lost'. I Corps knew their approximate location, but could not reach them. See also H. Liggett, *AEF. Ten Years Ago in France* (New York: Dodd, Mead & Co., 1928), p. 184.

13 J. J. Pershing, *My Experiences in the World War* (2 vols., New York: Frederick A. Stokes, 1931), II, p. 322.

14 G. von der Marwitz, *Weltkriegsbriefe*, ed. E. von Tschischwitz (Berlin: Steiniger-Verlage, 1940), p. 326.

15 'The Austro-Hungarian Note of October 7', in *USAWW*, X, pp. 14–15.

16 BA-MA: RH61/1035, 'Feldpost Postüberwachung beim AOK 5', 28 September 1918.

17 Group of Armies Gallwitz, 4 October 1918, in *USAWW*, IX, p. 536.

18 MHI: WWI 456, Second-Lieutenant H. Woehl, diary, 11 October 1918.

19 MHI: WWI 561, 'Experiences of Joseph D. Lawrence in the American Expeditionary Forces in Europe 1918–19', p. 96.

20 J. J. Pershing, *Final Report of Gen. John J. Pershing* (Washington, DC: Government Printing Office, 1919), p. 48.

21 IWM: 81/21/1, Account of A. J. Turner, p. 47.

22 Field Marshal Sir D. Haig, diary, 6 October 1918, in D. Haig, *War Diaries and Letters 1914–1918*, eds. G. Sheffield and J. Bourne (London: Weidenfeld & Nicolson, 2005), p. 470.

23 Wilfred Owen to Susan Owen, 10, 11 and 15 October 1918, in W. Owen, *Selected Letters*, ed. J. Bell (Oxford: Oxford University Press, 1985), pp. 354–6.

24 LAC: MG30 E100, Sir Arthur Currie Papers, Vol. 43, File 1914, diary, 9 October 1918.

25 LAC: MG30 E32, Corporal A. C. West, diary, 10 October 1918.

26 C. Mangin, *Lettres de guerre 1914–1918*, ed. L. Eugène (Paris: Fayard, 1950), pp. 305–6.

27 IWM: 78/29/1, 'A Field Artillery Officer, 1914–1919' by Colonel F. J. Rice, pp. 140–41.

28 CLIP: Memoirs of C. H. Savage.

29 JMO: 26 N 20/1, 'Journal de Marche de la 1ère Armée à partir du 1er janvier 1918 au 31 octobre 1918', pp. 513, 520, 523, 529 and 530.

30 J. P. Guéno and Y. Laplume (eds.), *Paroles de poilus: Lettres et carnets du front 1914–1918* (Paris: Radio France, 1998), pp. 529 and 532–3.

31 BA-MA: MSG2/5548, 'Josef', letters, 9 and 10 October 1918.

32 R. Stark, *Wings of War. A German Airman's Diary of the Last Year of the Great War*, trans. C. W. Sykes (London: Greenhill Books, 1988), pp. 185–7.

33 MHI: WWI 2832, 'Morgen Rot', by E. Kielmayer, diary, 5 and 15 October 1918.

34 The incident is discussed in T. Weber, *Hitler's First War. Adolf Hitler, the*

Men of the List Regiment, and the First World War (Oxford: Oxford University Press, 2010), pp. 220–21. See A. Hitler, *Mein Kampf*, trans. R. Manheim (London: Hutchinson, 1989; first publ. 1925), p. 183.

35 Crown Prince Wilhelm, *The Memoirs of the Crown Prince of Germany* (London: Thornton Butterworth, 1922), p. 214.

36 TNA: WO 157/166, Third Army Summary of Information, 2 October 1918.

37 Group of Armies Crown Prince Rupprecht to Fourth, Sixth and Seventeenth Armies, 14 September 1918, in *USAWW*, VI, p. 466.

38 Group of Armies German Crown Prince to Eighteenth Army, 13 October 1918, in *USAWW*, VII, p. 900.

13. 'A last struggle of despair'

1 'Memorandum for the Commanding General, First Army', 17 October 1918, in US Department for the Army, Historical Division, *United States Army in the World War, 1917–1919* (17 vols., Washington, DC: Government Printing Office, 1948 [hereafter *USAWW*]), X, p. 12.

2 E. M. House, *The Intimate Papers of Colonel House*, ed. C. Seymour (4 vols., London: Ernest Benn, 1928), IV, p. 83.

3 'Armistice Terms', 7 October 1918, in *USAWW*, X, pp. 4–5.

4 'President Wilson's Reply to the German Note of October 12, 1918', 14 October 1918, in *USAWW*, X, pp. 10–11. Wilson's reference to the sinking of passenger ships was probably prompted by the recent loss of two vessels, the steamer *Hirano Maru* and the Irish mail boat *Leinster*. Both were sunk (without warning) off the Irish coast between 4 and 10 October. Over 800 people were killed.

5 Prince Max of Baden, *The Memoirs of Prince Max of Baden*, trans. W. M. Calder and C. W. H. Sutton (2 vols., London: Constable, 1928), II, p. 89.

6 P. Scheidemann, *Memoirs of a Social Democrat*, trans. J. E. Michell (2 vols., London: Hodder & Stoughton, 1929), II, p. 511.

7 Crown Prince Wilhelm, *The Memoirs of the Crown Prince of Germany* (London: Thornton Butterworth, 1922), p. 219.

8 Prince Max, *Memoirs*, II, pp. 102–34.

9 BA-MA: MSG2/5792, 'Alfred', letter, 20 October 1918.

10 BA-MA: RH61/1035, 'Feldpost Postüberwachung beim AOK 5', 17 October 1918.

11 R. Stark, *Wings of War. A German Airman's Diary of the Last Year of the Great War*, trans. C. W. Sykes (London: Greenhill Books, 1988), pp. 198 and 201.

12 A. Hitler, *Mein Kampf*, trans. R. Manheim (London: Hutchinson, 1989; first publ. 1925), p. 184.

13 BA-MA: MSG2/10347, Leutnant K. Urmacher, letter, 17 October 1918.

14 BA-MA: MSG2/13746, Leutnant H. Mahler, diary, 8 and 29 October 1918.

15 Crown Prince Wilhelm, *Memoirs*, p. 216.

16 MHI: WWI 2832, 'Morgen Rot', by E. Kielmayer, diary, 18 October 1918.

17 'The German Reply to President Wilson's Note of October 14, 1918', 21 October 1918, in *USAWW*, X, pp. 15–16.

18 Scheidemann, *Memoirs*, II, pp. 516–18.

19 'President Wilson's Reply to the German Note of October 21, 1918', 24 October 1918, in *USAWW*, X, pp. 17–18.

20 Scheidemann, *Memoirs*, II, p. 522.

21 Crown Prince Rupprecht, *Mein Kriegstagebuch* (3 vols., Berlin: E. S. Mittler und Sohn, 1929), II, p. 465.

22 Supreme Headquarters to Group of Armies Gallwitz, 24 October 1918, in *USAWW*, X, p. 19.

23 E. von Ludendorff, *Concise Ludendorff Memoirs 1914–1918* (London: Hutchinson, 1933), p. 327.

24 Scheidemann, *Memoirs*, II, p. 525.

25 D. Lloyd George, *War Memoirs of David Lloyd George* (2 vols., London: Odhams Press, 1933–6), II, p. 1959.

26 'Notes on Conference Held at Senlis, October 25 1918', in *USAWW*, X, pp. 19–23.

27 J. J. Pershing, *My Experiences in the World War* (2 vols., New York: Frederick A. Stokes, 1931), II, pp. 361–2.

28 F. Foch, *The Memoirs of Marshal Foch*, trans. T. Bentley Mott (London: William Heinemann, 1931), pp. 539–41. The points were: the immediate evacuation of invaded territory; the surrender of 5,000 artillery pieces and 30,000 machine-guns; the evacuation of the left bank of the Rhine;

the cessation of any destruction and devastation to evacuated land; the delivery of 5,000 locomotives and 150,000 railway trucks in good condition; the delivery of 150 submarines; and the withdrawal of the surface fleet to the Baltic ports. Foch recommended that the naval blockade should stay in force until these conditions were met.

29 IWM: 92/36/1, 'The Wheels of Darkness', by Lieutenant R. G. Dixon, p. 83.

30 J. P. Guéno and Y. Laplume (eds.), *Paroles de poilus: Lettres et carnets du front 1914–1918* (Paris: Radio France, 1998), p. 501.

31 MHI: WWI 456, Second-Lieutenant H. Woehl, diary, 20 and 22 October 1918.

32 LAC: MG30 E100, Sir Arthur Currie Papers, Vol. 43, File 1914, diary, 20 October 1918.

33 IWM: 92/36/1, 'The Wheels of Darkness', pp. 133–4.

34 IWM: 06/30/1, Account of T. H. Holmes.

35 IWM: 99/13/1, 'Recollections of the Machine Gun Corps' by T. Brookbank, pp. 31 and 32.

36 LAC: RG41, Vol. 10, Testimony of R. H. Camp.

37 F. E. Noakes, *The Distant Drum. A Memoir of a Guardsman in the Great War* (Barnsley: Frontline Books, 2010), p. 181.

38 CWM: 58A 1154-4, K. C. MacGowan to his mother, 10 October 1918.

39 IWM: 81/21/1, Account of A. J. Turner, pp. 47–9 and 53.

14. *'Cowards die many times'*

1 MHI: WWI 2832, 'Morgen Rot', by E. Kielmayer, diary, 1 November 1918.

2 A. Niemann, *Revolution von oben – Umsturz von untern* (Berlin: Verlag für Kulturpolitik, 1928), pp. 184–5; P. von Hindenburg, *Out of My Life*, trans. F. A. Holt (London: Cassell & Company, 1920), p. 433.

3 M. Ludendorff, *My Married Life with Ludendorff*, trans. R. Somerset (London: Hutchinson, 1930), pp. 172–3.

4 W. Görlitz (ed.), *The Kaiser and His Court. The Diaries, Note Books and Letters of Admiral Georg Alexander von Müller, Chief of the Naval Cabinet, 1914–1918* (London: Macdonald & Co., 1961; first publ. 1959), p. 415.

5 One soldier from Württemberg simply wrote 'Ludendorff goes.' See BA-MA: MSG2/13746, Leutnant H. Mahler, diary, 27 October 1918.

6 BA-MA: MSG2/10347, Leutnant K. Urmacher, letter, 28 October 1918.

7 F. von Lossberg, *Meine Tätigkeit im Weltkrieg 1914–1918* (Berlin: E. S. Mittler und Sohn, 1939), p. 359.

8 Crown Prince Wilhelm, *The Memoirs of the Crown Prince of Germany* (London: Thornton Butterworth, 1922), p. 224.

9 W. Groener, *Lebenserinnerungen. Jugend. Generalstab. Weltkrieg* (Göttingen: Vandenhoeck & Ruprecht, 1957), pp. 440–42 and 444–5.

10 P. Scheidemann, *Memoirs of a Social Democrat*, trans. J. E. Michell (2 vols., London: Hodder & Stoughton, 1929), II, p. 526.

11 Görlitz (ed.), *The Kaiser and His Court*, pp. 416–17.

12 M. Balfour, *The Kaiser and His Times* (London: The Cresset Press, 1964), p. 403.

13 Kaiser Wilhelm cited in ibid., p. 402.

14 Prince Max of Baden, *The Memoirs of Prince Max of Baden*, trans. W. M. Calder and C. W. H. Sutton (2 vols., London: Constable, 1928), II, p. 255.

15 E. E. Mackin, *Suddenly We Didn't Want to Die. Memoirs of a World War I Marine* (Novato, Calif.: Presidio Press, 1993), p. 221.

16 IWM: 81/21/1, Account of A. J. Turner, p. 54.

17 Sir J. Edmonds and R. Maxwell-Hyslop (eds.), *Military Operations France and Belgium 1918*, V, *26th September–11th November. The Advance to Victory* (London: HMSO, 1947), p. 584.

18 Field Marshal Sir D. Haig, diary, 19 October 1918, in D. Haig, *War Diaries and Letters 1914–1918*, eds. G. Sheffield and J. Bourne (London: Weidenfeld & Nicolson, 2005), p. 475.

19 H. Liggett, *AEF. Ten Years Ago in France* (New York: Dodd, Mead & Co., 1928), p. 207.

20 G. S. Viereck (ed.), *As They Saw Us. Foch, Ludendorff and Other Leaders Write Our War History* (Cranbury, NJ: Scholar's Bookshelf, 2005; first publ. 1929), pp. 274–5.

21 G. von der Marwitz, *Weltkriegsbriefe*, ed. E. von Tschischwitz (Berlin: Steiniger-Verlage, 1940), p. 340.

22 MHI: WWI 8188 (Folder 8), 'A Private Saw It. My Memoirs of the First Division World War I', by H. L. McHenry, p. 79.

23 Liggett, *AEF*, p. 221.

24 CWM: 58A 1 20.3, General E. W. B. Morrison papers, 'Artillery Report on Mont Houy'.

25 T. Cook, *Shock Troops. Canadians Fighting the Great War 1917–1918* (Toronto: Penguin Canada, 2008), p. 559.

26 A. G. L. McNaughton, 'The Capture of Valenciennes: A Study in Co-ordination', *Canadian Defence Quarterly*, Vol. 10, No. 3 (April 1933), p. 292.

27 R. Stark, *Wings of War. A German Airman's Diary of the Last Year of the Great War*, trans. C. W. Sykes (London: Greenhill Books, 1988), p. 203.

28 Lossberg, *Meine Tätigkeit im Weltkrieg*, p. 358.

29 Between 18 July and 11 November the BEF captured 188,700 prisoners and 2,840 guns; as many as the French Army (139,000 prisoners and 1,880 guns) and the AEF (43,400 prisoners and 1,421 guns) combined. The Belgian Army captured 14,500 prisoners and 474 guns. Edmonds and Maxwell-Hyslop (eds.), *Military Operations France and Belgium 1918*, V, p. 557. See also W. Deist, 'The Military Collapse of the German Empire: The Reality behind the Stab-in-the-Back Myth', *War in History*, Vol. 3, No. 2 (April 1996), pp. 186–207 (p. 203).

30 D. von Kuhl, *Entstehung, Durchführung und Zusammenbruch der Offensive von 1918* (Berlin: M.B.H., 1927), pp. 210–11.

31 TNA: WO 157/167, 'Appreciation of the Situation on the Third Army Front on the 2nd November, 1918'.

32 A. Hitler, *Mein Kampf*, trans. R. Manheim (London: Hutchinson, 1989; first publ. 1925), p. 182.

33 TNA: WO 157/199, Fourth Army Summary of Information, 27 October 1918.

34 A. Mahncke, *For Kaiser and Hitler. The Memoirs of General Alfred Mahncke 1910–1945* (Pulborough: Tattered Flag, 2011), pp. 68–9.

35 Lossberg, *Meine Tätigkeit im Weltkrieg*, pp. 359–60.

36 Edmonds and Maxwell-Hyslop (eds.), *Military Operations France and Belgium 1918*, V, p. 463.

37 3rd Westphalian Regimental History cited in H. D. Du Pree, *The 38th (Welsh) Division in the Last Five Weeks of the Great War* (London: Royal Artillery Journal, 1933), p. 192.

38 Wilfred Owen to Susan Owen, 31 October 1918, in W. Owen, *Selected Letters*, ed. J. Bell (Oxford: Oxford University Press, 1985), pp. 361–2.

39 Details of attack taken from D. Hibberd, *Wilfred Owen. A New Biography* (London: Weidenfeld & Nicolson, 2002), pp. 364–6.

40 BA-MA: MSG2/1291, 'Die Letzte Schlacht, 4 November 1918', p. 5.

41 G. Gliddon, *VCs of the First World War. The Final Days: 1918* (Stroud: Sutton, 2000), p. 176.

42 Edmonds and Maxwell-Hyslop (eds.), *Military Operations France and Belgium 1918,* V, p. 476.

43 JMO: 26 N 20/2, 'Journal de Marche de la 1ère Armée du 1er novembre 1918 au 31 décembre 1918', p. 532. First Army also secured 4,000 prisoners.

44 BA-MA: MSG2/1291, 'Die Letzte Schlacht, 4 November 1918', pp. 9–13.

15. Armistice at Compiègne

1 Cited in G. Ritter, *The Sword and the Sceptre. The Problem of Militarism in Germany* (4 vols., London: Allen Lane, 1973), IV, p. 376.

2 M. Weygand, *Mémoires. Idéal vécu* (Paris: Flammarion, 1953), p. 639.

3 Department of State to General Headquarters AEF, 6 November 1918, in US Department for the Army, Historical Division, *United States Army in the World War, 1917–1919* (17 vols., Washington, DC: Government Printing Office, 1948, X, pp. 32–3.

4 These were Captain Ernst Vaneslow of the German Navy (chosen because he was a personal friend of Erzberger); Staff Captain Geyer; and a cavalry officer, Captain von Helldorf. B. Lowry, *Armistice 1918* (Kent, Ohio: Kent State University Press, 1996), p. 157.

5 Weygand, *Mémoires. Idéal vécu*, p. 639.

6 F. Foch, *The Memoirs of Marshal Foch*, trans. T. Bentley Mott (London: William Heinemann, 1931), pp. 545–55.

7 P. Scheidemann, *Memoirs of a Social Democrat*, trans. J. E. Michell (2 vols., London: Hodder & Stoughton, 1929), II, p. 557.

8 Prince Max of Baden, *The Memoirs of Prince Max of Baden*, trans. W. M. Calder and C. W. H. Sutton (2 vols., London: Constable, 1928), II, pp. 331 and 340–42.

9 Scheidemann, *Memoirs*, II, p. 562, 565 and 569.

10 Crown Prince Wilhelm, *The Memoirs of the Crown Prince of Germany* (London: Thornton Butterworth, 1922), pp. 232–3 and 239–40.

11 Prince Max, *Memoirs*, II, pp. 342–3.

12 Taken from M. Baumont, *The Fall of the Kaiser*, trans. E. I. James (London: George Allen & Unwin, 1931), Chapter 2.

13 Major-General Löffler, letter, 5 November 1918, cited in W. Groener, *Lebenserinnerungen. Jugend. Generalstab. Weltkrieg* (Göttingen: Vandenhoeck & Ruprecht, 1957), pp. 456–7.

14 'Denkschritt des Generals v.d. Schulenburg vom 26 August 1919', cited in A. Niemann, *Revolution von oben – Umsturz von untern* (Berlin: Verlag für Kulturpolitik, 1928), pp. 353–4.

15 Baumont, *The Fall of the Kaiser*, p. 97.

16 Groener, *Lebenserinnerungen*, pp. 460–61.

17 Heye's interview of the thirty-nine officers – the so-called *Armeeparlament* – has long been seen in an unfavourable light, with critics complaining that the men were not even given breakfast before they reported to Heye. Had they done so, it is claimed, they would not have been as downhearted and pessimistic and might have given a different response. Groener thought not. Although he admitted that it might have been better had they been allowed some time to recover from their journey, he believed that their response would not have been any different, and he was probably correct. A straw poll of nine staff officers from OHL delivered the same verdict. The men would fight on, but the Kaiser would have to resign and peace negotiations begin. Groener, *Lebenserinnerungen*, pp. 458–9. For a full discussion of the events in Spa on 9 November see S. Stephenson, *The Final Battle. Soldiers of the Western Front and the German Revolution of 1918* (Cambridge: Cambridge University Press, 2009), pp. 83–96.

18 Heye cited in Baumont, *The Fall of the Kaiser*, p. 111.

19 Prince Max, *Memoirs*, II, p. 360.

20 Crown Prince Wilhelm, *Memoirs*, p. 245.

21 Groener, *Lebenserinnerungen*, p. 463.

22 W. Guinness, *Staff Officer. The Diaries of Walter Guinness (First Lord Moyne) 1914–1918*, eds. B. Bond and S. Robbins (London: Leo Cooper, 1987), p. 239.

23 TNA: WO 95/180, 'Report on First Army Operations: 26th August–11 November, 1918', p. 74.

24 LAC: MG31 G30, File 7, W. B. Woods to Professor Desmond Morton, 14 June 1989.

25 C. Degelow, *Germany's Last Knight in the Air. The Memoirs of Major Carl*

Degelow, trans. and ed. P. Kilduff (London: William Kimber, 1979), pp. 175 and 184. Original emphasis.

26 G. von der Marwitz, *Weltkriegsbriefe*, ed. E. von Tschischwitz (Berlin: Steiniger-Verlage, 1940), p. 344.

27 JMO: 26 N 20/2, 'Journal de Marche de la 1ère Armée du 1er novembre 1918 au 31 décembre 1918', p. 535.

28 MHI: WWI 146 (Folder 1), 'The Last Kilometer: The Very Last', by J. E. Ausland, pp. 8–11.

29 BA-MA: MSG2/10347, Leutnant K. Urmacher, letter, 11 November 1918.

30 IWM: 06/62/1, Captain T. F. Grady, diary, 11 November 1918.

31 LAC: RG41, Vol. 12, Testimony of A. B. Goodmurphy.

32 See for example MHI: WWI 146 (Folder 1), 'The Last Kilometer: The Very Last', by J. E. Ausland, p. 11. George Marshall complained that 'Getting word to the troops to cease fighting and advancing at eleven o'clock, was quite a problem on some portions of the lines', particularly for those units which had crossed the Meuse, such as 89th and 90th US Divisions, at Stenay. G. C. Marshall, *Memoirs of My Services in the World War 1917–1918* (Boston: Houghton Mifflin, 1976), p. 199.

33 MHI: WWI 3345, Private F. W. Groves, Army Service Experiences Questionnaire.

34 IWM: 78/29/1, 'A Field Artillery Officer, 1914–1919' by Colonel F. J. Rice, pp. 169–70.

35 MHI: WWI 2450 (Folder 1), 'Memoirs of Clair Groover of Service in the US Army', p. 43.

36 Field Marshal Sir D. Haig, diary, 11 November 1918, in D. Haig, *War Diaries and Letters 1914–1918*, eds. G. Sheffield and J. Bourne (London: Weidenfeld & Nicolson, 2005), p. 487.

37 J. de Pierrefeu, *French Headquarters 1915–1918*, trans. Major C. J. C. Street (London: Geoffrey Bles, 1924), p. 307.

38 Sir G. Aston, *The Biography of the Late Marshal Foch* (London: Hutchinson, 1932), pp. 277–9.

Epilogue

1 IWM: 92/36/1, 'The Wheels of Darkness' by Lieutenant R. G. Dixon, pp. 138–9.

2 IWM: 06/30/1, Account of T. H. Holmes.

3 CWM: 58A 1 237.6, F. C. Teskey to his mother, 11 November 1918.

4 J. P. Guéno and Y. Laplume (eds.), *Paroles de poilus. Lettres et carnets du front 1914–1918* (Paris: Radio France, 1998), pp. 172–5.

5 BA-MA: MSG2/10347, Leutnant K. Urmacher, letter, 11 November 1918.

6 P. Scheidemann, *Memoirs of a Social Democrat*, trans. J. E. Michell (2 vols., London: Hodder & Stoughton, 1929), II, p. 595.

7 Although widely attributed to Fridrich Ebert, who addressed German troops in the centre of Berlin on 10 December 1918, he never used the phrase. He told them that their 'sacrifice and deeds' had been 'without equal' and that 'No enemy has conquered you.' S. Stephenson, *The Final Battle. Soldiers of the Western Front and the German Revolution of 1918* (Cambridge: Cambridge University Press, 2009), pp. 241–2.

8 A. Hitler, *Mein Kampf*, trans. R. Manheim (London: Hutchinson, 1989; first publ. 1925), p. 183.

9 See the account of F. J. Hodges, *Men of 18 in 1918* (Ilfracombe: A. H. Stockwell, 1988).

10 Crown Prince Rupprecht to Prince Max, 15 August 1918, in Prince Max of Baden, *The Memoirs of Prince Max of Baden*, trans. W. M. Calder and C. W. H. Sutton (2 vols., London: Constable, 1928), I, p. 320.

11 D. Stevenson, *With Our Backs to the Wall. Victory and Defeat in 1918* (London: Allen Lane, 2011), p. 239.

12 Wilfred Owen to Susan Owen, 4 or 5 October 1918, in W. Owen, *Selected Letters*, ed. J. Bell (Oxford: Oxford University Press, 1985), p. 351.

Index

Achiet-le-Grand 81
Achiet-le-Petit 80, 88
'Advance to Victory' see 'Hundred Days'
African Trench (German lines) 173
Ailette, River 74
air power
    Bristol Fighter aircraft 36
    crucial role at Amiens 36
    Division Aérienne 36, 40
    Fokker DVIIs aircraft 94
    played a key role 35–6
    RAF biplanes 53, 57
    Sopwith Camel fighter 36, 93–4
    Spad fighter aircraft 36
    superiority of Allies 93
    see also German Air Force; Royal Air
        Force (RAF)
Aire river 162
Aisne river
    Amiens comparison 74
    main body of French Army to move past
        95
    new offensive opened on 74
    and the Siegfried Line 143
    thick belt of enemy defences on 153–4
Albers, Leutnant 39–40, 46–7
Albert–Arras railway line 80
Albrecht of Württemberg, Duke 145–6, 246
Alenfeld, Leutnant Erich 249–51
Aleppo 226
Allenby, Sir Edmund 226
Allied prisoner-of-war camps 90
Allies
    acceptance of Wilson's Fourteen Points
        252
    advance depended on engineers 107–8
    Amiens always in their hands 29
    and the Armistice 275–8
    artillery bombardments had pounded
        into dust 244
    assault on 8 August deep into German
        lines 54
    at the mercy of enemies 21
    attacks to go on 78
    9 August a day of wasted opportunities
        56
    conference in Paris on 5 October 216–17
    constant air attacks from 93
    continued to jab away at German line
        181
    counter-attack plans 40
    counter-stroke on the Marne 40
    equality in numbers to Germans 25
    face to face with German defensive line
        167
    finally on their way 77
    flu brings grim resignation 19
    Foch co-ordinating the actions of 21, 25
    and the Hindenburg Line 80, 138–9
    learnt about secrecy the hard way 38
    let slip priceless advantage at Marne 278
    liberated most of western Belgium by 19
        October 220
    little to prevent from liberating all of
        Belgium 177
    meeting of Commanders-in-Chief at
        Foch's headquarters on 27 October
        226
    methods of attack improved 74
    and the 'mouse trap' 2–3, 5–6
    naval blockade of 15–16
    not be halted until German resistance
        impossible 228
    only just getting started in 1918 114
    operating in terrifying/dangerous
        chemical environment 102
    problems clearing vast array of German
        material 264–5
    rear lines of armies vibrant in September
        1918 134–5
    remarkable gains July–November 1918
        278
    shared a common goal of breaking
        German Army 200
    slowed down in wake of German
        destruction 263

Allies – *cont.*
    smashing blow at Amiens 97
    speed of Amiens advance slows 55
    strain of constant operations 92
    Supreme War Council 21
    tactical control of armies 22
    tactical learning curve of xxxiii
    use of gas 103, 106
    see also Western Front and various army
        entries
Alsace-Lorraine 216, 227, 244, 253
American Army see United States Army
American Civil War 152
American declaration of war (April 1917) 126
American Expeditionary Force (AEF) 26–7,
    165
    see also United States Army and various
        army entries
American Tank Corps 160
Amiens
    and Aisne comparison 74
    Allies' smashing blow 97
    always in Allied hands 29
    attack on 8 August 44–7
    battle of xxx, xxxii
    crucial link in Western Front 29–32
    crucial role of aircraft 36
    deception plan prior to 36
    Foch pleased by results 63, 137
    Foch's plans 64
    great test of training 56
    greatest defeat for German Army 70
    infantry, horses/tanks 41
    passage of 46th (North Midland)
        Division 133
    Pershing requested withdrawal of five
        US divisions after battle 127
    rail junction in range of enemy guns 25
    smashing blow of Allies 97
    speed of Allied advance slows 55
    suffered relatively lightly 28
Amiens–Roye road 46, 57
Anderson, Sergeant Hakon 165–6
Antwerp–Meuse Line 11, 112, 224, 238, 244
Argonne 128, 137–8, 143, 152–3, 158–60,
    204
Armeeparlament 260, 328n.17
Armentières 143, 207
Armin, General Sixt von 264
Armistice, the
    background to xxvi, xxx, xxxii
    brought forth mixed feelings 271–2,
        276–7
    and Foch 226, 266
    in force 267–70, 274, 329n.32
    Hitler's reaction 214
    most iconic event xxxiii
    negotiations begin 252–4, 260, 327n.4
    not a total victory for Allies 275–6
    offer on 1 October 196, 201
    Owen killed seven days before 250
    pointless and ultimately futile 278
    rumours circulate throughout Western
        Front 240
    US offer on 21 October 223–4
    war continues 262–4
    Wilson's conditions 216–17
Army Group Gallwitz 205
Arras xxix, 143
artillery
    bombardments pounded Allies into dust
        244
    counter-battery fire 35
    fought a demanding war 82–3
    patchy support in Amiens 59
    rail-mounted naval guns 33
    vital to operations 33–5
Asservillers 108
Ausland, John 265–6
Australian Corps
    5th Brigade 87
    1st Division 56
    5th Division 86
    and Amiens attack 36, 49
    capture of Mont Saint-Quentin 85–6
    crossing the Somme 95, 107
    feverish activity at calibration range
        34–5
    reputation of 31
    surprise raid on German positions 39
Austro-Hungary
    collapse of Empire 271
    naval blockade of 16
    soon to offer peace 205
    on the verge of capitulation by October
        1918 226
    weakening of the forces of 142
Avesnes 109, 251
Avesnes conference (September 1918) 112
Avre, River 30, 44

Bairnsfather, Bruce 20
Baker, Newton 131
Ball, E. F. (Padre) 174
Bapaume 64, 80, 89
Barricourt Heights 241–2, 264

Bavaria, King of 256
Bavarian Alpine Corps 58
Bazentin-le-Grand 88
Beaucamp xxvi, 171–4
Beaumont Hamel 84
Beaurevoir–Fonsomme Line 189, 208
Beier, Vice Sgt 46
Belgium
    final days xxxiii
    forces harrying retreating German
        armies 207
    German reserves at their thinnest 175
    little to prevent Allies from liberating all
        of 177
    western part liberated by Allies by 19
        October 220
Belleau Wood 115–16, 126
Bellenglise 185, 187
Bellicourt 144, 182
Below, General Otto von 79, 97
Berlin 15
Bertangles 108
Bertry 209
Bidet, Edmond 272
Bidet, Elise 272–3
Bill, Captain Charles xxix
Binarville 204
Binding, Rudolf 9, 92, 109, 148
Birmingham 'Pals' *see* 15/Royal Warwick
    Regiment (British)
Black Death 19
'Black Jack' *see* Pershing, General John
Blanc Mont ridge 126, 155
Blue Cross gas *see* tear gas
Blue Dotted Line 52
Blunden, Edmund xxv–xxvi
'Boche', the *see* German Army
Boehn, General Hans von
    Army Group faced bulk of British
        strength 175
    Army Groups of 145, 214, 247
    daily visits to the Siegfried Line 112
    and Lossberg 70, 88
    temporary residence at Avesnes 109
    and work on the Hermann Line 193–4
booby-traps 210
Boucanville 123
Bourlon Wood 167, 170
Braithwaite, Lieutenant-General Sir Walter
    185
Bray 63
Bridges, Major-General Tom 117
Brie 64, 107

Briey iron basin 137
Bristol Fighter aircraft 36
British Army
    and Amiens 29
    approaching total exhaustion at the
        Armistice 277
    capture of Jerusalem 142
    compelled to remain in the north 127
    facing devastated countryside in final
        weeks of August 1918 78
    finally knew how to fight effectively
        83–4
    guns in the Amiens sector 35
    Haig worried about exhausted state of 227
    harrying retreating German armies 207
    morale rose 'like mercury' as advance
        continued 100
    ready for renewed push in August 1918
        79
    tough resistance on northern coast of
        Greece 142
    see also Allies; British Expeditionary
        Force (BEF); Western Front
    ARMIES
    First
        breaks through at Canal du Nord 170
        breaks through Drocourt–Quéant
            Line 98–9
        Cambrai falls 208
        report on German destruction 263
        to breach Hindenburg Line 138
    Second 176
    Third 228
        attack on 21 August 1918 80–81, 88–9
        attack at Cambrai 135, 171, 173, 175,
            208
        Foch's plans 64
        Haig's plans 66–7
        and the Hindenburg Line 138, 170
    Fourth
        and Amiens 29–30, 34
        at the Drocourt–Quéant Line 99
        breaks into German rear areas 52
        crosses the Sambre–Oise canal on 4
            November
        establishes itself on the canal 187
        fifty miles from railheads by the
            Armistice 277
        heavy barrage at Amiens 45
        mounts major operations 17–24
            October 228
        no further attacks without artillery 65
        peace talk not allowed 207–8

British Army – *cont.*
    staff had complete plan of German
        defences 181–2, 316–17n.2
    three miles of ground gained on 9
        August 59
    CORPS
    III Corps
        at Albert 38
        secured left flank of Amiens attack 46
    IX Corps 185
    DIVISIONS
    5th 80, 108, 135, 171, 173
    6th (North Midland) 133, 185–8
    32nd 60
    37th 81–2
    38th Welsh 83, 232
    56th (London) 230
    66th 262
    BRIGADES
    13th 81, 173
    15th 172–3
    95th 173
    regiments
    1/6th North Staffordshire 186–8,
        317–18n.15
    1/Coldstream Guards 171
    1/Royal West Kents 171–2
    12 Glosters 81
    14/Royal Warwickshire 172, 190,
        318n.20
    15/Royal Warwickshire xxviii–xxix,
        80, 81, 136, 172–4, 190, 293n.4
    16/Lancashire Fusiliers 189
    BATTALIONS
    1st 52
    2/Manchesters 189, 207
    16/Royal Warwickshire 190
British Expeditionary Force (BEF)
    'Amiens method' standard operating
        procedure 79
    Anglophone focus xxxi
    benefited from RAF dropping boxes of
        ammunition 108
    by 1918 composed mainly of youthful
        conscripts 275
    growing reputation of Canadian/
        Australian Corps 31
    Haig tells Lloyd George on 19 October
        'never more efficient' 241
    manpower shortages in October 1918 191
    tactical proficiency of 85–6
    see also Allies; British Army; Western
        Front and various army groupings

British Government
    circulated 'British Military Policy,
        1918–19' 139
    needed convincing that victory near 140
British Military Mission 117
'British Military Policy, 1918–19', 139
British War Cabinet 101
Brunswick, Duke of 256
Bucher, Georg 9–10
Bulgaria 142, 195, 226
Bullard, Robert Lee 27
Byng, Sir Julian 79, 168, 170, 270

Calais 25
Cambrai
    attack towards 167
    Cambrai–Saint-Quentin line crucial 175
    Crown Prince Rupprecht comments on
        fighting 193
    falls on 9 October 208, 212, 214
    few tourists now xxxiii
    Gouzeaucourt repeatedly fought over
        xxv–xxvi
    great British objective 95, 135
    Haig comments on remarkable progress
        since 32–3
    heavy British attacks around 177
    and the Hindenburg Line 144, 170
    remained in German hands on 3 October
        194
    trucks commandeered 55
Cameron, Major-General George 153
Camp, R. H. 231
Canadian Corps
    in action on outskirts of Valenciennes
        242
    at Amiens 31, 36–7
    and the Drocourt–Quéant Line 95,
        98–101
    exhausted after breach of Hindenburg
        Line 188
    fighting at Framerville 53
    four miles inside the German lines 49
    and German destruction 263
    only 420 casualties at Mont Houy 243
    plan to cross Canal du Nord 168
    DIVISIONS
    1st 56, 101, 230–31
    2nd xxix, 56, 266
    3rd 56, 208
    4th 52, 60–61, 169
    BRIGADES
    11th 55

REGIMENTS
5th Mounted Rifles 37, 210
BATTALIONS
10th 44
18th 54–5
28th 266
47th 232
Canal du Nord
attack across 169–71
British decide to take advantage of 144
Currie's forces placed here 167–8
heavy British attacks around 177
Thomas Cotterill killed at xxix–xxx
Carignan-Mézières rail link 152
Carlepont 57
Carlowitz, General von 175
Carpenter, Lieutenant William 121
Central Powers 141–2, 226
Champagne fever *see* Flanders fever
Charleroi 238
Charleville 237
Charlton, Captain A. H. 186
Château de Bombon 24, 29–30, 62–3, 95, 141
Château de la Fraineuse 180
Château-Thierry 2, 25, 115
Chaulnes 56
Chauny 74
Chemin des Dames 14
Chenu, Lieutenant Charles 3–6, 119
Cheppy 160
Chipilly 30, 39
Chipilly–Rosières–Roye line 57
chlorine gas 102
Churchill, Winston 191
Clark, Brigadier-General J. A. 64–5
Clarke, Miss C. W. 159–60
Claudel, Major-General Henri 206
Clausewitz, Carl Philipp von 61
Clemenceau, Georges
brings back Mangin 75
conference on 16 October 216
description 20
Foch hands him Armistice conditions 270
Foch to provide report on military terms of armistice 226, 228
furious pronouncements of 14
visit to Montfaucon 166
and Wilson's Fourteen Points 200
Colt, Lieutenant-Colonel 81
Comines 213, 221
Composite Army C 128, 148

Congressional Medal of Honor 120
Cook, Tim 102
Corbie (Somme) 134
Cotterill, Florence xxx
Cotterill, George Thomas xxvi–xxviii, xxx, xxxiii, 80, 172, 293n.4
counter-battery fire 102, 105
Courcelles 80
Cox, Bertram Howard 48
Crown Council meeting 72–4
Crozat canal 57
Crutchley, Corporal 186
'culminating point' 61
Currie, Sir Arthur
agreed to mount operation to secure Mont Houy 242–3
and Andrew McNaughton 35
breaks through Drocourt–Quéant Line 98–100
Canadian troops exhausted 189
deception plan worked perfectly 54
description of 31–2
and fall of Cambrai 208
and the front 61, 64–5, 167–8, 170, 230–31
'neglect nothing' policy 31–2, 243
petitioned for earlier date of attack 41
Curtis, W. E. 44
Cuts 74
cyanosis 19

Dallas, Gregor xxxi
'Dead Man's Corner' 174
Debeney, General Eugène
attack on Montdidier 47
battle at Amiens 40
came to prominence under Pétain 77
captures Hangest and gains ground 59
convinced of the need to desist 66
feeling increasingly queasy 65
First Army criticized for hanging back 210–11
First Army gained sixteen kilometres of ground 265
forces did not attack on 29 September 191
forces moved up 77
and the Hindenburg Line 144
noble fatalism of 78–9
northern offensive 138
ordered by Foch to capture Roye 63
ordered to postpone attacks 67
sent two tank battalions 33

Debeney, General Eugène – *cont.*
  temporarily under orders of Haig 29–30
'deep penetration' 63
Degelow, Major Carl 93–4, 176–7, 264
Demicourt-Graincourt road 171
Department of War Neurosis, Bonn 111
desertion 9–10, 245
Distinguished Service Order xxix
Division Aérienne 36, 40
Dixon, Lieutenant R. G. 118–19, 228
Dominion corps 31–2
Douai 99, 220
'doughboys' 120–21
Doullens Town Hall 21
Downing, Sergeant Walter 49, 86
Drews, Dr 239–40
Drocourt–Quéant Line 95, 99–101, 143, 167
Drum, Hugh 154, 160–61
dug-outs 184
Duncan, G. S. 23
Dunkirk 25
Durrant, Colonel J. 85

Ebert, Friedrich 266, 274, 330n.7
Edwards, Major P. C. 174
electro-shock therapy 111–12
Elles, Hugh 38, 56
Elser, Sergeant 222
Erzberger, Matthias 252–5, 266
Étain 155
Éterpigny 107

Faulkner, Corporal Frank 1
Fayolle, General
  came to prominence under Pétain 77
  crushing blow to the German right flank
    6
  no question of giving Mangin every-
    thing 76
Fifth Army (Germany)
  at the front Apremon–Metz 128
  censor reported morale relatively bad
    205
  could muster only 190,000 men 151
  could no longer maintain sustainable
    resistance 238
  heavy losses at Argonne 162
  Marwitz in command 149, 152, 242
  to fall back to Hirson–Mézières line 238
First Meuse–Argonne cessation 204
Flanders
  attack on the Mount Kemmel sector 37
  front held by German Fourth Army 176

German Army position crumbled/
  collapsed on 28 September 176–8
German reserves there at their thinnest
  175
Ludendorff's Operation Hagen 14–15
Flanders fever 92
Foch, General Ferdinand
  Armistice negotiations 252–5
  attack towards Cambrai 167
  character of 20–22
  Clemenceau complains about Montfau-
    con 166
  concerned about Allies crossing
    Hindenburg Line 180
  concerned that OHL might sanction
    pre-emptive withdrawal 63
  decision to limit Saint-Mihiel operation
    137–8
  discussions with Haig 66, 191, 207, 226–7
  exhausting night drawing up Armistice
    266
  hated by Ludendorff 178–9
  headquarters of 24
  inspected American sector with
    Weygand/Pershing 140
  left Rethondes for Paris on 11 November
    270
  looked favourably on what had been
    achieved 94
  made Marshal of France 62
  meeting at Senlis of Allied Commanders-
    in-Chief on 27 October 226–8,
    323n.28
  meeting with three Allied commanders
    139
  ordered Debeney to capture Saint-
    Quentin 191
  and Pershing 131, 136–7
  preferred US forces under French
    command 128
  Prince Max blames him for Wilson's
    demands 218
  'series of movements' plan 25–7, 29–30
  sought to extend battle line further 95–6
  talk with Colonel House 278
  urged an attack on Chaulnes–Roye front
    67
  urged Pétain to grip his commanders 77
  wanted to capture road junctions near
    Roye 64
  working practices of 62–3
Foch, Germain 21
Fokker DVII aircraft 94

Foot, R. C. 81–3, 105–6
'Forester's House' 248
Forêt de Nieppe xxix
Fort Gironville 129
Foster, Arthur James 100
Fourteen Points (Wilson) 198–202, 223, 252, 319n.27
Fourth Army (Germany)
  held front in Flanders 176
  ordered to fall back from Lys 99
  troops to Amiens 60
Framerville 53–4, 182
France
  cooperation/coordination with UK 21–2
  dreaded Americans dictating a peace 217
  expectations from Americans 121
  final days xxxiii
  and the German Spring Offensive xxxi, 294n.10
  Marne losses 18
  number of guns at Armistice 33
  rapid increase in US manpower in 118
  Rheims victory 2
  shied away from occupation of Germany 278
  superior aircraft production 35–6
  warm initial perspective on US troops 119
  see also Allies; French Army; and various army entries
Franz Ferdinand, Archduke xxvii
French 15th Colonial Division 131
French Army
  active front length narrowed dramatically by last weeks of war 241
  and Amiens 29
  approaching total exhaustion at the Armistice 275, 277
  destined to stay in centre to cover Paris 127
  facing devastated countryside in final weeks of August 1918 78
  guns in the Amiens sector 35
  Haig worried about the exhausted state of 227
  harrying the retreating German armies 207
  majority supported armistice discussions 211–12
  Mangin's aggression/confidence not welcomed 76
  morale rose 'like mercury' as advance continued 100

old-fashioned methods disliked by Pershing 124–5
only two tank battalions 33
operations 8–29 August cost 100,000 casualties 95
relied heavily on their guns 83–4
to push forward, past River Aisne 95
tough resistance on northern coast of Greece 142
wasteful tactics dispensed with 75
worn out after four years of war 26
see also Allies; France; and various army entries
ARMIES
First
  aiming for the town of La Capelle 247
  and Amiens 29–30, 47
  criticized for hanging back 210–11
  did not attack on 29 September 1918
  encircled Montdidier 59
  gained sixteen kilometres of ground 265
  'hanging back' accusations 191
  marched into the village of Guise 250, 327n.43
  mounts major operations 17–24 October 228
  nearly 15,000 casualties during October 211
  objective of Stenay–Le Chesne–Attigny–Rethel 153
Second 151
Third 63
Fourth
  assistance to US Army at Argonne forest 153–4, 156
  impressively big, consisting of seven corps 154–5
  on the march for twenty-five nights in late October 229
  Pétain complains about lack of progress 191–2
  ready to go deep into German flank on 25 September 149
  to mount an attack west of the Meuse 137
Fifth 145
Sixth 6, 75
Tenth
  faced largest German Army Group 145
  and Hellé 23
  Mangin pleased with achievements of 76

French Army − *cont.*
  Operation Marneschutz-Reims 3
  CORPS
    IX 38
    X 65
    XVII 206
    XX 3
    XXXI 40, 47, 49
    XXXV 65
  DIVISIONS
    1st Moroccan 3
    154th 229
Frisby, Captain Cyril 171, 231
Fuchs, General-Leutnant Georg 128, 148

Gallwitz, Max von
  Army Groups of 145–6
  counter-attacks at Argonne 161
  did not replace Ludendorff 236–8
  initially sceptical about US troops
    150–51, 313n.2
  and Saint-Mihiel salient 128–9, 131–2
  saw Marwitz 10 November 264
gas 102–6, 173, 181, 191
George V, King 187
German Air Force
  on its knees by 30 October 264
  limitations of 175
  outflanked by RAF 93
  see also air power
German Armistice Commission 252–3, 261
German Army
  across the Canal du Nord 99
  acute shortage of horses 109
  Aisne attack another disaster 74
  Allies shared a common goal of breaking
    200
  Amiens a unique experience/greatest
    defeat 35, 49–50, 54, 61, 70–71
  approaching defeat on a grand scale
    242–6, 326n.29
  at long last seemed to be breaking apart 67
  battalion field strength poor by end of
    War 146
  commanders concerned about morale at
    Argonne 162
  continuation of fight would have been
    disastrous 276
  crumbling 73, 88
  decreasing quality of recruits being
    drafted into 111
  defences worn out by late October 222,
    230, 241

despair, depression and fear on 11
  November 266
in disarray, but benefited from falling
  back 86
divided into five Groups in the west 145
divisions back to last defensive positions
  in October 214
endurance of shellfire worst thing 110
experience of retreat tough 212
Foch believed they would break 63
gradual fall-back through Somme sector
  87
had limited, dwindling number of
  tenacious units 175
and Haig 24
harrowing day of Allied attacks on 27
  September 174
headquarters repeatedly moved back 108
and the Hindenburg Line 95, 143
imaginative and ingenious booby-traps
  of 210
increasingly experienced horror of
  mustard gas 106
long winter campaign expected in
  August 1918 79
Ludendorff's resignation meets mixed
  feelings 235
makes its way home 274–5, 330n.7
morale of 89, 91–3
needed to regroup 113
news of retreat spread quickly 97
nothing but chaos, disorganization,
  shellfire and fighting 192
position in Flanders crumbled with
  alarming speed 176
proclamation issued to on 24 October
  225
relied upon a system of defence in depth
  132
retreat caused Allied logistic problem
  106
and Saint-Mihiel salient 129–31
Saint-Quentin left in flames 208–9
speculation of retreat as far as Rhine 139
strain of Marne fighting 7, 9
suffering from Allied air attacks 93
tactical changes 32
unease and confusion on 9 August 57
units desperately tried to hold Saint-
  Quentin Canal 183
US understands why not defeated 115
withdrawal from exposed lines
  advocated 11

see also Germany; German Supreme
   Command (OHL); Western Front
ARMIES
Second
   at Hattencourt 58
   continually engaged, suffered heavy
      losses 148
   counted over 120 bombs fallen in
      Cambrai 93
   defeat due to enemy tanks/exhaustion
      50, 69
   devastating beginning to Amiens
      battle 44–5, 54
   fought well but removed from the
      canal 187
   issued October message, peace would
      bring worse devastation 245–6
   local counter-attacks on 9 September
      57
   Marwitz removed from command on
      22 September 148–9
   not in best of condition 38–40
   occupied line of the Sambre–Oise
      canal 247
   only three divisions completely fit for
      action 175
   retreat of led to outflanking of
      Eighteenth Army 70
   retreat to the Hindenburg Line 99
Third 128
Sixth
   all peaceful on 3 October 194
   ordered to fall back from Lys 99
   troops to Amiens 60
Ninth
   Army Group to withdraw and link up
      with 57
   Chief of Staff changed three times 113
   not yet engaged at Amiens 70
   retreat to the Hindenburg Line 99
   withdrawal of the right wing of 74
Seventeenth
   all peaceful on 3 October 194
   beginning to fall back 67
   occupied line of the Sambre–Oise
      canal 247
   plan for three corps to push forward
      against 79
   retreat to the Hindenburg Line 97, 99
   troops to Amiens 60
Eighteenth
   at Hattencourt 58
   division sent northwards 50

Fourth French Army on heels of 211
   measures to preserve strength 57
   occupied line of Sambre–Oise canal
      247
   only one division completely fit for
      action 175
   reaches outskirts of Roye 59
   reported exhaustion in divisions 193
   retreat to the Hindenburg Line 99
   Second Army's retreat led to outflank-
      ing of 70
   staggering casualties 54
   strengthened by three divisions 60
corps
   51st 187
   I Bavarian 182
   IV Reserve 187
   XIV Reserve 147
DIVISIONS
   1st Guard Reserve 99
   1st Guards 163
   2nd Guard Reserve 88, 99
   2nd Guards 146
   2nd Landwehr 161–2
   3rd Guards 162–3
   3rd Naval 175
   4th Bavarian 88
   5th Bavarian Reserve 161
   6th Cavalry 175, 192
   10th 129
   14th Bavarian 47
   21st Reserve 245
   26th Reserve 174–5
   27th Württemberg 39
   34th 192
   37th 161
   41st 39, 50, 52, 54
   43rd Reserve 39, 46
   54th Infantry 175
   79th Reserve 57
   111th 245
   117th 46
   221st 57
   Jäger 74, 171, 173, 175
REGIMENTS
   3rd Westphalian 247–8
   13/Hussars 192–3
   16/Reserve Infantry 213
   55th Infantry 88
   84th Infantry 175
   152nd 50–52
   153rd 146
   157th 46

German Army *–cont.*
  188th 170
  208th Artillery 194–5
  280th Field Artillery 249
German Medical History 19
German Spring Offensive (March 1918) 118, 127
German Supreme Command (OHL)
  and the Armistice decision 196–7, 207, 276
  could only shuffle exhausted divisions around 193
  disintegration becomes noticeable 246
  Foch concerned about sanction of pre-emptive withdrawal 63
  forbidden any retirement due to negotiations 242
  greatly overestimating army's capacity for resistance 70
  a hive of activity 141
  HQ at Spa in Belgium 67–8, 109
  knew that victory a long way off 7
  laziness/complacency among 40
  mood becoming progressively worse 113
  morale slumped again after Saint-Mihiel 131
  ordered Seventeenth Army's retreat to Hindenburg Line 97, 114
  pamphlets issued discouraging capture 147
  proposed Amiens attack 36–7
  sanctions withdrawal of Eighteenth/ Ninth Armies 99
  and serious decline in Germany's fighting power 69
  sought confirmation that Allies would keep to Fourteen Points 202
  US confirms OHL must go to gain peace 224
  wanted new defensive areas behind the line 112
  see also Germany; German Army
Germany
  aircraft production 36
  became clear that must do whatever it took to secure armistice 223
  collapse of Empire 271
  complete collapse of resistance in 1918 unlikely 277
  a country on the verge of revolution 274
  dream of German victory ended near Saint-Quentin 188
  dwindling reserves of manpower 14

  effects of naval blockade 16
  fatal amnesia regarding the Americans 151
  front-line position 155
  had played her last card by 1918 91, 114
  Haig feared that would not accept an armistice 227
  and influenza pandemic 18–19
  last offensive of 1–3, 5
  loyalty beginning to fracture in October 214
  nation/army starving by 1918 10
  Operation Marneschutz-Reims 2
  Ottoman Empire staunch/dependable ally 142
  peace with Russia at Brest-Litovsk 16–17
  position deteriorating, allies falling away 177
  questionable 1918 defeat xxxiii
  retreat from the Marne 17, 24
  revolution spreads on 6 November 254–5
  sailors mutiny at Kiel on 4 November 254
  Spring Offensive xxxi–xxxii, 28–9, 294n.10
  and the 'turnip winter' (1916–17) 15
  US warns that could only deal with real rulers of Germany 224
  and Wilson's demands 179, 201–2, 216–18, 222
  see also German Army; German Supreme Command (OHL)
Gillemont Farm 183
Goodmurphy, Arthur 267–8
Gouraud, Henri 154–6, 191, 241
Gouzeaucourt
  and 15/Royal Warwickshire Regiment 190
  death of Private Cotterill xxxiii
  fought over repeatedly xxv–xxvi, 171
  gaining an infamous reputation 171
  gas shelling of 173
  German evacuation of 175
Grady, Captain T. F. 120, 123, 158–9, 266
Graincourt 171
Grandpré 155
Grant, General Ulysses S. 152
Grasset, Colonel 42, 47
Great Britain *see* United Kingdom
grenades 85
Grenadier Guards (Britain) 80
Grévillers 81

Groener, General Wilhelm 237–8, 252, 257–61
Groover, First-Lieutenant 156–7, 164–5, 269
Groves, Frank 268
Guinness, Walter 262–3
Guise 250, 253
guns *see* artillery

Haeften, Colonel Hans von 71, 196
Hagen (operation) 15
Haig, Field Marshal Sir Douglas
  agrees Amiens attack 30
  Allied contingent commanders' meeting 24–7
  asks Byng to speak to Currie 168
  character of 23–4
  concerns in London about his command 101–2
  confident that Germans breaking 139–40
  convinced of the need to desist 66–7
  and Debeney 79
  delighted with achievements of Canadians 101
  devastating firepower now available to 181
  and Foch 6, 22, 63, 191, 207, 226–7
  furious attacks slowing down by 1 October 188
  keen to achieve tactical success on battlefield 36
  and Lloyd George 23, 241
  looked favourably on what had been achieved 94
  lunch with Alfred Milner 138–40
  meeting with battery commander Foot 82
  meeting in Cambrai on 11 November 269
  meetings with Rawlinson/Elles 32, 66
  and Pershing 127–8, 131
  petitioned for earlier date of attack 41
  problems of retreating German Army 262
  refuses an attack on the Chaulnes–Roye front 67
  responsible for breaching Hindenburg Line 138
  seven Victoria Crosses won on 27 September 1918 171
  Wilson's warnings to about sustaining heavy losses 191
  working with Pétain 22

Hallu 60
Ham 63, 95
Hamel, Battle of 31
Hattencourt 58
Hatzfeld, Hauptmann 50–52
Helldorf, Captain 254, 265
Hellé, Joseph 23
Helm, Captain Malcolm 5
Hermann, Guido 110–11
Hermann Line 112–13, 193–4, 214, 224
Hertling, Count von 70, 195
Heydebreck, Hauptmann von 93
Heye, Colonel Wilhelm 141, 257, 260, 328n.17
Hindenburg, Field Marshal Paul von
  at Spa on 9 November 257, 259–61
  breach falls to Haig's armies 138
  chaired meeting at Hôtel Britannique 70–71
  character of 11–15
  Crown Prince disapproves of Groener appointment 237
  furious telegram to Gallwitz 131–2
  gives thanks to Dr Hochheimer 140
  Hindenburg Line plans in 1916 143–5
  his usual stoical, uninterested self 68
  increasingly frustrated by indecision/ incompetence 148
  lost touch with the war by 1918 13
  Ludendorff calls for armistice offer 177, 179–80
  petitioned by von Hintze 113
  reaction to collapse of two Bulgarian divisions 142
  resignation on 26 October not accepted 234–5
Hindenburg Line
  Allies' 1918 attack plans 80
  Army Groups no option but to pull back forces 214
  and British forces 95, 108, 170, 207
  broken by 46th (North Midland) Division 133, 185–8
  concerns as to whether Allies could cross 180
  Debeney confident of breaking 79
  'end of the world' 135
  fast becoming anvil to break German armies 181
  fighting still continued after crossing of 210
  Foch haunted by the retreat to the 63
  German units move into 114, 192

Hindenburg Line – *cont.*
last German card remaining 97–9, 101
Lossberg advice to occupy and extend
70
main German defensive position xxvi, 11
in need of thorough refurbishment 114
question on whether it would hold 143
Saint-Quentin canal heavily protected
183
von Boehn reported on poor state of 112
Hindenburg reserve line *see* Beaurevoir-
Fonsomme Line
Hindenburg Support Line 171
Hintze, Admiral Paul von
appeal to Wilson to be followed by
political reform 179
appointment as Foreign Secretary 17
at Spa on 9 November 257
fourth part of Foch's offensives began on
26 September 181
Ludendorff withheld information from
113
meeting at Hôtel Britannique 70, 72–3
recognized need for new government
195
telegram from Ludendorff 143
Hirson railway junction 110
Hitler, Adolf 213–14, 221, 245, 274–5
Hochheimer, Dr 73, 140–41, 178
Holden, Second-Lieutenant Frank 20,
104–5, 121, 123, 202–3
Holmes, T. H. 84–5, 103–4, 134, 230–31
Hornaing 230
House, Colonel 216, 228, 278
Houthulst Forest 176
Hunding line 143, 214
Hundred Days xxx–xxxii, 294n.7
Hunter Liggett, Major-General 155–6, 165
Hutier, General Oskar von 50, 211
hysterical symptoms see shell-shock

Impey, Arthur 173
influenza pandemic xxxii, 10–11
influenza pandemic (first strain) 18–19
influenza pandemic (second strain)
death toll growing in the autumn 222
French army ravaged in August 1918 78
killer disease 19
stalked the German Army at War's end
245
Inspector-General of First Army's report
166
Irles 81

Iron Cross 13
Italian Army xxvii
Italy
Battle of Vittorio Veneto 226
final days xxxiii
front line xxviii, xxix
the 'mousetrap' 2

Jackson, Lance Corporal Thomas 171
Jagdstaffel 89, 93–4, 98, 176
John Summer's steel mill xxvii
Johnson, Brigadier-General Evan 161
Johnston, Clifford 106–7
Joliffe, Lieutenant-Colonel J. W. H. 169–70
Joncourt 189
Jones, Sergeant T. J. 172
Jones (Wilfred Owen's servant) 190

Kaiser Alexander Regiment 87
Karl, Cyrus 111
Kaufman Method 112
Kielmayer, Ernst 174–5, 194, 213, 222
Kirk, Second-Lieutenant James 250
Kretschmann, Major von 260
Krieghoff, Leutnant Hans 170
Kuhl, Major-General von 68–9, 224, 235–7,
245
Kühlmann, Richard von 16–17, 196

La Boisselle 84
La Capelle 247
La Harazée 155
Lansing, Robert 223–4
Lawrence, Second-Lieutenant Joseph 206–7
Le Cateau 109
Le Quesnel 52, 55–6
League of Nations 199
Lee, General Robert E. 152
Lejeune, Major-General John A. 126
Lewis guns 51
Liège 14
Liggett, Hunter 241–2, 277–8
Lille 220
Little Gibraltar see Montfaucon
Lloyd George, David
and 'a Christmas present for the empire'
142
clear that the end now in sight 226
conference on 16 October 216
and Haig 23, 241
personality 20
and Wilson's Fourteen Points 200
Löffler, Major-General 257–8

Lomme airfield 93–4
looting 9–10, 109
Lossberg, Major-General Friedrich Karl
    'Fritz' von
    advice at conference at Avesnes 112–13
    estimates 400,000 dead at Antwerp–
        Meuse Line 244
    formation of a new Army Group 69–70
    glad to leave Spa on 1 November 246–7
    great respect for Ludendorff 236
    position on Marne should be given up
        immediately 11
    'resilience/fighting spirit on the wane' 90
    went to the front every day 88
'lost battalion' *see* 308th Infantry Regiment
    (US)
Luce River 30
Ludendorff, General Erich von
    agreed no counter-attack at Saint-Mihiel
        128
    and the Allied counter-attack 7, 54
    Amiens one of worst experiences of war
        68–9
    attended conference at Avesnes 112–13
    call for Allied armistice offer 177–80,
        197–8, 316n.29
    changed Chief of Staff of Ninth Army
        three times 113–14
    character of 11–15
    in comparison to Groener 257
    could only hold centre on Western
        Front 175–7
    Council of War on 17 October 218
    devastating peace offensive on 21 March
        118
    and Dr Hochheimer 140–41
    dreams and illusions of 260
    headed back to OHL on 24 October 225
    the Hindenburg Line, last card
        remaining 97
    increasingly frustrated by indecision/
        incompetence 148
    lost confidence in the morale of his
        troops 71–3
    meeting with Prince Max on 9 October
        201
    never captured Amiens 29
    no reasons for any panic 90
    ordered formation of new Army Group
        69–70
    peace offensive a failure 110
    Prince Max loses confidence in him
        224

    Proclamation on 24 October 225–6
    reaction to collapse of two Bulgarian
        divisions 142–3
    refused to contemplate further
        withdrawals 70
    resigns on 26 October 234–7
    strain continued to mount 75
Ludendorff, Margarethe von 13, 178, 235
Ludwig, Paul 161–2
Lynch, Edward 58
Lys 99

MacArthur, Douglas 120, 130
Macdonell, Major-General Archibald 101
MacGowan, Keith 232
McHenry, Herbert L. 121, 242
Machine-Gun Corps (British) 231
    machine-guns 146, 161
Lewis guns 51, 85
Mackin, Elton 4–5, 115–16, 203, 240
McNaughton, Lieutenant-Colonel Andrew
    35, 168–9, 242–3
Mahncke, Alfred 246
Manancourt 105
Manchester Regiment xxix
Mangin, General Charles
    army deployed north of the Ourcq
        River 6
    new offensive by Tenth Army 74–7
    Operation Marneschutz-Reims 3
    prepared to move forward on Aisne 63
    shook with anger at state of Saint-
        Quentin 208–9
    warnings about fighting power of
        French Army 191
Marigny Château 115
Marne, Second Battle of
    Allied counter-stroke on 40
    Allies let slip priceless advantage 278
    American troops at 116
    beginnings xxxii, 1–2, 15
    enormous strain on German Army 7
    German retreat from 9, 14, 17–18, 25,
        30
    plans for attack 34
    saving of Paris 20
Maroilles 251
Marquion Line 167
Marshall, George 153–4, 165
Marshall, Major H. J. C. 133–4, 185, 188
Marwitz, General der Kavallerie Georg von
    der 38
    Chief of Staff blamed for failures 69

Marwitz, General – *cont.*
   commanders recommended immediate
      retreat 57
   complained his men endured unspeak-
      ably hard conditions 92–3
   ensured no bridges left standing 86
   favoured pulling back beyond Meuse in
      late October 242
   holding on at Romagne Heights 204–5
   idea of an Allied counter-attack 40
   loss of Mont Saint-Quentin a heavy
      blow 87–8
   removed from command of Second
      Army on 22 September 148–9
   underestimated value of armoured
      vehicles 50
   visit to the Argonne front 163–4
   went to see Gallwitz on 10 November
      264
   wondered at stupidity of Europe 148
   'masses of manoeuvre' 30
Massey-Beresford, Jack 82
Max, Prince
   announces abdication of the Kaiser 261
   clear that Kaiser must go 224
   cobbles together an Armistice Commis-
      sion 252
   furious at Ludendorff's political stunt
      224–5
   introduces Kaiser to new Cabinet 223
   letter from Crown Prince Rupprecht
      276
   loath to press the Emperor to resign
      238–40
   replaced von Hertling 195–7
   telegram to White House on 6 October
      200–202, 320n.7
   tries to hold country together on 8
      November 254–5
   and Wilson's note 217–18
Maxim machine-guns 115
Maze, Paul 41, 52–3, 55, 60, 135, 184
Meehan, Sergeant James 157
Megiddo, Battle of 226
Melun 23
Mende, Major 46
Metz 136
Meuse–Argonne front 120, 136, 151–4, 158,
   203, 203–4
Mézières 49, 95, 136–7, 153–5
Michel Line 112, 129, 143
Middle East 142, 226
Military Cross xxix, 189–90

Military Medal 100, 172
Miller, Lieutenant-Colonel G. S. xxix, 81,
   190
Mills bombs 85
Milner, Alfred 138–9
Minenwerfer mortar shells 263
Mohan, T. G. 42, 84
Molleville Farm 207
Moltke, Helmuth von 236
Monash, Sir John
   conference at Villers-Bretonneux 65
   description of last ten minutes before
      Amiens 42–3
   'feverish activity' in Australian Corps
      noted 34–5
   and the Hindenburg Line 144–5, 184, 186
   increasingly unhappy about situation on
      front 61
   most promising commander 31–2
   move towards Lihons delayed 56
   no costly attack from the west 86
   orchestration of military power
      compared to music 299n.22
   reluctant to leave château at Bertangles 108
   told that railway bridge at Péronne
      could be rebuilt 107
   troops pushing the enemy on 26 August
      86
Mons 247, 266, 272
Mont Houy 242–3
Mont Saint-Quentin 85–7, 95
Montdidier 30, 49, 59, 65
Montfaucon 152–3, 156–7, 164, 166, 269
Montgomery, Major-General Sir Archibald
   29–30, 87
Montmédy 150
Morgen, General-Leutnant Curt von 147
Morlancourt 30, 39
Mormal Forest 232
Moroccan *tirailleurs* 49
Mount Kemmel sector 37
Mouse Post 171
'mouse trap' 2–3, 5–6
Moyenneville 80
Mudros island 226
Müller, Georg von 197
mustard gas 102–6, 135, 181, 190
mutineers 194

Nazi Party 274–5
   see also Hitler, Adolf
Neuville-Bourjonval British cemetery xxxiii
New Zealand Division 136

Niemann, Major Alfred 235
1918. War and Peace (Dallas) xxxi
Nivelle offensive 22, 63
Noakes, Frederick 231–2
Norroy 104
northern Army Group (Germany) 57
Nouvron 74
Noyon, Canal du Nord 74, 94–5

Oberndorff, Count 253
Oise River 74, 145, 211
'Old Bill' (cartoon character) 20
Order of the Black Eagle 195
Orlando, Vittorio Emanuele 216
Orpen, Sir William 21, 62–3
Ors 248, 250, 279
Ottoman Empire 142, 142–3, 226, 271
Ourcq River 6
Owen, Wilfred 134–5, 189–90, 207–8, 248,
    250, 254, 279

Palestine xxxiii, 226
Paris 20, 25
Paris–Avricourt railway line 25
Passhaus, Karl 111–12
Patton, Colonel George S. 120, 160, 164
'peaceful penetration' 31
Peck, Colonel 230
Péronne 64, 86–7, 95, 107
Pershing, General John
    Allied contingent commanders' meeting
        24, 26–7
    attack at Argonne 160–61
    character of 26–7
    comments on US positions northwest of
        Verdun 152–4
    convinced that the Armistice premature
        277–8
    corps reaches the Meuse 242
    desired an American sector on Western
        Front 126–8
    fighting on the Meuse 'most desperate
        battle of our history' 207
    finally agreed US divisions to serve
        under British/French command 118
    forced to suspend operations in
        Meuse–Argonne 166
    forces particularly susceptible to gas
        attacks 104
    humiliated by primitive state of US avia-
        tion 117
    inspected American sector with Foch/
        Weygand 140

    meeting with Foch 226
    now involved in brutal attritional slog
        165
    renewed assault on 4 October 205
    requested withdrawal of five US
        divisions after Amiens 127
    and Saint-Mihiel operation 116, 129–31,
        136–7
    soldiers different to Allies 124–5
    three-hour bombardment at Étain 155
    US First Army refused to move in way
        he wanted 203–4
    US policy was to 'build distinctive army
        of our own' 117–18
Pétain, General Henri Philippe
    Allied contingent commanders' meeting
        24, 26–7
    character of 22
    concerned about state of French Army
        139
    could not push troops any harder 241
    discussions with Foch 63, 191–2, 226–7
    distrusted Mangin 75
    hails success of Aisne offensive 74
    looked favourably on what had been
        achieved 94
    meeting with Mangin 76
    not to attack at Étain 155
    praised capture of Blanc Mont ridge 126
    problems of retreating German Army
        262
    provided Pershing with guns 128
    refused to release troops 77
    spent 11 November at GQG 270
    would have disagreed with Pershing's
        methods 125
phosgene gas 102
phosphorus grenades 45
Picardy 80
Pierrefeu, Jean de 22
Piggott, Corporal 172
pistols 146
Plessen, General von 261
Plumer, General Sir Herbert 176, 269
poilus 124
Poincaré, Raymond 228
Ponsonby, Major-General John 108, 171,
    173
Pont-à-Mousson 143
Poperinghe 118
Pour le Mérite 14, 264
Price, George Lawrence 266–8
prisoner-of-war camps, Allied 90

Prussia 12–13, 148, 179, 223–4, 237–9, 257, 260–62
see also Germany
Ramicourt 189
Rawlinson, General Sir Henry
army crossed the Sambre–Oise canal on 4 November 250
artillery support to Debeney 191
conference at Villers-Bretonneux 65–6
convinced of the need to desist 66
difficulties at Saint-Quentin canal 185–6
and Foch's 'series of movements' 29–30
great hopes placed on the use of cavalry/tanks 52–3
and the Hindenburg Line 144
keen to achieve tactical success on battlefield 36, 40
northern offensive 138
not in favour of long, draining bombardment 34
ordered to postpone attacks 67
success of Amiens barrage 7, 45
Rayfield, Corporal Walter 100
Read, Herbert 183
Reinhardt, Walther 6–7
Reisinger, Leutnant 52
Rethondes, Compiègne 252
Rheims 1–2
Ribot, Alexandre 116
Rice, Major F. J. 37, 209, 268–9
rifles 161
Lee Enfield 85, 123
Mauser 45
Riqueval road bridge 186
Rollings, Lieutenant Ernest 182
Romagne Heights 204
Roselaere 194
Ross, Alexander 59
Ross, Major B. 266
Royal Air Force (RAF)
brought down surveillance aircraft 40
played a crucial role at Amiens 36
reaching further into German lines by late summer 1918 93
see also air power
Royal Engineers 108
Royal Navy 16
Royal Tank Corps (Britain) 182
Roye 56, 64–5
Roye-Chaulnes area 66
Rupprecht, Crown Prince
admired the patience of Kuhl 68–9
Army Group of 145

comments on fighting at Cambrai 193
complained about mood amongst Chiefs of Staff 113
complained individual divisions failing him 214
enemy still advancing along Amiens–Roye road 57
hears that Chancellor to be replaced 194
letter to Prince Max 276–7
and Ludendorff 141
meeting with officers on 30 September 193
rest to cure insomnia cut short 148
retreat to Antwerp–Meuse Line could not be delayed 238
told of slow retreat from Hermann Position 224–5
Russia xxxi, 12, 16–17, 271

Sailly-Laurette 39
Saint-Mihiel
battle at 25, 116, 127–32, 136–8, 311n.10
defeat of Composite Army C 148
inspected by Foch/Weygand/Pershing 140
and the Michel Line 143
a warning of American capability 151
written off by Germans as freakish accident 141
Saint-Quentin
Allies advancing towards 78
Foch orders Debeney to attack 191
German 34th Division defending 192
left in flames by Germans 208–9
and the Siegfried Line 143–4
Saint-Quentin canal
breached by 1/6th North Staffordshire Regiment 186–8
crossing concerns 166, 180
Foch's fourth blow lands on 167
heavily protected 183
most difficult sector of the front 138
pontoon bridges erected across 189
position of xxvi
Third Army advancing towards 135
Salonika
final days xxxiii
offensive 142
Sambre, Battle of 247–8
Sant'Anna Morosina xxvii
Sarajevo xxvii
Sassoon, Siegfried 135, 189
Savage, Charles Henry 37–8, 210

Savatier, General Eugène 119–20, 309n.9
Scheidemann, Philip 223–4, 238, 254–6, 261, 274
Schëuch, Heinrich von 219
Schlieffen, Count von 236, 244
Schneider medium tanks 6
Schreder, Oberleutnant 53–4
Schulenburg, Count Friedrich von der 238, 257–9
Schütt, Leutnant Richard 16, 90–91, 97
Schütt, Willy 91, 97
Sealand, Flintshire xxvii
Searcy, Corporal Earl 130
Sedan 155, 241
Selle, River 228
shell-shock 110–111
Siegfried Line 97, 112, 143
    see also Hindenburg Line
SmK ammunition, armour-piercing 52
Smut Trench 136, 171, 173
sneezing gas see tear gas
Social Democrats (Germany) 254–5
Soissons 1–2, 6
soixante-quinze field gun 123
Somme, battles of the
    attack in 1918 by 38th Welsh Division 83
    British cemeteries xxxiii
    German Army pounded 143
    memory-defining xxix
    offensive captured the imagination 279
    old battlefield re-entered 59–60, 78
    trench warfare xxxii
Somme, River 57, 63, 86, 95, 107
Sopwith Camel fighter aircraft 36, 93–4
Spa 140, 237–9, 246, 254, 256–7, 260
Spad fighter aircraft 36
Spanish Flu see influenza pandemics
'Spring Offensive' (Owen) 135
Stark, Rudolf 55, 89, 97–8, 108–9, 212, 220–21
Steinmüller, Paul 140
Stephenson, Scott 110
Stevenson, David xxx–xxxiii
stick grenades 161
stormtroopers xxxii
Stosstruppen (stormtroopers) xxxii
Strauss, Walter J. 183–4
Stürmer, Leutnant 48
submarine warfare 217–18
Suippe, River 155
Sulzbach, Herbert 7, 195
Summeral, Major-General Charles 125

Tank Corps 33, 38
tanks
    continued success at Amiens 50
    defeat for Germany at Amiens 50
    Haig shown a demonstration 32
    ideal for 1918, when available 84–5
    Mark IV 81
    Mark V 32–3, 51–2, 298–9nn.11,12
    Medium Mark A 32–3, 52–3, 164
    Renault 123, 160, 163
Tannenberg, Battle of 12
tear gas 104, 222
Teeton, Captain Percy 186
Terraine, John xxx
Teskey, Frank Clifton 272
Thiepval 84
'three day fever' see influenza pandemic (first strain)
To Win a War (Terraine) xxx
Toul 159
Trescault xxvi
Tschischwitz, Major-General Erich von 69
Turkey 271
Turkish Army 226
Turner, A. J. 83, 232–3, 240

Uhrmacher, Leutnant Karl 194–5
United Kingdom
    aircraft production 35–6
    cooperation/coordination with France 21–2
    and the German Spring Offensive xxxi–xxxii, 294n.10
    looked upon growing might of US with envy and fear 217
    number of guns by Armistice 33
    shied away from occupation of Germany 278
    see also Allies and Western Front
United States
    aircraft production 35
    Americans' expectations of France 121
    enthusiasm for war 26
    forces particularly susceptible to gas attacks 104
    and the German Spring Offensive xxxi, 294n.10
    Government responded swiftly to German note of 21 October 223–4
    lacked aircraft/facilities to support mass air operations 117
    lacked understanding of Great War 115

United States – *cont.*
　Mangin's aggression/confidence
　　welcomed 76
　Pétain agrees US should take strain 77
　powerful new ally 14
　rapid increase in US manpower in
　　France 118–19
　shied away from occupation of Germany
　　278
　war might be over before could
　　intervene in any strength 118
　welcomed into war in spring 1917 116
　see also Allies and Western Front
United States Air Force, 80th Wing 93
United States Army
　acquired healthy respect for Germans
　　123
　an unknown quantity 150–51
　battle of Saint-Mihiel 128–31, 137
　begins to tire 241
　differences between US and Allied
　　soldiers 123–4
　divisions contained 28,000 men 146
　'doughboys' term meaning 120–21
　encountered horror of mustard gas 104
　reached Sedan on 6–7 November 264
　scheduled to make attack on Saint-
　　Mihiel 95
　swept over German lines in late October
　　242
　see also Allies; Western Front; and
　　various army entries
　ARMIES
　First
　　at Saint-Mihiel 116, 138
　　began to concentrate northwest of
　　　Verdun 151–3
　　difficulties at Saint-Quentin Canal 185
　　effort to raise epic story of hard work
　　　126
　　Hunter Liggett takes command in late
　　　October 241
　　improvisation of medical staff 159
　　ready to go deep into German flank
　　　on 25 September 149
　　stubbornly refused to move in way
　　　Pershing wanted 203–4
　　sustained over 45,000 casualties at
　　　Argonne 165
　　to mount an attack west of the Meuse
　　　137
　CORPS
　　I 128, 155–6

　　II 183, 317n.6
　　III 156, 242
　　IV 128
　　V 128, 131, 153
　divisions
　　1st 3, 6, 125, 242
　　2nd 3, 6, 125–6, 130
　　77th 154
　　77th Liberty 203
　　82nd Division 123
　　107th Ammunition Train 165
　BRIGADE
　　1 Provisional Tank 160
　REGIMENTS
　　23rd Infantry 1
　　113th Infantry 206
　　136th Infantry 205
　　308th Infantry 203–4, 206, 320n.12
　　313th Infantry 156–7
　　328th Infantry 202
　BATTALIONS
　　5th Machine Gun 5
Urmacher, Leutnant Karl 221, 236, 273
US Evacuation Hospital, Toul 159

Valenciennes 242
Varennes 161, 202
Verdun 116, 279
Verdun, Battle of xxxii, 98
Versailles, Treaty of 278
Victoria Cross 100, 171, 231, 251
Victoria, Princess 11
Villers-Bretonneux 65, 133
Villers-Cotterêts forest 3
Villers-Plouich xxvi
Vimy Ridge, Battle of xxix, 31
Vince, Charles 28

war neurosis 110
'war prolongers' 214
Waters, Private George 186
Weimar Republic 274
Wellington Battalion 136
Wemyss, Admiral Rosslyn 253
West, Albert 208
Western Front
　air of anticipation settled upon 114
　Allies' superiority in July 1919, estimate
　　139
　Amiens a crucial link 29–32
　artillery vital to operations 33
　Australians captured one of most
　　formidable positions on 87

back and forth, through shattered woods and pock-marked slopes 165

Battle of the Sambre, last great offensives of war 247

begun to turn tide on in eighteen months 126

clear that the end now in sight 226

crumbling, Ludendorff could not hold the flanks 176–7

element of surprise returned 4

entering final stages in September 1918 133

final days xxxii

Forêt de Nieppe area xxix

German armies in headlong retreat by 9 November 263

German Army in full retreat by 1 November 244

German divisions drawn from and sent to Amiens 60

German hopes of making an indefinite stand to be ended 167

Germany accused of scorched-earth policy 222–3

Germany holding on 141

Germany's four defensive positions 143

a lottery of life and death 222

Ludendorff still felt breakthrough possible on 17 October 219

Meuse–Argonne battlefield comparison 152–3

Mont Houy attack equivalent to 'Dante's Inferno' 243

negotiations for an armistice since situation worsened 196

one of Germany's two arteries severed on 6–7 November 264

one of toughest days, 27 September 170

origin of name xxv

Pershing disillusioned about stalemate 166

rumours of armistice circulate through armies 240

Saint-Mihiel regarded as nasty thorn 128

a series of hard lessons for British/French 138

succession of hammer-blows on 112

taking of Vimy Ridge 31

twilight of xxxiii

unearthly walls of silence after the Armistice 271

see also Allies

Wetzell, Lieutenant-Colonel Georg 113–14

Weygand, Maxime 24–5, 95, 140, 252–4, 266, 270

Whippet tank *see* tanks, Medium Mark A

Whittlesey, Major Charles 120, 154, 203–4, 206

Wilhelm, Crown Prince

armies to fall back along Hirson–Mézières line 238

begged Kaiser not to appoint Groener 237

Charleville headquarters 237

claimed intensity of fighting purified German Army 222

comments that German order breaking down 109–110

drives to the front filled with bitterness 10–11

forces pulled back after Hindenburg line breach 214

held largest Army Group 145

'like a vast conflagration' 167

visit to the Argonne front 163–4

visit to his father on 9 November 256

Wilhelm II, Kaiser

abdication on 9 November 260–62, 274

accepts resignation of von Hertling 195

background of 11–12

black days became almost daily occurrences 132

confined to bed with arthritis/rheumatism 198

Crown Council meeting on 2 October 197

gives Marwitz command of Fifth Army 149

meeting at Hôtel Britannique 72–3

meets new Cabinet on 21 October 223

met Hindenburg and Ludendorff on 26 October 234–5

own position becoming untenable 238–40

refused to abdicate 255–9

replacement of Foreign Secretary 17

US entry meant he had lost the war 126

US insisted he must go 224

Wilhelm of Prussia, Prince Friedrich 11

Wilhöft, Wilhelm 111

Williams, Lieutenant-Colonel Ashby 121–3, 155–6

Williams, Private Ralph 5, 18

Wilmot, Major George xxix, 190

Wilson, Henry 191

Wilson, Joseph 200

Wilson, President Woodrow

Austro-Hungary note offering peace 205

Wilson, President Woodrow – *cont.*
  Fourteen Points as basis for peace
    negotiations 198, 199–201, 223, 252,
    319n.27
  further note expressing peace willing-
    ness 252
  German Supreme Command wanted to
    appeal to 196
  Ludendorff's planned approach to
    178–9
  New York speech on 4 July 1918 199
  opposition to too much interference in
    Germany 278
  response from Germany on 21 October
    222
  second note to Berlin on 16 October
    216–20, 322n.4
  third note to Berlin on 24 October 225,
    238
  unhappy about Haig's 'drafting' proposal
    117–18, 178–9, 196

Wilson, Sir Henry 101
Winterfeldt, Major General Hans von
  252–4
*With Our Backs to the Wall: Victory and Defeat
  in 1918* (Stevenson) xxxii–xxxiii
Woehl, Second-Lieutenant Harold 205,
  229
Woods, William 263
Wotan Line 143

York, Alvin 120
Ypres
  Allied attacks on 167, 176
  British cemeteries xxxiii
  First Battle captured imagination 279
  Fourth Battle of 176
  memory defining xxix
  trench warfare xxxii
  use of gas 102
Ypres Salient 118–19
Ytres 136, 190